NER
press

THE MOUNTAIN AND THE RIVER

Genesis, Postmodernism, and the Machine

Also by Albert Norton from New English Review Press:

Dangerous God: A Defense of Transcendent Truth (2021)

THE MOUNTAIN AND THE RIVER

Genesis, Postmodernism, and the Machine

Albert Norton, Jr.

Published by New English Review Press
a subsidiary of World Encounter Institute
PO Box 158397
Nashville, Tennessee 37215
&
27 Old Gloucester Street
London, England, WC1N 3AX

Cover Art and Design by Kendra Mallock

ISBN: 978-1-943003-81-5

Library of Congress Control Number: 2023934246

First Edition

NEW ENGLISH REVIEW PRESS
newenglishreview.org

Men have forgotten God; that's why all this has happened.
—Alexandr Solzhenitsyn, 1983

Contents

Introduction

IMAGINE YOU'RE walking through the woods on a crisp fall day. Strewn about the path before you is a woodland carpet of fallen leaves. They're a variety of leaf types in a variety of colors, now in varying degrees of decomposition. Pick up one leaf. It is unattached to the others because the carpet is not one whole thing. The leaf you pick up will be something in the family of yellows, reds, oranges, and browns, possibly vestiges of green here and there. It's not one color, it's many, and you readily distinguish among them. You can attach names to the colors just as you can the types. Perhaps you've picked up an oak leaf, somewhat like other oak leaves on the ground but unlike the hickories and maples. The leaves didn't grow up from the ground, they fell from the trees around you: an oak here, a maple there, a hickory beyond that. Those oaks are not all the same, but are of different varieties: post oak, black oak, red oak. Not just maples, but sugar maples and red maples. Pignut hickories, and mockernut.

In one visual sweep of a familiar scene, we encounter countless categories by which we make sense of things. We distinguish the whole from the disparate and delineate by categories and subcategories of color, and of leaves, and of trees, and of course we can continue the thought, distinguishing up from down; existence from non-existence; light from shadow, and in this way, apprehend innumerable other categories extant in our environment.

This is how we make sense of things: an ongoing process of differentiating this thing from that, and this resulting category from that, so that meaning emerges. The process is not just internal to us. The differentiations exist in the things themselves. Categories formed of identification and differentiation, both extant in the world and formed in our minds, enable us to apprehend reality. Intelligence is just that ability to categorize, in ever finer nuanced gradation. Thinking means division, differentiation, discrimination, discernment.

Categories by which we are able to think are implicit in many of the words we use to set them up: types, kinds, species, classes, patterns, symbols, universals, models, ideals. The process of differentiation by category involves boundaries, or constraints, or forms, by which we channel thought, and consequently also our actions and beliefs. We categorize into taxonomies, and taxonomies within taxonomies, so that we form entire architectures of understanding and belief and value, all by differentiating this kind of thing from that; this kind of idea from that; this kind of value from that.

Look up into the branches of that oak. That first large branch itself branches off, and that branch has branches, and so on. Each branch is a miniature of the form of the tree of which it is a part. This is a pattern, repeating at successive stages; that is, fractally. Fractal patterns exist in nature but also in our symbolic understanding of reality. We recognize and use symbols routinely, without pausing to consider their sophisticated function in denoting categories. A symbol is a representation of something else. It could be a straightforward substitution, like these typed letters and words for the concepts they convey, or it could represent complex interacting abstractions, as in mythology and religious imagery. Likewise universals, characteristics in common to all members of a class, the class itself being formed by differentiation of like with like and against unlike.

Distinguishing like from unlike is made possible by opposing characteristics in the things or ideas or values. We live in a reality of binary oppositions. The oppositions, and their binary nature, go all the way down, so to speak—they are not incidental to a particular kind of analysis but form the platform for all our existence. They enable distinctions into the categories by which we make sense of the world.

Hierarchies naturally emerge from this categorical thinking. We distinguish between oppositions of truth and falsity, and good and evil, and we are created to assign value to each, so that honesty is prized over dishonesty; courage over cowardice; compassion over indifference; and so on. Conceptual and value hierarchies form, and hierarchies within hierarchies, and all of our experience of life occurs inside these fractal and intersecting hierarchies.

The values are objective. Truth and falsity, for example, are objective; they exist in reality, extant and apart from us. Our relation to them may bend and twist in response to events and patterns of thought and vicissitudes of lived experience, but truth is truth regardless how I feel about it.

We can symbolize this categorical and hierarchical way of thinking as the mountain, in contrast to the river. The river is the opposite of hierarchy: levelling, changing, and fluid. Categories and hierarchies give form and meaning to our existence. If we imagine them as restraining rather than liberating, and conducive to narrowness of mind or obscurantism or meanness, then we might come to think of the categories, and the constraints by which they are formed, as shackles on our freedom. Perhaps they can be deconstructed. That deconstruction might take forms of philosophical critique whereby we re-evaluate assumptions built into the fabric of our shared experience. This is the postmodern mindset. Not about construction, but about deconstruction. At every level it is negation, an attempt at bending reality to the will.

This book is about the chasm between two worldviews: that of Genesis and that of postmodernism. The allegorical mountain and river aid our understanding of how these worldviews present in opposition. The mountain is built on the objective reality of differentiation and division; contrasts in things, concepts, and values, which develop into intricate architectures of meaning and purpose. It represents objectivity of truth, and morality, and beauty, and all the virtues to which we aspire. The river is the resting creative potential of formless existence. Mountain and river are internal subjective psychological dispositions in people, but they also manifest externally in cultures and abstractions of value. Both mountain and river perspectives exist in our reality but pushed out of balance they diminish us.

Why does this matter? Because Western civilization is at a precarious crossroad. The objectivity of truth and of right and wrong was a first principle until about the turn of the twentieth century, when postmodern ideas of truth-formation began to gain traction, and Christianity lost its grip on Western cultures in favor of secular ideologies. The result has been the bloodiest century in human history and the accelerated proliferation of oppressive ideologies. Postmodern critiques during this time have become general in the culture, like a virus escaped from the lab.

There's something wrong with us. We all feel it, and we're trying to do something about it. That something wrong is often described rather vaguely as "alienation," open-ended as to what about us is being alienated from what. The Genesis worldview tells us the alienation is a natural condition of our existence, unfortunately. It is the result of our moral agency and two-nature essence: spiritual and material. We are dust-formed but also God-breathed, and we live this life in the body conscious of a vaguely felt lack of completeness. If we reject the Genesis worldview, the sense of alienation does not go away, and so we grope around trying to explain it. Hence, postmodern theory.

The pagan world of antiquity gave way gradually in the West to Christianity. Now Christianity has given way to—what? What is the guiding ideal, if there is one at all? If we bother to describe the dominant worldview now, we tend to do so as a negation—secularism, atheism, irreligion, and so on—words to describe what we aren't, instead of what we are. "Postmodernism" is used in this work to characterize the philosophical trends contributing to the current dominant worldview. Postmodernism is primarily a tendentious critique of objectivity and of the existing hierarchies wrought by objectivity historically. Importantly, postmodernism is not, primarily, a propositional explanation of reality unto itself. It is more an attitudinal stance; a posture of resistance or rebellion or transgression rather than independent substance that can be set forth comprehensively.

It can nonetheless be described by its effects. We wring our hands over the breakdown of the family, deterioration of the rule of law, spreading malaise, a pervasive sense of hopelessness, and the drug-induced zombie apocalypse. These are symptoms in individuals which are attributable to the postmodern outlook. Socially, too, we experience worrying symptoms: concentrations of institutional political and commercial power, and a drive to collectivism through contrived metanarratives, the postmodern replacement for objective truth. Individual agency gives way to that collective, as in the original definition of fascism. Religion reduces to repetition of rites and practices with no hold on the human heart.

It doesn't have to be this way. It is possible to recover individual human dignity, and freedom, and toleration. It requires rediscovery of the objectivity of truth, and goodness, and beauty. It requires rejection of disastrous flirtations with postmodernist critique and negation. Religion is not for everyone, but the objectivity of truth that attends it must be reclaimed. And to do so, we must first understand the worldview that supports it. That is the Genesis worldview, in irreconcilable conflict with postmodernism.

CHAPTER ONE

Crisis of Meaning

W<small>E ALL FEEL</small> the need for a sense of purpose and meaning in our lives. We seek it out, sometimes in obvious and external ways, and sometimes only in the subjective consciousness. We can analogize this seeking to the desire for the mountain: stern, mastering, eternal, unchanging, immoveable, and resolute. The answer to our desire for meaning may seem heavy or even oppressive, as when the absoluteness of a demanding God seems more than we can bear. So we have a countervailing desire for the (analogous) river: frivolous, undemanding, temporal, fleeting, moving, and mutable.

Either extreme experienced in a sustained way can seem unbearable. We each live alone in little houses of consciousness, alive to social interaction or lack thereof, confronted in every moment with moral choice, simultaneously feeling lonely and desiring solitude. We desire meaning, but not just in the sense of having the world become more comprehensible. We desire meaning in the sense of finding purpose in our lives. Inside each of us is a burbling conviction of our own significance in a larger drama that yet remains invisible to us. That intuition of significance can be beaten down by circumstance, or drained away by ideologies which change the way we conceive ourselves as human beings. This draining away is happening to us now. It is the crisis of meaning of the postmodern age.

The mountain symbolizes hierarchy of value, and structure derived from forms imposing order on thought and actions, and incidental to that, our physical environment. It is the product of active agentic[1] execu-

---

1   The exercise of agency, sentience with volition directed to purposed ends. Human

tion: the formation of a goal and active purposeful movement toward it. It refers to the concentrated attention we (and God, if He exists) bring to the formation of structure, including physical things we build, but also mental constructs: whole architectures of meaning. This urge to build is an individual psychological disposition, but it also manifests socially. The figurative mountain is the result of mankind's search for meaning.

The river symbolizes fluid subjectivity and flat particularity. It is a flow of intuition and inference; of pre-creation potentiality. We can think of it as a contemplative and fecund precursor to action; the germ from which an idea grows; subjectivity, intuition, and a night-time dream-like state in contrast to the high noon of the mountain. It represents rest, creativity, anticipation. And yet it is the seething roil from which the mountain emerges.

Western societies have evolved so that many reflexively reject God, the Source of ultimate meaning. When and how did this happen? Weren't people generally more pious at some point, more concerned with what an active Maker thought of them? Yes, of course. Were they happier then compared to us now? Well, how do we define "happiness"? Surely not by the state of our technology. We might imagine our forebears' existence to have been oppressive, their social limitations unduly constraining compared to ours. But were they actually better or worse off subjectively? Did our ancestors thrive better with a fear of the Lord? Are we better off than they were, accounting for the wholeness of a person rather than superficial differences like relative material prosperity or modern conveniences?

When genuinely felt religion was on its way out, even skeptics worried over the consequences. This was the subject of Matthew Arnold's famous poem, "Dover Beach" (1867), for example, but it has been addressed more prosaically by many philosophers, most notably Friedrich Nietzsche, in the late nineteenth century. All of postmodern philosophy is about finding meaning if God, as the source of ultimate meaning, does not exist.

The phrase "disenchantment" is sometimes used to explain this problem. It is traceable to Friedrich Schiller,[2] but is more famously associated with Max Weber,[3] who contrasted rationalistic post-religious

---

beings are said to have "agency," meaning the ability to choose. "Moral agency," for example, means the ability to choose moral right or wrong. This and other terms are defined in the Glossary.

2   (1759-1805)

3   (1864-1920)

societies with previously religious, traditional ones in which "the world remains a great enchanted garden." Disenchantment is the sense of loss that craters into a crisis of meaning. Postmodern philosophy is, in large part, an unsuccessful effort at re-enchantment without God. Hartmut Rosa, a contemporary German sociologist (b. 1965), uses "resonance" in a similar way to describe the sense of living in a world for which there is objective meaning. Our obsession with control, he writes, means that we encounter the world as "points of aggression," against which we feel we have "to know, attain, conquer, master, or exploit." This is suggestive of Iain McGilchrist's thesis[4] that the left hemisphere of the brain exerts this sort of controlling feature of attention, which is necessary but must be "emissary" to the "master" of the right hemisphere, which enables a more fully integrated vision of reality that accommodates intuition and mystery. McGilchrist would hold that culturally, we have allowed the left hemisphere perspective to dominate, crowding out our ability to live with a larger sense of purpose and meaning.[5]

Disenchantment goes beyond the loss of a sense of mystery that necessarily accompanies belief in God. It means our mastering, controlling instincts take over and dominate, not just individually but socially. We become disconnected from the fuller meaning of life, lost in one narrow materialist aspect of it: the perception of self as controlling, with the result that on a social level, we are controlled. Disorder, chaos, and irresolution exist in ourselves and in our environment. We can't and don't control everything, individually or socially. It is important that we recognize the elusive and mysterious as features of our existence. If we would live more fully, we must have a disposition toward the sacred, that entire other-ness which we can never ourselves encompass. If we question the materialist premise that everything we know just is— somethingness as brute fact, we mentally truncate a vast arena of reality necessary to making us whole. Being does not explain itself. Some additional approach to reality is necessary, like anti-matter to matter; nothing to something; disorder to order. McGilchrist suggests we need an "un-word," not defined by reference to anything else, and suggests that words of religious traditions like tao, logos, Brahman, and God point to this ultimate ground of being, this "place for a power that underwrites

---

4 *The Matter With Things*, London: Perspectiva, 2021.

5 The author Rod Dreher is attuned to these movements in his blog at www.theamericanconservative.com, and at this writing is working on his own book "about disenchantment."

the existence of everything."[6]

A tipping point for loss of belief in God in the United States can reasonably be pegged to about the turn of the twentieth century; earlier in Europe. One could certainly argue for a little earlier or later, it's not the kind of thing one can pinpoint on a calendar. This tipping point marks the commencement of the postmodern era, during which philosophy moved forward with what amounted to an effort to rake back meaning after it was ceded to bankrupt ideologies like fascism, Marxism, humanism, misguided nationalism, and other variations of materialism.[7] For postmodernists, God is dead, and objectivity and hierarchy must be replaced with another ontology[8] more congenial to human flourishing.

Truth, goodness, and beauty are often referred to as irreducible transcendentals. But if these transcendent values originate in the singularity of God, what is good is also true and what is true is also beautiful. In *The Abolition of Man*,[9] C.S. Lewis wrote of their combination in the Tao, his referent (like one of McGilchrist's) for the ground of all being: objectivity in values and truth. In an essay based on works of Lewis and J.R.R. Tolkien, N.S. Lyons wrote:

> [A]ny conceivable ordered reality—physical or rational or moral—is only possible through unchanging laws; that which is good must conform to this Tao, and so that which is good must by definition first be that which is true. To pervert or obscure the truth of words, or anything which is true, is to attack the Truth writ large; i.e., the Tao, and thus begin to melt away all solid ground from which any stand at all can be mounted against the encroach of total meaninglessness and total disorder. In the end, no conception of human value—or any fixed truth—can then withstand this assault, and so we abolish ourselves along with our perception of reality, inhumanity triumphs over man,

---

6 *The Matter With Things*, vol. 2, p. 1200.

7 "Material" has already been used here in slightly different ways. It is a contrast to spiritual, as with the distinction between body and soul or nature and supernature. A "materialist" is one who subscribes to "materialism," the belief that physical things are all there is: no supernature, no soul, no spirit. All of reality is matter in motion, on this view, except that most materialists would allow also for a limited immaterial reality, as with concepts and values, that is nonetheless tied in some way to the material brain. The foregoing is the usual meaning for variants of "material" in this book, but a distinct meaning would be avarice or the prioritizing of physical comfort, especially when used to imply self-identification with one's possessions.

8 The philosophy of existence. To be discussed further.

9 Lewis, C.S. *The Abolition of Man*. New York: HarperOne 2000 (first published 1943).

and the void devours.[10]

The quest for an individual sense of meaning took on new urgency after the mid-twentieth-century wars. It was heightened by the ideologies that drove those hot wars and the ensuing Cold War. Hence, a variety of philosophical trends, some to deconstruct social attitudes thought to contribute to the conflicts; some to address the pointless anomie of crass consumerism; some to re-enchant with substitutes for transcendence[11] in various process philosophies.[12] Process philosophy operates in opposition to philosophy based in transcendence. Process philosophy is to postmodernism as transcendence is to religion. Process philosophies have several threads in common, enabling us to group them under the label "postmodernism."[13] We'll look at several, after considering generally the competing Genesis worldview.

The postmodern impulse arises upon rejection of God. God is at the pinnacle of the hierarchies of value represented by the mountain, but they emanate from Him; He's not a figurehead for our conception of the hierarchy. God is positionally at the pinnacle, but also functionally. He holds it up and sustains it. There is no hierarchy at all if there is no real basis upon which it comes into existence. God must be real, in other

---

10 Lyons, N.S., *A Prophecy of Evil: Tolkien, Lewis, and Technocratic Nihilism*, quoted in *The Upheaval* (theupheaval@substack.com) November 15, 2022.

11 We will have recurring need to refer to "transcendence." This means God as Source of ideals, values, meaning, and purpose, but a slightly different and slightly more vague meaning is merely that these features of our existence originate beyond this mortal and material plane. Transcendence and "immanence" stand in opposition. Immanence means the presence of God in the world, but a slightly different and slightly more vague meaning is that ideals, values, meaning, and purpose arise solely within this life in the body. Both are addressed in the Glossary and are discussed further in this book.

12 Process philosophies presuppose there is no God, and that ideals, values, meaning, and purpose are socially generated. Postmodernism consists principally in varieties of process philosophy to replace both meanings (previous footnote) of transcendence with the more vague meaning of immanence: that ideals, value, meaning, and purpose are self-contained within this physical life in the body, an "immanent frame" excluding a spiritual component of reality.

13 We should take note that "postmodern" is sometimes used only to describe the post-WWII thinking of philosophers like Jacques Derrida, Michel Foucault, Jean-Francois Lyotard, and a few others, especially in efforts to avoid metanarratives like Nazism. In this work, we cast the net somewhat more broadly, however, because what makes postmodernism postmodernism is, first and foremost, rejection of God. For Western societies as a whole, that mostly pre-dated the mid-century wars. Moreover, postmodern thinking rests significantly on philosophical pillars of Marxism, existentialism, and pragmatism, which were already well-developed before WWII.

words, to serve as the ultimate value to which all subordinate values attach. If we imagine God out of existence, we truncate the structural support for the hierarchy of values altogether, and it collapses. The resulting network of values becomes relatively flattened, like Christmas tree lights strewn about the floor once removed from the tree which held them up. If we disregard the tree, as an unhelpful hierarchical structure, we're left on our own to make sense of the mess on the floor. We can imagine them all interconnected but not vertically hierarchical, if we adopt the thinking of postmodernists.

The Christmas tree analogy illuminates the mountain analogy. The mountain is awesome, and represents a stepped-up hierarchy with a clear pinnacle at the morally highest positions, with more numerous but less consequential value and moral distinctions as one descends the mountain. The river, by contrast, is characterized by flow. It may be awesome, too, but in its own way—its ever-changing dynamism. It seeks the level, in contrast to the mountain. If it is the analogy for our understanding of value formation, we must grasp that it presents a levelled array of values, to be arranged by us according to the push and pull of social forces, changing in time as the river flows, each perception of value informed by those around it dynamically, and so relative to time and place and context, moment to moment. The river would yield process-formed truth and ethics. This is the direction of the process philosophy of postmodernism. The features of mountain and river exist in opposites, as in all of creation:

Mountain	River
Actual	Potential
Eternal	Changing
Absolute	Contingent
Hierarchical	Flat
Liberty	Equality
Masculine	Feminine
Substance	Process
Static	Dynamic
Stillness	Movement
Acting	Thinking
Objective	Subjective

Word	Image
Reason	Intuition
Constrained	Unconstrained
Prosecution	Defense
Execution	Planning
Tactical	Strategic
Attack	Entrap
Soldier	Priest
King	Philosopher

Postmodern philosophy rejects transcendence and looks to this-world replacement for it. It develops theory for finding purpose and meaning without transcendence; philosophies of becoming rather than being. Postmodern process philosophies examine the phenomena of natural human experience and sources meaning and purpose within it, instead of in God. The river model's psychological predisposition is typical in process philosophy.

Postmodernism is collectivist in perspective. Or "socialist," to contrast more neatly with the relevant opposition of "individualist." The river, as a whole, analogizes escape from hierarchical value formation. As the river flows, the moment-by-moment changing relation of values organically and of its own yields our understanding of right and wrong, and of truth and falsity. But this is entirely a collective undertaking. That is, the river is society. A river is a river because it is all the drops of water collectively. Surface tension binds them, in the same way intersubjectivity[14] of consciousness binds human beings. But the river as a river is irreducible.

The social element of our being, however, is not the totality of our being. In the Genesis model, the indivisible and irreducible element of moral accountability is the individual. Unquestionably, there are society-wide effects of individual moral decision-making, and the reverse

---

14 Defined in Glossary, but in addition, for a concise explanation of the phenomenon of intersubjectivity in human consciousness, see Norton, Albert, *Dangerous God: A Defense of Transcendent Truth*, Nashville: New English Review Press, 2021 (hereinafter *Dangerous God*), chapter 7. Intersubjectivity as the impetus for collectivist perspective is also discussed further in the present work, chapters 2 and 13. Note that "intersubjectivity," as used here, does not mean a collective consensus. Rather, it explains how mutual self- and other-awareness yields a sense of society in any group of people.

also is true: socially held values unquestionably affect how we individually address moral or truth questions. The picture of the river roiling and changing with the landscape is a picture of what society does, not what an individual exercising his moral agency does, if he or she aspires to the objective and transcendent truth and goodness of God. The river is a collectivist picture, in other words. In the postmodern imagination, the collective is presented as the aspirational totality of our vision: value formation does not exist apart from us, like with the mountain as a third point of reference in interactions among individuals. Values are instead understood as a social product.

The mountain relates to the tendencies toward building and order and hierarchy, and these are served by individualist linear rationality which in mankind can become untethered from objective principle. Unbalanced, this tendency can lead to dogmatism and authoritarianism. The river relates to tendencies toward relationship-building and emotional sensitivity and collectivism, and these are served by relativizing principle. Unbalanced, this tendency, too, can lead to dogmatism and authoritarianism, if from a different direction. The imbalance results from rejection of God, so that we either lose connection to first principles, or lose the principles themselves in an acid bath of relativism. In the current age, the dominance of the river disposition is more dangerous. The desire to preserve a Genesis understanding of reality is taken as mounting totalitarianism, but totalitarianism from the other direction is presented as the cure.

In this day, the degeneration of meaningfulness is for most people not really visible at ground level, so to speak. It is enervating rather than oppressive, so there's no rising up against it. We find ourselves too weary to think of fighting it. We may perceive in others, if not ourselves, a general sense that even if we have more material prosperity and opportunity, there is more despair, hopelessness, isolation, suspicion, and fear. The lightness of being hoped-for in a move to the river does not bring with it contentment or a feeling of real freedom. There is clearly a crisis of meaning, in the postmodern world, and it has all kinds of ill effects on us, individually and collectively. We tend to perceive the heavy weight of the mountain, and run from it, without perceiving the countervailing meaninglessness of the roiling river to which we run.

God is believed absent from reality, in our post-Christian world, but an eroded hierarchy of values based on Christian understanding remains. Postmodern philosophy and praxis generally reject hierarchies. Still, we intuit the need for hierarchy even as we reject it, and so we attempt to re-create it on our own. The mountain-substitute we build is a tower of hierarchy. Its values are human-derived, instead of God-provided. The Tower of Babel story in Genesis (chapter 11) warns us about this. Technological advances in an advanced prosperous society enable the scenario of frustration which will follow. There is a shift to collectivist perspective, which entails automation and loss of individual agency. Ceding agency to the collective means heightened individual insecurity and concern for safety. Without God and without self, society becomes our only refuge and source of identity. Increasing anxiety attends this shift, and it becomes unsustainable. The safety and security we seek in the herd is short-lived, and the system collapses. Instead of achieving oneness with the collective, we become splintered and antagonistic, speaking past each other, perhaps speaking the same sounds but with entirely different or even opposite meanings. Language fails. Our desire for unity, without God as the unifying principle, results in tribalism and strife.

This should sound familiar to anyone living in the West in the twenty-first century. We cannot self-create a world of meaning, and if we attempt it, we fail disastrously, ending with the very opposite of what we set out to attain. In this age the Tower of Babel story is played out in extreme ideologies of the right and left, both departing from transcendence, objectivity of truth, and universality of principle. Technological innovation drives greater interdependence. Greater interdependence means decreasing self-sufficiency. Decreasing self-sufficiency erodes personal agency. There is no God to look to, we think, so we're left with diminished agency, diminished confidence, and anxiety about what the world can now do to us. As in the city of Babel, our collectives splinter into irreconcilable factions, each muttering syllables of hate in language unintelligible to the other.

If truth is not objective, public discourse shifts away from appeal to principle and toward power negotiation. This takes place in words, the meaning-making medium between and among us. But words can be used to redescribe concepts, to distort meaning, to deliberately present half-truth or ambiguity, and to build false narrative to replace objective truth and morality. The power paradigm distorts language. Fraud and deceit corrupt the meanings of words. Language is deceitfully employed to advance ideology, for example, by using strategic ambiguity in word meanings. We may use some of the same words, like the English words "tolerance," "love," "freedom," and so on, but find we mean something completely different by them. The philosophy of many of the postmodernists is, in significant part, about deliberate confusion of language. The result is that we speak different languages, and so our efforts to communicate fail. We can't make ourselves understood to each other, just like with the people who built the city and Tower of Babel.

The confusion of language at Babel is often interpreted as having been undone at Pentecost, when different language-speakers with the Holy Spirit gained mutual intelligibility. Pentecost underscores the principle that common deference to objectivity of truth and value is the only cure against descent into mutual unintelligibility and resulting mutual suspicion. We build to futility if we misperceive the way human beings are and the way the world is. Genesis presents reality.

Postmodernism rejects the Genesis worldview. The objectivity of truth and falsity is rejected, as is the objectivity of right and wrong. In the postmodern vision, these are not transferred entirely to a subjective plane, however, in which we all live and move independently according to our self-constructed visions. Subjectivism in concepts and values is cast back onto an objective structure, because we can't help it, this is the way of the world, however it came into being. What we do is create new and artificial hierarchical structures of meaning, ideologies,[15] and regard these as socially operative. What begins as individual subjective wishful thinking becomes collective objective mandate. Again, a Tower of Babel doomed to destruction because it is out of phase with the reality of God-created human nature. We will have a mountain, one way or the other. We build towers of Babel upon rejecting God because we must; because by unimagining God, we don't thereby erase His creation. The tower rises because there is a value hierarchy in reality and in mankind. If we don't perceive it correctly, we build our own, but in doing so, we build to futility.

For many thinkers, this was the lesson of the mid-twentieth-century wars, in which hierarchies of meaning built around metanarratives[16] collapsed into ruinous chaos at the expense of millions upon millions of lives, and destitution and despair all around. The thought was that perhaps we're better off eradicating mountain-building. But inevitably,

---

15 Defined more thoroughly in the Glossary, but "ideology" carries a negative connotation. It is a system of cohering ideas, but all built on abstract theory attenuated from the true nature of things. It is theory built on false ideals or mistakes of fact about human nature. Two examples are communism and fascism.

16 A metanarrative is a set of principles supported by a narrative, in the way the Apostles' Creed is supported by the Bible. "The narrative" is fought over, in the postmodern age, because of the metanarrative principles the narrative implies. In chapter 23 *infra*, we consider the phenomenon of metanarrative more thoroughly.

we build new artificial mountains of ideology.

The Babel towers rose because God, the author of the real mountain, and the river too, was imagined dead. Postmodernism is, in part, a re-action to the mid-century disasters, but the groundwork for it had been in place for decades, particularly in the toxic philosophies of Marxism, existentialism, and pragmatism. Post-war thinkers wanted to dismantle ideologies but just replaced the existing ideologies with new ones. They are legion, like the demons ousted by Jesus, but there are common ele-ments, and by those common elements, they are grouped together here as "postmodernism."

But instead of trying to explain postmodernism now in the abstract, let's first understand essential elements of the Genesis worldview, the contrast by which we understand postmodernism.

CHAPTER TWO

In the Beginning

"**I**N THE BEGINNING, God created the heavens and the earth." These words opening the book of Genesis seem to come with a crescendo of timpani and clash of cymbals. The words are weighty. The phrase "in the beginning" signifies the beginning of a story to explain reality, and even beyond that, it is an assertion about "ontology," the nature of being itself. The first ten words of the Bible disclose fundamental features of existence, which will inform everything which comes after.

"In the beginning—," well, beginning of what? Of everything, we are to suppose, meaning there was Nothing before—"Nothing" capitalized here to indicate not merely an absence of a something, but complete and utter nothing, conceptually more difficult than we might think because it is a distinct metaphysics altogether, not a mere negation of the reality we think we know. We live in somethingness, like fish live in water, and so it is difficult to grasp Nothing. We tend to approach it by imagining vague somethingness, and then trying to negate that something. The resulting nothing-as-such substitutes for true Nothing, hampering our ability to see physical reality as proof of the spiritual reality behind it. The mental habit of negation may work its way into our architectures of meaning, as a buzz of negative critique or tendentiousness, whereby we assume hidden and nefarious systems arrayed against us. We will see how important this tendency is in the postmodern impulse.

"God." As difficult to conceive as Nothing. A singularity from which all differentiations emerge. A personality, we would say from our limited perspective, but omnipotent, omnipresent, omnibenevolent. We may struggle with belief in this entity/Being/concept/ultimate because our beliefs are formed around what we know and God is beyond our knowing except obliquely. We draw understanding from His revelations in word, creation, history, and our own most abstract conceptions.

"God created," and so is the pure actualization[1] from which all contingent reality emerges. In a first division there is God, and then all that God creates. Differentiation itself is thus an ontological feature of reality. Indeed, if we scroll back the innumerable divisions by which we apprehend reality, we mentally revert to the Singularity from which they are all birthed, and so God is a necessary first cause of all that differentiates and proceeds from Him.

"The heavens and the earth." A differentiation we can understand as a duality, the division of one into two which are opposites, each understandable by the opposite it is not. We will further investigate the ontological nature of dualistic differentiation, but for now, we can assign a working definition. Ontology is philosophical inquiry concerning existence. To say dualistic division is "ontological" is to say it is bound up in the very existence of things. Oppositional pairs are not just a way for us to describe things and concepts. Things and concepts exist because they differentiate from others in binary division.[2]

Successive differentiations are the continued creation of dualities, often layered and overlapping and complexly related, but ultimately reducible to binary opposition. To say that something exists at all (apart from God) is to say that it is the result of differentiation, and all differentiation is, at bottom, division between opposites. Ontological duality should not be forgotten when we observe further category differentiation, as when living things differentiate to plants and animals, and animals differentiate to vertebrates and invertebrates, and so on. All categorization begins with dualistic division, the starting point for any differentiation by which we make sense of reality.

We can take from the first sentence of the Bible a differentiation between God and not-God—between Absolute and contingent. Dualities are even more obvious in the divisions described by "heavens and the earth." They are both symbolic and literal. The phrase describes immaterial and material; ideas and things; abstractions and instantiations;

---

1 "Actualization" is used here in its Aristotelean sense, not in the sense of psychological achievement. Aristotle distinguished between actual and potential, in his theories of causation, and pure actualization represents the absolute, non-contingent, uncaused cause and unmoved mover.

2 Chapter 22 of Iain McGilchrist's *The Matter with Things* (London: Perspectiva Press, 2021) concerns "The Coincidentia Oppositorum," a more thorough presentation of the oppositional duality described here.

forces and matter; spirit and nature; God and creation; Mind and brain; sky and earth; order and disorder; and the ontological nature itself of division and differentiation opening out into the reality we know.

"Heavens" describes (among other things) the spiritual component of reality. "Earth:" physical material. Material and spiritual are in opposition, in the sense that each describes the other by negation. That which is material is all that is not spiritual though infused by spirit; that which is spiritual is all that is not material. Each side of the opposition, in this way, negatively describes its opposite. The principle of their opposition is the law of non-contradiction. Often attributed to Aristotle, it holds simply that contradictory propositions cannot both be true in the same way at the same time. The principle is so simple that it's easy to overlook its implications. For one thing, it implies the very ontological dualism discussed here. It favors an ontology of being over the ontologies of becoming favored by postmodern process philosophies.

The dual nature of mankind—spiritual and material—has been a cornerstone precept of Western civilization, at least since Christianity upended paganism as the primary way people thought about their own nature and their relationship to the divine. That has come into question gradually over time, but at an accelerating pace going into the twentieth century. Now, in the twenty-first, the default view is materialism, a monist[3] view that matter and energy are all there is. We nonetheless confusingly continue to use words linked to dualist metaphysics, like "spiritual" and "transcendent," and the word "metaphysical" itself. "Spiritual" may mean only deeply contemplative; "spirit" the animating feature of consciousness, "transcendent" may mean superlative in some way; "metaphysical" may relate only to division of tangible and ideal rather than material and spiritual. The original meaning of such words is leached out, in the new dispensation of monist metaphysics. Traditional Western religion, with its metaphysics of dualism, has been all but eradicated outside religious enclaves. This is a central element of the postmodernist worldview. It holds that mankind is of the dust only; that people are not God-breathed because there is no God. Postmodernism is a rejection of Genesis on this very fundamental level.

The spiritual realm is distinct from the physical cosmos, and yet it runs in and through the natural world. But it is not the same kind of substance as matter and energy, because it is not quantifiable or containable

---

3 The contrast to dualism, "monism" means all that exists is of one substance. So, for example, the material world is all there is (materialism) or spirit and matter are indivisible aspects of the same substance (pantheism).

or describable in the same way. The spiritual element of reality is not bounded by space and time. We might say matter and spirit coincide, or run together, or co-exist, but each of these phrases employs physical-ist language of space and time, so they're only analogous. We may say they are distinct in "substance," but that word, too, suggests materiality, unless carefully defined otherwise.[4] We may speak casually of a material reality and a spiritual reality, because of the ways they differ, but we should be careful in such usages not to then confuse the word "reality." If the dualist perspective is correct, it can be differentiated conceptually into material and spiritual, but "reality" encompasses both.

The monist view holds that all of reality is of one substance. This might be some irreducibly combined version of spiritual and material, as with Eastern pantheisms which imagine God and the universe being of one substance, and there being no God distinct from the world. Spiritual and material are not distinct, on this view. A question might be how living things are accounted for, given that all living things die. In Christian thought, living bodies can cease to exist in their biological forms, but the spiritual, being eternal, continues. This wouldn't make sense in a one-substance pantheistic vision, so typically pantheist religious views imagine the soul expanding to be one with the universe, or to again inhabit material form. Often Westerners who reject monotheisms will regard themselves as "spiritual but not religious," which could be taken as a vaguely monist, pantheist vision of reality.

Materialism is a monist belief, too. It is monist because the spiritual component of Christian duality is truncated, leaving only material and the energy by which forces act on material as the complete constituents of reality. This appears to be the default view in Western societies today. On this view, science is thought to be the only valid way of acquiring knowledge, but of course, science by definition is limited to the study of matter and energy.

Materialists often do not undertake to defend their monist view of reality, such as by offering an explanation of consciousness within the confines of materialism. Instead, because the West is relatively recently post-Christian, postmodern materialists tend to comprehend the dualist vision and simply cross off the portion they reject, not seeing the explanatory problems that result. It's easier to defend Christianity as a coherent view of reality than materialism, but people seldom defend materialism. They're more likely to criticize Christian dualism without

---

4   As with Baruch Spinoza (1632-1677), a pantheist who postulated God and material nature as being of one "substance." His was a monist, rather than dualist, perspective.

applying the same scrutiny to their position of materialist monism.

A materialist conceives immaterial thoughts and ideas as rooted in the physical workings of the brain, and concepts seemingly untethered to the physical, like virtue, beauty, and truth, and their opposites, as somehow emerging from that which is physical. On this view, truth and falsity are not objective realities existing apart from a person's perception of them. Instead, the individual generates the truth or falsity label and assigns it to the proposition in play, but of course, the individual's evaluation will be strongly affected by other physical inputs, especially those from the surrounding society. This post-Christian version of materialist metaphysics, combined with confusion about how materialism could explain the world, makes a person uniquely vulnerable to the postmodern suggestion that truth and falsity and right and wrong are not absolute, but are instead formed through collectivist process philosophy.

One of many problems with the one-substance or monist view of reality is its inadequate explanation for consciousness. Consciousness is a mysterious thing. We think of it as self-awareness co-located with the body, but beyond that, there is little we can say about it. How could a physical system of cognitive functioning give rise to conscious experience? Observation and reason do not answer that, and so there has long been a tradition of mind-body dualism to explain consciousness. Mind is in some way distinct from brain, and the mind of a person would seem to be of the same immaterial "substance," for want of a better word, as the Mind of God. A rich and complex body of philosophy develops the features of consciousness that are difficult to square with materialism. In this book, for example, we will emphasize the oddity of our ability to discern differentiating categories in physical and conceptual reality, and of the consistency of that discernment from person to person. We may overlook the phenomenon precisely because it is so fundamentally an organizing principle in our thinking that we may not pause to consider why it is so.

On the monist understanding, there is no transcendent God, no immaterial sentient agentic presence,[5] like angels or demons, and there is no afterlife because the mind is extinguished with the brain at death, or subsumed into universal collective mind with no individual soul. A dualist perspective allows for the truth of monotheistic religion, and also resolves some of the conundrums concerning mind as distinct from

---

5 Immaterial, meaning no physical body; sentient, meaning aware intelligence; agentic, meaning acting volitionally, and presence, signifying a distinct entity.

brain.

Most discussion of monist vs. dualist perspectives on consciousness begins with René Descartes (1596-1650). Descartes was a pivotal figure in history. Among his many contributions to early modern intellectual development was to set up a framework that came to be known as mind-body dualism: that there is an ontological duality of substance, physical and spiritual, and that human consciousness bestrides both, meaning it involves the physical brain, but resides also in the immaterial realm.

Descartes' thought promoted advances in theological thinking about the nature of physical people in a spirit-infused world, but it also hastened Enlightenment-era skepticism by sharpening the division between these two realms. By focusing on purely physical functioning as distinct in kind from mental, one can theorize away any remaining mystery concerning natural physical processes. Though there is no viable scientific explanation, perhaps consciousness nonetheless just emerges somehow from physical brain functioning, rather than co-existing in an ethereal spiritual realm. With this leap of faith, one can reject the idea of spiritual reality altogether.

If we admit of any possibility of mind/body dualism, we must next consider what the non-physical component of mind might be. Is it a physical psychic aura of some kind, around and among human beings? Or is it the immaterial, spiritual component of reality religions have proposed for thousands of years, recognized also by many philosophers until it became unfashionable in the postmodern era after the nineteenth century?

Genesis tells us mankind is made from dust, but not only from dust. He is God-breathed; that is, literally in-spirited by God, which means that people share in some way in the spiritual realm. We have one foot in the animal physical world, and one foot in the spiritual world. This is the distinction between "heavens and earth" in the opening line of the Bible, and the first man's dust and God-breathed origins—unmistakeable references to this duality.

There's still a great deal of mystery about this ontological dualism within mankind, but at a minimum, it means there is some kind of interactivity between the physical and spiritual realms. The interaction must take place in this strange thing we call consciousness, which is also the locus of rational thought because self-aware thinking is the essence of conscious experience. But what is a thought? It is immaterial, existing apart from the flashes of electricity in brain tissue even if in some sense it is connected. That is to say, a complex combination of neuronal impulses might be said to generate or capture or project the thought, but the content of the thought is nonetheless distinct from its physical capture, in the same way we might say a category is distinct from the things categorized; a pattern is distinct from the thing presented in a repeating way; and the concept of thought is distinct from the semantic content of a particular thought.

To express this a different way, consider that the content of a thought can be conveyed from one mind to another without any transfer of physical force or material. There might be physical processes involved in the transfer, of course, as when you articulate a thought which reverberates in air and pings my ears, setting up decodable electrical impulses to my brain. In that manner, the same thought then exists in both our physical brains. But still, the content of the thought itself is immaterial: unbounded by time and space.

It therefore doesn't work to imagine an impermeable barrier between material and immaterial—between brain and mind. Consciousness is best explained by understanding our thought life to exist, at least in part, in an immaterial realm. This is what Christianity necessarily holds, because if it were otherwise, there would be no point in praying, or in believing that God can and does intervene in this life in the body. Or that there are, in a spiritual realm, immaterial sentient agentic beings, "principalities and powers,"[6] who can have an impact, through thought, on what happens in the here and now of our daily physical reality.

The implications are large. If a thought is immaterial, it can be influenced by other thoughts also existing in that immaterial realm. This happens in normal interaction with others, when our immaterial thoughts are affected by the immaterial thoughts of others conveyed to us. But if the immaterial realm for thought is also spiritual in nature, then it can contain immaterial thought sourced in spiritual, rather than material, beings. If our minds operate in both physical and spiritual reality, our thoughts can be influenced by that spiritual reality. We are material, sentient, agentic beings. But our thoughts are immaterial. If immaterial sentient, agentic beings also exist, then the expression of thought by or among those beings may occupy the same immaterial realm our this-life thoughts do, such that we can be influenced by them.

A reasonable way to think about it is this. We have agency, including with respect to our thought-life, which means we can control the direction of our thoughts and be responsible for how we do so. It is

---

6 Ephesians 6:12.

the reason the Bible admonishes us to "take every thought captive" to obey Christ.[7] But also, in our thought-life, we are influenced by the expressed thoughts of others. If our mind operates immaterially not only in this-world movements of thought, but also in spiritual movements of thought, then our thoughts are exposed to influences there, including those of immaterial agentic beings which we may think of as demons or angels or other kinds of entities existing within spiritual reality.

Our consciousness is the locus of our subjectivity and also of the intersubjectivity we experience with others. Intersubjectivity is the mutual self-awareness between individuals which creates a distinct society. Is there, on some difficult-to-discern level, a sort of intersubjectivity between individuals and immaterial beings, including God? Apparently so, at least among mystics who seek God in prayer and seem especially sensitive to the spiritual. But on the other hand, the buzz of intersubjectivity in that realm is qualitatively different than what we experience among people socially. For most people, spiritual intersubjectivity is barely discernible.

A worthwhile question to ask is why. Why would an immediate sense of spiritual presence be withheld from us, or asking the same thing in reverse, why are we so obtuse as to not experience it like we do interaction in physical space-time with other people? The Bible seems repeatedly to set up the requirement that we avidly seek God. It is a feature of our physical existence that breaking out of it mentally to engage the spiritual is a matter of great effort. But that is a ponderable question concerning our spiritual life, not a disprover of our dual physical and spiritual natures.

Here's a poetic way to illustrate the dualist point. Roberto Calasso wrote of Solomon's temple building this way:

> [G]od is in the cloud, but men can build, give shape to, a place where that cloud can reside, or a tiny part of it, in the same way that they articulate words to celebrate he who is within the cloud. Everything takes place between cloud and House—and everything that happens is a consequence of that, which is to say, history.[8]

The cloud is immaterial spiritual reality, where God resides except as and when He condescends to manifest with us in space-time, as He did in the person of the Christ, and possibly at other times and plac-

---

7 2 Corinthians 10:5.

8 *The Book of Books*, New York: Farrah, Straus and Giroux, 2019, p. 57.

es. The House is the temple, of course, but it is physical and represents the physical reality in which the immaterial spiritual reality can reside. We consider temples "consecrated" for this reason, but Christ reminded us the presence of the cloud is more general than that. Our very body is a temple. The cloud-stuff resides in us. We are not little-g gods, but we are made in the image of God, which means we have one foot in both worlds. "Everything takes place between cloud and house." The interactivity of mind and Mind produces consciousness and is the arena in which human beings, material sentient agentic beings, conduct themselves. House and cloud together constitute reality. We should not consider the shambling physical body, the house, to be all there is to us. House and cloud together produce history, yours individually and ours together: all of human triumph and tragedy in space-time physical reality.

If this seems vague because it doesn't fit a scientistic paradigm, we might do well to consider how little we really understand even of physical reality. Far-reaching scientific inquiry still leaves us with basic imponderables. For example, what is gravity, really? The question is not how it affects physical things, like making water run downhill. Yes it describes relationships among physical things, but how and why? Yes it is a force, but of what is the force constituted? No one knows. Not only are basic scientific facts not as grounded as we may assume, but the meaning behind it all is entirely a mystery, without God. We use mathematics to describe relationships among physical things, but as with gravity, what exactly is mathematics, aside from a description of physical relationships? Stephen Hawking, an atheist, asked:

> What is it that breathes fire into the equations and makes a universe for them to describe? The usual approach of science of constructing a mathematical model cannot answer the questions of why there should be a universe for the model to describe. Why does the universe go to all the bother of existing?[9]

We can describe physical things and forces acting on them, all day long, but still not get to the bottom of reality, because we're only describing relationships among things to describe their extrinsic behaviors—not their intrinsic natures. Jean-Philippe Marceau wrote on this subject insightfully. The problem, he wrote, is that "physical ontology is

---

9 *A Brief History of Time*, Toronto: Bantam Books, 1988, p. 174.

empty."[10] If we delve more deeply into what we think we know about material things and energy, we come to realize we're merely repeating our descriptions of them without really explaining them. In this light, and in application of the logic concerning the mystery of consciousness, it seems inevitable that there is an immaterial reality, and it is the current tendency to presume atheist materialism that is unreasonable.

---

10 "Panpsychism and Neoplatonism: Re-Enchantment for Mathematicians and Physicists," *The Symbolic World*, May 29, 2022. Marceau adopted a neoplatonic stance by saying the universal substrate to explain physical things is not consciousness per se, but love, because love comes before consciousness.

CHAPTER THREE

Formless and Void

T HE SECOND SENTENCE in Genesis ought to create a sense of hushed expectancy:

The earth was without form and void, and darkness was over the face of the deep. And the Spirit of God was hovering over the face of the waters.[1]

We are peering in on the moment of creation. The earth formless and void means God-authored pre-creation potentiality. A substrate of formless matter and matterless form, a chaos and disorder not even substantive enough yet to be chaotic and disorderly. It is essential disorganization, a cauldron of potentiality. It is the ultimate sense of the river: sleeping, and dreaming, but with a tension suggesting an imminent bursting forth.

This language further describes, in mythical[2] terms, the moment of God's creation. The spirit of God hovers over the waters, the swirling pool of potentiality. He is about to draw it up, to give it form and substance through differentiation. A hierarchy of will and purpose and thought will swiftly ensue. The mountain rises up. The man rises from the woman's bed. The seed takes root. Day is born of night. Reason, purpose, will, meaning, and physical things spread to the horizons of God's dominion. God commands, on His own sole authority: *"Let there be light."*

---

1 Genesis 1:2.

2 "Mythical" does not mean fictitious. See chapter 6 infra.

36

In failing to see the mythological dimension to this poetry, one might ask how the earth could be the earth and yet "without form." Or how the somethingness of earth could be the nothingness of "void?" Mankind is not yet in the picture, and so neither is his perspective, so why does the earth appear in the first lines, and not the millions of planets and suns in the sky? "The deep" is water. How can water be contained, without a form to contain it? And what does it mean that God's spirit hovers over it?

We have to understand this text mythologically. The waters represent the fluid undifferentiated matrix out of which all physical things and concepts and ideals will form. It is unactualized potentiality. It is the locus of God's creation of order and form, but presently existing in disorder. If it were an aspect of human nature rather than pre-biotic potential, we might describe it as resting but contemplative, perhaps dreaming,[3] in a state of pre-wakefulness. The process of actualizing into physical and conceptual and spiritual reality is nascent, with God's spirit. God infuses that potentiality with His will, and it becomes actualized into the cosmos, and the earth, and mankind on the earth. The transition from unformed and chaotic, to formed and ordered, is transition from river to mountain.

Early mythology addressed itself to the question why there is order rather than chaos. The Babylonian creation myth would have been known to the writer(s) of Genesis chapter one, and he/they may have freely used some of the same symbolism, but with important differences to express a different theological point of view. In the Babylonian myth, "the waters" represent the seething turmoil of pure potentiality not yet actualized. It is disorder and chaos from which order and structure emerge.

A similar representation is likely intended in Genesis. Its writer(s) wrote as they did not because they were ignorant of science, or of science as it has progressed in our day, but because they weren't talking about things like whether there was a Big Bang or not. They weren't using empirical observation and measurement to try to explain the physical and spiritual reality we encounter. Instead, they were expressing a more significant point than the "how" of progression from simplicity to complexity. The point is that this reality comes from and belongs to

---

3 Recommended in this connection: David Gelernter, *Tides of Mind/Uncovering the Spectrum of Consciousness*, New York: Liveright, 2016. His project isn't to exegete Genesis on this point, but he does provide an in-depth look from a psychological, subjective perspective of the dream-like resting state in contrast to the hyper-real waking state.

God. Genesis opens with the assertion that in the beginning, God created the heavens and the earth. The next lines could have been about
the philosophical conundrums of somethingness and nothingness, but
instead it presupposes the existence of "the deep," and that's clearly water, just like the Babylonian substrate of disorder from which the land,
representing order, will emerge. This is about the mysteries of life force;
the movement from chaos to order; the defeat of entropy; the formation
of hierarchical structure. And all a creation of God.

Let's understand this very important word "form," in the context
of understanding the earth "formless and void." Most English translations of the relevant Bible passage use this word, though some will read
"order" instead. The transition from disorder to order corresponds to
the transition from formless to formed. Form creates order. If you fetch
water from the well, you're going to do it with a bucket of some kind,
because the bucket provides form to the water. The form is a necessary
constraint on the water. In the bucket, the water will assume a roughly
cylindrical shape that can be conveyed from the well, so long as you
have it in the form-inducing bucket. Until we provide a form to prevent
the water's entropic levelling, it is of no use. And yet we must have water
or die. The bucket is a constraint on the water. Constraint is what all
forms provide.

If you begin to think within the paradigm of forms providing constraint, as opposed to formlessness leaving all unconstrained (thematically, the mountain and the river, respectively), you begin to see the
ubiquity of forms. To start with the physical, every time you shape a material for some useful purpose, you're restraining the material in some
way. To build a house you might cut a tree, saw it into regular shapes,
measure and cut the pieces, and attach them according to mental forms,
a plan, so that roof, walls, and floor result. Every step in this process is
the application of constraint to material. In the physical world, you see
forms everywhere. Whenever you cut, sever, distill, separate, cook, or
carry material, or establish a position with respect to it, as with ladder
or scaffolding or parachute, you apply forms.

Behind all these constraining physical forms are forms of mind.
When you apply those forms to constrain material, you first formulate
the plan mentally. Mental forms necessarily precede their physical instantiations. You formulate a series of constraining processes and materials in the mind, so the material constraints are preceded by immaterial
ones. Constraints formed in the mind necessarily precede and facilitate
their imposition physically. Any physical form necessarily originates in

the mind.

This is relatively easy to see when the mind is the mind of a person engaged, as we must, in manipulating our environment, as with building a house or carrying a bucket of water. But what about the naturally occurring physical things on which we act? Re-consider that tree you were going to cut down and build your house with. Perhaps it grew naturally; in other words, it wasn't planted and cultivated by people according to human mental and then physical constraints of form. Instead God provided the form. The seed landed in the soil and took root. The roots spread in search of nutrient-laden water, helpfully pushing back soil and contributing to its friability and thus structural suitability for further plant life. The pushing forward of the roots constrains the soil, and of course the soil constrains the roots. As does the water content of the soil, attracting the root growth. The main stem grows, but not randomly; it is heliotropic. The plan, or pattern, embedded in the seed, includes constraints on the growth pattern so that it is sensitive to gravity, and contains the internal structure necessary to grow upward into the atmosphere without toppling over. The plan acting on these natural things originates first in mind: the Mind of God.

The significance of constraint to forms is this. We will find when we move more deeply into postmodern thought that it prominently involves critique of the constraining nature of forms to civilization. Constraint is the bugbear of logocentrism,[4] in the postmodern mind. The conviction is that we are more fulfilled, and less imbued with anxiety and fear, if we move from the mountain to the river; from greater to lesser constraint. Constraint is taken to be the signal feature of the "domination of logocentrism," in Freudian and Marcusean terms.[5] The central divide in contemporary politics is between the constrained and unconstrained outlook: those on the right, who embrace the necessity

---

4 We'll have much to say about "logocentrism," and it is defined in the Glossary. For now, we can understand it as the centrality of the word, but more deeply, the environment of rationality in which our conscious minds operate. It is the means by which thought proceeds to thought, logically, oriented in the direction of objective truth.

5 The phrase is prominent in *Eros and Civilization* (Boston: Beacon Press, 1955), Herbert Marcuse's dilation at mid-twentieth century on the metapsychology of Sigmund Freud, in which Marcuse seeks a corrective to structures of unfreedom thought to inhere in logocentric Western civilization. Freud (1856-1939) was a key figure in the development of disciplines of psychiatry, psychology, and neurology. He identified subconscious impulses in conflict with one another, and theorized repression of eros to sustain civilizational constraints. His vision is incorporated in the philosophies of many postmodern thinkers, including but not limited to Marcuse.

and utility of conceptual constraints—and those on the left who chafe at constraints and make it their business to attempt to remove them.[6]

It's not wrong to associate constraint with forms. It is wrong, however, to reflexively associate forms with oppression or domination. Forms, and their attendant constraints, are necessary to lift us out of animal stasis, as surely as stable footings are necessary to sustain a building. In the simplest natural thing, like the tree we've used as an example, we see the necessary existence of forms, but remember forms originate in mind. This is generally true; it is not merely true of forms imposed by mankind on its physical environment. A more general mind than that of individual people directs the imposition of forms in the natural environment. This is true for a tree but also for all trees, and all plants, and also rocks and atmosphere and deserts, jungles, seas, and the cosmos in its entirety, including mankind. Genesis tells us, in its opening lines, that that mind is the mind of God.

Aristotle conceived of physical things as an inseparable combination of matter and form. Formless matter is meaningless, because form is a necessary definitional descriptor of matter. Matterless form is inconceivable for an opposite reason: it is so meaning-full that it exceeds human conception. It is the mind of God, and, as such, describes the pre-physical imprint placed by God on what will be, with that imprint, matter. Matterless form is the idea of form in the abstract; divine design existing before, and instantiating, the physical; the spirit of God hovering over the waters.

Does the language of the second verse of Genesis[7] tell us events sequential to the preceding statement that in the beginning God created the heavens and the earth? That is, did God first create everything *ex nihilo*, as might be inferred from the opening assertion, such that what comes next in the text is a subsequent stage of creation? Or is the second statement a sort of qualifier to the first? If the latter, then God begins with a dream-like state of disordered potentiality, and begins to build hierarchies of complexity in the physical universe, and upon creation

---

6 Thomas Sowell used the terms "constrained" and "unconstrained" to describe competing visions of human nature that play out in the left/right divide in politics and culture, in *A Conflict of Visions: Ideological Origins of Political Struggles*, New York: Basic Books, 2007 (first published 1987 by William Morrow & Co.).

7 This is the conventional way to reference specific passages in the Bible. We should remember, however, that chapter and verse designations are not inspired; that is, the original text did not include them, nor section headings, nor paragraph breaks. They're helpful, but we should be careful how much we infer from them, in the same way we're careful about nuanced differences in translation.

of partially God-like mind in mankind, a hierarchy in concepts, ideas, ideals, and values.

One school of thought places the act of creation in God's commanding, "Let there be light." If that is correct, then the first sentence ("in the beginning God created the heavens and the earth") is just declarative of what is going to be further described. But the very next thing described is the formless and void features of the earth. This refers to something, not nothing, so this could mean God created from material that was already in place. If that is what is meant, it doesn't change the fundamental significance of these first acts of creation, but it does leave a loose end for our modern, scientific minds. If something was already there when God began His work of creation, then who or what created that? Genesis doesn't attempt to answer how material might have existed before God acted upon it, either because there wasn't any, or because that's simply not what we're reading about here. Genesis is setting up a worldview that will sharply contrast with pagan worldviews of people groups around the Hebrews, and it's explaining theology, not exclusively science nor history.

All is in darkness until God speaks light into existence. Light is crucial to biology on the earth, but we should understand this also metaphorically. Light means understanding. Darkness means ignorance, obfuscation, confusion, misunderstanding—and is the default state until that majestic moment when God will speak light into the world. The God-to-mankind message of Genesis is a message about message; information about information; language about language. God speaks the world into existence and Genesis speaks to us about His speaking.

Mankind, made in the image of God, speaks too, to God and to each other. But we don't always speak to each other with understanding. Our Babel towers are frustrated by lack of understanding. Our failures to understand one another are explained in Genesis, if we have ears to hear. We should understand the relation behind the Tower of Babel story to be the centrality of language and understanding in Genesis as a whole. This will be important to grasping the postmodern departure from the Genesis worldview, when we discuss the substantive nature of postmodern critique, and the "hermeneutics of suspicion," and the function of contrived social narrative, and the purposeful obfuscation by postmodern disinformation.

"Void" is the term used to describe the state of the earth before creation, in many English interpretations of the Bible. But the phrases "desolate emptiness" and "empty" are used in others. To say the earth was without form is significant. How could the earth be without form and yet be the earth? "Void" means absence, so how could the earth be both present and void?

We're to grasp a mood, a sensibility, a receptiveness to the idea of the earth in an incompletely formed state. What we're not to try to do is picture a physical transformation according to scientific formula. Not that the current laws of physics did not apply to what we're reading about. Maybe yes, maybe no. But certainly we're to understand that God was present at the beginning. He is not bound by the laws of physics, He authored them. Whatever chaotic movement of material occurred, God was in control, "hovering over the face of the waters."

What we're reading about in these particular lines is not the transition from non-existence to existence, but rather the formation of order from chaos. These may coincide; that is, one way of looking at creation is the transition from true Nothing to something, and another way of looking at it is the transition from chaos to order. We think in chronological terms, however, because we're time-bound creatures, and from our way of thinking, there would be step one in time, creation from Nothing ("*ex nihilo*"), followed by step two in time, development of order from primal material. This primal state would be Augustine's "inexpressibly profound abyss,"[8] a difficult to conceive "formless matter:"[9] no physical essence as yet, but rather essential mutability.

Christian tradition holds that God created the physical heavens and earth *ex nihilo*. We often think of nothingness as mere absence (or "void") rather than true Nothing.[10] True Nothing can be a difficult thing to grasp, from our physical platform of somethingness. We tend to think of nothing as being the absence of some particular something. To think of empty space with no earth as being space-minus-earth means we're thinking of "nothing" by first thinking of a something (earth) and subtracting it. That's negation, not true Nothing—a distinction that will be important when we try to contrast postmodern thinking to the worldview of Genesis.

If we allow ourselves to think unconstrainedly about whether God exists, we should first untether this tendency to negation. Stop thinking about whether the God you imagine exists or not. Stop thinking about whether the supernatural reality you imagine does or does not super-

---

8 *Confessions*, 12:3.

9 *Confessions*, 12:3-5; and Aristotle's *Metaphysics*.

10 *Dangerous God*, chapter 19; Norton, Albert, *Intuition of Significance/Evidence Against Materialism and for God*, Eugene, OR: Resource Publications, 2020, Chapter 3.

vene upon physical reality. Instead, try to think of true Nothingness, first. It's hard to do. This is different than mere absence of something. Don't imagine God, then cross him off in your imagination. Don't imagine the cosmos, then cross it off. You can't fully imagine true Nothing because you're using something, your brain, to try to imagine it. We tend to start our contemplation of Nothing with a something.

To imagine true Nothing, we have to hold in the mind a pre-creation state, a nothingness so complete there are no mental tools with which to grasp it. We have to try to imagine without allowing a something to form in the imagination, not even a dark and vague and formless something. The pre-imagination imagining is like pre-creation reality, in which "The earth was without form and void, and darkness was over the face of the deep."

Attempting to imagine true Nothing might help us see the mistake we make psychologically in our tendency to engage a negation. We don't formulate propositions of truth *ex nihilo*. Instead, we take existing propositions and accept or reject them. We don't create like God does. We cancel things and ideas from the somethingness we encounter, and consider that creating. We engage a negation, "nothing-as-such,"[11] meaning a nothing that is really a something, but a something that is vague and formless and void-seeming. This is what we do when we describe ourselves by what we're not, as with the labels "a-theist," "a-gnostic," "not religious," and so on. This same mistake of thinking is made on subjects more prosaic than ultimate metaphysics, by the way, as when we identify as anti-fascist or anti-racist; anytime we place our identity in a negation.

The tendency to engage negation is a significant element, not to be overlooked, in the direction of postmodern thinking beginning especially in the twentieth century. It is a rebellious or transgressive disposition wherein one doesn't really feel alive except in proximity to the fires of destruction. Life and meaning are thought to be a product of intellectual revolutionary frenzy, which might be described like this:

> To the question, 'Your idea of happiness?' Marx replied, 'To fight.' To the question, 'Why do you fight?' we reply that our idea of happiness requires it.[12]

---

11   In David Bentley Hart's phrasing, in *The Experience of God/Being, Consciousness, Bliss*. New Haven, CT: Yale University Press, 2013.

12   Anarchist literature by Anonymous dubbed "The Invisible Committee," *To Our Friends* (2014).

This is an ongoing attitude of negation and transgression, an attitude that pre-exists the question purportedly addressed. Revolution for the sake of revolution. It is an attitude born in the river, with hostility to the mountain, insisting on devolution to chaos and disorder in a vague hope that a better creation will arise out of it. Whatever it will be, at least it's not what we have now.

CHAPTER FOUR

What is Reality?

T O SAY SOMETHING is "real" is to say it is part of reality. We have just considered true Nothing, but Nothing is, by definition, not part of reality. Only the concept of it is, and only to facilitate imagining a boundary to reality.

Whenever we set out to identify anything, we do so by distinguishing it from that which it is not. Identity and differentiation are two sides of the same coin. This is a feature of ontological dualism we will further address anon, which is in turn established on the principle of non-contradiction. If we are trying to say what reality is, we do so on the basis of differentiating between what is and what is not reality. But "reality" would seem to be so all-encompassing as to defy that differentiation. "Reality" must have boundaries, else we cannot grasp it at all. But establishing boundaries means dividing between two real things, which means we've cut out of reality some of that which is real.

A way to try to avoid this conceptual black hole is to narrow the definition of "real" to that which is part of reality but not merely ideal, or merely conceptual. But that's not sufficient, either, because there is a sense in which everything is reducible to mere ideal. We have no hesitation saying rocks are real, for example, but what about the idea of rocks, or the conceptual criteria by which we differentiate rocks from other things? Are the rocks real but not the concepts we employ to recognize them as rocks? We find that the most obvious and widest-scope concept we can come up with, reality, is actually difficult to define.

A good example of this difficulty is with mathematics. Is mathematics "real?" There are actually two schools of thought. On the one hand, it's purely an abstraction, and only the abstraction itself is real. When we contemplate the relationships among numbers, and work out mathematical puzzles, we are dealing entirely with non-physical ideals. On that basis, one might say mathematics is not real. On the other hand, mathematical relationships are necessary to do science, which is the study of material things, and we have no trouble saying material things (like rocks) are real.

We might say mathematics is "instantiated" in tangible things, but how? Do rocks and dirt and water and sky disclose mathematical relationships, or are those relationships superimposed on them by us? If mathematics is just a mental tool we use to describe tangible things, how is the descriptive fit so perfect? There is such identity between concept and tangible reality that they would seem to be of the same substance, both descriptive and constitutive.[1] This is an evaluation of the reality of mathematics on the basis of a "formalist" perspective (meaning confined to itself as a logic system) in contrast to a Platonic or idealist perspective.

Even if we regard mathematics as solely a self-contained logic system of relationships, why isn't it still real? We conceive of mathematics in the material arena, our brains, so that is real even on a physical, tangible level. But even if mathematics were purely an ideal, not even accessible by our physical brains, wouldn't we still regard it as real? It would seem to be real, even if it is solely a self-contained logic system of relationships. It constitutes forms by which we understand physical and mental constructs. In that way, it is like other mental forms that come to us unbidden and seemingly unsupported, like categories by which we group like with like and separate unlike from unlike. These are philosophical universals, by which we address the problem of the one and the many; unity and multiplicity; identification and difference. And these are as "real" as mathematics.

The philosophical study of consciousness, especially as relating to the current technological age, opens the door to several related inquiries concerning what reality is. David Chalmers provides a good summary, citing thinkers behind various formulations of what makes something "real," in *Reality +: Virtual Worlds and the Problems of Philosophy.*[2] He cites several alternative definitions, depending on the subject matter of the candidate for inclusion in reality.

On what basis would we hinge reality strictly on tangible things? We have no trouble ascribing real-ness to all manner of purely conceptual

---

1 See *Dangerous God*, Chapter 2.

2 New York: W.W. Norton, 2022, especially Chapter 6.

things, like virtues and truth and beauty. Materialists hold that, as Carl Sagan famously said, "the cosmos is all that is or ever was or ever will be." But physical things and forces cannot be all there is, because even if there were no God, there would nonetheless be immaterial things that are unquestionably "real," like truth and beauty, and also concepts and virtues and vices. At a minimum, materialists would have to soften their materialist stance to say these immaterial conceptual realities somehow emerge out of that which is physical.[3] They exist separately; on a higher plane of abstraction:

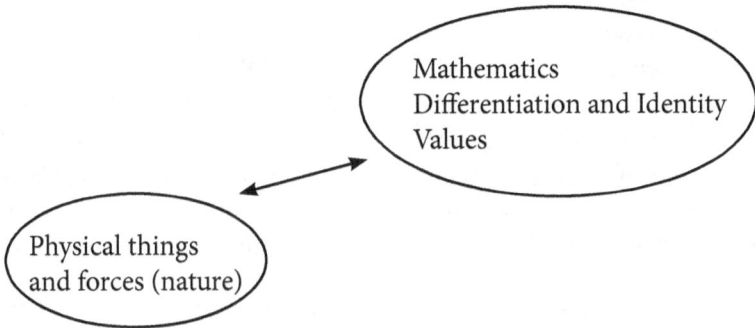

On a still higher plane, we would place spiritual reality; that is, a realm (for lack of a better word) not bounded by time and space like the cosmos or the immaterial concepts and virtues manifested therein; a realm in which reside God and such other supernatural beings as may exist, such as angels. It is (or includes) heaven and hell.

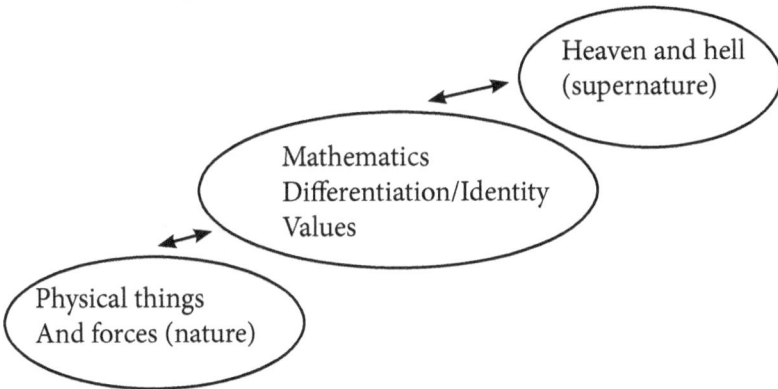

---

3 Unless, perhaps, they adopt eliminative materialism, denying reality to anything outside the brain, therefore no mind and no concept floating free from the buzz of brain activity.

Most who hold a generally materialist point of view would none-theless agree that concepts and values are in some sense "real," because, though immaterial, they are perceived or generated or in some other way connected to the physical brain. Religious concepts also, they might agree, are real (though not true) in the sense that they likewise emerge out of the workings of the brain, perhaps as informed by complex emo-tional elements like fear of death, which also originate in the body in response to the physical environment. But they would say "no" to the content of those immaterial concepts which point to a spiritual compo-nent of reality.

The religious point of view, by contrast, would hold that the spiritual realm is even more fundamental, more "real," than concepts and phys-ical things and forces. C.S. Lewis illustrated this idea in *The Great Di-vorce*[4] by describing grass in a purgatory or approach to heaven so real it hurt the feet of visitors not yet hardened to the reality of heaven. Christ's Advent was a manifestation of spiritual reality in the physical world, and He was just as physical as the people with whom He interacted, but also an Author of the greater reality beyond. We can think of the relationship of the differentiated planes of reality as nested, like this:

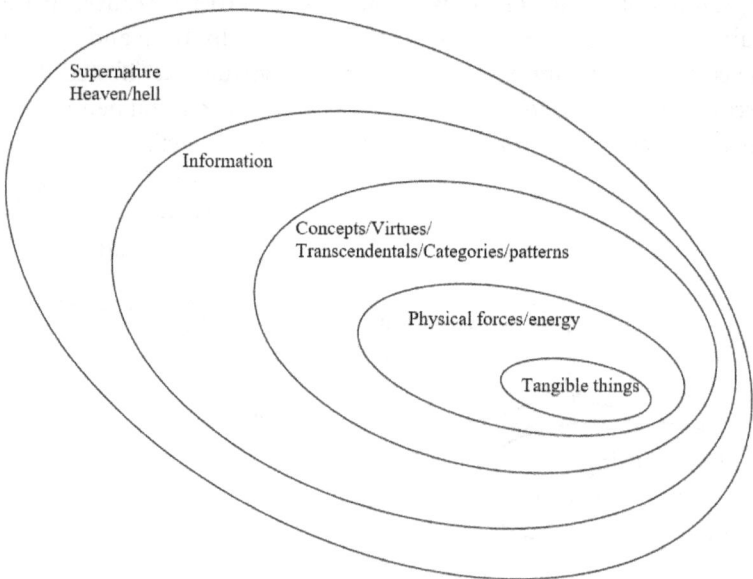

Supernature
Heaven/hell

Information

Concepts/Virtues/
Transcendentals/Categories/patterns

Physical forces/energy

Tangible things

---

4   New York: Harper Collins, 2001 (originally published in the UK, 1946).

Imagine the smallest oval of tangible things as being like an island. It's surrounded by water, so it appears to be the only non-water thing around. But we know there is a terrain of earth material under the surface of the water, too. We could map out the contours of the underwater terrain. Each of the successive ovals might be another depth of underwater terrain, all supporting the island. The above-surface land is real, but so are the unseen levels of terrain beneath it. In fact, the subsurface terrain is necessary to sustain the island above water, where we can see it. The point is that there is an unseen reality, and that unseen reality can be thought of as more "real" than the seen reality of the island.[5]

The monotheisms presuppose a metaphysical dualism of nature and super-nature, but there is another sense in which reality is a metaphysical dualism. Just as there is a dualistic divide between nature and spirit, there is a dualistic divide between real and ideal. What is the most "real" thing you can think of? Let's say you're taking your favorite walk through the woods. The path you're on, the air you breathe, the trees or shrubs around you are all certainly real. You can experience them through your physical bodily senses, and your body is real too.

But there's something more out there than those physical, tangible things, isn't there? Physical forces act on those physical things. These include electromagnetism, by which those tangible things are visible, and the nuclear forces, by which things hold together, and gravity, by which things are differentiated. Physical reality is a combination of matter and the forces acting on it: matter in motion.

But there's still more to call "real." On that path through the woods, how about concepts that may facilitate our appreciation of the physical things? The fallen leaves are down; the bare branches are up. "Up" and "down" are real, though they aren't tangible in the same way as the leaves and branches. Likewise, innumerable concepts that describe physical features, though it's not quite correct to say they're instantiated in physical things. The tops of the trees are "up," but we wouldn't say that upness is instantiated physically. It's a handy spatial pointer, but it says little about the subject other than its physical position relative to something else.

Color, shape, distance, texture, and beauty, and specifics of those like "green-ness" or "hardness" also describe features of this environment, and we can say they exist in some of the things on this walk, but they're universals; that is, they form a set distinct from but overlapping

---

5 "Now faith is the assurance of things hoped for, the conviction of things unseen." Hebrews 11:1.

these particular instantiations. The set of red things partially overlaps with the set of autumn leaves, and apples, and Ferraris. Color and density are real, both as descriptors of physical things and as concepts unto themselves.

Now, what about those trees? There are oak trees, hickories, and maples. These are taxonomical divisions; a type of category. Each tree is an individual, but the individuals appear in families and those families appear in larger families: a telescoping series of classifications. An oak tree is an oak tree and not a hickory, because there are differences between the types. And also similarities within them; both identity and differentiation apply in the categorizing.

If we dive deeper, we learn there are sub-categories within the category of oak, and sub-categories of hickory, and those sub-categories, too, are defined both by identification and by difference each from the other. Categories differentiate but also aggregate to common identity— the same phenomenon looked at two different ways. Categories are real, because they have meaning apart from the things or concepts they divide and aggregate.

Narratives are also "real" (as distinct from true). Narratives are stories, selective collections of facts and inferences expressing some point of understanding. They constitute differentiators, too, and a cohesive logic of identity, because every combination of words excludes all the other combinations that could take the narrative in a wholly different direction. We would refer to a story as having a "point" or a "moral" because certain facts and inferences are assembled into the story and some are left out to accomplish the purpose for which the narrative is composed. The division between included and excluded is what forms the story, and that division categorizes, just like mathematics and plant taxonomy and universals like redness and hardness and oppositional concepts like up and down, and physical things distinguished from conceptual, and forces distinguished from material they act on. Even the most illogical narrative can express something real, as in Lewis Carroll's *Jabberwocky*, showing us how the alliterative quality of form-driven symbols suggests a logic behind story-telling more generally. Narratives can be more or less rooted in fact, and more or less rooted in logical inferences from facts. They are sophisticated abstract representations, in comparison to a simpler differentiating category, like a quilt pattern. Metanarratives are the principles that distill from narrative. This type of differentiator will prove important, as we contrast the postmodern and Genesis world-views.

Philosophers down through the ages have wrestled with the distinction between ideal and real. We would describe as "idealistic" someone who aspires to ideals of virtue, such as courage, honesty, or self-discipline, or someone who works toward a laudable social vision. No person is perfectly courageous, honest, or self-disciplined, and yet those virtues are real things. Why do we try to act in accordance with these non-material ideals? Is a concept like "honesty," a property or trait emergent in some way from the physical body or brain? Or, is this moral aspiration supernaturally imparted to me and to my kind from a God who authors it and lays it upon our hearts as a natural law, which we experience as conscience?

Those realms of various ideals can be understood as heavens, in contrast to the earthly realm of physical existence. At the time of writing Genesis, mankind had certainly been wrestling for some time with the nature of "things" which don't directly manifest in our physical world, but are nonetheless real. So even apart from the metaphysical differentiation between natural and supernatural, the "heavens and earth" of Genesis must also refer to that real/ideal differentiation that philosophers have long grappled with. Heavens and earth are presented in the conjunctive, in the opening lines of Genesis, to signify all that is.

What is the most fundamental thing in reality? What would we describe as the substrate from which all else is derived? It's typical of us to think in terms of physical things at a ground level of "realness," and then consider more ethereal abstractions as in some way emerging from the hard rock of realness. The arrows, on this way of thinking, progress from more real to less:

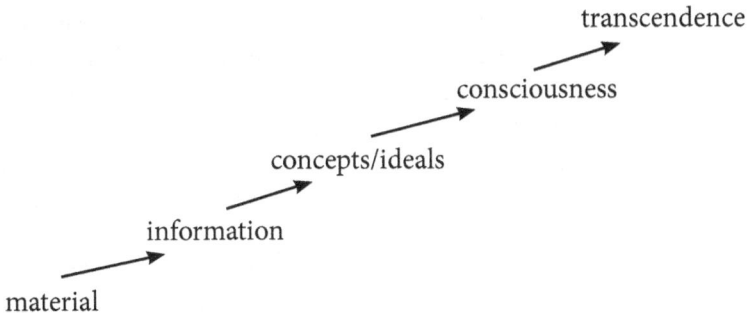

But why assume material is the most basic constituent of reality? As an expression of the "realness" of things, perhaps that's backwards. Perhaps a transcendent reality of universal Mind precedes human consciousness, and our ability to think abstractly, and the production of information, and perhaps it is embodied in the seeking mind of mankind:

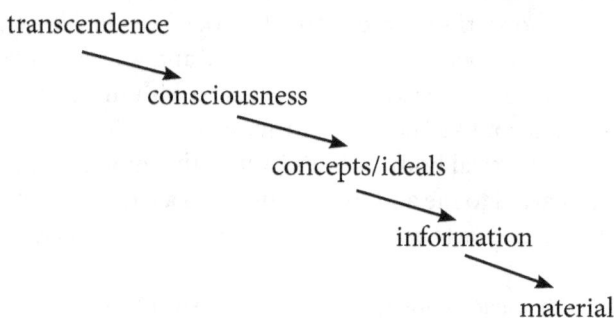

transcendence

consciousness

concepts/ideals

information

material

The most real thing is not diamond-hard physical objects. The most real thing is transcendently imbued consciousness by which we apprehend ideas; the word; logos; information; communication. This is the significance of the ontological differentiators in the innumerable categories and patterns in our physical and conceptual worlds.

"Informational realism" means information is a real and extant part of the universe, in the same way as mathematical realism and other conceptual entities are understood to be, like the universals, categories, symbols, etc., we have been discussing. Physicist Archibald Wheeler famously posited "it from bit," a shorthand way of suggesting tangible reality is derived more fundamentally from immaterial information; that we live in a "participatory universe."[6] It is certainly an intriguing idea that quantum physics might yield further understanding of informational realism. But whether Wheeler's particular speculation is right or not, informational realism is properly inferred in the Genesis worldview, because all of physical reality is generated from God, unfolding in successive oppositions we apprehend as differentiating categories. The tension generated in those oppositions generates meaning. Meaning in the sense of semantic information. Information can be understood as the primary constituent of reality, such that to say God spoke the world into existence is more than metaphor.

We tend to think of reality as primarily resting on matter, with information, concepts, and even spiritual components resting on that substrate of reality. But it is suggested here that this is so only as a result of shifts in paradigm over long periods of civilization. To grasp the signif-

---

6 See, e.g., "It From Bit: What Did John Archibald Wheeler Get Right—and Wrong?" *Mind Matters News,* May 20, 2021 (mindmatters.ai).

icance of a paradigm shift, let's first turn to some accessible examples. Here's one: consider the decimal system we use in everyday practical math. The non-integer .1 means one-tenth, as the word "decimal" denotes. That's a base-ten system. But why do we use base-ten? Why not base 8 or something else? If we were to shift to a base-8 system, it would seem strange and unfamiliar at first. To understand things, we'd tend to translate back to the base-ten system our usual paradigm requires. But a base-8 system would be just as valid. Here's another example: when we undertake learning a new language, and we learn its words and sentence structure, we get to a tipping point at which we're no longer translating in our heads, but actually thinking in the new language. It's a new paradigm. Another example: we're used to thinking that science is the source of all understanding and that because science is the study of material things, material things are all that exist. But that's a mistake; it's the result of channeling all of our understanding through processes of science, which is limited to the study of material things, so that we assume away any spiritual reality at the outset. That results in a materialist paradigm.

So with those examples, let's look again at the paradigm of informational realism. Our materialist presumptions lead us to think of matter as being the most "real," and then we imagine concepts and ideals and virtues, and so on, as being in some way emergent from matter, or that part of matter which comprises our brains. But in doing so, we forget that the hardest matter we can think of—perhaps a diamond—is actually mostly space, because we know it is composed of a combination of particles separated by space; in fact, by volume, more space than particles. So most of what we call matter is not even matter, and even more importantly, we know what we know of matter because of *information* about it. We don't see atomic and sub-atomic particles, but we know they're there because our scientific advances have revealed this *information*. And when we perceive matter, we are not experiencing it directly, but only over the medium of our consciousness, and what we perceive is, first, *information*. That information derives from pervasive differentiation and identity of things and concepts, the categories by which we make sense of the world.

A way to understand this primacy of information is to consider the intentionality of our consciousness as an exercise of attaching attention to relationships already extant in the world. This includes sensory but also intellectual perception, but let's illustrate with objects in our environment, perceived through vision. When we see objects in our environment, we see them differentiated. We distinguish rock from not-rock, animal from tree, tree type from tree type, on the basis of how they're different. But every object is not unique. They are identifiable to like things, so we see a rock not only as distinct from things that are not rocks, but also as identified to other rocks—a member of the broad category "rock." An animal is not just distinct from a tree, it is like other animals. An oak tree is not just distinguishable from maples, it is also identifiable to other oaks. Objects are not merely sorted into categories by the exercise of the intentionality of our consciousness. The categories exist in the objects themselves. When we perceive the objects, we perceive their categories. Perceiving their categories means perceiving the differences in category. Perceiving differences means perceiving relationships: this not that; this with that.

In a sense, we participate with objects in the course of perceiving them. We are able to navigate among objects like rocks and animals and trees because they are meaningful. "Meaning" as semantic content; as information, arising from differentiation and division. Perceiving like with like and against unlike means perceiving relationships among objects. The relationships inform us about the object and thus generate meaning, and it is that meaning that we first perceive. Information—rock/not rock, animal/tree, tree type/tree type—is what we see, not just matter. Objects don't exist separated from information about the objects. Even the brute fact of existence is information. Matter is inseparable from information, and the information is what makes matter perceivable. If you open your eyes and see a rock, or an animal, or a tree, you are seeing first the meaningfulness of those objects. They are "meaningful" because their very existence generates meaning. Category inheres in existence, it is not a feature of the object sorted separately. Categories generate information, and it is that information that we observe. That meaning-making is more fundamental to the existence of the object than its physical composition or the ocular physics involved in our perception of it.

Thus, it can truly be said that we perceive information before objects. Meaning precedes matter. It follows that information is the more fundamental element of nature: bits, not subatomic particles nor joules, nor seconds of time. William Dembski suggests that "the proper object of study is not particles, but the information that passes between entities—entities in turn defined by their ability to communicate information." Indeed, "information is poised to replace matter 'as the primary "stuff" of the world."[7]

From the beginning, mankind has tried to make sense of how anything in the cosmos can be differentiated from every other thing. An example of this inquiry in art: in Raphael's famous *School of Athens* painting, the two central figures are Plato, pointing up, and Aristotle, pointing down. They're not simply emphasizing heavens and earth, respectively. They're disagreeing about the source of the elusive principle by which we discern universal categories and not just particulars.

The School of Athens by Raphael (cropped).

Plato argued that we differentiate among things in our environment according to an ethereal Form by which we recognize specific instantiations. There is a Platonic ideal horse, for example, and actual horses we encounter are instantiations of the ideal. The ideal serves as the means by which we distinguish horses from other kinds of things. He therefore points up, from the actual perceived horse, to the immaterial ideal of a horse.

Aristotle pointed down. There are no ideals by which we group like things, he held. Instead, matter and form are united in the thing itself, and we group like things—like horses—because horsiness is the essential nature of what we observe. Horses are distinguishable from other

---

7 *Being as Communion/A Metaphysics of Information*, New York: Ashgate Publishing, 2014, preface, p. xiv. Dembski quotes Paul Davies, "It From Bit?" *New Scientist* 161, January 30, 1999. In *Being as Communion*, Dembski argues that "Information is produced as certain possibilities are realized to the exclusion of others within a matrix of possibility." (p. 37).

kinds of things because their material and form is bound up in their causal existence.

Aristotle and Plato are key figures in the long philosophical struggle to explain universals, properties which hold like things with like despite their instantiations in differentiated things and concepts. Universals refer to the strange fact that we can discern commonality among disparate things. We instantly know the category horse, without having seen and compared all the horses in the world. A universal property combines them, and there is a differentiation between universals, a categorizer that causes them to make sense to us as instances of type. The project of attempting to explain universals was overthrown altogether by nominalists like William of Ockham (1287-1347) but was taken up again in philosophical realism, which takes the universals to be existing properties of reality.

It's simple enough to say the categories, or universals, are "real," but what does that mean? Do we point up, or point down, or say vaguely that categories are just out there, or with the nominalists that they don't exist at all? None of these answer the question, really, but Genesis does: we know things because God makes the forms; their "essential nature" is conveyed by Him. He provides the universal differentiators by which we apply reason to our experience of the world, and discern among types of things and concepts and hierarchies of value.

We discern categories, we don't create them, in other words. They are ontological, meaning they inhere in the existence of the thing we discern as being categorically distinct from other kinds or types or species or patterns and so on. We're familiar with categorical animal taxonomies, so let's use that as an example. "Species" means a type of living thing distinguished by category telescopically from higher orders of type. Bears are a species of animal, but if we want to refer to a particular animal rather than the species, we might refer to a "specific" bear. The very phrasing—"species"/"specific"—encompasses the ontological significance of the category the bear represents. "Bearness" as distinct from whale-ness or seal-ness is inseparable from the existence of the bear itself. The taxonomy is not superimposed on all undifferentiated animals. It exists in the animals themselves. And exists in us, in our ability to distinguish among the categories.

Likewise other kinds of categorical differentiators, like symbols, patterns, and metaphors. There is a universal called "pattern," for example, of which there are innumerable instances in our world. Patterns exist so pervasively in nature that one could never complete a catalogue of them.

We could begin with the pattern of spring following winter, and annual circuits of the sun, and 24-hour cycles of day and night, just as the opening lines of Genesis attest. And then we can proceed to the patterns of leaf forms and spreading flows of waters and the draw and heave of waves on the beach, and the electric awareness of youth that gives way to weariness in old age.

God's act of creation by "this-not-that" division means that all of creation can be described in innumerable oppositions, rather than as an endless catalogue of paired things. "The heavens and the earth" is inclusive of all reality, and subdivisions of that reality are identifiable by categorizing oppositions. "The heavens and the earth" is not merely a recital of two things created by God. Each is what it is because it is not the other thing. Each pole is defined by its opposite. The heavens/earth opposition typologically announces the unfolding oppositions by which all of creation comes into existence.

A visual: imagine an undifferentiated field of gray. It's in a box, here, but imagine it has no borders and extends indefinitely in every direction.

We can differentiate into black and white, an opposition. So far, it's still simple, but overly simple, in the way we use "binary thinking" pejoratively to criticize unsophisticated analysis.

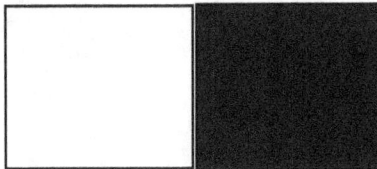

Our world is much more complicated than this, however. It presents to us in innumerable binaries. And so we make further divisions. White can be opposed to a slightly darker color. Black to a slightly lighter one, and those shades can be contrasted with another middle shade, and each of those can be placed in opposition with each of the others; as with black/not-black; gray/not-gray, and so on:

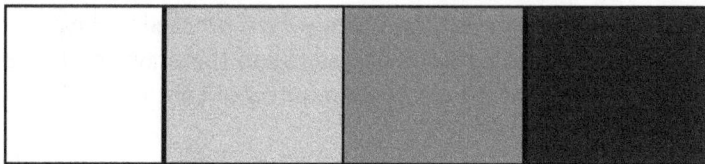

We proceed quickly to additional binaries layered on binaries, pro-liferating the differentiations we can make for greater and more refined understanding. Starting with the black/white/gray motif, we can con-tinue until we've achieved a nuanced delineation of blacks and white and grays, in ever more complex presentation, and a recognizable image emerges from these innumerable oppositions creating categories inside categories. The resulting image conveys meaning—in the picture below, a small pine clinging tenaciously to a rocky exposed cliff-top in the Pis-gah National Forest of North Carolina:

Photo by Greg Norton.

And we needn't stop there. We can expand our binary differenti-ations to include color, in its infinite shades, each contrasted with all the others, and then add differentiations on a third spatial dimension, sculpture rather than a picture. And then additional differentiations for a fourth dimension, time, so there is movement. And then we can add differentiations for more types of things, animals and people, and cities, the earth, the cosmos. And then differentiations for cognition, purpose, and moral values, in ever-increasing complexity and meaning, all on the basis of expanding and interlocking binary differentiations. In this way, we ascend to the full reality we know, and by God's grace, a renewed appreciation for the Author of it all.

CHAPTER FIVE

Form and Hierarchy

I N THE LAST CHAPTER we considered whether information could be a more fundamental constituent of reality than even matter or energy. Information, the word, relates to the form of things: in-formation. It gives shape to ideas which can then be communicated, in turn developing structure in the mind of the receiver of the communication. In classical philosophy, forms were central to the idealism of Plato. For Aristotle, form inhered in the "formal cause," among the types of cause necessary to understand an object. Information provides mental form or structure to our thinking, which may then manifest in physical products of mind.

"Form" constitutes constraint, whereby like is differentiated from unlike so as to be identified with like. It is therefore a boundary or point of division in oppositions from which meaning emerges. Form is another way to describe the differentiations of category, universals, symbols, narrative, and so on. Forms create the boundaries between one physical thing and another; one concept and another; one value and another; and all these stacked and overlapping and intersecting in complex and hierarchical ways. Forms produce meaning.

Consider as an immediate example of form-creating differentiations the letters on this page. They are symbols, arranged so that differences between them produce meaning. Each letter constrains the others, in the same way a retaining wall constrains earth movement, or a pillar constrains a ceiling from collapse. It is the differentiation (or we might say clash, or collision) between letters which produces a particular sound in a syllable; and the clash between syllables produces words. Then, the combination of words in a sentence produces meaning that doesn't exist in each word or letter separately. It is the constraining difference from letter to letter, syllable to syllable, word to word, and so on, that produces meaning. The collisions in speech or writing repeat at larger and larger scales with increasing complexity and nuanced meaning. And all arranged logically, on a direction arrow of objective truth, or else we discern the absence of logic or truth because discerning truth means also discerning deviations from it.

An awesome mountain landscape is awesome because it is meaningful, and it is meaningful because it contains innumerable visual and conceptual differentiations, as does our perception of it. The differentiations separate categories of scale, light, and color; peak from peak, peak from valley, vegetation from rock, color from color, light from shadow, sky from earth, and so on. Your intelligent mind discerns all this and the mountainscape itself projects it. Meaning—from intelligent Mind—was infused into that landscape before you ever encountered it. And if you find it beautiful, that is yet another layer of meaning generated by the whole. The "alphabet" of that meaning is form, by which categories are bounded, beginning with the spatial differentiator of plane and lift that makes the mountain a mountain.

A subset of the categorical distinctions we make has to do with values, by which we make moral judgments. We routinely distinguish between negligence and intent, for example, arising out of the same facts. An old saw has it that even a dog knows the difference between being kicked and being tripped over. We form our hierarchies of value by making conceptual distinctions in oppositions. Instead of "this-not-that," we can regard them as "this-above-that" distinctions. We make value judgments when we impute moral preference to the binary formed by the differentiation.

We impute value preference on the basis of God-imbued conscience. We say good is preferable to evil; honesty to dishonesty; courage to cowardice; rectitude to promiscuity; and so on. And yet, people choose dishonesty and cowardice and promiscuity all the time. We may become confused or deliberately choose evil, but we do not thereby throw over discernment of right and of wrong. Hypocrisy is the homage that vice pays to virtue, after all.[1] Even in failing to discern which is which in a morally ambiguous situation—that is, failing to continually double-down in moral differentiation to discern what is right—we nonetheless invoke moral value judgments. We know which values to aspire to,

---

1 A saying attributed to François de La Rochefoucauld (1630-1680).

even if we fail in our aspiration.

The source of values we ascribe to oppositions is properly basic, in the language of epistemology.[2] That is to say, prizing honesty over dishonesty (for example) is a function of the moral sense that God lays on the hearts of mankind, part of our "essential nature," in Aristotelean terms, or the ideal form of person as truth-speaker, in Platonic. Something is "properly basic" if it does not depend on other things in our calculation of how anybody knows anything. Philosopher Alvin Plantinga argues that intuition of the existence of God is epistemically "basic," for example.[3]

What this means is that some kinds of oppositions involve inherently a sort of "privileging," to use a postmodern term, and that privileging comes from a source distinct from reason (though certainly refined by reason). It is a value distinction already there in the human heart, when encountering, for example, the honest/dishonest binary. Subject to manipulation and abuse, of course, as is everything, but already there. When a card sharp cheats you out of the rent money, he's back-handedly invoking moral principles, not erasing them.

For value-laden oppositions, the value ascribed to one side of the opposition does not entirely come from the opposition itself. Moral values have a distinct source, God-given natural law. This is important because we need not be apologetic for "privileging" one moral value over another—honesty over dishonesty, in our example. And we need not take at face value the unproved assertion repeated by postmodernists (like Jacques Derrida) that the fact of binary opposition itself somehow supplies the privileging.

Among the universals pervading our world are truth (and falsity). They exist in ideal and precede our evaluation of a particular expression. Without truth and falsity as objective realities, we are not able to engage in discussion with others. Communication is possible only because speaker and listener both appeal to the criterion of truth. Truth is the compass arrow for a succession of expressions, in that they are linked "logically;" a transcending application of the logos. In this way, it is possible for us to find the same things beautiful, or the same moral good, or the same logic in a sequence of thoughts. And in this way, we

---

2 Epistemology is the philosophy of knowledge, attempting to answer the question "how do we know" about anything.

3 Plantinga, Alvin, *Knowledge and Christian Belief*. Grand Rapids, MI: Eerdman's, 2015. Discussed also in Norton, Albert, *Intuition of Significance/Evidence Against Materialism and for God*. Eugene, OR: Resource Publications, 2020.

can understand one another in speech.

In the unfolding "days" of creation in Genesis, the narrative moves rapidly from utter Nothingness, to chaos and disorder, to organization and order, to differentiation in kinds, to highly complex systems in the cosmos and in living things on the earth, culminating in mankind. How do these accumulated differentiations become hierarchical and form the intelligence-revealing world, and mankind's moral agency exercised within it, and the resulting structures of value we internalize and live by, and which form the civilization we know?

We live in a society with all manner of mutual social expectations based on what is perceived to be morally right and wrong, with wrongs ranging from a social slight at tea to rape or murder. Hierarchical moral value is differentiated: honesty over dishonesty; sexual rectitude over licentiousness; kindness over meanness; independence over dependence; fullness of life over mere breathing. We live inside a complex matrix comprised of myriad and overlapping value-laden oppositions from which moral values emerge. It provides form and structure to our existence. We may attempt deconstruction, but it is the fabric of God-created reality, not amenable to human deconstruction. In the postmodern world, we may attempt reversal or recalibration of values, but doing so introduces unnecessary strife. Ultimately, we fail in attempts to re-orient form- and structure-inducing fundamental values.

This form-created structure can be thought of as a series of boundaries differentiating thoughts and deeds, which we accept and internalize. By them we are oriented to the good, the true, and the beautiful, and by them we recognize evil, falsity, and ugliness. These structural boundaries include, by their nature, restrictions, including impingements on our freedom, if freedom is to be defined as unimpeded personal autonomy in all things. We value freedom as a positive good, so should we reject all moral and intellectual boundaries to our existence? Think what that would mean. It would mean never undertaking anything we don't want in the moment. That would mean no self-sacrifice, ever, including sacrifice we make today for a better tomorrow, as when we exercise self-discipline or work to a better future or refrain from words and deeds destructive to self or others. We can just decide not to get out of bed in the morning, and see how that works out for us.

It is restraint on freedom from which we learn self-discipline. It is the honoring of boundaries—forms—that enables us to channel our energies in positive and productive ways. If you don't save money, you'll remain enslaved to a paycheck. If you don't exercise and don't avoid drugs and smoking, your freedom will sooner be curtailed by health limitations. If you don't pursue life-long learning, you'll live in a dark closet of ignorance. If you don't observe personal and social boundaries, you'll be isolated and rejected. We self-impose constraints for other goods. And we live inside constraints imposed by others, in order to sustain personal relationships and citizenship and liberty. We live with all manner of limitations on our freedom. This is not something to complain about. It's the way life is and must be.

Those constraints can be thought of as forms for building a better life. We used the analogy of building a house, applying constraints and forms to constituent materials. We can think of the project of building a life the same way. Our lives are shaped by forms, and constraints, and boundaries, imposed to achieve a beautiful edifice instead of random junk. Constraints or forms or limits formed in differentiation include those which apply individually, but also those which apply collectively, to enable peaceful social living. We have criminal laws that place a floor on acceptable human conduct, in the exercise of freedom. We have civil laws, the rules governing certain social interactions. We have cultural norms of conduct that, if transgressed, invite opprobrium. We have legal jurisdictions, with territorial boundaries. These also constitute forms, or barriers, or restrictions, on our exercise of personal freedom. We may sometimes disagree on whether they are effective or necessary or even moral, but none of them are optional; they are binding on us whether we personally embrace them or not.

Religion, too, prescribes forms for our conduct and for our thought-life and for our spiritual growth. This is necessarily a collection of forms imposed individually, subjectively, and voluntarily; that is, from the inside out. They call for affirmative belief in the divine, rather than mere acquiescence, but what is belief? How is religious belief different than, say, belief in the territorial boundary of the country we live in?

We say we believe in this or that thing or idea, but this means more than acknowledging the thing or idea's mere existence. If we believe, we acknowledge existence in accord with what the thing itself is, objectively, and to determine that, we employ universal categories of thought. Anyone might say "I believe in God," if God is perceived frozen in that state of hovering over the formless and void, creating no constraining types or ideals or categories by which we apprehend Him or the reality He creates. This would be a vague acquiescence to the necessity of some impelling force to time and space and material within it, but with no demands on human beings.

Religious belief requires special mention, among civilizing forms, because religious doctrine informs and explains vertical binary differentiations enmeshed in the structural matrix of our society. It does not merely inform, but is fundamental to, value hierarchies and architectures of meaning. Even when Christian religion is largely abandoned, as it is now in the West, its values still inform that architecture for a time, but as the basis for those values fade, so too do the values themselves, and the architecture of meaning Christianity produced becomes transmuted into something else. This is the effect of postmodern process philosophy replacing religious transcendence.

In liberal Western societies, we can reject religious creeds, but if we accept them, we do so because we believe them to be true, and to warrant self-restraint accordingly. Not because of church traditions disapproving of this or that conduct—or not only that, more accurately—but because God knows my interior being, authors my conscience, and sits in judgment at the gate between this life and the next. If we willingly internalize self-control because we correctly perceive the God-full nature of reality, then fewer external controls are necessary socially, and greater individual liberty is possible. Individual self-restraint, for religious moral reasons or secular ethical reasons, is necessary to well-being in this life.

As religion fades, so does the architecture for its hierarchy of values, so that values collapse in the vacuum left behind, or are replaced by ideologies like those of scientistic materialism or Marxism or fascism or hedonistic will to power or some other vision of collectivist New Man. The new ideologies needn't be invented and wedged into place as fully-formed structures, as with Nazism. More likely, they are selective principles emerging from the dry bones left after a process of postmodern deconstruction. In this way bigotry, for example, can become the greatest sin, and victimhood valorized.

At this moment in history, in the waning days of Christianity in the West, deconstruction of the hierarchy of values wrought by Christianity occurs through the leftist impulse. In the course of the gradual wearing-down of Christianity, a gradual build-up of a replacement ideology comes into being, creating its own structural hierarchies to replace those deconstructed. What we are merging into is a kind of technocratic Maoism: automated, collectivist, Godless, morally relativist, and pointless—but not without structure. External structure, imposed collectively from the top down, is the new trend. It replaces the hierarchy of ideals naturally developed from the bottom up; that is, by individuals looking outside themselves to objective truth and goodness, and by which liberal society is made possible by individual self-restraint.

The significance of structure is revealed, as Genesis describes the unfolding of reality. We can picture its deconstruction this way, employing again oppositions that create meaning. Consider John Lennon's song "Imagine." He asks us to imagine there's no heaven and no hell; no countries; no possessions; no religion. What will follow from this, he sings, is an absence of greed and hunger and killing, and we'll then share all the world in peace and "be as one." This song is a poetic anthem for those living a critique of God and of the logos and of reason; a devolution away from the mountain and toward the river. Its imagined but vaguely-stated utopian ideal is the antithesis of the structure we see in reality, and as revealed in Genesis.

Lennon's oneness is achieved by removal of all boundaries. Not just national borders, he's imagining a world without rancorous divisions by race or tribe or philosophy, in addition to all restrictions that inhibit personal freedom. Certainly, we'd like to diminish racism, xenophobia, and tribalism; these are among negative values in a Christian-structured value hierarchy, too. Removal of boundaries in the abstract, however, as Lennon imagines, would mean removal of the structure upon which civilization is built.

Consider, for example, our practice of imposing on children the effort of learning to read. By living inside the boundaries of study-time to master the written language, they will, as they grow, live more fully. That's an example, and there are innumerable others. An important one, not so obvious in the present age, has to do with sex. Self-restraint of sex to its place inside opposite-sex marriage is mostly abandoned outside conservative religious enclaves, so much so that it is difficult for many to see its utility in strengthening marriage, rearing children, and inculcating values necessary to liberal civilization. Boundaries to freedom can be onerous and excessive, but some boundaries are necessary for longer-term benefit. This would apply to any short-term sacrifice for long-term gain. The moral strictures of Christianity are, at their most fundamental level, about that very thing: sacrifice of base impulses as a form, or boundary, for higher good.

The Genesis division of heavens and earth is not a one-off instance of division. It sets a pattern for all of existence. An illustration, again using the hypothetical walk through the woods. If you are a silviculturist or an agronomist or an ecologist, you might begin to see the woods as one large organism, with oppositional features in its various parts. Or perhaps you see as an artist: subtle differentiation in color, value, structure, and texture, which might be rendered in some medium with your artistic interpretational spin. Or you're a theist and ponder the mystery of a numinous presence in the living things around you. Or you're a biologist interested in sorting the number and variety of living things by contrasting each from the others. These are all different ways to sort one's thoughts about these same woods, and all lead to further questions and observations.

But now suppose you are a reductionist materialist, and begin to contemplate that what you're seeing, fundamentally, is a collection of atoms and subatomic particles. Only a few more than a hundred different kinds of atoms, but combined in complicated ways to form the variety of material things you see. You might wonder where these atoms and particles originated from, before coalescing in the myriad ways you see before you. Perhaps they're stardust. Perhaps they originated in the Big Bang which was, in turn, a quantum blip. You might wonder at how and why these particular combinations of atoms ended up here. But most of all, you're intent on seeing reality in the raw, so to speak, in its most fundamental, irreducible way. You may feel this gives you the surest grasp on reality.

But what if your understanding of the most irreducible element of reality is all wrong? What if the simplest building block of everything in these woods (and by extension from this analogy, the cosmos) is something other than atoms? Are you really seeing the most "real" reality? In a previous chapter, we considered the possibility that information is even more fundamental than the particles comprising the trees and soil and atmosphere. You can't hold information in your hand, but it's certainly real. Its existence preceded the existence of physical things because differentiation generates meaning and forms discernibly distinct physical things. Everything comes into existence in oppositional differentiation which gives rise to semantic meaning which enables you to perceive the woods (and the cosmos) and to contemplate the various ways to think about what you perceive.

To try to remove boundaries on a fundamental level is to deconstruct all that is best about us. It amounts to deconstructing civilization. The boundaries include things like a conception of objective (rather than relative) truth, and norms of behavior inculcated in the family and reinforced in society. The structure of civilization is built up this way into an intricate value hierarchy. It forms the basis of logocentric Western civilization, which is in turn built on the text of the Bible and informed by the philosophical traditions of the Greeks.

In Lennon's "Imagine," we're to imagine those boundaries thinning into nonexistence, and the structures they maintained crumbling. But ultimately, that's impossible. Civilization may suffer from a rush down the mountain to the river, but reality will not be overthrown. The structure-producing forms and constraints are part of the fabric of reality, not an oppressive construct from the ancients of the West evolved to benefit the powerful. Genesis and like texts do not create reality, but rather describe it. We can imagine, like Lennon does, a new reality, but the existing one cannot be deconstructed except in our minds, and to the end of regrettable loss.

It can be critiqued, however. Critique consists not just in this one song, but in the idea it expresses, which is repeated in postmodern culture in innumerable ways. The river impulse Lennon exemplifies is part of reality, too, if not the utopia he imagines it leads us to. The impulse to critique can—and to deconstruct does—result in corrosive wearing-down of the structures of civilization built by unavoidable divisions.

Lennon would have us climb the ladder of those real civilizational structures, and then kick the ladder away in order to live in oneness, peace, and harmony. Except that we wouldn't. The continuing presence of the ladder is necessary to sustain all this. It is the hierarchy built to sustain civilization, including that part of civilization that critiques civilization. Without the hierarchy, we'd soon descend to squalor, madness, self-absorption, meanness, arrogance, small-mindedness. We escape those bad things precisely because of the hierarchy existing in oppositional division in our physical reality, and in our minds, and proceeding from the mind of God. We build beautiful things with forms. If we go too far in our zeal to remove overly constricting boundaries, we collapse also the values those boundaries support. This process can accelerate and build momentum until we descend into chaos, disorder, and misery, as has happened countless times in history, on large scales and small. It is the historically monotonous collapse of human towers of Babel. It's one thing to clear debris from the scaffolding of civilization. It's quite another to destroy that scaffolding altogether.

CHAPTER SIX

Mythos and Logos

T HE MOUNTAIN: rational, value-laden, and hierarchical. The river: aesthetic, relational, creative. Genesis discloses elements of both mountain and river. They are features of individual subjective psychology, but they are also features within civilizations. The claim is made here that ignoring one at the expense of the other leads to individual strife and civilizational decline.

Postmodernism is the headlong rush to the river, abandoning the mountain altogether. It is primarily a critique of the Genesis worldview, in particular its logocentric mountain features. To understand the distinction between Genesis and postmodernism, it is helpful to understand the ways of knowing which result from the text of Genesis and the civilization Genesis-based religion established in the West upon vanquishing paganism. From this perspective, we can better critique the critique that is postmodernism.

Logocentrism is the centering of the "*logos.*" *Logos* means "word," but also stands in for reason, or reason expressed in words, or logic, or it might even be used to describe God himself, as when we want to emphasize His speaking meaning into the world. These usages differ according to context, but are interrelated.

We should understand the unavoidable connection between creation and *logos.* We think of creation primarily as that which is physical, being bounded and formed by the three dimensions of space and that of time. Then we think of metaphysics—non-physical concepts and abstractions—as deriving from the physical. Mind from matter. But it's really the other way around: matter from Mind. The physical world of space-time is contingent on the metaphysical world beyond: ideals and concepts and ultimately super-nature. When God speaks the world into existence, He makes the word visual and time-bound; a material "book." We can read that book just like we can read the books of human prophets God in some way inspired. Both forms of revelation are "word" spoken by God into space-time. In this way the Greeks were more right than they knew, when they spoke of the logos as universal divine reason oriented to eternal and unchanging truth.

The word "logic" derives from *logos* because logical thinking is taken to mean the expression, in words, of a thought which leads "logically" to another thought. Imagine sentences linked with the word "therefore:"

> The earth turns relative to the sun. *Therefore,* part of the earth is in shadow and part in daylight at any one moment. *Therefore,* if we are stationary on earth we experience cycles of light and darkness.

The first sentence seems to demand the second, and the second the third. But why? What is the criterion by which we say these sentences are linked? We might say simple logic, but what does that mean? Compare this sequence:

> The earth turns relative to the sun. *Therefore,* the sun winks on and off randomly. *Therefore,* light is called "day" and dark is called "night."

Hunh? Syntactically these two sequences are similar, but the second makes no sense whatsoever. Neither of the "therefore" sentences follows logically from the one preceding it. We can easily see that, but how? On what basis do we perceive that logic impels the successive conclusions in the first sequence, but not the second?

In a logical sequence, there is a "because" element: sentence one somehow causes the thought in sentence two, which somehow causes the thought in sentence three. What is the cause? The sun continually radiates light, so we can reason that rotation of the earth would expose different parts of it at a time. That "makes sense;" it is logical. There is an ordering principle between the two thoughts, the rationality connecting proposition to proposition. We say the sentences are rationally linked because there is a consistent ordering principle for the linkage. The ordering principle is truth. Sentence two logically follows from sentence one if it is true and necessarily true from the premises set forth in sentence one. Sentence one "causes" sentence two because the move from proposition to proposition is in the direction of truth.

But who decides? What enables you to test my logic by deciding for yourself whether the sequence I utter is connected by logical inferences? For that matter, how can anyone communicate any remotely complex thought to anyone else, without both speaker and hearer employing logic—importantly, *the same logic*—to the same message? How is there a commonality to my employment of reason and yours, so that we can communicate? Imagine each of us speaking gibberish while the other shakes his head in exasperation. There would be no point in speaking at all. Normally, we do "make sense" to each other, and when we don't, it's precisely because we discern the break in logical connections, again proving their accessibility to us collectively through the logos.

For there to be mutually understood language, the ordering criteria for logic—truth—must be accessible to us both. It is therefore objective, not a product of our respective inner psyches. The speaker and the discerning listener appeal to the same truth criterion in expressing themselves logically or in testing the logic spoken by the other.

Even apart from person-to-person communication, objective truth serves as the ordering criterion to reason, as when we perceive the common principle of gravity in water flowing downhill and an apple falling from a tree. Precisely because truth is objective and external, we can link these phenomena and apply the universal concept of gravity to these otherwise unlike events. In the same way, objective truth is proven out in all universals, those expressed in types, patterns, symbols, models, and ideals resulting from differentiation and identity in the world and in our thoughts.

Likewise in our discourse, even as we disagree about whether what is said is logical, we both appeal to the objective truth criterion for ordering successive inferences. Through a process of debate, we can drill down to more fundamental precepts on which we might disagree, but all the while the flag of objective truth stands above the debate. If truth is not objective, logic does not apply, and we can't make ourselves understood to each other, just like with the people who built the city and Tower of Babel. When someone argues that truth is not objective, ignore him. The statement—asserted as objectively true—contradicts its own premise.

The logos—understood variously as logic, reason, rationality, objectivity, the word, and God—is fundamental to Western civilization. Language is understood to hold meaning by virtue of its relationship to fundamental reality. The cosmos and our more immediate physical environments are objectively real, and so is our internal ability to perceive it. And so is our ability to reason from what we observe, and to express and understand that reason one to another. We further perceive concepts, ideals, and values as being objective, though more abstract. We understand that certain qualities of physical things may share abstract commonalities—universals—and we perceive those to be objectively real, too. In short, Western civilization is logocentric. In this age, logos is the air we breathe; it is rational and pragmatic and rooted in language as contrasted with image. It is especially helpful to understanding the "how" of unfolding material processes, as with science, but our current over-emphasis on empiricism and rationality can lead us to ignore the "why" of meaning and purpose.

It is possible to attempt to imagine away logocentrism as an unnecessary super-structure of thought applied to text or interpersonal communication or nature. This has been a project of postmodernism, in fact, so much so that "logocentrism," the word, is often used pejoratively as shorthand for internalized repression, or preservation of a nefarious structure of domination of oppressed people groups. Logocentrism depends upon objectivity and eternality of truth and right and wrong. It conflicts, therefore, with the relativism of postmodern process philosophies which place generation of truth and ethics in social process. Critique of logocentrism is, therefore, a central project of postmodernism. To understand the critique, we have to understand the thing being critiqued. What is critiqued is the Genesis worldview, which reveals the mountain logocentrism described here.

The mythos/story way of knowing was the primary way the ancients imparted truth. It began to give way with the Greek philosophers, many of whom advanced, implicitly or explicitly (as with Heraclitus), the idea of the logos, by which rationality and empiricism began to take on greater prominence as against the mythos of the ancients. The logos came to mean intelligibility that permeates the universe in some way, a pattern of rationality discernible by thinking beings. The logos rests on oppositional tensions of change and multiplicity and the meaning they produce.

Heraclitus (c. 500 B.C.) tried to reconcile that against the appearance of unity, permanence, and harmony. "We step into, and we do not step into, the same rivers," he famously wrote. The river you first step into is not the same river you next step into, because the water which comprised the river has changed between steps. And yet it is the same river. Heraclitus's river is conceptually both the one and the many, one problem of universals with which philosophers have engaged as long as there has been philosophy. If we deny the organizing principle that unifies the two steps, that would mean the river as an entity distinct from other rivers is an illusion; that we ought to stop using the same name for the rivers at Thebes and Cairo. But that denial violates our common sense. The Nile is the Nile in both places. Red is the same color in both apples and Ferraris. Beauty in the abstract inheres in both the Tetons and the Grand Canyon. Truth and falsity and goodness and evil reside in otherwise unlike situations, things, and concepts. And it is so with universals more generally: dualities, categories, taxonomies, patterns, and symbols which generate differentiators from which meaning emerges. The meaning emerging from the edges of these differentiators is the logos, the reality of the intelligibility of the universe, and, as such, the direction-driver for our thoughts toward objective truth, the exercise of which we call "logic."

The concept of the logos came to be associated also with systematic theology in Judaism and then Christianity. Upon the Ascension of the Christ, the project of further systematizing theology commenced with the Gospel writers and Paul, but continued as a philosophical enterprise intensely through the Medieval Ages. With the Renaissance and Reformation, the project expanded to reconciling heterodoxy, including the increasing skepticism, deism, and materialism through the early modern era into the Enlightenment period. The modern era, usually tagged as commencing around 1600, was marked especially by the advance of science, followed by technology, followed by a gradual shift from agrarian society toward industrialization, and concomitantly, away from subsistence living, for most, to increasing prosperity. The objectivity of the logos was the principal underpinning of science. Successes of science spurred increasing reliance on the logos as the principal way of knowing, so much so that logos has largely crowded out the mythos way of knowing.

In the late modern and postmodern eras, it became increasingly difficult to understand ancient texts expressed in myth, even as newer mythos expressions have developed, such as with entertainment superhero pantheons, social narrative, and the symbology of postmodern ideologies. Mythos relies more heavily on the river than the mountain. It is a way of knowing by means of contemplation through promptings of liturgy or figurative language or symbolism or imagery to express deep truths about the nature of reality, especially those truths not directly accessible by empirical observation. In this way, one makes sense of the medieval congregant willingly kneeling in a cold cathedral, surrounded by icons expressing ethereal spiritual reality, raptly attentive to the priest facing forward murmuring in ancient language while handling symbolic instruments of the Eucharist, performing, by his actions, re-enactment of divine Presence.

It is crucial to grasp that "myth" is not synonymous with "fiction." A myth is a story that reveals deep truths; often an allegorical narrative. The story is the vehicle for conveying those deep truths, but the facts of the story need not be literally true in order to do so. Indeed, the nature of the truths might be obscured in a story of mundane details and propositional assertions. This might well be the case, for example, with truths relating to spiritual reality or intuitions or features of human nature difficult to express in empirical terms. Traditional fairy tales convey expressions of human nature, or of dangers extant in the world, or of super-nature, or of moral values. Their messages are conveyed even to children, who can internalize, if not articulate, their deep meanings. If you tell a child about Little Red Riding Hood, or Cinderella, or Rapunzel, or Santa Claus, these are received as just stories, and yet they convey deep meaning that persists in the child's understanding even when he or she casts off their literal facticity.

In this day, the whole Christian story is often treated as myth in the sense of being fictitious. Elements of the story are rejected because they contravene materialist assumptions about reality. This includes most notably the Resurrection, but also other events Christians call "miracles" precisely because they occur outside the order generally imposed (by God) on natural processes in creation. Some elements present as implausible, if one is overly devoted to an empiricist expression of reality in the *logos* saturation of culture since modern times.

Because of our tendency to look for science-based accuracy, we tend to overlook the validity of the *mythos* way of knowing. Myth in the Bible conveys deep truth by allegorical narrative, not falsehoods. Because, in this age, we do not slip easily from logos to mythos, we tend to insist on application entirely of one or the other. Many who reject the Christian story do so because it has elements of mythos, and that for them means falsity, which seems to invalidate the whole story. Others gradually reject Christianity because they expand the Christian story's mythos elements so much that it erodes the necessity even of hard facts like the Resurrection, rendering the whole story irrelevant.

This all-or-nothing tendency exists for some Christians, also, who insist, for example, on a literal six days of creation only because modernity informs them that the logos way of knowing alone can be countenanced. Their fear, understandably enough, is that the line between logos and mythos may be unclear in a given text, with the result that the presence of any allegorical rendering means we must dismiss the entire story as non-factual. The thinking would be: if there was not a literal six days of creation, or if the sun was not stopped in the sky, or if Jonah was not in the belly of a fish for three days, or if Noah did not house all species on his ark, then why not treat the redemption story of Jesus as allegorical, too? In this way, we can step on a slippery slope and end up modern-day gnostics, and then pagans, and then perceive ourselves as animals in a mechanistic world with the unfortunate burden of aware-ness of our meaninglessness.

We should resist this tendency to be locked into a logos way of knowing, rejecting mythos at every turn, even as we preserve the nec-essary facts of the Hebrew stories of captivity, exodus, and redemption, and the culmination of that story writ large across history in the Advent of the God-man who redeems mankind despite God's justice. If we in-sist on a literal reading of the first eleven chapters of Genesis, the depth and richness of its idealized structures, allegories, metaphors, analogies, and symbolism may elude us. We wouldn't really understand what it is saying to us. We should embrace a mythos way of knowing as well as the logos, as Christians, and reject the accusation that mythos is the equivalent of unreal.

Mythos is alive and well in the secular world, after all. It exists most obviously in our popular entertainments, in which tapestries of moral order and deep truth are presented at every turn. Who would dare say that George Eliot's *Middlemarch*, or Mark Twain's *Huckleberry Finn*, or Kazuo Ishiguro's *Never Let Me Go*, carry no weight of meaning because they are novels, and therefore fictional? Why do *The Lord of the Rings* movies enthrall? Obviously, they convey deep truths, and we are en-riched if we plumb their depths rather than dismiss them out of hand as irrelevant fictions.

Indeed, in the postmodern era, we are witnessing a new kind of mythos arising against the backdrop of scientific application of lo-gos. This is postmodern metanarrative, ominously different from the metanarrative of religion because untethered from objective fact, and tethered instead to socially constructed "truth." Metanarratives are im-portant to understanding the fraud at the heart of the postmodern worl-dview, so we will devote a chapter to a discussion of it in that context. Until then, we need a working definition. Metanarratives are the prin-ciples underlying narratives. Narratives are general storylines we repeat to ourselves, intending them as short-hand summaries of fact to support the metanarrative. The Santa Claus story is a narrative. Its metanarrative is joy derived from universal goodwill, generosity, and giving. Religion is a metanarrative, too, and so is the ideology composed of the variants of postmodernism.

Metanarratives support totalizing worldviews in which we're taught to see the unseen. Religion is a metanarrative on the same definition, but there are important differences between religion and postmodern ideologies. For one, the monotheisms disclose that the line between justice and injustice runs through every heart. Every person can be an oppressor and can be oppressed. Postmodern ideologies, by contrast, rest on spurious narratives formed to spur rebellion against putative injustice in social structures. The line between good and evil runs between historically formed groups, in this imagining, rather than individuals. There are oppressors and oppressed: good and evil people, grouped accordingly. Moral agency is individual, but that agency is imagined absent in postmodern ideology, and replaced with group identity. The group is imagined to have agency rather than individuals. In this way, postmodern ideology would extinguish mankind's God-imaged status.

The Genesis story is a narrative to express truth not readily accessible to us simply from empirical observation. It explains a reality beyond nature, which supervenes upon the physical world, infusing it with light literally but also metaphorically. God said "Let there be light," and there was light.[1] So we have light from the sun, by which we can see everything else. That's pretty significant, but is that it? Is there nothing more to be learned from this statement? How about "light" as metaphor for understanding? For human consciousness? Responsible interpretation of Genesis has for millennia included this understanding; it shouldn't be excluded because "light" does not literally refer to the logos and attendant conscious awareness.

In the first chapter of Genesis, there is a series of assertions about creation occurring in "days." What do the "days" mean? To say something about that, we should place the question in a larger context of interpretation. The Bible as a whole is full of symbols, metaphors, parables, and analogies that are not intended to be taken as propositionally true. Moreover, it is not one book, but many compiled, by different authors with different purposes over millennia, though all inspired and deemed canonical. Parts are written in a more matter-of-fact way, as

---

1 Genesis 1:3.

with the theology of Paul or the Acts of the Apostles. Others are written in a deeply mythos expression of truth not so empirically accessible, as with Revelation and Genesis. The texts cannot all be read the same way. There is a tension here between logos and mythos, and there is not always a clear dividing line between them as one moves from text to text.

A central hermeneutical question will be whether we take a text as a straightforward rendition of facts, or in a more symbolic way. The "slippery slope" concern is that if we concede one text as figurative, then why isn't the whole Bible figurative, in the sense that it teaches moral lessons but only in the realm of the ideal, unmoored from physical reality? This would be a problem, in fact, the same problem the Gnostics never resolved. Religious belief would be an idealistic add-on to reality, not something really pertinent to our everyday lives, and so easily ignore-able, especially when it illuminates some of our desires as transgressions against the order God created. To be relevant, it has to connect to the physical world we live in at present. And so it's important to understand the interaction between mythos and logos. God condescended to cross the divide between spirit and nature in the person of Jesus, who lived bodily, was tortured bodily, died in the body, and was bodily resurrected. "If Christ has not been raised, then our preaching is in vain and your faith is in vain."[2] The Bible is about heaven, of course, but it's about the earth, too. "In the beginning, God created the heavens and the earth." The Bible is about God, but is a revelation to man, so it's about the place they meet. The Christ had to be among us as a person rather than spirit only.

The danger of forcing an empiricist reading is at least two-fold. One, it squeezes out deep meaning that only metaphor and symbolism can provide. We're left with a denatured storyline seemingly unconnected to reality, which is unable to fully express the deep significance of mankind's connection to God. Two, on that kind of reading, it appears to have inconsistencies which from an empiricist perspective renders it suspect. How does God separate light from dark, when we know the sun radiates light continuously? How does God separate light from dark on both day one and day four? How is there an expanse between waters, when we know rain comes from moisture condensed in clouds, not from a reservoir above the sky? How does vegetation appear on day three, if day and night is created on day four?

The "days" structure of Genesis either means creation in six 24-hour

---

2 1 Corinthians 15:14.

days, or in six epochs, or else the "days" are not intended as sequential at all, but rather serve as a device to differentiate acts of creation hierarchically for greater depth of understanding. The story is symbolically true. It would seem that even the peculiar sequencing of events itself has symbolic meaning, as with a fractally repeating sequence of higher order over lower.

We have to be careful not to have the cart before the horse. The text should drive our conclusions, not the other way around. If the Bible is true, and it says God spoke the world into existence, then the physical world is a revelation of truth just like the Bible. This consideration in approaching texts like Genesis is not an accommodationist exercise of negotiating Biblical text against scientific speculation concerning origins. It is an exercise of properly distinguishing mythos and logos ways of knowing in Biblical text. It's literally true that in His creation, God separated the light from the darkness, for us here on the surface of the earth, but it's also metaphorically true, in that God thereby also separated understanding from obfuscation, and order from disorder, and being from non-being, all on axes of dualistic opposition.

The narratives of the first few chapters of Genesis in some cases overlap, and in some cases run parallel. The literary structure of Genesis reveals that it is not to be read as a rigidly sequential narrative. We know that with certainty for many reasons, but one is that the same events are related in different ways without any transition. So with the creation of mankind: on day six, God created mankind in His own image, male and female, for purposes of then explaining mankind's relationship to the rest of creation. The narrative will then turn to God's sabbath and then the Garden of Eden, before returning again to creation of mankind. The same events are looked at from different angles and for different purposes and with differing degrees of mythological style.

When we read the opening chapters of Genesis, we can derive understanding from its mythological expression. We derive deep meaning from densely concise words artfully placed in poetry, without demanding that the poetry unfold like the instruction manual for assembling a bicycle; as if we were to follow after God and try to make a world ourselves based on His model. Poetry can impart deeper meaning than prose.

CHAPTER SEVEN

Male and Female

I N THE OPENING lines of Genesis, God simply declares the world to be, "and it was so." God speaks all this into existence, His word made material, as it will later be made flesh in the person of Jesus. And then God declares His creation "good." This likely means a moral good; that is, creation itself being a morally good thing, as opposed to merely satisfactorily performed. This, of course, is the pre-fall creation, before mankind's acquisition of moral awareness. The fall introduced corruption but did not reverse the moral good of creation.

Upon creation of earth and seas, plants and animals follow logically. What stands out in the narrative is the emphasis on seeds. God creates living things with the capacity to reproduce in their kinds, because the living individuals will die. Death and reproduction go together because a person's life in the body is finite, yet mankind as a whole continues in existence through history. The theme of death and regeneration through seeds recurs in the Bible, for example: "unless a grain of wheat falls into the earth and dies, it remains alone; but if it dies, it bears much fruit."[1] Jesus refers here to His own death as a necessary seed for His Resurrection, and the resulting propagation of the word of reconciliation with God.

The seed is the recompense for natural death. In people, it requires both man and woman, and the woman is the natural and only body in which the seed is nourished. A man and a woman belong together in this most fundamental of ways, two in sexual opposition to bring forth new life. Meaning is generated ontologically in the sexual opposition.

---

1   John 12:24.

As with a particular man and particular woman, so with mankind, the species. Opposite sex mating is necessary to the continued existence of mankind, a fact obvious yet obscured by misuse of sexual function.

The notion that sexual function might be misused is mostly eliminated in the postmodern era, in which the self-evident value of marriage, monogamy, and non-marital chastity is questioned and even regarded suspiciously. Why is this? It is a function of our departure from the natural to the artificial, and from the individual to the social. These devolutions go together. Sexual mating is the natural means by which we propagate down through the ages, so that we are naturally, biologically, connected to the first man and woman, and in that way to all other people, including progeny in generations which follow us.

The when and how of God's creation of the man (as opposed to mankind) is provided in mythological language. There is symbolic significance to the male/female difference arising from the fact that the woman was created in the garden, and the man outside of it. This is suggestive of man's outward-looking perspective, as with engagement in business and politics, in contrast to woman's traditionally more inward-looking emphasis on home and family. Agentic, assertive, and dominating, on the part of the man; communal, cooperative, and nurturing, on the part of the woman. These tendencies are reflected in the body and in the sex act by which male and female come together. The male assertive outwardly; the female receptive inwardly. The man instantiating; the woman embodying. The man actualizing matterless form; the woman potentiating formless matter. The mountain predominating in the man; the river in the woman.

God is neither male nor female. Both derive from him. Sex-specific traits are nascent in Him. What this must mean is that neither male (or masculinity) nor female (or femininity) are superior or inferior to the other. The essential equality of men and women before God is established here, though men and women may relate differently to God by virtue of essential differences in nature, or by ways in which we socially idealize those essential differences in our religious rituals or God-mindful customs and social norms.

We're used to thinking of God as male in part because the male was created first, with the female a "helper" (or better, "sustainer") to him. The "help" is in continued propagation of mankind, this shouldn't be read to mean she is merely an assistant of some sort. Traits identified as more predominantly male are the most visible in God's acts of creation: traits like authority, execution, and justice. But really, traits associated with the feminine are equally necessary and present in the creation as well: wisdom, creativity, and mercy. We might do better in our apprehension of God if we don't reflexively consider His character in terms of maleness. We might come to better appreciate the feminine in creation.

Importantly, both male and female are created in the image of God. Both are responsible for their actions; both have moral agency; both partake of God-like moral responsibility and earthly creation; both inhabit the liminal space between metaphorical heavens and earth. And yet they are quite distinct, comprising a polarity within mankind. Each requires the other, for the project of reproduction so thoroughly emphasized in the first chapters of Genesis, and for subduing and filling the earth as God commands. That mutual need is basic biology, but the mutual need goes well beyond the reproductive imperative. Male and female are drawn each to the other by mutual need beyond mating pairs of humans. Beneficial male/female tension runs through all our social lives.

Among the ways we can think of mutual interdependence of man and woman is in complementary characteristics commonly associated with each. These are both positive and negative. Traits associated with masculinity include decisiveness, strength, reason, determination, order, hierarchy, protectiveness, aggression, building, destruction, self-indulgence, rashness, monomania, cruelty. With femininity: caring, nurturing, supportiveness, relationship-building, creativity, indulgence of sentiment, indecision, worry, fearfulness. A partial sorting out of sex-predominant traits like these exist as between men and women, but of course they are all traits that can be found in some degree among all people.

Initially the creation of mankind in Genesis involves only man, not yet woman, and woman will be made from man. Possibly this is to emphasize sex differences, of which male characteristics are better signified by his appearing first, as with man's more assertive and visible agency. God's fundamental task for mankind was to exercise dominion over the earth. We see the man alone exercising that function at first, by naming the animals, and interestingly, God watching "to see what [the man] would call them," thus demonstrating man's agency. This is significant because naming is a differentiator, and therefore a creative and information-producing act.

Even this exercise of dominion is not sufficient, however, to overcome the lack felt by the man because no companion like him—meaning, one with the same intelligent conscious awareness—exists among those he names. Mankind is distinct from the animals in a way that is essential to humanity. Self-awareness, or "metacognition," means mankind in its God-breathed aspect responsible for moral discernment. The intersubjectivity of human consciousness[2] results in human society, impossible without woman.

Exercising dominion over the earth means to subdue and fill it, and subduing and filling correspond respectively to male and female traits and functions, and subduing necessarily comes first. Mankind's place in the world must be established, with chaos and disorder and danger pushed to the boundaries as much as possible, before the male/female regenerative function can be established.

In churches trying to hang on to some understanding of male and female in the puzzling postmodern age, it is common to speak of male "leadership" or "headship" as being the difficult square peg we must somehow accommodate. But Genesis doesn't set forth roles that must be dogmatically followed. It just explains how men and women are different in function, and everything follows from that. As Alastair Roberts put it:

> It is less a matter of the man having authority over the woman as one of the woman following his lead. As the man forms, names, tames, establishes the foundations, and guards the boundaries, she brings life, communion, glory, and completion. Neither sex accomplishes their task alone, but must rely upon, cooperate with, and assist the other.[3]

This describes male/female difference through a lens of love rather than power. If power is the operative paradigm, Genesis can be twisted to read like validation of male hegemony over women. But if love is the operative paradigm, then it describes man and woman giving of their respective natures, each to the other, to accomplish the work set before them. Love vs. power corresponds to Genesis vs. postmodern worldviews.

Much debate occurs these days about whether the "Adam first" feature of Genesis justifies patriarchy. On that question, we should probably first query what is meant by "patriarchy." In the context of current

---

2   Concerning intersubjectivity, see chapter 13, infra, and *Dangerous God*, chapter 7. Intersubjectivity does not mean social consensus, but rather the mechanism of mutual subjective awareness from which one's social awareness emerges.

3   "The Music and the Meaning of Male and Female," *Primer*, Issue 03, (Fellowship of Independent Evangelical Churches) 2018, p. 12.

debates over gender roles, it means systemic preference for men in society: a part of the Marxist and Structuralist systemic unfairness criticized by feminists. To be fair to the anti-patriarchy point of view, it is true that most Western societies are or have been patriarchal in a legal sense, as when men were preferred in inheritance of property. Patriarchy is the reason wives traditionally take the husband's surname for their own, in marriage. Historically, women's work outside the home was limited by social custom.

Most cultures have long valued a wife's deference to the husband's leadership of the family, while devaluing a husband's refusal or inability to take it up, as when we say, disapprovingly, "she wears the pants in the family." Are these circumstances what is meant by "patriarchy?" Or is it something more sinister, like women having inherently less worth before God, or being regarded as second-class citizens by nature, or being considered unreliable or frivolous or lesser in some other way?

We should really distinguish between two different ways of "othering" women from the male perspective. One perspective is that patriarchal male dominance can only be oppressive and must be eradicated wherever it is encountered by minimizing sex difference in favor of presumptive sameness, and imposing this view as a socially created cultural norm. But another view is that masculine traits are necessary to fully enable feminine traits, and feminine to enable masculine, each complementing the other, and each enabling the other to be more than they would be in isolation, with society as a whole enriched by the full flowering of both in bonds of love rather than wariness in power struggle.

We would do well to reconsider the reflexively pejorative use of "patriarchy." One could as well ascribe "patriarchy" to the fact of God's agentic act of creation, His visible and deliberate act of creating all that we know. He created, first, Adam. And then He creates anew in succeeding generations, including the "patriarchs," who in obedience founded the faith that pierced the pagan world and culminated in the Advent: Transcendence leading and being fulfilled in Immanence. Transcendence and immanence are a duality understandable by their opposition, but both manifestations of God to us. Transcendence is perceived by us in, among other things, idealistic value hierarchy, which we find symbolized in the vertical portion of the Christian cross. Immanence is felt by us in, among other things, conscience-driven love for others, symbolized in the horizontal portion of the cross. The mountain and the river must be allowed to co-exist. The transcendent coincides with the agentic and purposeful element of our being; the immanent with the receptive and creative.

Imagine you're again walking down that favorite path through the woods. It's you doing the walking, exercising your purposeful, agentic, self-will to do so. But that's not enough to propel you down that path. You can't do it alone. Suppose you were unconnected to the earth, hovering above it, moving your legs but going nowhere. You need the solid earth, to pull you to itself and to resist the push of your feet, and only then does your act of self-will actually serve to propel you forward. The walk requires your self-will and the earth's receptivity.

God hovers over the waters. He actualizes the universe and all that is in it, from the swirling pool of potentiality represented by the waters. Creation requires both the matterless form of His creative act, and the formless matter of the potential upon which He acts. He creates both heaven and earth; ideal and material; both necessary but neither sufficient. Reality unfolds in this dualistic way, and the dualism of male and female corresponds. Genesis presents masculine and feminine as among the fundamental dualities of existence.

The immanence of God is concerned with the horizontal; with this-world relationships and this-world realization of values. Women tend more to experience of God immanent; men to God transcendent. It is for this reason that men tend to be more oriented to things and ideas than to people; more likely to pursue theory and ideals but also with greater tendency to self-isolation or cruelty. And it is for this reason that women are more oriented to people and the relationships which bind them; more likely to pursue practical needs with empathy but potentially unwilling to apply harsh-seeming principle. That there is any perceptible difference in men and women at all means they have distinct purposes.

The connection of creation to human concepts of masculine and feminine is described thusly by Anthony Esolen:

> The feminine tendency is toward the immanent, the personal; and its danger is emotionalism. The masculine tendency is toward the transcendent, the beyond-personal; and its danger is abstraction. [¶] But if we have to order the two tendencies, the one that should govern the other is the transcendent; it is the leader. The risk in seeing the divine as immanent in all things is that we may lose ourselves in the things and call divine what is just powerful feeling. Thus we must rise to the vision of the divine.[4]

---

4 Esolen, Anthony. *No Apologies/Why Civilization Depends on the Strength of Men.*

Practical realism grounds us but alone keeps us only grounded, so that we become concerned only with the here and now of personal needs; an exclusively horizontal outlook. Idealism requires a look up, but alone removes us from practical necessities, so that we become concerned only with the theoretical and abstract; an exclusively vertical outlook. Ideals unfold vertically in a stratified way, creating a hierarchy culminating in the ineffable and unseen. Patriarchy corresponds to this inevitable hierarchy. We experience spiritual immanence because we first experience spiritual transcendence. "Patriarchy" is not to be reflexively reviled. To the contrary (again, adopting Esolen's words):

> [P]atriarchy is a function of hope. Think of the hopelessness of the secular world, which has set its face in stubborn self-destruction against the figure of the father, and ultimately against the fatherhood of God. . . . It is not just a gray life without fathers. It is a severely restricted life, bound to the present, not a culture but a mirthless floating along with the suggestions of mass phenomena. Perhaps we may put it this way: be governed by fathers, or let the tiller go, and the ship floats wherever the water takes it. It has no direction: no past, and therefore no future.[5]

In the same way, if we dispatch God from the imagination, the mind-"imaged" Oneness from which all else emerges, we are left only with horizontal experience uninformed by hierarchical objective value formation. There would be no direction to our wanderings; only intensely felt sense of the present, the relational, and the subjective. The jettisoning of God from our understanding of reality corresponds to the jettisoning of male/female difference in our understanding of who we are as a people. "Patriarchy," the word, can be dispensed with, if it is so poisoned by feminism as to obstruct sound understanding. But the concept cannot be. It is the right relation of men and women so that they flourish together. To abandon it is to pit the sexes each against the other so that neither can be to the other what it naturally should be.

To reconsider "patriarchy" in this light is not to say that the modern relaxation of rigid traditional sex roles is bad. Neither Genesis nor the rest of the Bible explicating the Genesis worldview demands that women not work outside the home, for example. But it is to say that differences in how life is lived, as between men and women, are to be expected as the result of free choices and expressions of preference. There

---

Washington, D.C.: Regnery Gateway, 2022, p. 154.

5   Ibid., p. 110.

is much to be said for preserving traditions surrounding sex roles, so long as there is yet room for the exercise of personal liberty without shame or ostracism.

Here's an example. Once upon a time it seemed perfectly natural for an unmarried young woman to voice as a life goal her desire to marry and have children. Now such a sentiment, given voice, would be frowned upon. Instead, in the prosperous West at least, a young woman is expected to behave career-wise like a man, and keep family-oriented ambitions to herself. The social expectation is that marriage and children are to be considered incidental, optional add-ons to their life goals. If it is objectively true that sex differences are more inherent than socially formed, however; and if it is true that most women have more communal than agentic values; and if it is true that marriage and children are naturally more central to a woman's concerns than a man's, then feminist presumptions in the current culture frustrate women's desires more than they satisfy.

People tend to approach the question of sex differences with binary thinking—as we always approach everything—but without properly doubling down on that binary thinking to derive more nuanced values concerning, in this instance, the male/female binary. At one pole is essential sameness: a presumption that men and women are essentially the same in every material respect, so that to form differing social expectations on the basis of sex is always and everywhere wrong. At the opposite pole is essential difference: a presumption that male and female differences are so thorough-going that they essentially belong to different societies altogether, except as reproduction necessitates. Neither fits the Genesis worldview.

Adam was made from dust but was God-breathed. Eve was formed from the rib of Adam. Whatever else we may get from this story of their creation, we should see a poetic way of describing the mutual need of a man for a woman and a woman for a man, specifically in marriage. Marriage is about the combined being, the reassembly of the man and woman in one entity, after their divergence from the person of God in the beginning. For children that may come to the union, that reassembly provides a balanced model of God's love expressed in immanence and transcendence; and of His authority, as both male and female are comprised in God. Children have the benefit of that model until they come to accept the reality of God on their own, and the attendant hierarchy of objective values God authors. The family headed by man and woman is thus the locus of inculcating ongoing allegiance to objective and transcendent values, and the sense of immanence which expresses and gives life to those values.

The second chapter of Genesis describes the connection of a particular man and woman, but we can infer from it the more general richness of society resulting from male/female differences. The man and the woman are distinct human beings yet drawn into an exclusive pairing, marriage, wherein the husband so regards the wife that she is "bone of my bones and flesh of my flesh." This way of thinking reflects the man's enwrapping himself around his wife, making her very self his home, returning her to his body, so to speak. That is the significance of the woman being made from the man. This way of thinking is built (by God) into the man's psyche. He and his wife are of one flesh, as they are in the sex act. Children may result, and they are of one flesh in a different sense, to both mother and father, and so all a family.

It is the man, not God, who says "this at last is bone of my bones and flesh of my flesh." It is not an admonition from God to the man that he should think this way. Genesis is not saying here how we ought to behave. It is, like all the paradigm-setting stories of Genesis, about how things are. Obviously, not all men and women marry, and there's no reason from this text to suppose all should. But Genesis tells us marriage is a natural and proper calling, central to understanding how we regard male/female differences generally, whether we are married or not. Marriage is central to the story of male and female creation but is expressed in such a way that male/female difference should inform our regard of members of the opposite sex even outside of marriage. We have all observed and experienced male/female tension, positive and negative, ubiquitous in social situations. It is the oppositional nature of male and female that supplies this tension. Because of that opposition, same-sex gatherings are quite different from mixed-sex gatherings.

Sex difference is not a socially imposed construct. It is ontological. Just as human beings are a distinct category from animals, so women are categorically distinct from men. Existence and category coincide, and we know this because in the first instant of observation and cognition, the world presents to us in differentiations, divisions, categories, typologies, patterns, symbols, and so on, as we have discussed in previous chapters. We would be mentally helpless were it otherwise; indeed, there would be no consciousness within which to discern or not discern categories, were it otherwise. We've considered biological taxonomy as categories by which the world is formed and makes sense to us. The taxonomical divisions are ontological; that is, bound up in the very existence of the creatures we discern. If you encounter a bear in the woods, you don't have to sort taxonomical classifications to figure out what you've encountered. A bear is a bear and not an antelope or a chair. The bear-ness of the thing is as fundamental a category as that of animal and mineral; mineral and atmosphere; existence and non-existence. As with categories of objects, and with categories of animals; and with categories of species—so with categories of sex. We have no trouble saying a person can't choose to be another species. Sex within our species is no more open to revision.

Within the transsexual/transgender movement, many reflexively buy into the notion that gender is not ontological but rather a matter of self-construction, even to the point of medical intervention to modify outward sex indicators. In this way, we can become convinced that that most fundamental of binaries, male and female, can be reversed or dispensed with altogether, at individual will. It is an article of faith among many that sex and gender must be infinitely malleable, because to think otherwise is to be traitor to the principle that we are entirely autonomous and that we can entirely self-actualize. This perspective of fluid sex mutability is self-refuting, however, because the existence of the categories is necessary to affirming them, as with the Ls, Bs, and Gs of the alphabet soup, or to denying them, as with the Ts and Qs.

The loss of sex normativity is incalculable for everyone, and not just for individuals who directly deny it. Esolen, again:

> Modern man, having denied that there is any meaning in created things, finds that his own mind falls to ruin, and he can no longer affirm any meaning in his own body, his sex. He is far from being grateful that there are such creatures as boys and girls. He is made wary and snappish by reminders of that fact. At best he retains a superficial appreciation for their peculiar forms of handsomeness. But he has been taught to acknowledge nothing more—not the far sight of the boy on the bow of the ship of life, or the deep tenderness of the girl who is made for protecting what is small and infinitely precious.[6]

Human male and female are a foundational polarity in creation. Before throwing over this understanding of reality, we'd do well to understand what we're throwing over. Genesis sets a paradigm for how we are to understand reality, rather than instructing us on how to change it. The postmodern worldview is sufficiently distinct from the reality

---

6 "The Unbearable Burden of Being," *Chronicles*, December 1, 2019.

Genesis describes that we must reject one or the other.

CHAPTER EIGHT

Sexuality

"**T**HE MAN AND his wife were both naked and were not ashamed." This last line in what we call chapter 2 of Genesis is about sex.[1] This must be said because there are alternative explanations out there, for which nakedness is symbolic of something else. Let's touch on those and get some context before coming back to sex.

After this note about nakedness, we read about mankind's disobedient transgression of God's command, and its consequences. So the reference to nakedness serves to explain a state of mind the man and the woman had before that transgression. The transgression is often referred to as "the Fall," meaning mankind's lapse into a state of awareness of sin. This is the state of mankind we know now. So there was an introduced corruption which changed the relationship with God. There was a state of relative innocence, before eating of the tree of the knowledge of good and evil.

Some mythological or psychological interpretation of the Genesis story focuses on the eye-opening nature of the event of disobedience. The theory might be that it is an explanation for full human consciousness, for example, or an explanation for the internal moral conscience upon removal from direct communion with God. It has been suggested that mankind becomes aware of its vulnerability in its environment outside the garden as a result of the Fall, and awareness of nakedness sym-

---

1   "What we call" chapter 2 because Genesis wasn't written under inspiration with chapter breaks. Those were added later. This line could as well have been the first line of chapter 3, because it commences the story of the Fall, but on the other hand one could argue that stylistically its placement at the end of 2 lends some drama and therefore emphasis to the centrality of sex in the awareness of sin that marks the Fall.

bolizes that awareness of vulnerability. The fig leaf can be seen as a move to moral agency, as opposed to consciousness in the abstract.

All these explanations are likely true. They indicate expansive understanding of what it must mean to suddenly have knowledge of good and evil, the moral awareness unique to human beings. But it is immediately following this statement about unashamed nakedness that we're told how the relationship of God to mankind changed. So when we read "the man and his wife were both naked and not ashamed," we are to understand that nakedness unaccompanied by shame was an essential element of their pre-Fall relationship to God.

We should not overlook that the reference to nakedness relates specifically to human sexuality, and so sexual sin is not incidental to the corruption introduced by the Fall. In the sex act, man and woman reprise their unity in the mind of God but also re-affirm the oppositional sex separation in God's creation. The very act by which we come into physical being is the sex act, requiring sexual opposition, and the sex act is inseparable from new life. From this we would be right to infer that sexual sin, including especially the repudiation or reversal of the otherness of sex differentiation, manifests most clearly the corruption in mankind's relationship to God.

What makes a person a person? Physically, the sex act of parents. But metaphysically, moral agency, the exercise of the will concerning good and evil. Human beings are defined by their choice in not acting merely on animal impulse. Their metacognition, or conscious self-awareness, coincides with their moral agency; their decision-making based on discovered moral value. Animals are not sexually immoral. Human beings can be, because sexual sin means choosing animal impulse over God-imbued conscience. Sexual sin is a failure of the exercise of self-will to choose principle over impulse. It is a lapse into animal nature rather than uniquely human moral discernment, and in the context of the very act by which we physically come into being. Rectitude in exercise of our sexuality is deference to the God-breathed portion of our make-up; that part of us that is of the heavens rather than the earth.

We can infer that sexual sin is most fundamental in the breach of relationship to God because the events of the Fall are preceded by just one sentence about the nature of mankind beforehand, and it has to do with the absence of shame in nakedness. It might have been instead a statement about selfishness resulting in "other-ing" our neighbor, what the postmodern world deems more fundamental. But it isn't. The fig leaf signifies awareness not just of moral responsibility, but moral responsibility specifically with respect to sex. Its use is a first attempt at sexual restraint because the first man and woman have discovered the need for sexual restraint. Naked man and woman feel shame, not just exposure, and shame different in kind than would result from selfishness.

Which is worse, today: being called out for bigotry, or for sexual dalliance? The answer is obvious. You might actually be applauded for sexual sin, depending on the circumstances. But bigotry? Racial prejudice? Nationalistic chauvinism? Never. Indeed, in our world, in a short amount of time, social group intolerance has overtaken sexual sin as more shame-inducing. There are other groups of sins, of course, like theft and fraud and violence. It is not as though those kinds of sin are, or were, acceptable. Murder has always been about as bad a thing as one can do, and yet it carries a different quality of shame, and ostracism, and judgment, as compared to bigotry in postmodern times, or sexual sin in earlier times. Sexual sin and bigotry are not necessarily among the overtly criminal acts which must result in punishment separating the offender from society in some way. Instead, they strike at the standing of a person in society. In earlier times, adultery or fornication or homosexual acts might or might not trigger criminal prosecution, but would certainly result in shame and disgrace. Today the same kind of shame and disgrace attaches to acts or attitudes taken to signal bigotry. This is a fundamental difference between the Genesis and postmodern worldviews, as to what conduct is counted as evil.

As noted, a "merging" of male and female occurs in sex. That is a re-merging, we might say, of the merged male and female in the mind of God. So when two become one, as we say of a husband and wife in marriage, they combine attributes of their respective sex. In this way, their merger in marriage, symbolized quite graphically in the sex act, is a merger in the direction of the unified Godhead whence they both came. Unitary and complete in male and female ideals, in God; particular and affected with sin, in the married individuals.

Much is made in postmodern philosophy about the need to overcome alterity[2]—whether the word "alterity" is used or not—so as to re-center moral values around openness to others through empathy, overcoming the boundary of "otherness" that manifests most egregiously in xenophobia and racism. One could come to see the male/female difference as a form of alterity that can be overcome, hence the

---

2 For present purposes, it is sufficient to define "alterity" as the felt sense of otherness we have among others; the basis for empathy. Expanded upon especially in Chapter 13 infra.

curious drive to validate a person's choosing of their sex. This seems to be of a part with the river sentiment of process philosophy, "making transcendence horizontal,"[3] as with socially generated morality aimed at striking down all boundaries, including the boundary between male and female. Acceptance of one's natural sex is to respect a boundary imposed by transcendent truth. Sex identification outside that boundary is the most fundamental breach of boundary possible, and therefore especially prized in the postmodern mind as emphatic rejection of the Genesis first principles, and emblematic of boundary destruction and self-creation more generally.

Why do we say a husband and wife "consummate" their marriage on their wedding night? It's because marriage exists in ideal (the wedding) but also in the body (the wedding night). The bodily marriage may produce children because it is a union of oppositional natural sex difference, and not a partnership between any two people. Children are distinct lives in the body, continuing in existence after the sex act which forms them bodily, just as marriage is an idealized life distinct from the two who comprise it.

Male and female are different also in that masculinity is brought to the union by man; femininity by woman, the two elements comprised in whole, in complementarity, in God. Genesis tells us the man was made from dirt; the woman from the man. Man was made outside the garden; woman within it. Man can be alone, but is less isolated, less lonely, and less in need of a "helper" (or better, "sustainer," as in some translations) with woman. Part of man is taken out of him and placed in the woman, so that he is henceforth incomplete without her. We tend to think this incompleteness means only loneliness, because God said "it is not good for the man to be alone,"[4] but this is all within the explanation of life-regeneration on the earth. God's purposes for humanity cannot be achieved by the man alone.

Though the woman's being taken out of man suggests that she, too, is incomplete without man even more directly sustaining her, it also must mean that she is different from man, and an independent being. Men and women are different kinds of human beings, that's for certain. The man is to leave his father and mother and join his wife, Genesis tells us. A similar injunction is not imposed for the wife. Why? It likely has

---

3 Del Noce, Augusto, "The Shadow of Tomorrow," an essay contained in *The Crisis of Modernity*, transl. Carlo Lancellotti, Montreal: McGill-Queen's University Press, 2014, p. 103 (originally published in Italy in 1970).

4 Genesis 2:18.

to do with the differing predominant attributes of men and women. As Alastair Roberts put it, "the bonds of human relationship and communion are chiefly formed by and in women."[5] The woman doesn't need to be told a new generational divide is undertaken, in marriage. This is among the differences between men and women that make them fitted for each other.

In the Genesis story there is a moment, at least, when the man exists but not yet the woman. Is this symbolically significant? We can imagine man prior to the advent of the woman as being mankind comprising both male and female attributes, as yet undifferentiated. The woman being taken out of man highlights the fundamental division, wherein softer, communitarian, empathetic inclinations are diminished in man, and emerge in woman with a lesser degree of his agentic and aggressive inclinations.

Socially, both men and women together are needed for full flourishing. Woman is made from man in the same way the flowering of a tree is different in kind than the growth of the trunk. The flower adorns or crowns the tree. This is likely what the Apostle Paul meant, when he wrote "woman is the glory of man."[6] The reverse is not true: man is not the glory of woman. We know this is true instinctively. Paul is often taken in these times as a misogynist, but he correctly understood Genesis and recognized a woman's uniqueness in creation. He also acknowledged that man is made for woman, and woman for man, a fundamental truth that sounds like heresy in the divisive postmodern age. He goes on to write about head coverings in worship, in a way confusing to modern ears. The head covering represented acknowledgement of male authority, but it also represented woman's nature as crowning glory to man. It may even have been a cultural practice that the privilege of head covering be stripped from some women, with Paul writing to restore it, consistent with his teaching to eliminate moral stratification among those who were new in Christ.[7]

As in everything, greater understanding comes from greater differentiation and division, and with that greater understanding, greater appreciation for differences. Men and women are different, and essentially different. Instead of attempting to put both in one category, as modern feminism does, perhaps we'd be happier and better people if we accepted

5 "The Music and the Meaning of Male and Female," *Primer*, Issue 03, (Fellowship of Independent Evangelical Churches) 2018.

6 1 Corinthians 11:7.

7 Sarah Ruden, *Paul Among the People*, New York: Image Books, 2010, pp. 85-88.

the categorical opposition, and then found greater differentiation within those categories, for greater understanding and a richer life experience. Neither men nor women fully understand themselves, except when seen in opposition to the other, as with all binary oppositions. A man understands himself and his place in the world better because he can see it through the eyes of the Other, woman. And likewise in reverse, for women.

Woman is the crowning glory of man, Genesis teaches, not because she is superior to him, but because she is more refined, attracted to beauty, and more communitarian commitment than man. Why do women generally care more about how another person feels than do men, generally? Why does she care less, typically, about how physical things work? Because she is made differently than a man, obviously, and the differences cohere with this notion of man as the solid stem from which the flower grows. Exceptions, as with masculine-seeming women, prove the rule rather than invalidate it. Effeminacy in some men does not mean there's an absence of essential difference between men and women.

If we're to take this explanation of the relationship between men and women in Genesis seriously, and Genesis certainly suggests we should, then we also ought to consider that a woman's need for a man is as strong or stronger than a man's for a woman. A woman alone might feel bereft, but in the postmodern world we pretend not to notice a single woman's sense of social isolation, perhaps because she herself doggedly lives out a postmodern lie about the relationship of men to women. Women in general are sustained by male influence in society; and men by female influence. We would expect a sense of incompleteness in an all-male or all-female community.

To modern ears, how does this sound? Not like the common sense it would seem in earlier and wiser times. It offends because it runs counter to a metanarrative of female independence. A woman needs a man like a fish needs a bicycle, after all; never mind the legions of lonely individual men and women living without opposite-sex companionship, separated by the bankrupt feminist ideology of patriarchal oppression. It's not that women can't survive without men, but that they miss out on the wholeness of their design. They don't flower in the same way as if they stood on the shoulders of a man. The same principle applies for men, except that men and women differently conceive the benefit of the other in marriage. Each party to the marriage (or as a sex collectively, to co-existence in society) brings something the other lacks. Not just personality difference, but sex difference. There's survival, and there's flourishing, and these are two different things. As a society we've lost track of all the little ways we've learned to rationalize and accommodate to the loss of opposite-sex companionship marriage provides, as the best model for living whole, and the best model for men and women co-existing generally in society to their mutual benefit rather than living in hostility.

People were given the creation mandate, in Genesis, to fill and subdue the earth. It's noteworthy that people and not animals were given this mandate. Animals will fill any time not mating or eating with sloth. People don't, unless they give themselves over entirely to their animal nature. Genesis helps us understand the driving force in mankind to build and improve and conquer and procreate. This drive is from God; it is the source of our ambitions as a people, not Schopenhauer's general will, not Nietzsche's will to power, not Freud's eros. We have places we want to go; things we want to do. Ambition is the name of the horse we ride to get there, though we must remember that we provide the direction, not the horse.[8] The drive to do and to be is in everyone, but it looks different, from person to person. Again, Genesis is about how things are, not how they should be. Man was made to cultivate God's garden. Woman, created in it, sustains it and nurtures offspring and community within it. Her ambition is inwardly garden-directed, while man's is outwardly to protect it. As always, the boundary provides the meaning; in this case the boundary of the garden, symbolically. Men want to conquer the world. Women want to beautify the garden and hedge it in. Of course, these are broad categories, but that doesn't mean they're wrong. A man and woman could do the same jobs in corporate America, for example, both ambitious but with their ambitions serving ultimately different aims.

If this discussion seems off, in light of the zeitgeist, why? Possibly because the postmodern world teaches us to think in terms of power rather than love. All of postmodern deconstruction is about dethroning putatively wrongly attained power with a differently formulated power of the collective. It's the resentment of Cain, wrought up against Abel. In that story (Genesis chapter 4), there's no real reason given why Abel prospered as compared to Cain. It's just the way things are. But also the way things are is to harbor unfounded resentment, so much so that, like Cain, we strike out without justification even while we consider our-

---

8 This word picture courtesy of a skit by one of the women's houses at King's College, New York, 2015. It has stuck with your author these intervening years but without sufficient recall, alas, to better attribute it.

selves the ones wronged. The sin of Cain, unfounded resentment, is in all of us. Sometimes expressed in enraged spouse abuse. Sometimes in race riots. Sometimes in confusing equality with sameness.

Love is the alternative. It's possible to look at the world through a lens of love rather than power, but it takes some effort, because we are ornery in our not-Godness, just as Genesis teaches. All of God's revelation is showing love to us. We have thorns in the garden, now, but we have a garden. God provides but requires us to work for His provision. We have the story of His people, constantly becoming enslaved to the power paradigm before being returned by God to the love paradigm. And most of all, we have the Redeemer, and the grand turn-about, wherein woman, who said yes to the Deceiver, then says yes to God, and so woman, made from man, delivers the man who is God; and the God of love sacrifices for mankind in rebuke to the pagans who sacrificed other people to appease false gods of power.

If we think in a paradigm of love rather than power, what does that mean to the division of man and woman? How would women regard men, socially, and vice versa? How does an individual man treat a woman, if he treats her in love rather than authority and power? And how does a woman treat a man, if power struggle is not the ruling principle? Think of it. They might each build the other up instead of tearing down, and that building might be enabled by acknowledging the essential sex differences that should enrich us rather than divide us.

Love is eternal. Power is of this world. God chose the weak of this world to shame the powerful. Love might mean putting another first; an idea anathema to the world's first principle of power. When we witness eternal forms of success, through love, we are likely to make that a priority in our lives. We too often don't see it, however, especially in this power-driven postmodern age. And so success on the world's terms seems to be all there is, and we choose to live inside a massive Squid Game.

CHAPTER NINE

Sex Differences

W HAT DISTINGUISHES male and female? What, if anything, inheres in their sex, and what, if anything, do we add as a matter of socially developed cultural norms? The language used to examine this question varies, depending on context. It's a subset of the long-standing nature/nurture conundrum. We might say some differences are "hard-wired," and some are matters of social convention. We might say some elements of one's sex are "essential," meaning necessary to the category of male or female. We might say some differences are mere "social constructs" rather than biology. These characterizations are ways to ascribe certain attributes of each sex to "socialized" difference in contrast to inherent or essential difference. Let's pose the question this way: what differences in male and female exist categorically, and what differences do we socially construct?

In previous chapters we discussed categories in the abstract, not just those of male and female, and we considered what makes a category a category. Categories are universals, and universals are features of our minds and our environment that are difficult to explain philosophically, but which unquestionably comprise reality and make it comprehensible to us. They are types of differentiators, from which meaning emerges. It is not to be taken for granted that from our first spark of cognition reality unfolds categorically, enabling us to make sense of things. Infinite intertwined and overlapping differentiators ontologically comprise the reality we perceive, and the differentiations produce meaning. This is true more specifically of the differentiation between the categories of male and female.

If you assemble on your driveway a Ford, a Chevrolet, a Buick, and a pony, you'd have a collection of four automobiles, right? Well, no, of course not. A pony does not fit into the category "automobile." In the process of gathering automobiles, you exclude some things and include others. Fords and Chevrolets differ, but they're both types of automobiles, and so they both belong in the category. The pony does not. There is a boundary to this category; that's what makes it a category. The boundary is a fence which serves both to include and exclude. Essentialism, in this context, means that which is necessary for inclusion in the category: a conveyance with four wheels and an engine. All manner of non-essential things may also be included, without violating the boundary that forms the category.

To be clear, a "category" encompasses types, kinds, species, classes, patterns, symbols, universals, models, and ideals, the subject of much of our discussion thus far. A category is real, meaning that it exists in reality distinct from our mental perceptions. If you collect automobiles on your driveway, the automobiles are certainly real enough, but in addition, their categorization as such is real. Like mathematics and virtues and aspirations and abstractions and ideals, the category is a real feature of reality, it is not made unreal by virtue of being intangible. The categories didn't have to exist. They were created with the things categorized. The boundary between automobiles and other things that are not automobiles is an extant, real feature of the collection on your driveway, and the category is not made unreal by that pony ambling about amongst the cars.

Human beings are a category of like things. That category is nested in others, in telescoping fashion: hominids, primates, mammals, and so on. But also there are categories, exactly two of them, nested within the category of human being: male and female. There is a boundary between the categories male and female, a fence which includes some humans in the male category and some in the female category. There are essential features which place a person in one category or the other, and unlike with the collection of cars on the driveway, the categories are not mankind-created.

Essentialism in this context refers to those features which make a person one or the other. We can argue about what is essential to the respective categories, but not that there are such features by which we differentiate them. Reproductive biology is the most obvious point of differentiation. The existence of rare intersex individuals does not negate the category; they rather serve as the exception that proves the rule. This point of differentiation is natural in the most obvious sense: it is the seed and nurture for the seed by which these living things regenerate in like living things, though each contributing individual eventually dies.

In Genesis, the male/female differentiation is recognized and emphasized, and that differentiation is shown to have foundational spiritual significance. God did not merely create mankind, but created mankind in His own image, God-breathed, and "male and female He created them." Genesis doesn't conflict with nature, but rather describes it. The categories of male and female present to us in biology, we don't make them up and impose them on subgroups of human beings. Categories pre-exist in physical reality, and as with all things, this reality presents in binary opposition. Male and female are not merely two separate categories, they are two separate categories in opposition, meaning each defines the other, according to the tension between them. We know male by its opposition to female, and female by its opposition to male.

Because the oppositional differentiation is essential to natural procreation, we must understand it as essential to the very existence of human beings. Existence, recall, is a matter of "ontology," and duality in physical things, concepts, and values is ontological. Ontological dualism is the basis of reality, and the oppositional duality of man and woman is an obvious and primordial example of ontological dualism. It is emphasized in Genesis in the same way heavens and earth are: not merely a binary opposition, but an ineradicably necessary one.

Does postmodern thought deviate from these truths? Yes and no. No in the sense that one cannot deviate from them, ultimately, because they're unchangeable reality. Genesis tells us how things are. But yes in the sense that postmodern thinking is hostile to boundaries in general, including even fixed boundaries like that between male and female.

A protest is made in these strange times against reproductive biology as an essential feature of each category, hence, "non-binary" rejection of the categories. Rejection of the categories means rejecting the boundaries which form them. The proposition of "non-binary" sex would seem to be eradication of the boundary altogether, but actually it sets up a new and hostile one: a boundary between gendered and ungendered humans. It is an attempted rejection of male/female categories, and the formation of a new ungendered category. It is not an opt-out from the reality of categorical differentiation. All of the new and various gender and attraction-based classifications actually depend on the male/female binary, even if only in the form of negation.

To investigate the degree to which sex differences are inherent or socially constructed, we can start by understanding polar opposite views.

One is that all observable sex differences are entirely natural, only marginally shaped by social influences. The opposite point of view is that all sex differences are social in origin, except for unarguable biological reproductive differences, and even those can be trivialized in this era of advances in medical technology. This latter point of view is prevalent in the postmodern era, explaining existing gender differences as a matter of roles created by social conditioning. On this understanding, women, for example, do not prioritize child-rearing more than men because of their essential nature. Rather, doing so traditionally brought social approval, and not doing so, disapproval.

What are the internal sex differences, as opposed to the obvious external differences? We feel we know them when we see them, but it takes some thought to classify them in a meaningful way. One way to classify them relates to "communal" as opposed to "agentic" traits, as does David Geary in a recent essay at *Quillette*.[1] Women have more "communal" traits, "manifested by selflessness, concern with others, and a desire to be at one with others." Men, on the other hand, tend more to "agentic" traits: "self-assertion, self-expansion, and the urge to master."

Sex differences have not always been a point of controversy. Quite to the contrary, most cultures celebrate those differences, and re-express them in gendered customs, norms, language, and traditions. Far from thinking of gender norms as restrictive, most cultures in history have regarded the difference as liberating. A woman in such a culture can lean into her inclinations as a woman, unapologetically, recognizing that some human values are better reflected in traits more predominant in men. And likewise for men, who can better enjoy the female contribution to our shared experience, understanding that certain human values are better reflected in distinctively female traits. The underlying idea is that men and women are not in competition; that the full flowering of humanity requires both; and that no one person can contain all the positive and negative traits of the combined sexes within humanity.

We should be wary of the assumption that there is no utility to reinforcement of sex roles or sex identity. If there is any natural sex difference at all (and one cannot seriously deny all sex difference), then it could be we're better off socially enhancing those differences rather than minimizing them. Societies the world over have generated all manner of differences not strictly necessary to reproductive function, to celebrate

---

1 "The Real Causes of Human Sex Differences," *Quillette,* October 2020, citing other theorists including A.H. Eagly, *Sex Differences in Social Behavior: A Social-role Interpretation*, Hillsdale, NJ: Erlbaum, 1987.

and further enhance the difference. Why would we reflexively take so-cially constructed sex differences to be a bad thing?

We readily observe male and female differences that go well beyond procreative function, and even beyond outward physical differences. How much of it is essential to the categories of male and female? This has been an ongoing debate in the West, especially in the last century. Feminist theory, for the most part, develops around this question: To what degree are the attributes we describe as "womanly" or "manly" a function of essential sex difference, and how much is socially formed? Is a woman more likely to be nurturing and caring than a man because it is essential to the nature of a woman, or because society teaches women they should live out those values?

In postmodern thought, categories like male and female are suspect to the extent that they are socially formed rather than essential to the category. Minimizing the socially formed aspect of sex difference means bringing male and female closer to sameness, which is thought to be an improvement. Feminism is about reducing male/female difference. Likewise, transgenderism. In the zeal to reduce the male/female distinc-tion, the urge in the postmodern era is to attribute as much sex differ-ence as possible to social construct, leaving only natural insemination to sex essentialism until that, too, can be overcome through technology.

Because men and women are said to be "socialized" differently, this is taken to mean most manifestations of difference are socially construct-ed. Social constructs are considered the only reason for, by way of exam-ple, disparities in male vs. female participation in various professions, as with women being under-represented on oil rigs, and over-represented as hospital nurses. Feminist ideology holds socialized differences as in-authentic or motivated by power interests, and essential sex differences as minimal, to the conclusion that men and women are more alike than previous generations supposed.

But why would socialized differences be presumed to perpetuate power interests, and on what basis do we conclude essential differences are minimal? These questions are typically skipped over because they don't serve the postmodern project of re-making mankind. It might well be that men and women have been purposely socialized differently, historically, to enhance sex differences to enrich life experience, rather than to perpetuate power interests. Perhaps our forebears were wiser than we give them credit for, and leaned into sex differences because that was understood to make life better.

And, it might well be that essential biological differences have a greater effect on sex differences than we tend to think. It could be that differences attributed to social construct are more minimal than we imagine; that our tendency to attribute sex difference to social construct is overstated. Indeed, our placement of sex difference in the social construct category may itself be a social construct.[2] Perhaps because the social construct explanation for difference is a refrain repeated ad nauseam to remake mankind according to neo-Marxist, postmodern vision.

The social construct explanation for difference in male and female attributes is part of a larger socialist-leaning predilection in postmodernists, generally. "Socialist" is used here in contrast to "individualist," to describe a perspective, one that starts with "we" rather than "I," on nearly any subject. That perspective partially coincides with "socialism" in its more traditional understanding, to mean communal sharing of means of production and a paradigm of exploitative oppression and resentful reactive transgression to bring about the communitarian ideal. If male and female attributes are socially constructed, then they can be socially deconstructed. In this way, we can engage in social engineering to bring about a better and more equitable world, it is thought. If the differentiation is natural, however, rather than socially constructed, the social engineering brings about strife and distrust and division, instead, but this is overlooked in the headlong rush to embrace the approved social narrative.

If sex differences are entirely socially constructed, the thinking goes, then the value of equal economic opportunity can replace values associated with traditional sex differences. That's the feminist position. If you are a woman with career ambitions, and don't want to be held back by claims on your energies from traditional sex roles, you might be inclined to adopt the minimally essentialist point of view. The truth about sex differences is what it is objectively, however. The common postmodern corruption in thinking is pragmatism, by which we fixate on a goal and then adopt a "truth" designed to get us there. In Genesis reality, by contrast, we discover truth, we don't create it. We shouldn't say gender roles are socially constructed just because that conclusion serves some other goal like career ambition. If a particular woman values agentic traits in herself over communal ones, it doesn't follow that agentic and communal traits are merely assigned, socially, to men and women, respectively.

---

2 Michael Rectenwald said it best in 2017: "Gender is not a social construction. The social construction is the idea that gender is a social construction." https://www.michaelrectenwald.com/quoted-sayings.

Why would we not say it's postmodern society which socializes sex roles and sex identity, to make people less categorical sexually, and even more fluid in their sexual identity? It could well be that sex differences we take to be socially constructed are actually more rooted in nature than we think, and if so, our culture forces us to reject that which is most natural and healthful for us.

And as we consider this question, here's a related one. If socialization in matters of sex and gender is wrong, why are we actively engaged in it by re-directing socialization efforts in the direction of sameness? If the answer is to reverse the putative socialization that previously occurred, then why? And when does it stop? What is the goal to be brought about by reversed socialization? At what point do we say the socialization to reverse socialization is complete?

Suppose essential differences are in fact confined to reproduction, and all remaining differences are in fact socially constructed. This would suggest sex differences are enhanced (or exaggerated, one might say) by social custom. What is the basis for criticism, though? Why shouldn't we enhance or exaggerate sex difference? Why is that worse than minimizing it?

The answer prevalent in this age is that socially constructed differences exist only to keep women rigidly inside sex-defined roles to protect the interests of men. That is the reason, really the only one, to adopt the extreme social-construct position of feminism. But obviously, all men didn't get together to intentionally conspire against women, so this means males, perhaps unwittingly, participate in a hegemonic system of domination just by living in society, and societies have—since the beginning of time—evolved social barriers to perpetuate that male hegemony. The male conspiracy is unspoken, in other words, and is reinforced down through the generations in man-made social structures now collectively labeled "patriarchy." This point of view means our motivations in male/female relations arise primarily from self-interest rather than love, a power struggle necessary because the traditional father/husband role is all take and no give, and women are systemically subjugated.

That answer is difficult to square with actual love and the obvious benefits of sex-role differences in rearing the next generation, however, and so there is cognitive dissonance concerning feminist theory. The dissonance manifests culturally and politically, but also individually. Among other difficulties it creates is frustration in efforts toward marriage. The low-voltage buzz of hostility now existing between the sexes results in a paucity of like-minded marriage prospects, and increased strife if and when marriage is nonetheless achieved. Perhaps we are better off if we embrace socially constructed sex differences that enhance personal and social benefits of natural differences in sex. Maybe feminist ideology gets in the way of our getting along. It might be the disease rather than the cure.

Unfortunately, feminists who insist sex differences are merely social constructs also insist their point of view be held collectively, because if the problem is social constructs, then re-orientation of social constructs is the cure. All of society must change, on their view, so that social approval and disapproval mechanisms affirm careerist feminism or LGBTQ ideology without dissent. "The personal is political." Freedom of individual thought and choice on this subject is increasingly rendered intolerable.

To be clear, this is but a specific of a larger trend in the postmodern world. All claims to truth are seen as bids for power, in accord with thinkers like Michel Foucault, and all stable categories (like men and women and marriage) are seen as manipulative or oppressively restrictive. It is not enough to hold the social construct view privately and get on with one's life accordingly. Belief in sex roles as wholly socially contrived must be enforced as a social orthodoxy, with public institutions evolved to catechize that orthodoxy. This, ironically, involves a truth claim, so in the postmodern world, it ought to be regarded as a mere bid for power, but this one escapes the Eye of Sauron.

Principles of sexual attraction and sex identity are invoked or rejected haphazardly among variants of LGBTQ, etc., pragmatically to advance power in social discourse. The inconsistencies in theory and interests among the members of this coalition are dissolved in the shared political goal of de-normalizing heteronormativity. Conflicts in theory are diverted onto "intersectionality," to obscure theoretical inconsistencies in the coalition. The important thing for all of them is to first overthrow norms for marriage, family, and children.

Confusion over essential and socially constructed sex differences contributes to the transsexual phenomenon. When a person forms a self-identity that deviates from his or her physical indicators of sex, he or she typically does so believing the opposite sex is his/her real essence. This isn't a rejection of male/female categories, nor is it a rejection of the idea that something is essential to the category. Quite to the contrary, transitioning from one sex to the other depends on the existence of the categories.

The prevailing expectation among transsexuals is that society must normalize a person's subjective belief that gender is essential, and that gender is distinct from sex. But natural categories of sex (as opposed to socially constructed ones) are the basis for same-sex attraction just as they are for opposite-sex attraction. In this way, the transsexual movement is potentially disruptive and hostile to other LGB+ categories of sex attraction and identity. This is often overlooked, however, because intersectionality in postmodern political and cultural engagement strategically assures cohesiveness of the coalition. Its constituents remain united against the real enemy, those who hold to a paradigm of love rather than power, and to the centrality of sex in regeneration of mankind, and to families as the venue for the passing on of hierarchical values, including those relating to the proper place of sex; that is, those who hold to a Genesis worldview.

CHAPTER TEN

Good and Evil

I N PRECEDING CHAPTERS we considered male and female as an essential opposition in the creation of the world. The male/female distinction is inextricably bound up in the first sin, mankind's disobedience to God. God told Adam, before the creation of Eve, that he was not to eat of the tree of the knowledge of good and evil. Good and evil existed, therefore, but mankind was ignorant of it. We can assume a child-like innocence with respect to evil.

We should also understand the nature of the relationship between mankind and God, in light of the command. There is no indication at first of their shaking a fist at God over it. The command came from their Creator. God's authority is a given. Neither the man nor the woman questions it, initially. We can infer a close relationship, in which it would be natural for the man and the woman to walk with God in the garden in the cool of the day,[1] and that closeness would be like that of a small child to its parents, so thoroughly enveloped in love that defiance and independence are as yet far from the child's mind.

Our relationship to God is sullied, however, by our disobedience, then and now. That disobedience is possible because God made us with agency. Mankind chose moral agency over an innocent relationship with God.[2] Mankind chose this because God enabled it, and God enabled it by making mankind with moral agency; that is, in His image. Consciousness of good and evil makes mankind guilty upon choosing evil. We learn something of the power of God in the consequence of

---

1   Genesis 3:8.

2   Genesis 3:6.

separation from Him when we choose evil, as we inevitably do. He is the source of goodness but also of justice, and therefore cannot abide any stain, no matter how small. It is for this reason that the difficult thing to explain in this world is not evil, but good. Why is evil the default state of the world? Because we have attenuated our fellowship with the Creator of good. Our will to seek God is corrupted, so we look in the wrong places for our continued well-being. We continually kick against the goads, the boundaries and constraints God fixes in our world.

The story of the disruption of our relationship to God is stated in a few dense sentences, set forth in what is now the third chapter of Genesis. The crafty serpent inveigled the first woman to eat the forbidden fruit. Why the woman? That the woman rather than the man was approached by the serpent must be meaningful, regardless how literally or metaphorically one reads the passage. Eve acts. She eats of the fruit while Adam stands passively with her. When we read of God's confrontation of the pair, we find Him first calling for Adam, not Eve. Adam then tries to lay the fault on Eve, hiding behind her skirts, so to speak. God admonishes Adam for "listen[ing] to the voice of your wife." Is he not supposed to listen to his wife? What this means is that Adam, uniquely, was expected to exercise male traits of decisiveness and moral leadership along with protectiveness for the "bone of my bones and flesh of my flesh." He didn't sin by simply listening. The sin of Adam was his passivity, counter to what was expected of him specifically as a man. Men miss the mark if they do not embrace and act on their distinctiveness as men.

Eve is admonished for her affirmative act, and as with Adam, God's admonition is specific to her as a woman, not just as a morally responsible person. Women bear children, not men, and God made child-bearing painful. Moreover, God inserted a level of strife between men and women, in that woman's "desire shall be contrary to your husband, but he shall rule over you."[3] The precise meaning of this curse is often debated, but we can at a minimum infer ongoing tension between husband and wife, which we experience in male/female relationships to this day. The man asserts dominance in their shared journey, and the woman chafes at it, tempted to undermine it, and is frustrated whether she succeeds or not—frustrated at his leadership, if he leads; frustrated at his lack of leadership, if he does not.

The man is a man and the woman a woman not just because of different origin stories, and different reproductive functions, but because

---

3   Genesis 3:16.

of other observable differences expressed universally. The man and the woman are designed for different roles and functions with respect to the other. We read in Genesis that certain traits are designed into man, and he is expected to act accordingly. His agentic and dominating and outward-looking traits are not bugs, but features, to use modern computer parlance. Likewise, a woman's communal, agreeable and inward-looking traits are not mere observable differences from the male perspective, but are unavoidable and expected. These form social boundaries. We can resent them or celebrate them, but we can't erase them. Genesis tells us how things are, not how they should be, so if we come up with a plan that differs from the reality disclosed in Genesis, we do so at our peril. And if we decide we have a better plan than God's, then we can dismiss Genesis in favor of a postmodern conception of sex as entirely socially constructed, and see how poorly that works out for us.

Just as the male/female polarity is foundational to mankind and to God's creation, so it is foundational to the introduction of evil in a creation otherwise declared "good." The event that caused banishment from the garden was disobedience, and reversal in sex-specific traits was integral to that act of disobedience. It is not incidental to the story that the serpent approached the woman; that she reached for the fruit; and that the man was passive. Disorder in our world arises from muddling male and female difference, then and now.

The disobedience of Adam and Eve was the catastrophic "Fall," whereby people lost their innocence as they gained moral responsibility. Their eyes were opened to their sin. The penalty for disobedience is death, and we read that the first couple was turned out of the garden before they could eat of the tree of life, so they would die eventually. Traditional Jewish and Christian belief has been that there was an idyll with God that was abruptly and catastrophically disrupted by mankind's sin; and that we have lived in that fallen state ever since.

That is not the end of our story, however, because the Bible speaks of a coming redemption from that state. Christians believe Jesus of Nazareth to be the Redeemer. The nature of the redemption is to be reconciliation with God, despite His unwavering justice, either in heaven following this life, or in heaven upon our bodily resurrection, or in a resurrected state in a new earthly millennium, or some combination of these. The Bible's language of redemption supports reading Genesis with an event of moral falling away from God, rather than as simply an allegorical way of describing the presence of evil in mankind's nature.

Apart from the centrality of male and female difference in the story of the Fall, we should note that it came about from twisting words and meaning. We will observe a similar strategy in advances of postmodern philosophy. The serpent that will entice Eve is "crafty" in the ESV translation; "subtil" in the KJV; "cunning" in the NASB. The serpent is often associated with the devil, though in this passage in Genesis, it's just called a crafty serpent. The Bible in other places speaks of angels and demons and idols and false gods and the sinful foolishness of people, as with Adam and Eve in this story. Whether individual supernatural beings are involved in these episodes or not, certainly there is a bad idea, a twisting of the moral sense that taints a seemingly good thing into something horrible. We do this all the time. We take good ideas and twist them into something unrecognizable, and heap bad ideas on top of bad ideas until we have a catastrophe on our hands. We do this because our thinking is corrupted by sin; by evil inclination from which we need to be freed. We fail less frequently and catastrophically if we accept the reality of hierarchical value formation rather than build our own pathetic towers of Babel.

It's a small step from an internal bad idea to a spirit of some sort bringing trouble to us from outside. The line separating human frailty and demonic influence is thin, so much so that one can stand in for the other without undue violence to one's more nuanced theological beliefs. There is no sense in Genesis that Adam and Eve are off the hook because "the devil made me do it." Quite to the contrary, their fault is in not resisting the serpent, whether he represents mankind's sin nature, or a spiritual presence of craftiness, or an individuated demon, or the prince of the power of the air, satan. "We do not wrestle against flesh and blood, but against the rulers, against the authorities, against the cosmic powers over this present darkness, against the spiritual forces of evil in the heavenly places."[4] The fact of external influences on us, from whatever source, does not absolve us from our wrongdoing. We have the responsibility to exercise our moral agency well.

The serpent's manner of corruption is the twisting of words. "Did God actually say, 'You shall not eat of any tree in the garden?'" This is a lie, but a "subtil" one. God did prohibit eating from one tree (not "any"), but suspicion and doubt is cast also by couching this as if the serpent were merely questioning the accuracy of his understanding, rather than insinuating unreasonable harshness on the part of God. And the subject matter the serpent chooses to bring up is God's one prohibition, as if

4 Ephesians 6:12.

it were unjust, despite his having made the man and woman from dirt and having placed them in His garden. This is how we are. We chafe at even the mildest constraint, forgetting the almost limitless freedom we otherwise enjoy. We know Eve is taken in because in responding, she adds her own touch of resentment: "neither shall you touch it, lest you die," something God did not say, but the implication with this twist is that this is certainly a harsh penalty for something that could happen even accidentally. Thus, the serpent mixes a truth with an ambiguous half-truth and an omission so important as to be fraudulent. Yes, their eyes would be open to knowing good and evil. That was true, and it happened. The ambiguous half-truth was "you will not surely die." True that they would not drop dead on the spot, but untrue that death would not eventually come, as their lives in the body would end and lifetimes thereafter would rapidly decrease in duration. And the omission: with knowledge of good and evil would come moral responsibility, the inevitable casting out of the garden because mankind, not being God, inevitably will use its moral agency to choose evil over good, even if only one time, in one small way, and separation from a wholly just God results. The separation results because we are God-breathed, and so we bear His standard of justice even as we are unable to attain it.

The instrumentality of that first catastrophic sin is language. Once again language has a central function in the unfolding story of Genesis. God "let there be light" in understanding, and spoke the world into existence. He created the physical reality we know, and set his God-imaged creation, mankind, to the task of naming the animals, attaching words to the beings over which he was given dominion. God spoke to man, in words, His decree that mankind not eat of the tree, and through language, mankind was induced to do so anyway. The speaking inducement was from the serpent, which we should take to represent the principalities and powers arrayed against us. Words are their weapons, not to create anew, but to corrupt what God speaks. Our task is, therefore, to demand of the word a straight uncorrupted delivery, to avoid important omissions or half-truths or ambiguities that skew meaning. Our first duty is to simply tell the truth, and not participate in lies by silence, and to speak and act with discipline against mischaracterization, ambiguity, and strategic omission. And not to be taken in when others employ these forms of deceit.

We will see that subtle deception is the principal project of postmodern technique. This first sin, brought about through deception in words, is the type for later sins, in complex patterns and myriad presentations, all constituting the principalities and powers, the systems of ideas that take us away from truth rather than delivering us to it. So it is in postmodernism, far down the trail of human misery from these first deceptions spoken by the serpent.

This separation of man from God, and our susceptibility to the wiles of those lying serpents, begins an exodus that continues to this day. Exodus is, of course, the next book of the Bible, about delivery of the people of God from their slavery in Egypt. That Exodus is actual but also metaphorical, delivery of us from sin to redemption; from the corrupting world to the haven of restored promise in a place God has prepared for us; it is victory over enemies and over the self, fallen prey again and again to enslaving systems of the world. The Exodus from Egypt sets a pattern for us individually and collectively, and it is the central theme of the Bible.[5]

The exodus of the book of Exodus is necessitated by this first event of enslavement, through words, in Genesis. Genesis sets up the need for exodus as the continual searching for redemption. It also establishes certain patterns that will repeat in human nature and in societies, in the stories of Cain and Abel, Noah and the Flood, the Tower of Babel, and others. Then commencing with the appearance of Abraham, we begin to see successive exoduses undertaken, followed by the enslavement in Egypt, and then a repeating pattern of exoduses, all through the Old Testament and into the New, as when Mary and Joseph flee to Egypt to avoid the slaughter of the innocents. Then Christ appears, the Redeemer who puts an end to the repeating pattern of exodus.

The Exodus from Egypt seemingly ends when Joshua crosses the Jordan with the people, but then a new exodus commences, as the people become entangled with the gods of the locals in Canaan. We can think of those gods as typical pagan gods and their worshipers as people following the pagan way of thinking that the Hebrews were supposed to be breaking from, but we can also equate them with spiritual entities, whether invisibly hovering in the air about us, as we commonly conceive them, or manifesting only in the thought processes that produce bad ideas corrupting good intentions; the principalities and powers that bedevil us today whether we think of them as literal demons or not. Our world is still inhabited by serpents who "speak" to us because it is

---

5 In *Echoes of Exodus/Tracing Themes of Redemption through Scripture* (Wheaton, IL: Crossway, 2018), Alastair Roberts and Andrew Wilson establish this theme, tracing repeating patterns of exodus not just in the delivery with Moses from Egypt, but repeating thematically throughout the Bible.

through words that corrupting bad ideas are propagated. This is a true state of affairs whether we acknowledge demons as spiritual beings like angels, or merely as descriptive of word-based intellectual manifestations in the corrupted thinking in human beings.

Joshua has a word for the Hebrews still spiritually entangled with pagan gods once the Jordan had been crossed: "choose this day whom you will serve," the pagan gods or the real God.[6] This means choosing one or the other, of course, rather than having a foot in each camp. But it means more than that. Choosing God means choosing truth. Choosing the pagan gods doesn't mean merely choosing a different religion. It means choosing untruth, or rather half-truths, ambiguities, and omissions that amount to lies that deter us from the truth available from the true God, who sent His word, His literal word in stone, from the midst of blinding light atop a literal mountain, and His personal Word in the flesh—the Redeemer Himself. We "choose this day" every day. We are on a continual exodus from corrupting untruth to truth, fleeing artful lies. This is an exercise in words, in the messages and information that floods our world but is corruptible in it, infecting us if we are not vigilant; if we do not choose truth all day every day and understand that this is our central purpose in life.

If we have the beginning of an understanding of Genesis, it would seem puzzling that we're puzzled by evil. The presence of evil in the world seems to be the foremost reason people reject God. Why would a good God allow evil in the world? This seems offensive to some, who then conclude either that there is no God, or that He is not good, and so does not deserve worship. If this were a real thought process, we would have to be aghast at the unimaginably unbridled hubris of second-guessing the Creator of the universe. But it's not a real thought process; it's a declaration that follows the rejection of God. That is, people don't consider the presence of evil and then reject God. They reject God and then consider the presence of evil to justify it.

"Dear Sir: Regarding your article 'What's Wrong with the World?' *I am.* Yours truly, G.K. Chesterton." I am. I am what's wrong with the world. The reason I am what's wrong with the world is that I am not God. But we are made in the image of God, and that means we have a continual yearning for what is beyond this earthly veil, and a part of us unrequited in this lesser world. C.S. Lewis: "If we find ourselves with a desire that nothing in this world can satisfy, the most probable explana-

6 Joshua 24:19.

tion is that we were made for another world." We are not like the ants and camels and apes. We have one foot here and one foot there. And so, we live with a sense of unease, or dissatisfaction.

But that is not the only reason I am what's wrong with the world. The same *Imago Dei* means that we have moral agency, and because we are not God, we use it imperfectly. There is evil in the world because we choose it. If God eliminated evil, He would also eliminate human moral agency, which would mean we wouldn't recognize or choose evil, but we also wouldn't recognize or choose good. We would be exactly like the ants and camels and apes, and we would not have the spiritual equipment to recognize evil as evil and so would be unable to make the accusation against God. Why is there evil in the world? There's something wrong with the question. God did not inject evil into the world, he injected mankind, free moral agents, into the world.

Explaining evil is not the hard thing. Explaining good is. Why is there any good in the world? Why are we sometimes flooded with a sudden sense of ultimate immanent Presence? There is good in our every waking moment and we did nothing to earn it. This is a glass-half-full outlook instead of a glass-half-empty. But it's also the result of going deeper on the nature of the question. The moment we ask why there is evil, we give away the fact that we are able to discern evil and good. We have moral vision. That moral vision is more than evolved tendencies to prefer one kind of conduct over another. Even if we were the products of mindless naturalistic evolution, evolved preferences—for, say, sociability—would not explain the moral authority for the preference: why we consider it morally good rather than merely preferable.

And finally, if there were no evil, there would be no good because these are concepts that exist only in opposition, each to the other. As with all of creation. Reality unfolds from ontological dualism, in which every thing, concept, and value acquires meaning from its opposite, in innumerable overlapping and telescoping oppositions. Good stands in opposition to evil. If we knew no evil, we would know no good. The concept of either would be literally meaningless. For this reason, it is every bit as reasonable to ask why there is good in the world, as to ask why there is evil.

Genesis provides understanding but the Genesis worldview stands in contrast to the postmodern. What does the latter say about good and evil? Relevant features of postmodern thought are: resolute atheism (obviously in contrast to Genesis); the blurring of boundaries and the consequent dilution of universals (in contrast to the ontological structure and dualism of Genesis); advocacy through redirection of language (exactly the truth corruption just discussed); and a shift of perspective from the individual to social groups (a move away from moral agency). Postmodern thought supposes morality to be socially constructed, and insists on deceitful narrative to support its metanarrative, ironically for the purpose of deconstructing metanarratives, so long as the metanarrative to be deconstructed is religion or logocentrism, or "capitalism" or "fascism" tendentiously defined.

Because Genesis is about reality, however, it is not to be dispensed with because competing theologies emerge. To be consistent, there would be no moral absolutes in postmodernism, but postmodernism is not consistent, it can only depart so far from the reality that is Genesis, so it posits new moral absolutes that are socially constructed. Chief among them is the boundary erasure between self and other. Alterity in the abstract is to be overcome, and any who stand in the way of this ultimate goal must be scapegoated and un-personed, creating, ironically, an alterity more final and complete. Oppositions, especially if they impose restraints on personal autonomy, must be erased, even the most fundamental oppositions, like male and female; absolute and contingent; nothing and something; good and evil.

CHAPTER ELEVEN

Postmodernism

Do you know the TV game show *Family Feud*? Two families compete to guess the answers to various questions. The answers are ranked responses provided in surveys. A team scores more points by correctly guessing higher-ranked survey responses. There are some subtler strategy points, but generally a team does better by correctly guessing how the larger society would respond to the question. Group identification is an element of the game, and another is the curious basis on which an answer is considered the "right" answer. Not that it is objectively true, but that it matches what the larger society says is true. It's all for entertainment and fun, but the game's format is suggestive. Groups are squared off to get closest to "truth," that truth being what the social consensus dictates. This is a reasonable starting point for apprehending in broad outline what postmodern philosophy is about.

Postmodern philosophy is a collection of theories which hold in common a rejection of objective truth and morality.[1] Postmodernism more generally is not just the theory but the practice—praxis—by which theory is deployed into the culture. A few common elements include these:

1) Resolute atheism. Postmodernists typically don't so much refute religious claims as ignore them, but their theories presuppose religious

---

1   We have suggested that the postmodern era commenced at around the turn of the twentieth century, and obviously many thinkers since then have not rejected objective truth and morality. So, this definition of postmodernism does not embrace all philosophy since 1900. But the dominant secular philosophy since that time shares certain elements, included here, and that is what is meant in this work by "postmodernism."

irrelevance and reject transcendence.

2) A blurring of boundaries. This entails resistance to universals, to categorical thinking, and to polarities in thought generally, but in particular opposes alterity—the "otherness" of people or people groups.

3) Resolute leftism, both in the political sense and in the personal, an instinctive resistance to hierarchy and structure-forming social norms. Group rather than individual orientation and an attitude of rebellion, resistance, dissent, suspicion, negation and critique.

4) Neo-Marxism. Grouping people according to an oppressor/oppressed paradigm to encourage resentment so as to dismantle social norms thought to perpetuate power structures, and a presumption of historical progress to utopia.

5) Socialism, both in the collectivist economic sense, and in the personal perspective sense: the "we," rather than "I" perspective. This results in the self being partially subsumed into a Machine collective of neo-fascism.

6) Anti-fascism, but with the important qualifier that "fascism" just means antipathy to capitalism in its bourgeois cultural manifestations, as with dehumanizing "Fordism"[2] and consumerist self-identity. Postmodern theory produces fascism in its original meaning of subsumption of the self into the collective.

7) Opposition to metanarratives[3] that rest on transcendence, objectivity, and logocentric idealism, and ideological methods for deconstructing them.

Postmodernism is not merely next in time after an era labelled modern. It constitutes a major shift in outlook that breaks from three eras that preceded it. In the first, paganism was dominant. In the second, monotheism. In the third, modernism, still imbued with monotheistic religious thinking before the postmodern era.

Though principles of forbearance and temperance existed in pagan societies, the pagan view of reality took forbearance only so far. The "merry dance of paganism" meant an earthy freedom from the burden

---

2 After Henry Ford, associated with assembly-line automated production. The label is intended to suggest capitalism transforms human beings into capital just like the machines they operate.

3 Some thinkers who are postmodernists as defined here would object to the label "postmodernist" because they would confine that term to theories which explicitly reject metanarratives, and would deem it inapplicable to theories encompassing other combinations of the elements summarized here.

of meaningfulness which transcendence induces. The price of that sense of freedom was to be paid in the bloody currency of appeasement of the gods, the worship of whom served to cohere tribal people groups and regulate society through ritual.

The ancient Hebrews represented a stark departure from paganism. The Genesis story of Abraham nearly sacrificing Isaac signals this break. Child sacrifice (and human sacrifice more generally) was repudiated, but the idea of sacrifice in the abstract was not. In secular psychological terms, sacrifice would mean the distinctly human trait of rationally foregoing pleasure today in order to build for tomorrow—forbearance as a virtue, as with the channeling of the sex drive in marriage. In religious terms, the concept of sacrifice went further, signaling a future reconciliation with God necessitated by the expulsion from the garden related in the third chapter of Genesis.

The Hebrew story is one long expression of the coming reconciliation with God, which culminated in the Advent of the Christ at a moment in history propitious for the Hebrew sundering of paganism to spread to the Western world more generally. The earliest centuries following the Resurrection marked the transition from paganism to monotheism, in the West. This brought profound change. Most relevant to our thesis, it underscored a dualist way of thinking of metaphysics: the natural and spiritual worlds, in which the spiritual runs in and through the natural, transcending it such that God is both transcendent and immanent within time- and space-bound reality.

Within the natural world, there is a lesser metaphysical dualism, between space-occupying physical things, on the one hand, and on the other, concepts, values, and abstractions like categories and universals. This was a stratification in our understanding of reality that enabled ever more refined thinking in science and ethics. This was an advance of reason. In the Enlightenment era, following closely on the heels of the commencement of the modern era, c. 1600, the triumphs of reason seemed to crowd out the more mystical elements of the religious story from which scientific reasoning arose. The mountain eclipsed the river. Some thinkers of the seventeenth and eighteenth centuries relapsed to a pagan-era deism or materialism. Over the course of the nineteenth century, their influence increased, in some quarters, but religion limped along on fideistic[4] or mystical impulses, abetted by the romanticism

---

4   Fideism: "ya just gotta believe." Knowledge follows from faith, rather than faith from knowledge. "The fear of the Lord is the beginning of wisdom," (Proverbs 9:10) and "the fear of the Lord is the beginning of knowledge" (Proverbs 1:7). But these precepts are

of the age. The candle had sputtered out, however, by the turn of the twentieth century. At this point, there was a hard break between secular philosophy and theology, and even philosophers who had not thrown over religion entirely hewed to a vague mysticism which devalued the significance of Christ's Advent and Resurrection.

Upon the putative demise of God, the stage was set for a re-evaluation of basic principles of ontology and epistemology in a reality imagined to be Godless or God-indifferent. This was the birth of the postmodern era. Postmodernism does not return to the pagan pantheon but would retain its social ritualism and its earthy sexual freedom. It rejects the monotheist religious principles of metaphysical dualism transcended by a personal God immanently. It is materialist, but presupposes a Hegelian historical teleology to mankind's development.[5] It is neo-Marxist in dividing social groups. Social metanarrative replaces God, and like God seems to exist apart from us individually.

We have used the analogy of mountain and river to express distinctions that manifest in the world but also in our interior, individual, psychological dispositions. These are tendencies to right and left, respectively, but recall that Genesis discloses both in our understanding of reality. Our thesis (one of them, anyway) is that a venture too far from either moves us toward totalitarianism, whether we think of it as coming from the right (e.g., Nazism) or the left (e.g., Maoism). Both are socialist and, at the extremes, are indistinguishable in all the ways that matter. Postmodernism tends toward illiberal fascism.

The push and pull for dominance in the social "conversation" is also a social negotiation of what truth is. It is torn from objective moorings, stewed subjectively, and projected onto a society-wide screen, so to speak, by the socialist impulse through which the self is subsumed into the collective. From there, the social truth becomes steadily larger and more dominating until it presses out of existence the worldview of Genesis entirely. If God is rejected *a priori*, and with Him a concept of objectivity in truth and morality, then all truth is internal and subjective

---

sometimes taken to eradicate the need for evidence altogether, substituting a distorted idea of "faith" in place of simply being persuaded to truth. How does one have faith without first being persuaded to the truth which is the object of that faith? These are among the paradoxes of religious belief a mature believer must negotiate. It is a "paradox" rather than a contradiction because one must have humility concerning the spiritual realm we presently perceive but dimly. For a sophisticated understanding of fideism, consider the work of William of Ockham (1285-1347).

5 Georg Wilhelm Friedrich Hegel (1770-1831), considered more thoroughly in chapter 12.

yet applied socially.

This happens because postmodernism provides a theory of reality, not actual reality. Genesis is reality and postmodernism is a means of forming artificial social constructs. Genesis objectivity places a third point between us, to which we both appeal, in discussing what is true, or what is right and wrong. If you and I both believe in God as Author of truth, but we disagree about what is true, we both appeal to that third point, so to speak. We're two points of a triangle, appealing to the third point in our discourse.

But if there is no God, and further, if truth is not objective, then how does our discourse work? Do we simply remove that third point, and engage in perennial tug-of-war? Even as we say with our mouths there is no objective truth, truth remains objective, and we continue to appeal to a third point, except that in postmodern imagining, that third point is social metanarrative. Our conception of truth is formed subjectively, in postmodernism, but because truth retains its objectivity regardless of our theorizing, we substitute a social objectivity, a metanarrative socially negotiated, and we both appeal to that social "consensus" as proof for the correctness of our point of view. We stop arguing about what is objectively true, and argue instead about what society expresses as true. This is why we live in the game show *Family Feud*.

And this is why language is so important in postmodernism. Language is the medium for the struggle. The goal is to win the point, not to find objective truth. To win the point means to have the social "consensus" narrative match our subjective truth-formation. This involves sniffing the wind for the acceptable range of disagreement within the contrived narrative, to shift its boundaries ever leftward. Manipulation of language to introduce ambiguity, or to change meaning, or to soften rhetoric, or to mischaracterize facts is considered fair game, rather than fraudulent, in this way of thinking. It's the serpent in the garden.

In the late nineteenth and early twentieth centuries, many thinkers considered religion a false social construct. Some regarded it as benign, but others regard it with hostility. They understood that if religion is false, then there is no God to embody truth, still less to author it. It was a short step, therefore, to reconsidering the objectivity of truth. Inroads were made into the concept of objectivity with existentialism and philosophical pragmatism, unmooring our idea of "truth" away from simply that which corresponds to the way things are. Truth was no longer absolute nor ontological, nor objective, nor eternal; but contingent, relative, and changeable in service to some other goal. Typically, that goal has been socialist utopia. Truth was no longer an irreducible transcendental, upon imagining God out of existence.

As with truth (and falsity), so with goodness (and evil). These have, in the same way, been demoted from their status as irreducible transcendentals, in the postmodern age. Morality, like truth, was traditionally understood to originate with God, who informs the conscience. But if there is no God, whence the conscience? If it is an evolved instinct in human beings, perhaps because natural selection hard-wires the Golden Rule, why would we suppose it is mutable through collectivist political influence? Evolved morality lacks authoritativeness, so we might become convinced that it can be set aside on the ground that reason trumps instinctual misgivings. This way of thinking relativizes the dictates of conscience, so that we can begin to think of all our instincts of good and evil as products of social negotiation, malleable according to evolving social dictates. As in early feminism, therefore, "the personal is political."

Philosophies of existentialism and pragmatism ushered in a re-thinking of morality in the postmodern era. In atheistic existentialism, the self is created by the self. Our lives are to be spent in that act of self-creation, and our sense of morality is a part of that project; it is not prescribed for us but is instead generated from within. While this understanding of existentialism is principally individualistic, philosophical pragmatism is overtly social. Social reform is the goal, and what advances us to the goal is therefore deemed true and right, because morality, like truth, is formed in social action. The individualism of existentialist thinking, and the socialism of pragmatist thinking, are linked in postmodernism because the self that does the individualistic thinking is subsumed into the collective. We tend to social conformity even as we cling to individuality of expression in peripheral, inconsequential ways. Pragmatist morality is that which seeks social harmony through elimination of boundaries among people; that which prioritizes deconstruction of alterity; and that which advances leftist political aims as attacks on what is conceived to be restrictive and repressive hierarchical value formation associated with false claims of objective truth and morality, most particularly exemplified in religion.

Religious belief is inimical to postmodernism. Not only because postmodernism is philosophically atheist and religion obviously is not. And not only because energy seems to postmodernists to be wasted in empty religious genuflection. Rather, because of the Judeo-Christian insistence on objectivity of truth and morality, originating from, residing in, authored by, and inseparable from almighty God, the unchanging and eternal Maker of heaven and earth, exactly as we read in Genesis. There is a philosophical split, therefore, between those who hold to objective truth and morality, on the one hand, and those who believe truth and morality to be situationally relative, on the other.

The problem with postmodernism is that it is collectivist, so the virus can't be quarantined. It is about how "we" should think so as to bring about desired collective ends. That means everything—*everything*—is political. One goal is to make us unfree to disagree with the postmodern metanarrative because it is necessarily held socially. The point is to rid us of the logocentric Genesis worldview held individually.

Postmodernists mostly ignore religion rather than try to refute it, and in this atmosphere, people who are tepidly Christian tend to form *a la carte* beliefs poorly informed by the religious traditions to which they subscribe, if they subscribe to any at all. The trouble with *a la carte* beliefs, unaided by revelation, is that we can assemble them and call that assemblage "my" reality. That actually makes some sense if truth is not extant in the universe but is generated internally and projected outward. It is consistent with the postmodern paradigm, in other words. If truth originates with me, that might begin to make as much sense as evaluating purportedly objective truth propositions of established religion. Maybe everyone gets their own planet when they die. I might adopt this view as a kind of "luxury belief"[6] and combine it with others systematically. It can spread through the kind of process philosophy invoked by postmodernists. This kind of thought progression makes sense if truth originates internally, or through the roil of social interactions. It's not goofy if it's true, and finding it to be true as a matter of postmodern process philosophy means not evaluating it as an objective proposition. This is how a cult would get traction, and also how totalitarianism becomes conceivable and even inevitable.

The cultish aspect of the postmodern worldview arises in part from its echoes in the esoteric metaphysics of Gnosticism. The Gnostic outlook results from failure to balance mountain and river tendencies, and it has ancient roots. As Christianity spread, theologians undertook to understand the dualistic reality of nature and spirit systematically; that is, in a way that all the parts of the belief system fit together. Some of those were of a Gnostic inclination. Gnostics, including some who con-

---

6 As with Rob Henderson's identification of certain progressive-left pieties adopted as a form of virtue or status-signaling. See https://quillette.com/2019/11/16/thorstein-ve-blens-theory-of-the-leisure-class-a-status-update/.

sidered themselves Christian but were deeply heretical, came to adopt a monist view that the spiritual is the only worthwhile constituent of reality, with material, like the body, being insignificant or even illusory. For this reason, what they did with the corrupted body didn't matter, and they tended to extremes of ascetism or hedonism. Gnostics sought esoteric knowledge; that is, they looked for dispensation of special knowledge from the unseen spirit world, to be manifested in their own intuition.

There are parallels to what we're seeing in the postmodern era. People living under a postmodern dispensation likewise seek esoteric knowledge, but the source of that knowledge is not the spirit world, but rather discernment of social movements, a phenomenon of the direction of history as meant by Hegel followed by Marx. They still look to the unseen, but the unseen is conceptual rather than spiritual. And then, they imagine they have special knowledge from their discernment, a sense that they are "on the right side of history." Things aren't true and good because of universal value. They're true and good because the *zeitgeist* tells them so.

The process of discernment includes a psychological disposition toward negation and critique applied to ferret out systemic social injustice, for example, as that wrought by patriarchy, heteronormative hegemony, or systemic racism. This disposition supports the postmodern vogue for eradicating barriers wherever they are found, including, but not limited to, categorical male/female difference. That disposition seems to recur in prominence historically in societies; it didn't begin with Karl Marx. The disposition to intuit power-seeking social systems stems from a felt sense of alienation, the same ineradicable human condition for which Christianity provided hope, but upon the death of Christianity, that sense of alienation is addressed in competing totalizing worldviews like Marxism and its postmodern variants, all operating on a paradigm of power rather than love.

The metanarrative of socialist progressivism is the source of gnosis. Upon receiving this esoteric awareness, one is awakened to the presence of unseen systems in the world protecting power interests. This awakening makes one "woke." The gnosis includes awareness of these social structures but also an awareness of self, distinct from oppressive categories, so that we imagine we create ourselves, and that self we create is our "true" self. The true self is not discerned from the spirit world, as with the Gnosticism of the ancients, but rather in existential self-creation.

Viewed from the non-woke outside, however, that self-creation is limited, because the self being created is social, and essentially so. Rather than generating the self entirely from within, as with theoretical existentialism, the self is formed in reference to a social metanarrative. The social metanarrative supports gnostic self-expression but only insofar as it conforms to the metanarrative. This limitation on self-creation seems rational in a worldview in which the self is increasingly subsumed into the collective (as we will see below).

On this way of thinking, one's true essence is not confined by objective categories or bourgeois social conventions. It is confined, however, by the postmodern metanarrative which replaces objectivity and universality of values. In this way, a female may consider her true self to be male, contrary to the indications of her body, and because the body is insignificant in consideration of essence, it may be modified, the thinking goes, to match that true essence as technology permits. Objectivity of categories must be rejected well before the chain of gnostic inferences leads one to consider "identifying" as the other natural sex.

As with truth, so with questions of morality, more likely to be termed "ethics" to avoid a hint of divinely imbued conscience. We can form our ideas of right and wrong without evaluating them against objective truth, other than the "truth" claimed and communicated by society, again through process philosophy attempting to replace a transcendent source with socially approved "truth." In this way, one can become convinced of, and reinforced in, one's evaluation of morality on the basis of society's collective say-so, which is in turn derived not from objective right and wrong, but from crowd-derived labelling of right and wrong.

Postmodernism is about deconstruction of hierarchy, but actually produces a new hierarchy, with a new source: social "consensus." "Consensus" doesn't mean unanimous assent; it is rather a term of art to mean, in a circular way, those who don't dissent. That is the opposite of consensus, but the thought is that dissenting views can be excluded because they're irrational, and given pragmatist premises, that seems to make sense. Rationality corresponds to truth, but truth is now socially formed, so rationality corresponds to assent to social metanarrative, and that becomes social "consensus." Agreement makes one rational; being rational makes one agree. Disagreement makes one irrational; being irrational makes one dissent. In this way, non-conforming dissenters are simply dismissed from the relevant pool considered to form the "consensus." Consensus exists by re-definition: it is the consensus of socialists. The exclusion tactics of John Rawls and Richard Rorty prevail. Let the irrational dissenters go off to hug their guns and pray to their imaginary friend. They're not to be counted.

The insidious nature of the Machine we will consider[7] is just this bogus consensus-formation. The danger of the Machine is that it represents the perspective of a social elite that is impervious to the desires, and often the interests, of putatively self-governing citizens within Western democracies. Those in positions of power don't act conspiratorially to advance self-interest. They act as they do because they are believers in a particular notion of collective progress advanced in narrative. The social narrative takes on a life of its own. The resulting contrived general will is formed by individuals who act in concert not because they're conspiring against the non-elite public, but because they find meaning and purpose in advancing the collective narrative. Their actions seem validated by the conviction that they know what's best for all of us, and diligently pursue it for the greater good. The narrative is taken to mean consensus, and the consensus is a self-reinforcing thing. It is managed by serious, morally superior people taking care of the unwashed and unenlightened. The elites who run the Machine wholly buy into the narrative misconceived as consensus because it proves they're good persons, engaged in what is ultimately public service, on the right side of historical movements, advancing us to some ill-defined but better place. Because of this moral earnestness, the elite lever-pullers of the Machine are impervious to the criticism that their machinations amount to ideological repression, which is anathema to individual freedom. The narrative and its metanarrative pronounce what is good, so dissent is evil, and properly excluded from the "consensus."

This is why illiberal public commentators can seem so oblivious and self-absorbed in their relentless pressing of socialist pieties. The thought, apparently, is that we can regard the hard-left point of view as a consensus so long as only socially engaged "good" people are counted. In this way, the religious hierarchy of values is not systematically disassembled, but rather ignored like a dead branch on an otherwise thriving tree. Instead of looking to God for authority, we look to the social consensus, and measure the correctness of propositions of truth and morality by that authority.

To be complete, we should consider the third of the irreducible transcendentals: beauty. It differs from truth and goodness in an important way. When discussing truth and goodness, we can more readily perceive the distinction between objectivity, on the one hand, and subjectivity

---

7   Beginning in Chapter 15, but especially Chapter 24.

and relativity, on the other. Relativism makes truth and goodness malleable in service to ideology because it can be distorted, and the distortions projected to a metanarrative. Beauty is more intractable to this kind of shift. Unlike with truth and goodness, beauty is beauty and can't be moved off its objectivity. Brutalist Bauhaus architecture, for example, is objectively ugly, and few seriously contend otherwise. It exists to dull the value-identifying intellect, to misdirect us from the transcendence which beauty implies.

Art points beyond itself to something. If not transcendence, then to some other vision like social or political statements. Art can serve as propaganda to advance ideology. But art purely for the sake of beauty is passé, among postmodernists, precisely because it calls to mind transcendent truth. The first casualty of totalitarianism is always belief in God and the dualist metaphysics such belief implies. Better to eradicate art entirely or manage it so that it points only to political aims rather than transcendence. The effort to make beauty relativistic—in the same way philosophy attempts to make truth and goodness relativistic—fails because beauty is more hard-wired as a reality for us. Attempts to subjugate art to ideology tend to be more clumsy than subjugation of truth and morality. Even the most hardened socialists may look on the *Pietà* and weep.

Philosophy on the subject of aesthetics has not cured this problem in postmodernism. An example can be found in the aesthetics arguments made by Frankfurt School postmodernist Herbert Marcuse. Citing the work of Friedrich Schiller (1759-1805), Marcuse takes note[8] of Schiller's distinction between the "form impulse" and "sensuous impulse"[9] in making art, and argues for invoking the sensuous impulse to the exclusion of the form impulse, in order to express one's break from the logocentric repression he thinks the "form impulse" represents. He recognizes the oppositional tension, therefore, but wants to eliminate one side of this duality in service to his project of remaking mankind—a cultural and political project that requires denying the transcendence that the form impulse and sensuous impulse together would point us to. The sensuous impulse prioritizes intuition, sentiment, creativity, in-

---

8   Marcuse, Herbert, *Eros and Civilization,* pp. 186-87.

9   This might recall to mind other philosophical oppositions like matter/form, substance/essence, potential/actual, and René Guénon's quality/quantity, in addition, of course, to the spirit/formless void of Genesis. All, like the mountain/river analogy of the present work, are similar efforts to capture in words the surprise of there being anything at all.

dulgence, and license. It is essentially passive and receptive. The form impulse prioritizes structure, hierarchy, principle, and reason. It is essentially active, mastering, and domineering. These correspond to the feminine and the masculine; the dream-like state of potentiality and the alert state of actualization. River and mountain. The sensuous impulse is the unconstrained vision of human nature, more prevalent on the political left. The form impulse is the constrained vision, more prevalent on the political right.[10] Schiller saw culture as arising from the interaction of these two impulses, as applied to oppositions of sensuousness and reason; matter and form; nature and freedom; particular and universal.[11] Marcuse wanted to collapse that duality.

Aesthetics means art, of course, like architecture, painting, sculpture, drama, and music. But it also means something more central to your everyday life. Why do you spend some effort picking out clothes; why do you arrange your table and the food on your plate in an appealing way; why do you arrange your furniture just so. Postmodernists, and especially those of the Frankfurt School, had a lot to say about aesthetics. There has to be a sense that aesthetics is a hard-wired element of our being, and perhaps a human motivator on a deep level like religion, so possibly a candidate for replacing religion. Beauty presents a problem upon rejecting God, because what is the point of it, if there is no animating Presence superintending this life in the body, to which the beauty points? Marcuse and his ilk commandeer aesthetics to try to make it do something else, namely to restore meaning to life when it so obviously is missing because we've rejected the only Author of it, and so have turned our face against the whole of immaterial reality. Life without distraction, like aesthetics, is matter in motion, coalescing from molecular combinations into you, with all your quirks and foibles and passing glories, and then de-coalescing into inert compounds, dust to dust, with no breath of God in the process, and you evanesce into the cosmos of oblivion. A whisper of a moment, then gone. How does anything matter, in this vision of reality?

Art points us to the transcendent, but doesn't replace it. Denial of the transcendent to which art points means that art must be meaningful unto itself. But that project must fail. Beauty always points beyond itself to the transcendent. The only way to avoid the transcendent is to

---

10 The terminology used in Thomas Sowell's *A Conflict of Visions: Ideological Origins of Political Struggles*, New York: Basic Books, 2007 (first published 1987 by William Morrow & Co.).

11 *Eros and Civilization*, p. 186.

remove the beauty from art, and that's what most postmodern art does. In place of art, we're presented splashes of color or novel arrangements of meaningless shapes, but presented in traditional formats like framed canvas or pedestal. Imagine bad hotel art, the kind that is nailed to the wall though perhaps with a light above it to signify "this is art." It might as well be a canvas that is blank but for bearing those words. It alludes to traditional formats for art but without beauty. In this way, the idea of art remains but without its attendant pointing to the transcendent.

An irony in postmodern art is that it's often produced as a feature of corporatist branding and marketing, imagination-free faux sophistication, serving as one little unimaginative money tributary to the money river to the money funnel for the corporation, which is owned on public markets and so another kind of corporation, and the public at large is another kind of corporation. "Corporatism" is the vehicle for reduction of people to the dreaded Fordism decried by neo-Marxists, but for some reason, the ultimate corporatism of socialism is invisible to socialists. Socialism is the direction of inauthentic art-lite simulacra, not the cure for it.

All art should point beyond itself to the transcendent, not inward or political, as with statement art, and not in a gnostic way as with postmodern art—gnostic because one must be privy to the high-level social consensus concerning art because that's the only quasi-meaning the "art" acquires because it doesn't project beauty on its own. Social construct concerning the presentation crowds out the necessity of transcendence in art.

Aesthetics in the postmodern world is not for beauty to point beyond itself to the transcendent, but for utility of social expression, hence, brutalist human warehousing and gritty stone expressionism and feminist/queer statement art that reminds us that power prevails, in this world, and between people the only value is lack of boundary that would otherwise serve to separate mediocrity from sublimity. We're all to be reduced to identical gray pennants flapping in the wind, none above the other, until all are tattered and torn and beaten down, leaving only a concrete gray Soviet wall: dingy, weather-beaten, blocking light, oppressively reminding us that brute power alone matters.

Social aesthetics as a substitute for beauty just isn't working out. Insistence on "socialism" continues, though no one can ever say what socialism is, outside the context of old-school Marxist theory. It certainly doesn't mean what Marx meant; that's long been discredited. The ideology beyond activist art is "neo" Marxism because like the old-school kind, it employs atheism, collectivism, skepticism about bourgeois so-cial structure, discontent generally, and group division. No one is an old-school Marxist anymore, but some may accept "neo-Marxist," or "cultural Marxist,"[12] or "socialist," or more likely, just "anti-capitalist" or "leftist" or "progressive." The labels are enormously vague and therefore enormously helpful to conveying what is really just a subjective psycho-logical disposition, basically low-voltage anger at the way things are. (Or high voltage, in the case of terrorist groups like Antifa.)

The vapid and infantile elements of Western culture sometimes give rise to the label "capitalism." Such elements are reasonably hated by left-ists or anyone else. But that's not capitalism, and the real object of hatred is the pointlessness of life upon removal of God. Meaninglessness is a major problem. It saps our strength. Aesthetics soothe the nerves a bit, but don't replace genuine transcendence, and eventually we realize it and give up on aesthetics, which means, remember, not just your flow-er-arranging hobby, but the expression of your individual humanity. It means no more ambition to contribute positively to the lifting up of the world, because that is only possible if rooted in the overflowing prodi-gality of the God-enriched soul.

Socialism for people who throw the word out thoughtlessly really just means the desired overthrow of gaudy consumerist frivolity among the prosperous, and the selfishness or haughtiness imagined to attend it. "Fascism" is taken as meanness of spirit that stands against communi-tarian fellow-feeling and harmony. Socialists imagine "fascism" by this definition to be an ineradicable endemic feature of capitalism, rather than the original sin of humanity. That's a blunder. Capitalism/fascism (on this definition) is the new original sin, and it is fought with the same fervor (and techniques, sometimes) as the original-original sin under-stood in Christianity. Hence, the pungent overbearing moralism evident in postmodern society.

---

12 Fine distinctions are sometimes made among "neo-Marxism," "cultural Marxism" and "critical theory." All employ a combination of the elements of Marxism discussed here, adapted to twentieth- and twenty-first-century social realities, and the distinc-tions may be useful among postmodern theorists in certain contexts. For purposes of the present thesis, the distinctions are overly nuanced and unhelpful to understanding the broader tendencies of negation, critique, socialism, and hostility to transcendence and logocentrism. It may be helpful for the reader to know there are attempts to mar-ginalize the phrase and concept of "cultural Marxism" by calling it far-right conspiracy theory. That's nonsense, however, easily disproved by reading prominent neo-Marxists themselves, writers like Antonio Gramsci, Herbert Marcuse, Theodor Adorno, and György Lukács.

CHAPTER TWELVE

Dialectic

OR MORE THAN a hundred years now, in the postmodern era, thinkers have been trying to rake back meaning for life after God is declared "dead." Postmodernists attempt to replace transcendence with process philosophies to "make transcendence horizontal," in Augusto Del Noce's phrasing. A process philosophy is one in which, having assumed away transcendence, ideals are thought to be generated immanently through social processes.

Marxism is a form of process philosophy, and serves as the template for later process philosophies of the twentieth and twenty-first centuries which comprise postmodernism, several of which we will address in later chapters. To understand the pervasive Marxist cast on postmodernism, it's helpful to take a step back to one of Marx's intellectual forebears, Friedrich Hegel.[1] Hegel is properly associated with the historicism that found its way into Marx's thought, and which now pervades Western thinking. Put simply, historicism is the habit of thinking of history as purposeful unto itself; that it is taking us somewhere. History, thus, is teleological. But not in the Christian sense that God's purpose and design is played out in history. Rather, the purposefulness of history is self-generated, through the process by which ideas are birthed and mutate. In this way, history itself can be thought of as a living, idea-generating phenomenon.

Hegel famously identified an oppositional dualistic process to the evolution of ideas, which he termed abstract and negative, which are then resolved in the concrete. Other philosophers would use the terms

---

1   Georg Wilhelm Friedrich Hegel, 1770-1831.

thesis and antithesis, which are then resolved in synthesis, which is then treated as new thesis, and the process repeats. There is some question whether the repeating three-step process as described by Hegel and Marx are the same, but in any event, a strict application of logic may not be applied to either, depending on the question submitted to the dialectic process. It would seem the concepts identified as thesis and antithesis, and the basis on which synthesis is said to result, derive from source(s) other than logical necessity. The elements of the three-part analysis may have advocacy or rhetorical purposes, as also the choice of subject matter submitted to the process.

More important than the logical precision by which syntheses are derived is the process itself. Synthesis becomes the new thesis, to which antithesis is applied, to yield a new synthesis, and the process repeats, mutating ideals over time. It means concepts and ideals necessarily evolve. This is a source of relativism in truth and morality. Perhaps the ultimate expression of Hegelian dialectic is in the dichotomy of being and non-being, which he resolved in immanent "becoming," in contrast to the eternal and unchanging "being" of transcendence and objectivity. Thus, process becomes the source of truth and morality and ideals more generally, in place of God, who declared "I Am" to reveal Himself as the ground of all being.

The thesis/antithesis "dialectic" process means that society progresses through history. Progress describes the teleological purpose in historicist thinking. Notably, the purpose and direction to history inhere in the dialectical process itself; it is not pulled along, so to speak, by some identifiable future goal, as with the Christian eschaton. It is pushed rather than pulled, we might say, and the push is called "progress;" adherents of this way of thinking are known as "progressives." Hence, modern-day "progressives" insist on an ever-leftward evolution in politics and culture without a particular end-point in mind. Politics and culture, now intertwined (perhaps through this very process), can "progress" without identifying what they progress toward. It is a utopian vision, meaning we'll find out when we get there. It is a form of faith, in other words, but "faith" as secularists mis-define the word: belief without the necessity of an object of belief.

Words like "historicism," "progressivism," "teleology," and "dialectic" all describe a sense in which history is substantive rather than merely descriptive; that is, alive, having internal direction though it is externally undirected. This sense is abetted by the biological theory of naturalistic evolution, and by technological progress, which by its nature builds upon itself. It would certainly feel like "turning back the clock" if we were suddenly without the innovations of electricity, telephones, internet, and so on.

Importantly, this sense of history as a living thing is so built into our way of thinking now that it obtains even for those who would say they reject both religion and Marxism. Marxism has a teleology of the dialectic in history. Religion has a teleology of God's purposes shaping history. So an atheist who is not a Marxist should reject the historicism of both. History ought to be instead simply a record of events, lifetimes following upon lifetimes and one event or movement after another, without a sense that they together take us in a particular direction. But that's not what we see. The sense that history lives and has direction and progresses obtains even for those who reject both God and Marxism. In this way, the Marxist premise of progressivism prevails even without the Marxist label, and we normalize the concept of process-derived truth.

Because there is no target to which we progress other than a vague sense of utopia, progressivism does not describe objectively positive change, but rather the change necessary to generate the arc of history; change for the sake of change because history is alive. History itself contains Hegel's geist, or world-spirit, replacing the spirit of God. Both fascism and communism are forms of ideal to be generated by the "progressive" impulse. They are both conceptions of the utopia to which the arc of history takes us. They are more alike than different, united in Hegelian historicism.

In this way, history itself takes the place of God. Process takes the place of transcendence. It is the reason modern political progressives will complain that a conservative policy "takes us backward," or puts us "on the wrong side of history." In exasperation, a progressive might say, "I can't believe we're still having this discussion in 2023," or whatever year it happens to be. The implicit assumption is that the matter is settled and we should move on; the matter should not be dredged up and "relitigated," because to do so is an offense to the progressivist, historicist imperative. These kinds of protestations often puzzle conservatives, who by contrast are more likely to look to objective and eternal truth. Something can be right or wrong objectively, it doesn't matter what year or century we're in, or whether the matter has been debated before.

Hegelian historicism is implicit in all postmodern process philosophy, whether acknowledged or not. It functions as the driving force of process, continuing the dynamism of philosophical becoming (our river) in place of philosophical being (our mountain). The dynamic push to the process is necessary upon removal of God from philosophy. The presumption of Hegel's historicism is implicit in the varieties of process philosophy we will consider in later chapters.

The idea of historical progress has not always been so pervasively the operating system of our understanding of the world and our place in it. There was an important break in this way of thinking between medieval and modern times. The "dark ages" weren't really dark, but they weren't progressive in the way we now count progress. Progress was to be an individual thing, as with individual moral improvement on eternal principles identified to God. The idea of a good society would follow—social change was not foregrounded as the object of our striving. Those times were also steeply hierarchical, objective value development being paralleled by class stratification and hierarchy among God's regents in the one Church.

Gradually, this period of Western history gave way, however, with influences of the Renaissance followed closely by Reformation and Enlightenment periods of history. The very fact that we attach those names to historical movements of ideas means a shift in our attention from individual progress before God to collective progress as a society on humanist terms. The Renaissance meant re-birth, of course, but re-birth of classical influences, a way of recapturing certain values of the great ancient civilizations, especially those of Egypt, Greece, and Rome. Those values had arisen in a climate of paganism, however, and the Renaissance didn't mean a reversion to paganism. Rather, it was a necessary loosening of the mountain tendency of medieval times dwelling too extensively on justice, guilt, and shame, and insufficiently on mercy, forgiveness, and freedom. The movement was an adjustment in the direction of the river, continuing to recognize our importance to God, but from an adjusted and better angle.

This necessarily coincided with an increasing centering of this-world human interests and concerns over heavenly ones; a move away from transcendence toward immanence; from the mountain to the river. It wasn't a sudden overthrow of God; far from it. The Reformation was in large part born of desire for genuine rapprochement with God in place of the religion some came to see as representing ossified and hegemonic human hierarchy.

The Renaissance period flowed into the Reformation period which flowed into the Enlightenment period. In what sense was the Enlightenment enlightened? How was light that didn't previously exist shined upon Western civilization? There was a loosening of religious dogma, but also a relative levelling of social hierarchy. One could say Enlightenment meant realization of equal human worth, in place of the stratification that previously obtained. But it was also a period in which religious skepticism was increasingly tolerated, and religious skepticism followed upon discoveries of science. Natural processes increasingly came to explain the physical world we know, in place of movements of spiritual good and evil. Scientific advances made for technological advances, and life became easier, even for common people. The Enlightenment period was "enlightened" by the idea of human progress birthed with modern times, c. 1600, following its gestation through the Renaissance and Reformation periods.

For more facile thinkers, science explained everything religion formerly seemed to, and so out with religion; in with science and progress. This was the backdrop for the thinking of Hegel. Like with the French Revolution and the United States' Declaration of Independence, Hegel's thought was a product of the Enlightenment. Science is process, and its fruits are manifest. The upheaval wrought by scientific materialism continued to sort out through the nineteenth century, and by the end of that century, the apparent death of God was inescapable, to many, and so also any sense of purpose and meaning. Progress, as the new god, was thin gruel for the deep hunger human beings had for the real God, however. The material fruits of relative prosperity could not replace God as the ultimate Source of all meaning.

In stepped God-absent ideologies, to inaugurate the bloodiest century in human history, and the continued collapse of our conception of the self as God-breathed beings. All is fluidity, flex, and flow. New searches for meaning have characterized Western reality since about the turn of the twentieth century, but aside from marginalized religious enclaves, the scope of inquiry was blinkered to exclude the transcendent. The postmodern era has been a fruitless search for meaning in the immanent; in process; ever under the watchful eye of the god Progress.

In this very work, we've taken some effort to see how perceiving oppositions in reality produces meaning, so perhaps the Hegelian dialectical approach is valid? To consider this, we have to understand the purposes for differentiation and identification in our perception of things and ideas. There are actually two radically opposed ways (dichotomy always being in play) to understand the process of differentiation and identification. One is rational. The other is dialectical. It is crucial that we understand how they differ.

We have already considered the process of ongoing differentiation and identification as the rational process by which we continually, and with ever greater refinement, group like with like and unlike against unlike in the exercise of logic. This is a function of the logos, by which our thoughts proceed: not helter-skelter, but in a straight line oriented toward objective truth. The degree to which we discern the arrow of logos is the degree to which we are able to discover truth. Without that orientation, we would have no criterion for supposing one thought "logically" follows another. This understanding of ordinary rationality presupposes transcendence; if not manifested in God, at least in the objectivity of ideal toward which rational thought proceeds.

The dialectic, by contrast, presupposes immanence. Assuredly not God's movement in the world, but immanence in the sense of truth emerging from this-world process. The mental process of differentiation and identification toward objective truth is replaced with syntheses of oppositions of thesis and antithesis through process of critique. The synthesis may then itself be critiqued, and this process is ongoing. What results is not capital-T truth, because the objectivity of truth is already assumed away. Instead, what results is a synthesis of ideas regarded as socially operative. The point is not to debate what is objectively true, but to rely on the dialectic engine to generate the flow of ideas in history.

Of course, the necessary objectivity of our normal cognition is not abandoned in dialectical thinking. It underlies even operation of the dialectic, but on an individual level by which syntheses can be asserted so that theory is formed. Critique operates on a social level, in that theory is formed in social engagement, and then the resulting theory is dialectically contrasted with social practice and resolved in "praxis" to react against offensive norms of society. It is fundamentally reactionary, a process for dismantling what is, with no idea what to replace it with other than "progress" toward an ill-defined utopia. This dialectical technique is foundational to Marxism.

This process also amounts to "faith" as it is incorrectly understood by atheists: unreasoned belief in belief itself. This is why Marxism is so often described, pejoratively, as "religious" in character. That may appeal to religious skeptics who are also Marxism skeptics, but it is a deeply pejorative account of religion because it supposes human belief attached to airy (and fictional) myth instead of the God of the universe who is more real than the physical things we mistake for ultimate reality.

Neo-Marxists take pride in their willingness to critique Marxism itself, hence a shift away from doctrinaire economic materialism, in application of the dialectical. The dialectic came to be applied more generally to all the ideals of Western civilization. Some peg the beginning of this shift to Antonio Gramsci,[2] who wrote in the early twentieth century, and that's reasonable enough as a marker in the evolution of Marxist ideas. Gramsci theorized cultural hegemony by the capitalist class to reinforce bourgeois values. Critiquing the narrow application of Marxist dialectic to economic determinism, Gramsci and other neo-Marxists expanded dialectical critique to cultural traditions. This mutation of Marxism into cultural critique accelerated upon egregious failures of traditional Marxist theory, as in the Soviet Union and later, China.

Now, the voices of neo-Marxist process philosophy are legion. Postmodernism is essentially Marxist, as we will see, and one way it is Marxist is its employment of this-world immanence in reflexive application of the dialectic. This means Hegelian historicism. It means a social, rather than individual, perspective. It means our goal is not to discover goodness, truth, and beauty breathed into the world by God, but rather to generate it ourselves, and to do so collectively.

Process philosophies employ Marxist thinking, if not in traditional dialectics, then in some related form of social process. Philosophies of process—of becoming rather than being—are irreconcilable with philosophies or theologies of transcendence. They represent non-overlapping ways of looking at the world. If we are caught up in any form of dialectical reasoning, we've departed from God's superintendence of history and have embraced instead the worldview of reduced "immanence"—not the immanence of the Spirit of God in the world, but rather temporal, this-world immanence of mankind-generated ideals.

---

2 (1891-1937).

CHAPTER THIRTEEN

Alterity

THE GENESIS MODEL starts with a nothingness from which hierarchies emerge through differentiation in our thinking whereby we make ever finer distinctions toward a goal of truth. Postmodernism is the reverse: differentiation must be eliminated and society deconstructed because it is deemed currently constructed on principles of capitalism, religious metanarrative, and "fascism." "Fascism" is in quote marks because postmodernism essentially is fascism; the word is a false flag. Equality, understood as sameness, is presumed the *summum bonum* of our existence.

Breaking down boundaries and constricting forms sounds good, but it is a repudiation of differentiation (or "judgment," in the right sense) on grounds that it will produce harmony and peace and brotherly love and so on, instead of the evils of hierarchies. It is the old story of left vs. right. The left is so dominant that in the common imagination, hierarchies are to be erased wherever they are found. But they're simply replaced with new hierarchies, because that is human nature, and the new hierarchies are founded on the shaky ground of "consensus"-formed ideology.

The battleground ultimately is ontological dualism. Reality understood in dualistic polarities includes the subset philosophical concept of alterity. Alterity refers to the subjective, psychological sense of separateness from other sentient entities—people, of course, but it could relate to separateness from God, if we believe Him to exist. It is necessary to our own ability to form an identity, based not just on subjective experience of self, but on subjective experience of self as not-other. Person-to-person alterity is the phenomenon of our awareness of our distinctness from other self-aware beings. To fully grasp that distinctness, we must imagine looking out on the world from the other's point of view. Alterity is an instance of the ubiquitous binary divisions of opposed meaning. There is me, you, not-me, not-you, and innumerable divisions of like nature operating socially, in the same way oppositions more generally operate physically, conceptually, and spiritually.

Alterity is "otherness," we might say, the sense of separation we feel from other people, but in contexts in which meaning and identity is derived from the me/God, me/you, me/society, me/culture distinctions. In this usage, it is important in much postmodern thought which examines and critiques our way of addressing alterity as a source for social disharmony or abuse. In a colonialist era, for example, it is theorized that there were collisions of culture with negative consequences for the colonized because of ill-considered "other-ing" by the colonizers.

Subjective alterity is inevitable, however, and is not unto itself problematic. Destroying alterity in the name of elimination of barriers between people is misguided. Tolerance should be the goal, not sameness, but sameness is the outcome if we are successful at breaking down boundaries altogether. If the boundary between individuals is broken down across racial, sexual, cultural, national, religious, and historical lines, at some point, we're just the same. And maybe that's the idea, or maybe that's just the natural outcome, of the collectivist engine of assault on alterity. No more distinctions, therefore, no more me; no more you.

The opening lines of the Bible establish ultimate alterity principles, especially in our perceiving God as wholly "other" to ourselves. That fundamental principle of alterity is necessary to understanding our individual relationship with other people in our world, and indeed of understanding reality in general, because it is but one instance of the pervasive oppositional polarities by which we begin to make sense of anything and everything.

Take, for example, the clash of East and West on the American continents. European settlers of what is now the United States encountered natives, "Indians," as wholly other, a radical alterity which, it was sometimes argued, self-justified the Indians' subjugation. There is another way of looking at this, though. The Indians certainly perceived the otherness of new Americans in just as radical a form. It wasn't alterity in the abstract, in other words, which caused conflict. It was an age-old desire for conquest and territory and domination. It was played out in slow-motion, we might say, as European-Americans pushed west on the North American continent, so it wasn't thought of exclusively in warlike, us-vs.-them terms. There were fitful and often futile efforts by European-Americans to make "them" more like "us" in order to co-exist, and there were similarly efforts—ill-conceived and half-hearted efforts, perhaps—to preserve difference as by setting aside territory in the reservation system. Those efforts were attempts to either overcome or acknowledge alterity.

An understanding of alterity among human beings is nonetheless helpful, because it is the basis upon which we can grasp the Golden Rule: we should do to or for others as we would have them do to or for us. We have to be aware of alterity as a phenomenon in order to also grasp the means by which it is routinely transcended in interpersonal relations. There is a real and extant intersubjectivity which employs, rather than subverts, alterity.[1]

Intersubjectivity describes the social aspect of human consciousness. Other people are not objects in my environment, like rocks and houses and trees. They are subjects, with the same kind of subjective self- and other-awareness that I possess. You are aware of objects, but you're also aware of your own subjective awareness, and you're aware that others are similarly self- and other-aware, and a sort of interactive play-back occurs. Your subjectivity and mine intermingle in a buzz of "intersubjectivity."

That intersubjective mingling is social awareness, in which I am not only aware of your subjectivity, and therefore aware of your awareness of mine; but the mutual awareness creates another dimension. It lives, in a manner of speaking, distinct from both of us, acquiring form and content distinct from that of its members. This is social awareness, through which we perceive social narrative and metanarrative. It is why we so readily and instinctively relate ourselves to our conceptions of collectively aware society. That is, our intersubjectivity does not only mean mutual awareness of subjectivity, but also we conceive a social awareness distinct from both of us. It is important to remember, however, that social awareness is not the same as consensus. It is more accurately an individual's awareness of the content of a social narrative that the individual may or may not share. Hence, competing narratives, and on the part of collectivists, frustration that some hold out against the social

---

1 Emmanuel Levinas, in *Alterity and Transcendence*, theorizes a form of transcendence arising out of this intersubjectivity, replacing the transcendence of a putative God. All of postmodernism is about constructing a reality without transcendence, or, in Levinas's case, constructing something called transcendence, but without real transcendence. Levinas's effort is another instance of "transcendence made horizontal;" a postmodern process philosophy.

narrative they prefer.

Intersubjectivity is the reason human beings are social on an essential level. It is an ineluctable element of our consciousness. The particular quality of consciousness held by human beings, alone among other living things, allows for the combined might of social groups, directed to purposes good or ill. This feature of human consciousness allows for metanarratives, either as benign, bottom-up organic development of philosophies and religion, or contrived systems of thought untethered to accurate conception of God; top-down ideologies coercively deployed for purposes of control.

Alterity is a valid and necessary concept in understanding the complete otherness of God, so that we can successfully remove our conception of Him from pagan misconceptions of supernatural beings existing somewhere in-between the ultimate fully actualized Source of all being, and others like me walking around on the earth for a season with all my foibles and idiosyncrasies. Alterity as applied to the God/man division is the basis upon which we correctly conceive our relationship to God.

With that understanding of subjectivity, intersubjectivity, and social awareness, we can compare the Genesis and postmodern worldviews, particularly concerning sensitivity to alterity. In the Genesis worldview, there is no thought of breaching the person-to-person divide. To the contrary, God as Mediator is such because individuality results in division which requires buffering of person-to-person (and group-to-group) interactions through God-authored principles of virtue to the end of peace. The categorical distinction between any two people is preserved. Difference is mediated, not eliminated, and so individuality is preserved, and fraternity is maintained, from mutual appeal to the same Source of authority. We are each of us coaxed by the conscience, by the Holy Spirit, and by traditions founded on doctrine, to extend the hand of peace toward others, so much so that in the Christian tradition, we are instructed to love others as ourselves, and even to love our enemies. Loving one another requires individuation wherein there is first a self—an "I"—to do the loving, and another like me to receive the love.

In the postmodern vision, by contrast, peace comes through eliminating difference, which means compromising individuality by merging into the collective. The expectation is that we seek out the collective mind and bend to the historicist *geist*[2] on questions that might otherwise divide. In this way, we become more in accord with the collective

---

2 The social awareness envisioned by Hegel, but incorporating also his historicist (or teleological) perspective which was taken up in the historical progressions of Marx.

mind, seeking to know it better and conform ourselves to it, in the way Christians of yesteryear sought out the mind of God, in order to conform theirs to His. Given postmodernist conceptions of reality, this collectivist way of thinking may seem freeing, but for those who renounce it in favor of objectivity, there is social opprobrium and even legal pressure to forswear it in favor of the god socialism.

This is the sense in which human interaction is central to the postmodern mentality, though typically stated more vaguely (i.e., less categorically) than it is here. In postmodernism, the obsession is with alterity itself, rather than how it might be bridged while preserving the individual self. If traditional religion is about bridges between islands, postmodernism is about merging the islands. A poetic way of considering it is in the title of Ernest Hemingway's posthumously published *Islands in the Stream*. In existentialist fashion, we lament the divide and struggle in the currents of emotion cutting us off each from the other, and we look with anguish to the other shores, exquisitely alone among others. A universal oneness of mankind seems to be the answer to this angst of loneliness, again as with the Tower of Babel. The psychological root of postmodern collectivism is a simplistic hope that it will ameliorate individual loneliness. It actually has the opposite effect, however, making loneliness endemic, and loneliness is, as Hannah Arendt[3] and others have observed, a signal feature of encroaching totalitarianism.

The Genesis answer to loneliness is a structure of relationships beginning with the joining of man and woman in marriage. A complex hierarchy of relationships radiates out from it, in family, friendships, commerce, parish, nationality, and so on. Postmodernism is an attempted top-down view of humanity, the collective constructed to mitigate a sense of loss, which is in turn blamed on individualism. Genesis, by contrast, places that sense of loss in the individual, and its mitigation is the outworking of innumerable rhizomatic human interactions, resulting in a society which actually does mitigate loneliness rather than merely absorbing the agency of individuals instead.

In binary terms, alterity is the opposition of me and you, and a postmodern precept is that it must be collapsed. Nationalism, citizenship, and territorial borders are seen as instances of perpetuating division and promoting alterity, so these kinds of concepts are instinctively resisted by those infected with the postmodern virus.

---

3 1906-1975. Arendt was a philosopher and political theorist of the twentieth century, who survived the holocaust and wrote from that experience in works like *The Origins of Totalitarianism*, 1951.

Isn't it a good thing, though, to overcome alterity? Isn't tribalism always and everywhere a bad thing? Some careful thinking is called for here, doubling down on categorical binary oppositions rather than broad-brush elimination of categories wherever they're found. The fascination with racism and anti-colonialism and nationalism, seen as foundational evils, has itself an evil side. We don't feel the same affection for everyone we know. Our ties to other people vary according to the nature of the relationship. You feel differently about your sibling than you do a stranger you've never met. That's not a bad thing. It's a necessary thing. There is no love without this differentiation in affections. We might feel a general sense of "we are the world" cheerfulness about the unknown billions that populate this planet along with ourselves. But that's hardly love. Love means—and requires—deeply knowing another.[4] The degree of love we feel for other people depends on the strength of personal relationship, and so it varies, diminishing in outer circles of relationship, increasing in inner circles. Typically, we love (and are loyal to) our spouse most, then perhaps immediate family, then perhaps long-time close friends. As to your best friend, you might say he's "like a brother" precisely because you want to say the relationship is more akin to what is expected in a closer concentric ring of relationship. Rings of affection radiating outward after that include acquaintances, colleagues, neighbors, and countrymen. If you're a Yorkshireman, you'll be pleased to run into another in some far-off venue. What could be more natural than that? And in like vein, why be apologetic that you love your countryman more than someone across the sea, even if you've never met either?

The point is not merely that differing degrees of attachment to others is the way things are. The point is also that this is the way things should be. Apart from the sheer impossibility of loving literally everyone, if you could love everyone the same, that's the same as saying you love no one at all. Now if we examine the fascination with alterity that obtains on the postmodern left, we see that this is exactly the trend: it is toward loving no one at all. We can see this by looking at the most sensitive relationships—sensitive because they make us the most vulnerable—our families. It's a horrible thing to be abandoned or abused by those positioned to love you the most, but it's horrible precisely because there, the opposite should be and normally is true: intense love expressed in time and resources and sacrifice. The kind of love that is necessary to form an

---

4 Knowing as a prerequisite of love is explicated more thoroughly in Norton, Albert, *Intuition of Significance*, pp. 97-100.

emotionally healthy human being. Serious emotional wounds can result from the abuse in close relationships like those inside a family. But the cure is to eliminate the abuse by appeal to higher principle, not to eliminate the relationship, thinning out the depth of love one experiences in favor of vague social attachment.

And yet, an affirmative and intentional undertaking is made to undermine the family, in postmodern theory.[5] Why? It's in part because of this sensitivity to alterity. Love is thought to be a zero-sum resource, and more of it spent in the family means less of it to spend on humanity in the abstract. Close, tight relationships are suspect. Moreover, in the postmodern mind, they normalize the tendency to preserve our best love for kith and kin, and thereby, so the thinking goes, contributes to the kind of suspicious mistrust and opportunism that plays out in racism, colonialism, nationalist populism, and other such bugbears of the deconstructionist left.

In the postmodern imagination, the me/you divide is one instance of unnecessarily divisive, either/or binary opposition. The culprit, in postmodernism, is categorical thinking, which enables polar divisions. So categories also are suspect, and presumptively appropriate for deconstruction. Categories mean taxonomical thinking, whereby we employ binary oppositions and formulate criteria for discernment of meaning, much like scaffolding and forms are used for construction of buildings. We employ universals in our thinking, to group like things with like, so as to distinguish them from unlike. This is binary thinking, however, which makes it suspect to the postmodern mind.

This is not to say that oversimplification into broad-brush categories is better. Oversimplification means use of binary oppositions in conceptual thinking in a brutish, unrefined way. This kind of thinking enables one to see male and female as almost distinct species, for example, rather than two types of the same species made for each other in interesting ways. The solution to over-simplistic thinking is more refined categorical thinking. Likewise, with the category of the person. We're not all the same, available to be subsumed in a universal mind. Better to celebrate differences as well as commonalities, for full flourishing individually and socially.

---

5 This is well-described by Carl Trueman in his *The Rise and Triumph of the Modern Self*, Wheaton, IL: Crossway, 2020, e.g., p. 263. Trueman uses the phrase "expressive individualism" to contain the existentialist impulse to creation of meaning in the individual, but "individualism" contrasts with "socialism," or "collectivism." His "individualism" might better be understood as "subjectivism."

A subject differs from an object because a subject is a being with subjective self-awareness. We perceive other people not as objects, but as subjects: another like me. Another person in your environment is instantly recognizable to you as a specific instance of the category of person, of which you also are a member. Because of that common membership, and your conscious self-awareness, you recognize conscious self-awareness on the part of that other person, too. Knowing that other person has subjective self-awareness, you also know he is aware of your self-awareness, just as you are of his. Instantly, that intersubjectivity creates a collective awareness, a society, even if only a society of two. With more information about the other's background, various clues from the circumstances of the encounter, a common culture arises, borrowing from the social background of each. You believe the other person exists, of course, but you believe that other person exists as a person, not a bear or a chair or an undifferentiated blob of color and movement. I believe in that person's existence, but specifically existence as a person with subjective self-awareness like mine; as one who grasps, interactively with me, our mutual self-awareness.

This phenomenon of intersubjectivity is the reason we experience a frisson in the company of another person that we do not experience alone with mere objects or animals in our environment. Imagine you're hiking a mountain trail and you believe yourself to be alone, but then you look up and see someone approaching. Instantly, the environment feels different, even if you both just continue in opposite directions. Or consider the imagery in Daniel Defoe's *Robinson Crusoe*, that electric moment when Crusoe, shipwrecked and alone, espies Friday's footprint in the sand. Many works of literature depict this phenomenon. It is a staple of shipwreck plots, like *Robinson Crusoe*, but also of last-man-on-earth plots, like this author's *Another Like Me*.[6]

With that background, let's turn to religious belief. Why does genuine Christianity feel particularly difficult to pursue now as compared to, say, fifty years ago? One reason is that in most churches—those that don't push hard to the left, at least—politics has been verboten. Or if not deliberately screened out, at least frowned upon, because perhaps it will discourage would-be believers. There is something to say for that. Christ wasn't a Republican or Democrat. Religion speaks to something far more important; something transcendent of the political gripes of the moment.

---

6   Dallas: eLectio Publishing, 2017.

On the other hand, we must recognize that the barbarians at the door of the church are of a different sort, now, since commencement of the postmodern era. The church no longer coexists with the polis in a combined center of light and life. Instead, the civilizing membrane that surrounds the true church has worn thin. Those outside tolerate only begrudgingly, if they tolerate at all. And even those within look around at their co-religionists with suspicion and sometimes with hostility, wringing their hands at their lack of corporate power. Creedal splintering has weakened the church from the inside, but this is as nothing compared to the ideological strongholds arrayed against it on the outside. The church no longer takes up a place inside the city walls, so to speak. The polis instead makes peace with the barbarians, and the church in its parts is scattered about, inside and outside, trying to make sense of it all.

A way to think about this is to appreciate history in broad swaths. The Jews introduced to the world the ontology of being and transcendence, in the form of God the great "I Am." This was a repudiation of the ontology of becoming and immanence that was paganism and which is now postmodernism. The fire of transcendence burned in Jewish redoubt within the pagan darkness until it exploded into the Western world and beyond through Christianity. It only gradually lost momentum in the eras of Renaissance, Reformation, and Enlightenment.

That momentum slowed until a tipping point was reached. That tipping point was in about 1900, though one could certainly make a valid case for a somewhat earlier or later time. The point is that Christianity, and with it the transcendent worldview wrested from paganism, became weary and complacent and self-doubting and vulnerable. This was the commencement of the postmodern era, in which paganism is resurgent—not with gods assigned to concepts and natural processes, as in pre-Christian days of yore, but in materialist ontologies of becoming and immanence.

Before the postmodern era, accommodation between pluralist democratic culture and government, on the one hand, and religion on the other, has been sometimes bumpy but mostly workable, each friendly but not intimate with the other. It's different now, and it's different because postmodern ideology is affirmatively anti-Christian and employs politics to propagate itself to the exclusion of Christianity. In the postmodern era, our most fundamental conceptions of reality are negotiated socially, so society; the polis—politics—seems the only arena in which to address anything meaningful. But genuine Christianity, not dependent on social process, is excluded from the discussion at the outset.

Just as Christianity was a successful assault on paganism, now post-modern ideology is an assault on Christianity. Whether postmodern ideology succeeds at vanquishing Christianity among most inhabitants of liberal Western societies remains to be seen. Perhaps it's too late to change the current trajectory; perhaps not. Perhaps the church retreats to its redoubts and those only nominally in step out. Whatever happens will be the result of irreconcilable ideological conflict, however, and it won't be easy on individuals who genuinely seek Christ. We must understand postmodern ideology to see that it is irreconcilable with Christianity, just as paganism was, and also that it is entirely at home within democracies not limited by individualistic principle. The church cannot ignore politics because in this day, democratic political systems are the host for the anti-Christian postmodern virus.

How? And why? As we will see, the ideology is essentially collectivist. We might say that socialist collectivism is the ideology, but that's too simple. We're not living in a simple linear tug-of-war between lesser or greater degrees of individualism and socialism in economic matters. At stake is the threat of an all-encompassing kind of collectivism, in which the self is subsumed into the collective, as with old-school fascism, but the collective has a purpose and direction of its own, inimical to religions of transcendence in general, and certainly to Christianity.

Believing in God doesn't just mean belief that God exists. It means believing in certain features of that existence. We form certain beliefs about God, perhaps from our catechism, perhaps from the wider culture, or perhaps our own imagination. The God we say we believe in is not an abstraction, but a God with certain attributes, and to "believe" in God means not merely to accept His existence in the abstract, but to believe the combination of things we understand to be encompassed in our word "God."

Belief in God as understood by Jews and Christians means belief in One who, though unseen, has awareness of me far beyond even my own self-awareness. As with belief in the existence of another person, we believe in God as God; that is as a subject, One with subjective self-awareness; One with whom I might develop mutual self-awareness as I would another person in my environment. But God is "unseen," meaning our perception of Him is through imagination—not that he is imaginary, but that because He is unseen, we must image Him in our minds in order to perceive His presence. That image cannot be visual in the same way we hold a mental picture of mother or father or friend. He is unseen, so the "image" is of God's attributes, attested through natural and written revelation, and our experience of life, and of course in the person of the Christ.

Understanding the essential subjectivity of God and of ourselves, we begin to find inevitable a kind of intersubjectivity with Him. Just as we participate in a shared, mutual other-consciousness with people, we can do so also with God. If we perceive God as here with us, though not bodily, and understand that He has self- and other-awareness with all people, we may also come to understand that He loves us despite knowing our interior minds, including that part we keep hidden from other people. To know that He loves despite knowing us so well opens a door to perceiving love on a scale we cannot know if we put away all spiritual aspiration and grunt along animal-like through this life, giving and getting affection transactionally.

But we don't experience intersubjectivity with God in the immediate physical sense we do with other people. Instead, we have to ascend another plane, so to speak, to reach beyond the physical world and develop sensitivity to another. That other is "the heavens," a spiritual realm distinct from the physical, as disclosed in Genesis beginning with its first line. Reality is a duality of heavens and earth; natural and spiritual; each made comprehensible by contrast to the other. In this life in the body, we live on the physical plane, but something of the heavens is in us, and it creates a yearning for transcendence. This yearning is endemic to human beings.[7] We see it everywhere, if we understand it for what it is. Whether we acknowledge God or not, we express this yearning by engaging in art, music, philosophy, innovation, the pursuit of excellence, compassion, and loving when we know our love is not reciprocated. We don't yearn for what we already have. We yearn for what is missing, and we call it "yearning" rather than merely "wanting" because the thing we yearn for is not clearly defined. We hardly know what it is we want. Many intuit, or reason their way to, an understanding that it must be that part of our make-up imputed from that other realm, and so we go looking for God.

Finding Him means believing in Him as He is, therefore believing certain things about Him. We have to know what is true about Him, therefore, and that means understanding—as well as possible in this life—the full scope of God-authored and -inhabited reality. And that means understanding the opposite version of reality, the principalities and powers arrayed against us in the materialist and postmodern theo-

---

7 *Intuition of Significance*, Chapter 16.

ries of an imagined God-less reality.

We make sense of things by differentiation, grouping like with like and so on, but in this one instance, there is no differentiation. No grouping of like with like. There is no category to which God belongs. Indeed, from our perspective, this is the signal feature of His existence, His very unlikeness to anything else: the singularity, whence comes all categories and instantiations. This is disclosed to us in the first lines of Genesis. If we could play the film of creation in reverse, we would see multiplicity merging to oneness; types and kinds reverting to fewer and fewer types and kinds; divisions unified; male and female merged; and all condensing to the one shining seed from which all things grow: God alone, uncaused, wholly actualized, and non-contingent.

So we have to "image" God with attributes we do not share. We do so through intellectual acuity and perhaps from heightening our instinctual spiritual acuity through spiritual exercise. We live in a time-bound world of contingent, caused things, yet we grope after the ineffable. We do so because when God made us, He put His spark in us, just as Genesis discloses. We exist between the heavens and the earth.

CHAPTER FOURTEEN

Hermeneutics of Suspicion

T HE POSTMODERN worldview rejects notions of spiritual or metaphysical dualism as fantastical inventions of a more primitive time. The postmodernist project is an attempt to explain the phenomena of human experience without such inventions. God is rejected *a priori* in postmodern thinking.

Indeed, there is a posture of negation in the whole of postmodernism. It consists largely in critique. This critique is often said to be critique of Enlightenment rationalism, and that's true enough. But Enlightenment rationalism is a product of centuries of pervasive Christian influence in the Western world. That Christian influence is largely responsible for the logocentric rationalist impulse and objectivity and hierarchical value formation and ontological dualism that postmodernism reacts against. Postmodernism rests on a foundation of skepticism. It is not a comprehensive explanation of reality, as with the Christian worldview we have sketched. It is more about saying what is not true, than what is.

This critique tends to be more than a questioning of popular verities. It is instead cynical, in the sense that it is mistrustful even of good faith in the opposing point of view, and involves building one's own substantive beliefs on that negation. Contemporary German philosopher Peter Sloterdijk, although writing in the postmodern era from a Nietzschean outlook, departs from other postmodernists in that he is critical of the critiques, recognizing them as such and calling them "cynical."[1] He de-

---

1 Sloterdijk, Peter, *Critique of Cynical Reason*, New York: Verso, 1988. More recently, this was a theme of *Cynical Theories* (Pluckrose, Helen and James Lindsay, Durham, NC: Pitchstone, 2020) targeted to the critical theories subset of "applied" postmodernism.

scribes Rainer Maria Rilke's poem, "The Archaic Torso of Apollo,"[2] as declarative and form-inducing and therefore likely inimical to the "anti-authoritarian reflexes"[3] of contemporary postmodern thought. This is a rare recognition that postmodernism is a negative stance against Enlightenment rationalism informed by a God-decreed value hierarchy rather than a body of affirmative thought complete unto itself. Sloterdijk described it as "enlightened false consciousness," a sensibility or mood characterized by doubt, yet the dominant mode in culture since the mid-twentieth century.

Postmodernism's posture of negation is rooted in a "hermeneutics of suspicion" directed at religion. The phrase is attributed to Paul Ricoeur in his work *Freud and Philosophy*.[4] Ricoeur noted a common spirit in the works of Marx, Nietzsche, and Freud; namely a desire to unmask hidden delusions in individual and social consciousness—an outlook of suspicion.

If Marx, Freud, and Nietzsche employed a hermeneutics of suspicion, to be followed by others of the Marxist disposition, what did those hermeneutics replace? What is the opposite of a hermeneutic of suspicion? Paul Ricoeur suggested a hermeneutics of restoration. As explicated by Ruthellen Josselson,[5] the hermeneutics of restoration is characterized by:

> . . . a willingness to listen, to absorb as much as possible the message in its given form and it respects the symbol, understood as a cultural mechanism for our apprehension of reality, as a place of revelation. This type of hermeneutics is animated by faith.[6]

The interpreter's task, in this hermeneutic, is "one of distilling, elucidating, and illuminating the intended meanings of the informant[.]"[7] The hermeneutics of suspicion, by contrast:

---

2 "The Archaic Torso of Apollo," a poem by Rainer Maria Rilke, provides the title of Sloterdijk's book, *You Must Change Your Life*, Cambridge, UK: Polity, 2013 (originally published in German, 2009).

3 Ibid., p. 19.

4 Subtitled *An Essay on Interpretation*, New Haven: Yale University Press, 1970.

5 Josselson, Ruthellen, *The Hermeneutics of Faith and the Hermeneutics of Suspicion*, Narrative Inquiry 14 (John Benjamins Publishing), 2004 (https://doi.org/10.1075/ni).

6 Ibid., p. 3.

7 Ibid., p. 5.

[M]ay be approached as the demystification of meaning presented to the interpreter in the form of a disguise.[8]

The interpreter's task in this hermeneutic is "discovering meanings that lie hidden in false consciousness."[9]

The significance of suspicion as a hermeneutic by which one evaluates a proposition is this. It means one approaches certain propositions not with healthy skepticism in order to deeply evaluate, but rather to interpret the proposition on the assumption of some hidden interest not reflected in the proposition itself. It imposes a lens of suspicion on a proposition so as to cast it in negative light even before undertaking an evaluation of it. You say there's a God only because you accept it blindly; you're afraid of change; you're afraid of death; you're afraid your social or material interests would be damaged if belief in God goes by the boards. In this way, the proposition—that God is—never gets reached. The critique only goes one way. The focus is on the possibility of hidden agendas in the proposer rather than the merits of the proposition itself. The hermeneutics of suspicion is most obviously (but not exclusively, as we will see) applied to the tenets of religion, but in whatever context it is applied, it shuts off critical thinking rather than encourage it.

Marx rejected religion and believed it so self-evidently false that it must exist for some purpose other than its stated creeds. So, he set about to unmask its purposes, finding it to be an integral part of a social structure to placate the laborer into willing acceptance of his oppression at the hands of the industrial capitalist:

> The foundation of irreligious criticism is: *Man makes religion*, religion does not make man. Religion is, indeed, the self-consciousness and self-esteem of man who has either not yet won through to himself, or has already lost himself again. But man is no abstract being squatting outside the world. Man *is the world of man*—state, society. This state and this society produce religion, which is an inverted consciousness of the world, because they are an *inverted world*.

> Religion is the general theory of this world, its encyclopaedic compendium, its logic in popular form, its spiritual *point d'honneur*, its enthusiasm, its moral sanction, its solemn complement, and its universal basis of consolation and justification. It is the *fantastic realization* of the human essence since the human essence has not acquired any true

---

8   Ibid., p. 3.
9   Ibid., p. 5.

reality. The struggle against religion is, therefore, indirectly the *struggle against that world* whose spiritual *aroma* is religion.

Religious suffering is, at one and the same time, the *expression* of real suffering and a *protest* against real suffering. Religion is the sigh of the oppressed creature, the heart of a heartless world, and the soul of soulless conditions. It is the *opium* of the people.

The abolition of religion as the *illusory* happiness of the people is the demand for their *real* happiness. To call on them to give up their illusions about their condition is to call on them *to give up a condition that requires illusions*. The criticism of religion is, therefore, in embryo, *the criticism of that vale of tears* of which religion is the *halo*.[10]

Nietzsche similarly approached religion with a view to unmasking its illegitimate functions. He believed it induced a slave morality in its adherents, with the result of repressing the innate will to power, by which he meant not necessarily domination, but the driving life force by which one excels in life. The servility he believed he saw in Christianity had the effect of suppressing this more natural and healthful impulse, he held.

Freud believed religion to be an internal illusion, socially reinforced, devised to explain the puzzling external world. It was actually a form of neurosis, in his view, getting in the way of a mentally healthful way of looking at the world. He also seemed to be critical of the in-group aspect of religious practice, as representing divisive re-tribalization. He wrote about religion:

> The whole thing is so patently infantile, so foreign to reality, that to anyone with a friendly attitude to humanity it is painful to think that the great majority of mortals will never be able to rise above this view of life. It is still more humiliating to discover how a large number of people living today, who cannot but see that this religion is not tenable, nevertheless try to defend it piece by piece in a series of pitiful rearguard actions. Religions, at any rate, have never overlooked the part played in civilization by a sense of guilt. Furthermore—a point which I failed to appreciate elsewhere—they claim to redeem mankind from this sense of guilt, which they call sin.[11]

---

10   Marx, Karl, *Introduction, A Contribution to the Critique of Hegel's Philosophy of Right*, translated by A. Jolin and J. O'Malley, Cambridge Press, 1970 (first published 1843). Emphases in Marx's text.

11   Freud, Sigmund, *Civilization and Its Discontents*, London: Penguin, 2002 (first pub-

These thinkers certainly had visions of reality at odds with religion, but they weren't comprehensive in nature. That is, they weren't developing an alternative to monotheistic religion through spiritual monism or the monism[12] of dispirited reductive materialism.[13] Even Marx, who inaugurated the dialectical materialism pursued in Sisyphean fashion by communists of various stripes for two centuries, had little to say about materialism as such—as a comprehensive explanation for all of reality. His was a social perspective, in which we first subtract God, and then follow the social dialectic in its evolution to a liberating communism through intermediate historical stages.

This is not to say these thinkers' contributions to philosophy were not significant—they were—but their mentions of religion were by way of sweeping it from the world stage, not replacing it with a developed materialism. They left religion as an erasure from the full picture of humanity. A negation. That stance of negation continues to this day among postmodern thinkers. When religion is addressed at all, it is couched in terms of pathology which the postmodern outlook might cure. And, the stance of negation is applied more generally, apart from religion, to social norms and institutions of prosperous Western liberalism drained of transcendence, typically labeled "capitalism" pejoratively, or even "fascism."

Now it must be said there is nothing wrong with critique *per se.* Indeed, critique is the method by which we make division and delineation in ever finer shades so that meaning emerges from the difference in shades. Critique could as well be described as the process of discernment enabled by ontological dualism, as described (hopefully) pervasively in the present work. When we try to understand the nature of evil, for example, we do so by contrasting good, and move to a process of examining each in light of the other.

Negation is distinct from opposition. No meaningful contrast emerges from x and not-x. This is merely a statement and its negation. In the same way, a meaningful contrast of opposites does not occur between theism and atheism, because atheism is not a substantive explanation for reality like theism. It is not a thing unto itself. It is merely not-x; a negation of the theist proposition x.

Meaning emerges from the clash of oppositions, but is often ob-

---

lished 1930).

12 As with the spirituality adduced by Baruch Spinoza (1632-1677) or those who espouse variants of Hinduism or Buddhism.

13 As with scientistic "New Atheism" authors popular in recent years.

scured in mere negation. If a person rejects theism, he is an atheist, expressing an absence that hints at a present worldview by saying
whatever the worldview is, it excludes this arena of thought. Critiquing
theism without defending the opposing metaphysics of materialism is
the sound of one hand clapping. Upon rejecting theism, one must then
explain reality without it. We cannot remove the planks from the floor
but still stand on it. There is a difference between critique offered from
an opposing point of view, and critique offered from a position floating
in space, so to speak.

Postmodern critique applies to religion, as noted, but also more
generally to the rationalist impulse and objectivity and hierarchical
value formation and ontological dualism that arise out of the Genesis
world-view. The instinctual levelling flow of the river is not enough because it is merely "not-x," urged upon us by postmodernists as a de-
sirable devolution from bad old ways of hierarchical social structures
built on hyper-rationalism. Postmodern critique is not mere critique,
but substantive, in other words, though the substance is vague. It is development of substance by negation: ceaseless evolving "theory" which
attempts to exclude rationality, objectivity, and hierarchy.

To reiterate, there is nothing wrong with critique *per se*. "Critical
thinking" is a skill we should develop and inculcate in our children. Another word for "critical thinking" is thinking. It's what we all do all the
time, and the more incisive and discerning we are, the better. A certain
level of skepticism must be brought to any analysis, else it's not analysis
at all, but bovine acceptance.

On the other hand, we must distinguish critical thinking from presumptive rejection, because that is the opposite of critical thinking. The
posture of critique as adopted by postmodernists colors the subject matter of what is being critiqued rather than neutrally evaluating it. Insight
into how is expressed by Rita Felski, a specialist on the role of suspicion
in literary criticism.[14] Among other features of postmodern critique, it:

> . . .rails against authority; . . . conceives of itself as coming from be-
> low, or being situated at the margins; it is the natural ally of excluded
> groups and subjugated knowledges; it is not just a form of knowledge
> but a call to action.[15]

---

14 English.as.virginia.edu/felski.
15 Felski, Rita, "Critique and the Hermeneutics of Suspicion," *M/C Journal* 15(1), 2011.
(https://doi.org/10.5204/mcj.431.)

It possesses, moreover, a "'partisan though not uncritical identification' with oppositional social movements."[16] And, most tellingly:

> *Critique does not tolerate rivals.* Declaring itself uniquely equipped to diagnose the perils and pitfalls of representation, critique often chafes at the presence of other forms of thought. Ruling out the possibility of peaceful co-existence or even mutual indifference, it insists that those who do not embrace its tenets must be denying or disavowing them. In this manner, whatever is different from critique is turned into the photographic negative of critique—evidence of an irrefutable lack or culpable absence. To refuse to be critical is to be uncritical; a judgment whose overtones of naiveté, apathy, complacency, submissiveness, and sheer stupidity seem impossible to shrug off. In short, critique thinks of itself as exceptional. It is not one path, but the only conceivable path.[17]

Hence, the contempt held by the hard left for those not similarly entrenched in an attitude of negation. How does "critique," in the ordinary sense of the word, have "tenets" at all? Because critique in the ordinary sense of the word is not in play. Postmodern "hermeneutics of suspicion" are not merely hermeneutics, they are a substantive polemical opposition to the God proposition and to the logocentric Genesis worldview as a whole.

If you want to push back against a proposition, you must have your feet planted on another proposition. The friction is what enables the push-back and the comparison that enables truth to emerge. So there is a difference between testing a proposition by pushing back, and employing methods of "critique" to erect what amounts to an *a priori* barrier to fair evaluation in the first place. We should be careful not to hermetically seal off dangerous ideas, and call that critical thinking. Critical thinking means deep evaluation, not preemptive skepticism to prevent it.

This distinction comes into play in one subset of postmodernism, critical theory, sometimes called "applied postmodernism." Critical theory is not simply the mental process of healthy skepticism, but rather artificial constraints we place on certain ideas to cancel them or prevent their spread. It is a species of the hermeneutics of suspicion. It is not fair critique, but a polemical methodology. Critical theory means approaching a feature of our social reality not with healthy skepticism in order to deeply evaluate it, but rather to detect hidden agendas existing

---

16 Ibid., quoting Nancy Fraser, "What's Critical about Critical Theory? The Case of Habermas and Gender," *New German Critique* 35, 1985, p. 97.

17 Ibid.

to preserve power interests, in order to liberate us from them. The fix is in, in this kind of analysis. It's advocacy, not evaluation. It is Marxist at its core because it shifts our perspective from universal values to group interests.

To explain this, we need to be specific about what is meant by post-modern critical theory. Critical legal theory supposes laws are enacted to preserve power interests or to sway outcomes through rigid legal doctrines that have the effect of further marginalizing already marginalized groups. It critiques the notion that objective legal principles equally applied have an equal outcome. Instead, so the theory goes, objective legal principles actually preserve status quo power interests. It's not (necessarily) that a particular law is unequal in principle, but that it may marginalize in practice. Suppose the principle is freedom of association, universally applicable. Freedom of association also means freedom of dissociation, because these are two sides of the same coin. Freedom of association in the context of a social reality of racism may result in active discrimination by race. An unequal outcome from an equally-applied legal principle.[18]

Natural law consists in universal principles derived from absolute values. Positive law, by contrast, is not rooted in universals but in practical political aims. It is the idea that all law is and should be man-made, for man-invented ends. Critical legal theory begins with the presupposition that even universal legal principles, founded in natural law, may benefit the powerful to the detriment of the weak. In this example, the universal principle of freedom of association benefits the established powerful and so positive law may be generated to diminish natural law freedom (of association, in this instance) and equality (through affirmative action, in this instance). And so likewise with critical theory applied in other "social justice" contexts. These include theories of systemic racism, heteronormativity, patriarchy, and nationalism. Intersectionality unites these as various modes of putative oppression.

Critical race theory is, at the time of this writing, a hot-button topic, particularly when it comes up in efforts to indoctrinate children in public schools. Critical race theory is a means of looking at social attitudes

---

18 This was the dynamic in play in early jurisprudence compromising freedom of association in favor of non-discriminatory public accommodation, as in Heart of Atlanta Hotel v. United States, 379 U.S. 241 (1964). It is also the dynamic in play more recently in various court cases testing the proposition that a baker or florist (two actual examples) can decline to do business that affirms homosexual unions as normative, or to be celebrated.

about race through the hermeneutics of suspicion. That is, implicit racism is imputed to all white people, and "systemic racism" explains all racial disparities in social outcomes, disregarding more proximate causes like single parenthood, illiteracy, addiction, criminality, and so on. It is a good thing to root out vestiges of actual racism, but critical race theory seeks only to reverse the polarity of the presumed oppression rather than eliminate it. Instead of equalizing, it resegregates, divides, creates mutual suspicion, and replaces the equality principle with a power principle, such as by re-institutionalizing racial preferences.

Once upon a time, we operated on a principle of individualism, with a moral referent in God, or if not God, at least objective right and wrong, to which we all appealed in our public debates. On that basis, American society in general determined that it was about equality and therefore racial emancipation, and a historical legacy to the contrary had to be overcome. There was a point A (where we started on race) and a point B, where we ought to be. One could call this the MLK paradigm, because Martin Luther King, Jr. incited moral courage inside this framework, as with his "I have a dream" speech: "I have a dream that my four little children will one day live in a nation where they will not be judged by the color of their skin but by the content of their character." Perhaps King said it this way only because he was a product of his times. We won't know because he was assassinated in 1968. But clearly, this dream presupposes equality, not a power reversal for racial discrimination. It was a call to honor universal principles.

The MLK paradigm has given way to critical race theory. CRT is given legs, so to speak, by other postmodern techniques, especially formation of the social metanarrative to replace objective truth and objective right and wrong. It has happened in a short time, so that anyone of a certain age can easily trace the shift from the MLK to the CRT paradigms. With CRT the objective principle of equality is jettisoned in favor of a social metanarrative, and as a result, the MLK project is interrupted by devolution to racial self-identification, mutual suspicion, resegregation, misplaced collective guilt, revived racism, identity (rather than principle) politics, and self-defeating entitlement and victimhood neuroses.

This form of critical theory rests further on a theory of collective guilt and collective victimization. Just as all black people are thought to be victims by virtue of the putatively systemic nature of racism, so all white people are guilty of the victimization. The right way to think about the proposition of collective guilt was articulated by death camp survivor and psychiatrist Viktor Frankl: "collective guilt does not exist,"

he said, in reference to Germans and Austrians alive during the Holocaust.[19] And likewise, Auschwitz survivor and author Primo Levi. In a
postscript to his book *The Truce*, Levi wrote:

> My personal temperament is not inclined to hatred. I regard it as bes-
> tial, crude, and prefer on the contrary that my actions and thoughts,
> as far as possible, should be the product of reason . . . . Even less do I
> accept hatred as directed collectively at an ethnic group, for example,
> all the Germans; if I accepted it, I would feel that I was following the
> precepts of Nazism, which was founded precisely on national and ra-
> cial hatred.[20]

And what about the church? On critical race theory, it is confused.
The theory seems to hold out a promise of racial progress, and most
people are in favor of that. But the promise is a lie. What often goes
missing in Christian evaluation of critical race theory is how it simply
rejects Christianity. We must be careful not to strain out a gnat and
choke on a camel. That's what churches do when they reject the "critical
race theory" label but embrace its premises. In at least five fundamental
ways, critical race theory is anathema to Christianity.

One, the cherished principle of equality is a product of the Judeo-Christian worldview. It is for that reason incorporated into the
foundational principles for Western liberal democracies. The principle
of equality is so much a part of our cultural values that it would be easy
to forget it has not always been so. For millennia societies have assumed
a stratification in the worth of human beings. Judaism and then Christianity changed that. We should preserve the principle of equality by re-
membering that our story is emancipation from slavery, not the bondage
that necessitated it, nor the bondage of people groups all through history. Critical race theory upends the principle of equality. In the name of
righting past inequalities, we install new ones, by classifying people by
race, imputing oppressor or oppressed status to them, and labelling the
groups exploiter or victim. The classification of oppressed victim diminishes its members further, re-conceiving them in presumed dependency
on a putatively superior race to fix things for them. The classification of
privilege induces false guilt but presumed superiority over the victim

---

19 "Collective guilt does not exist," a speech by Viktor Frankl in 1988, is available on
YouTube, https://www.youtube.com/watch?v=leGKtWlwHt4.

20 *The Truce*, New York: Abacus, 2003, postscript note 1. *The Truce* is published in
one volume with *If This is a Man*, about Levi's experience of Auschwitz.

class. It's racist.

Two, the Jewish and Christian traditions rest on a paradigm primarily of love rather than power, starting with God's creation and care in Genesis, and culminating in the sacrifice of God for man rather than the reverse that obtained in paganism operating on a power principle. Critical race theory reverses the love principle back in favor of the power principle. The idea is that systemic racism rests on white power, and can only be reversed by a shift to black power. Both are horrible ideas. Power is allowed to push out love.

Three, Christianity necessarily depends on an individualist perspective. We have salvation or we don't individually. We acquire moral agency, in the Genesis story, individually and not collectively. Individual consciousness precedes the intersubjectivity which creates society. We are personally responsible to God, and God is personal to us. Critical race theory depends on a socialist perspective. It identifies people by racial group in the process of according distinct duties and privileges by group, thereby diminishing or eliminating the individual agency plainly identified in Genesis.

Four, critical race theory is obviously a severe blow to unity. Social unity is important, but here we're considering a Christian response specifically, so let's consider unity within the church. Christ came to divide, not to unite, but he meant division with respect to those who follow Him and those who don't. Among those who do, His church, there is to be unity in Him. The first move of critical race theory is to divide both society and the church within it: you poor oppressed victimized black people on this side, to await your social redemption by whites; you brutish privileged white people on the other side, to expiate your sins in hard-left activism. How is this not disunifying? Suddenly, both sides of this divide look on each other with mutual suspicion and renewed distrust rather than embracing their commonality of faith and their brotherhood in humanity.

Five, and perhaps most obviously, critical race theory requires us to throw over the absoluteness and eternality of God in favor of the fickle relativist temporality of social metanarrative. Instead of looking up to God for moral direction, we are to look to social narrative to figure out what's right and wrong. The social narrative is a compilation of ignored facts, half-truths, deliberate ambiguities, and misdirection to prop up an ideology in opposition to Christianity. It is the language misdirection of the serpent in the garden. God is dethroned and social "consensus" is deified in His place.

CHAPTER FIFTEEN

Structuralism

A MANIFESTATION OF the hermeneutics of suspicion is "Structuralism," a school of thought that identifies social structures existing to uphold power interests systemically behind the scenes. Structuralism recognizes binary differentiation and employs it as a linguistic method to destabilize objective meaning to language or to explain social differences anthropologically or to "deconstruct" logocentrism.

We should distinguish the binary structure of reality that is among the theses of the present work, from the analysis of binary opposition in the "Structuralism" of thinkers like Marx, Ferdinand de Saussure, Claude Lévi-Strauss, Roland Barthes and many others. Jacques Derrida and other "post-structuralists" belong on that list as well, because their methods of "Deconstruction" presuppose the construction theorized by the Structuralists.

Structuralism errs in several ways. First, it imputes to certain binary oppositions meaning that is not necessitated just by virtue of the opposition itself. Second, it correctly concludes that binary oppositions generate meaning, but ignores the God who creates with them for that purpose. Third, it wrongly imputes nefarious motives hidden in social structures by the powerful. Fourth, it removes the primacy of individual autonomy, re-setting our platform for understanding to the collective.

The essence of Structuralism is the idea that our social environment is not what it seems. There are invisible structures in place which define us. Human behavior we observe in the world around us is primarily explainable upon interrogating social structures in which individuals operate. The structures are the accumulation of unconscious motivations and underlying causes that are more fundamental than individual conscious decisions in explaining human behavior.

Thus, Marxism is a kind of structuralism, because it supposes a social structure evolved to protect the interests of capitalists, those who own the means of production. Workers are among the means of production, in Marxist imagination, scarcely less so than a machine or a factory. Though the workers seem to make conscious decisions, for example, about their own continued employment, their decisions are tightly circumscribed by the structure of the society they live in. They are not truly free agents, therefore. "Life is determined not by consciousness, but consciousness by life," Marx wrote, in *The German Ideology* (published 1932, written c. 1846).

The complexity of modern life, in its institutions, law, philosophies, religion, morality, and so on, are to Marxists determined by conditions of life. They constitute structures which define and reinforce classes in society. The ruling classes are affected by the structures of society just as are the working classes, but the structures protect their interests at the expense of workers'. The classes themselves are formed by the structure, and their respective members perpetuate the resulting ruler/ruled dichotomy unconsciously. The thoughts and decision-making of all classes are determined by social situation, whether individuals realize it or not. Marx thought the differing situations among the classes would eventually prompt the lower classes to revolt, to assert their interests in contrast to those of ruling classes. In this way the structures of society, he thought, would be disrupted in a more just direction.

Clearly, there is a structure to society, and one can certainly say that structure is manifested in social institutions, traditions, culture, law, religion, and commerce. That structure is a natural result of the operation of innumerable value oppositions that form value hierarchies which those institutions reflect. What's wrong with the Marxist way of thinking, however, is the removal of human agency, consistent with Marxists' militant materialist atheism.[1] A central tenet of Marxism is social and historical determinism. Human behaviors are deemed the product solely of material conditions created and perpetuated by social structures, rather than being the product of individual exercises of agency.

So, a worker on the factory floor is made resentful by the Marxist technique of seeing through to the structural protection of monied capitalist interests. A resentful member of a racial minority may believe he perceives systemic (that is, structural) racism. A feminist attacks the

---

1 See, Gary Saul Morson, "Among the Disbelievers," *Commentary Magazine*, Oct. 15, 2018 (www.commentarymagazine.com).

structure of patriarchy. A resentful sexual minority opposes heteronormativity. These groups have disparate and sometimes conflicting goals, but share the common goal of de-structuring society to something imagined vaguely to be more congenial to their outlook.

Postmodernism is essentially Marxist, and Marxism means looking out on the world and seeing its faults instead of its glories. It's perceived to be a world full of cramped little minds deterministically drawing excluding boundaries around personal and group interests. Postmodernists would remedy this by improving the hearts of people, and the heart of mankind, just as the Soviet goal was the New Man of Leninist communism. The postmodern way is to throw down the boundaries and hierarchies and judgments and intolerances that impede the makeover of people and society. Thus, its adherents agitate to bring about collectivist change, and it is always a collectivist undertaking because it is thought to be social structures that must be undone, with individual moral decisions following, deterministically.

Because of this outlook, the Genesis worldview is largely invisible or incomprehensible to postmodernists, except as a form of inexplicable superstition. It does not manifest as collectivist political activism, and therefore, is perceived as only resistance borne of generalized fear-driven conservatism. Those on the left, therefore, tend to be dismissive of politically conservative thought rather than engaging it on its merits. Political conservatism (or classical liberalism) centers on individual rather than political change; with bottom-up rather than top-down improvement following, in the exercise of personal agency. Because Western liberal societies are founded on individual freedom, current (classically) liberal thought seems overly accepting of things as they are.

This is a key difference between the worldview of Marxist group identity movements, on the one hand, and the Jewish and Christian worldview, on the other. The paradigm-setting stories of Genesis establish a structure that passively results from individual moral decision-making. It is a bottom-up perspective, considered sociologically. Individuals are to exercise their moral agency in a positive direction toward their Creator. The accumulated effect of this individual moral decision-making tends toward a more just and equitable society. Imagine a flower seed (the individual), which is nurtured by the gardener (the family), but it grows upward in conditions conducive to thriving (society which acknowledges God). The flower is not pulled up from the top.

By contrast, the Marxist perspective is top-down, sociologically. The growth of the flower comes not from the germ of seed within, but solely from external conditions which can be changed to affect the flower, along with all other flowers. We're to imagine group power negotiation in society, which incidentally redounds to the benefit of the individual. Rather than erasing subtly hegemonic ruling classes, however, new ruling classes wearing a "for-the-people" mask invariably arise, and are invariably more brutal.

These worldviews are in utter opposition. Genesis is not a blueprint for creating a just society. It is an explanation of how things truly are. Social theories fail when they re-imagine reality in ways contrary to the reality Genesis discloses to us. Some that are totalizing in scope, like Marxism and fascism, fail dramatically and consistently and at great cost. The bridle-high bloodshed of the twentieth-century wars is definitive proof of these facts.

The Marxist way of thinking diminishes personal autonomy because it re-locates one's perspective from self to the collective. This perspective is alarmingly common now. Many people reflexively approach every question asking what "we" should do about it, instead of minding their own business. On top of that, the collectivism generally takes the form of government action, with its coercive power and ever-present tendency to tyranny, and that combined with other ideologically aligned and partnered power centers of Wall Street, big tech, big media, which we will refer to collectively as "the Machine." The correct word for this social structure is "fascism." Fascism is the all-embracing exercise of government power aligned ideologically with powerful commercial interests. The word "fascism" is associated with right-wing totalitarianism, and, of course, Marxism is considered leftist. But at the extremes, there is no practical difference between right-wing and left-wing tyranny. Today, burgeoning fascism is dominant in the United States, but it comes from the Marxist ideological left.

Postmodern political activism is relentlessly collectivist in a larger sense. In the individual consciousness, Marxism teaches that we perceive ourselves first as members of the collective because social structures create material conditions which define us. This is the reason Marxists can brook no dissent, and why tyranny and oppression inevitably follow upon Marxist innovation. Abandonment of God is the root cause of the discord and horrors that follow upon Marxist thinking, but this shift in consciousness from an individual to a collective perspective at least partly explains how. Aleksandr Solzhenitsyn was quite literally correct when he said of the Soviet experience:

If I were asked today to formulate as concisely as possible the main cause of the ruinous Revolution that swallowed up some sixty million of our people, I could not put it more accurately than to repeat: Men have forgotten God; that's why all this has happened.[2]

Religion unquestionably creates and maintains social structures. And those structures are based on deriving meaning from oppositions. Indeed, one Structuralist, Edmund Leach, asserts that "mediation between opposites is precisely what religious thinking is all about."[3] The present work is not a brief against structuralism in the abstract, or structuralism rightly understood, but only against the collectivist Structuralism (or Post-structuralism) of postmodernist philosophers like Jacques Derrida. Key foundations of a religion-informed social structure are established in Genesis, and that is the subject of our inquiry. But that structure fundamentally includes the principle of personal, not collective, moral responsibility.

Ferdinand de Saussure (1857-1913) was a philosopher who looked for structure in linguistic systems, and he started specifically with the notion of binary opposition as creating meaning. This either/or way of looking at things was picked up by anthropologist Claude Lévi-Strauss (1908-2009) and other thinkers looking at cultures comparatively, like Roland Barthes (1915-1980). Their starting point was to recognize binary oppositions in reality, but this was not new to the twentieth century, nor to Structuralism as a philosophical enterprise. Its roots are ancient, considered in the philosophies of Heraclitus, Parmenides, Aristotle, and the I Ching of the fourth century BC, and later in the thought of Gottfried Wilhelm Leibniz (1646-1716) and mythologist Joseph Campbell (1904-1987).[4]

In very simple situations, one can follow how meaning emerges from a particular this-not-that opposition, but very quickly, overlapping oppositions create infinite shades of gray, so that it would be nearly impossible to reduce even a simple proposition like "it is raining" to all its constituent oppositional pairings which generate the meaning. Instead, we start with the notion that binary oppositions populate our thinking life and infer that they are fundamental to reality—and to our thinking—all the way down, so to speak. There's nothing wrong with that, as

---

2 Templeton Address, London 1983.

3 Leach, Edmund, and D. Alan Aycock, *Structuralist Interpretations of Biblical Myth*, NY: Cambridge University Press, 1983, p. 16.

4 See *Dangerous God*, chapter 1.

far as it goes, but this way of thinking can be corrupted, and that's what happened among the Structuralists. Somewhere along the way, their analyses take on meaning not generated by the oppositions themselves.

The ultimate point for language deconstructionists is that the written or spoken word is not reliable unto itself; it is structurally a form of polemic to veil power interests and transmute them into a deceitful but persuasive logos structure. This is a deeply suspicious approach to how society is organized, imputing nefarious purpose to language rather than taking it at face value. It manifests a backward definition of "critical thinking," imputing substantively negative meaning to the logos, the word, and to other semiotic "language."

The Deconstruction technique only works on those who breathe logocentric reality. As Marxist critique expands, the world of logocentric thinkers contracts, so there are fewer rubes left to take the bait. We all become suspicious of words (and other communicative expression), and so there is no one left to listen besides the true wretched of the earth Marxism supposedly protects: people on the margins who are puzzled and befuddled; people who struggle with straightforward communication, let alone the meaning behind the meaning postmodernists believe they detect. Language loses its effectiveness, whether it's thought to camouflage power interests or is taken as straightforward expression. As communicative power of words decreases, their volume—in number and loudness—increases in a crescendo of nonsense and frustration into a widening gyre, whipped about through society with passionate intensity. It becomes a content-less force, real power emerging from where power was falsely thought hidden. Sound and fury signifying nothing but chaos and disorder and destruction, ceasing only when entropically spent. We inherit the whirlwind as understanding fails and the Tower of Babel collapses once again.

Structuralist binary opposition was central to the thinking of the post-structuralists, most notably Jacques Derrida, who believed they hid oppressions which could be extinguished by collapsing or reversing the oppositions. So, for example, Derrida would suppose that the opposition of male and female involves a privileging of the male half of the binary. But where does that privileging come from? Why would a consideration of the male/female binary cause us to think of the male as superior? It doesn't really. This isn't to say no one privileges male over female. Obviously, that happens. But it is to say that the privilege, when it exists, does not arise merely from the opposition. It's imported, so to speak, from among a person's particular prejudices or bad ideas.

Not from the mere fact of the binary opposition. Another example: racial bigotry is sometimes attributed to "binary thinking." The thinking might be that racial black and white are polar opposites (as the words "black" and "white" seem to imply), and to this opposition one can attach another, inferior and superior, respectively. But why associate these polarities? Reason should tell us there is no basis upon which to infer racial superiority or inferiority from racial difference.

This thinking error is important because it introduces a taint to binary thinking (all thinking) that needn't be there. The introduction of presumptive privileging and depriviliging to social binary oppositions serves polemical purposes only, which is to say it is a species of fraud. Far from removing oppression (for example, by men over women, or heterosexual over homosexual, or white over black), it institutionalizes ongoing group division and never-ending scrimmage for power. Women, for example, are the oppressed vis-à-vis men, by this way of thinking, and a standing lobby against anything considered contrary to female group interests is established. Remember, it is the structure against the oppressed half of the binary that must be attacked, and attacked on an all-in collective consensus basis, even if that "consensus" is coerced rather than genuine unanimous assent.

In the case of privileged-male/oppressed-female deconstruction, this means a sustained critique of "the patriarchy," a term which is then recalibrated for ever more radical ends as gains are made. Initially, it means something not reasonably arguable, like paying women less for the same job. Then the structure called "patriarchy" shifts in meaning, with a medium-range goal being sameness in roles for women and men in all arenas of life including the most private, like marriage. One can point to some positive gain, as with overcoming unjustified exclusion of women, but also the negative consequences of loneliness, opposite-sex wariness, a diminished venue for child-rearing, and general war between the sexes, ideologically separating male from female, which are, after all, created by God for each other. This climate may improve the lives of ambitious careerists but results in unmeasurable loneliness and disappointment and unhappiness for many others.

As with patriarchy, so with heteronormativity. First, the idea of individuals within society who are same-sex attracted is discarded in favor of homosexuals as a social group with a political platform. The social group is combined with other sexual minorities, referred to as LGBTQ or some variant. That group is conceived to be in the role of oppressed, so the structure of society resulting in that oppression is identified: het-

eronormativity. Then, the social struggle ensues, oppressed versus oppressor, in an institutionalized, collectivized, ongoing battle against the
putatively oppressive structure. At first, that means something unobjectionable, like stigmatizing gay-bashing in its verbal and literal forms.
But antagonism to heteronormativity will also mean rejection of the
mom-pop-kids family model with sex-specific roles. There's a partial
alliance with feminism, in this way. There is a target on the back of the
family unit, and that is certainly contrary to the structure of Genesis. As
with the institutionalized group division on male/female lines, there can
be no dissent from LGBTQ orthodoxy. Remember, repression of dissent
is a signal feature of Marxist methodology.

As with patriarchy and heteronormativity, so with systemic racism.
The putatively oppressed group is readily visible based on skin color,
and is comprised of descendants of truly oppressed people. It's reasonable to suppose there are lasting ill effects of Jim Crow because some of
the oppressions have had intergenerational impact. But that's a long way
from saying racism is systemic. "Racism" means animus based on race.
That's not what we're observing in lingering effects of past actual racism.
Statistical disparities in measures of flourishing as between blacks and
whites cannot be reflexively attributed to past racism. There is a causal
link to wrong-headed socialist public policy, but it is ignored because
socialism must be counted as the cure, not the disease. Ill-conceived
government social engineering contributes to general civilizational decline, which naturally affects more vulnerable people more severely. But
as with feminism and gay activism, on this front, too, no dissent is allowed from the Marxist orthodoxy.

As with patriarchy, heteronormativity, and systemic racism, so with
"nationalism" or "populism," or "colonialism," or "xenophobia," somewhat vague descriptors for a desire to overcome other-ness wherever
it is found. "Nationalism" is really an all-purpose word that relates to
boundaries in general—anything that divides people groups and runs
counter to the anti-colonialist narrative or the multicultural outlook. It
is marked by patriotism deemed excessive, or any view of immigration
policy more restrictive than whatever state it currently has. These various evil structures form a kind of intersectionality in the postmodern
mind. Nationalism amounts to an overlay on the other kinds of groups
that consider themselves aggrieved by the various oppressive structures
to society.

The structures thought to preserve power interests are opposed by
grievance groups that overlap and intersect, hence "intersectionality" on

the putative victim side. These groups are constituted of those deemed to have standing to oppose a particular power structure: women, with respect to patriarchy; sexual minorities, with respect to heteronormativity; racial minorities, with respect to systemic racism; leftists generally, with respect to nationalism. Conceptual intersectionality exists to leverage the various groups with standing. Groups with standing to oppose one type of purported oppression stand in solidarity with groups opposing another, because Marxist critique binds them. This is why to some it makes sense to cry "racism" even about a controversy that has nothing to do with race.

In this way of thinking, a word deployed to combine all the evil structures of patriarchy, etc., is "capitalism," or sometimes "late capitalism" to suggest it's on its way out. Capitalism is much more than economic freedom, in this usage. It is a stand-in for all the various oppressor interests believed protected by liberal Western society as it is. Those interests comprise a kind of countervailing intersectionality: men, with respect to patriarchy; heterosexuals, with respect to heteronormativity; white people, with respect to systemic racism; and comfortably bigoted privileged Westerners, with respect to nationalism. This dark-mirror structural intersectionality is thought to exist to preserve elites' standing, and a bourgeois class fearful of change. And so, the intersectionality of the oppressed is justified to oppose it. Critical theory is the chief technique of argumentation employed by these grievance groups. "Capitalism," in this hydra-headed definition, is the collective term for what is being critiqued. Critical theory is the postmodern mechanism by which putative oppressors, their victims, and intersections of grievance groups are identified and arrayed against patriarchy, heteronormativity, systemic racism, and nationalism.

Those with a Genesis worldview are rightly opposed to oppression, of course, regardless of the identity of the people oppressed. That makes them vulnerable to Marxist theory if they don't recognize it as a mechanism for shifting allegiance from universal principle to social group power. For an example involving systemic racism, critical theory works on sensitivity to actual racism; that is, it gets traction precisely because most people are opposed to racism, and are therefore susceptible to the suggestion of systemic racism. Once sold on systemic racism, the thinking might be that perhaps it's not so bad to shift some power to black people, for a change. Lost in this thinking is that power should not be the driving force in the first place. According to Genesis, and the Bible as a whole, the medium for social interaction should be love, not power.

Christians may innocently embrace critical race theory without understanding it is a postmodern technique for dismantling the God-sovereign worldview upon which Christianity is based, installing unceasing ideological warfare in its place. Critical race theory is one of several interlocking critical theories which are together a universal acid to decompose the Christian worldview in its entirety.

To close out this section distinguishing "Structuralism" from the small-s structure revealed in Genesis, let's revisit the more common errors of Structuralism. Four were suggested. First, we are asked to imagine a privileging taking place just by virtue of the oppositional nature of things. That may seem like a subtle point, but it's important because doing so weaponizes the fallacies of Structuralism. It enables Derrida and disciples like Hélène Cixous to imagine a hidden structure to society favoring men at the expense of women, for example, which then must be collectively deconstructed, regardless what individual women may have to say about it. Derrida can say men keep women down because of the "present" phallus privileged as against the supposedly "absent" genitalia of women. This is nonsense on stilts, but suffices to support the theory of male privilege arising just from the fact of male/female binary.

A second flaw in Stucturalist thinking is atheist presumption. Genesis tells us that God created all that we know, and we can see that creation flows outward from God in binaries. If we truncate the God origin, in our imaginations, where does that leave us? It leaves us still with binaries, but no direction. Binary oppositions are thought to create meaning all by themselves, like words hanging in the air with no Speaker. Mankind has no agency, therefore, and we're stuck in pointless determinism, waiting for the clock to wind down, so we can return to oblivion. Even if we don't get this connection and still imagine people to be decision-making creatures, without God, the only direction for that decision-making is socialist utopia. We're all irrational stimulus-responders, objects of socialist theory-making manipulation. And that in the direction of malleable values which have no reason to be valued, because the objective nature of the values is removed. There is no reason to say society should be more just, for example, but we do anyway. The reason, of course, is that God is real. But because He is disavowed, our moral sense can be distorted by power-seeking exploiters of social theory. Justice means what our betters tell us it means.

A third flaw is the imputation of nefarious motives in social structures. To use a simplistic pre-French Revolution example, church and aristocracy tacitly conspire to preserve their ruling privileges by intellectually reinforcing lower class deference to dogma and social hierarchy. That may sound intentional and nefarious, but what if it's not? Suppose the religious dogma happens to be true? And social hierarchy a natural development in any society? The point is not that France should turn the clock back 250 years. The point is that the social structures embodied in aristocracy and religion back then need not have been artificially created to protect power groups. Social structures are never simply deconstructed. They are only replaced with other structures. Individualism is replaced with collectivism. Capitalism with coercive political power. Religion with atheist political activism. Liberalism with illiberalism.

Fourth, the premise of both Structuralism and its post-Structuralist critiques is that the relevant structure is that of society, not the individual self. Solzhenitsyn famously observed that the line between good and evil runs through every heart. That means we individually fight evil within ourselves; it is not a battle between people-groups. That's what Genesis teaches. That's what Jesus came to repair. Postmodernists do not advocate such soul-searching as the way to root out evil. Instead, they interrogate social structures, to remove evil from the top down by social engineering. You can thereby imagine you've put off your personal moral responsibility, but you also put off your personal autonomy. It will be confined to empty titillation and gluttony. This shift is internal; consciousness removed from the platform of self to the collective. The collective is imagined as the hyperreal social metanarrative replacing religious metanarrative. One gives up personal guilt, but also personal triumph, trading the highs and lows for a narcotic middle ground, lurching zombie-like with the social in-group, fueled by the comforting certainty of smug moral self-righteousness just by virtue of belonging.

CHAPTER SIXTEEN

Frankfurt School

"**G**od is dead," wrote Friedrich Nietzsche in the late nine-teenth century. He referred not only to the monotheists' God, but also to any metaphysical gesture toward a reality beyond space and time. So no Platonic forms or mathematical realism or informational realism and no virtues or ideals or categories as being real in any meaningful way. All of those concepts, not just spiritual truth, go out the window.

Together they constituted transcendence, the sense of something beyond immediate space-time experience. Transcendence and the logo-centrism it creates are the real target of postmodernism, and postmodern philosophy proceeds on the question of how to make sense of reality without it. This is why postmodernism is a move to the river. All the process philosophy discussed here, phrased as "liquid modernity" or "flow" or "rhizomes" or "transcendence made horizontal" or "pragmatism," are really about how to manufacture a suitable substitute for transcendence without re-climbing the mountain to get it.

The ultimate expression of transcendence is God, and the nature/spirit dualism by which we begin to perceive Him. Once God is out of the picture, what replaces Him? This, too, was a question Nietzsche raised, and philosophy in the nineteenth and early twentieth century tried to answer it. We continue to search for universal meaning, but mainstream secular thinkers no longer accept what came to be considered mere inventions of religion. Religious propositions in postmodern thinking, for the most part, were ignored *a priori*, as if they'd never existed, except as a back-room pot of ideas to dip into once in a while, only to provide contrast for new ways of thinking.

Nietzsche seemed to understand that eliminating religion would not eliminate violence, because people would square off about other metanarratives instead. Indeed, in *Will to Power*, he foresaw the bloody brutality that would come in the twentieth century. The death of God meant the death of ready-made answers of grand metanarratives. The thought was that people are scared and lazy, they're part of the herd, and they're going to seek for something else to find meaning, if it isn't found in religion.

So: out with religion, in with ideology. "Ideology," in this context, doesn't mean simply a set of coherent principles applicable in sociology or politics. It carries a pejorative. Ideologies are top-down theories to which culture is fitted rather than the other way around: culture developed organically and without coercion from the bottom up. Marxism and fascism are ideologies. The story of the twentieth century is one of ideologies trying to fill the void left by the death of religion.

Marx questioned why oppressive and exploitative economic and class systems could not be undone, and set about theorizing how they might be. This is an instinct of deconstruction, and ideologies on the left have continued this deconstruction enterprise. They are Marxist, or neo-Marxist, for at least that reason. Deconstruction was thought a good thing, on the grounds that what's being deconstructed is an evil system. But is it a system constructed to preserve the interests of exploiters and oppressors or merely a natural result of unalterable human nature? If conflict and division is endemic to mankind, then it won't be fixed by top-down ideology, whether we regard it to be of the right or left. If the structure of Western civilization is a corruption by the powerful, however, deconstruction of it seems a necessary first step. Hence, the Marxist deconstruction project at the heart of all left-wing philosophy, including, but certainly not limited to, that of the Frankfurt School.

The philosophers grouped as the "Frankfurt School" retained Marxism in this sense despite the evident failures of hard-left ideology readily apparent by the mid-twentieth century. Marxist thought had by then evolved from Marx's classical capitalist/proletariat theory to what is now referred to as cultural Marxism and neo-Marxism, but Marxist methodologies of critique of capitalism are retained. "Capitalism," likewise, had shifted in meaning, however, to include the dominant cultural system of the liberal West which, it was thought, perpetuated systems of oppression that could and should be deconstructed, to start over with something better: societies in which people were freed from the alienation wrought by crass commercialism and from commodifying transactions which demeaned people and isolated them and robbed them of a sense of community. To get there, it was necessary to first subvert existing Western values.

To achieve its aims, Frankfurt School philosophers critiqued much that was taken for granted in mainstream culture. The centrality of the family was questioned, because traditional values upholding class structures were inculcated in the family. Sexual revolution was a part of that project, but it was also intended to reverse the repression of eros believed to be contained in cultural norms of chastity and monogamy. Obviously, this project was counter to the structure of the healthy civilization we would expect if the truths contained in Genesis formed the foundation of society, as it long had before the twentieth century. Genesis tells us how things are, remember, not how they should be, but Genesis was irrelevant to thinkers of the twentieth century outside religious enclaves. Truth and goodness and even beauty, and all the subordinate transcendentals to those, are formed socially and philosophically, according to the postmodernists, and the Genesis model of reality is easily set to one side in a world in which God is dead, and so the project was to excise remaining tendrils of belief in objectivity where they conflict with the vision of a rejuvenated mankind built on the ashes of religion.

The objectivity of religion as evinced in Genesis would also be an obstacle to the Frankfurt School critique of reason. There are limits to reason, so we're to put our energies into practical matters at hand, not in ethereal theory. The emphasis was to be on lived experience, rather than reflection, as suggested by Albert Camus' *Myth of Sisyphus*. The idea is that it's even perhaps arrogant to attempt to impose reason on the universe. It's time, such thinkers believed, to accept the absurdity of the universe; to emphasize process over substance and becoming over being.

Importantly for thinkers in the Frankfurt school, we're to avoid group identity. That was the problem with the Nazis, after all, building an affirming narrative of in-group struggle against out-group villains, like the Jews, scapegoated for being "other" to vigorous and virtuous Aryans. Group identity arises in ideologies, and so must be combatted; hence, the emphasis on individualism. Note: this is a significant difference from Genesis-based Christian and Jewish religion, also—not because Jews and Christians embrace hostility through ethnic and other barriers, but because Jewish and Christian believers ideally wouldn't run away from the inevitability of group identification. They seek to overcome the division by appeal to over-arching moral principle, as we read in the story of the Good Samaritan, which allows for transcending group difference in favor of universal principle, rather than trying to artificially collapse or eradicate the group difference.

As we've seen in the last half-century, however, the post-war idea of avoiding group identity has been stood on its head. Frankfurt School ideals of re-directing eros into a levelled river of process philosophy clashed with other strands of Marxism which emphasized social-group conflict. Marxist theory resting on group identity triumphed; hence, identity politics. But the Frankfurt School was certainly not vanquished, unfortunately. It succeeded, if one can call its effects a success, in significant deterioration of the family and in self-worship.

Ideologies promote an us-versus-them mentality. In the interwar and immediately post-war period, existentialism had traction in part because it was an attempt at an anti-ideology stance. Thus, existentialists would resist right-wing tyranny at mid-century, but not on the basis of religion. Religion, too, was an ideological metanarrative, and besides, God was dead. Existentialists generally wanted group identity broken because it was thought to support unhealthy ideologies on the right. But of course, in the latter part of the twentieth and the early twenty-first centuries, group identity has again reasserted itself, this time in ideologies of the left. Group identity politics was not eradicated, according to existentialist vision, because the emerging ideology was socialist rather than individualist (as were both fascism and communism). In the "we" perspective, group identity is unavoidable.

Ideological strife follows socialism like illness follows infection. The "we" perspective erodes individual agency and purpose and meaning in life, so it must be replaced with a revivifying transfusion of group identification. And that, in turn, requires the tension of opposition to the group. Opposition can be created, if it doesn't already exist, to give meaning and purpose to one's life once we've unimagined God. Where would Antifa be without putative fascists? Where would white supremacists be without black nationalists? The point is not really to break down the opposition. Quite the opposite. It has to be sustained, even if only in exaggerated form in the imagination, because it supports one's own need for moral earnestness and purpose. Otherwise, we abandon the meaning-making of rational reflection, and are left with pointless process only, like animals.

The opposition for postmodern ideologies is often generalized to "capitalism." The ideologues don't mean free trade economics in which capital concentration naturally occurs because some people pursue wealth more avidly or more capably. They mean a way of thinking that is a holdover from economic Marxism; that is, it's not just economics, it's a system of structural interest protection that goes beyond economics. Capitalism is equated with "fascism," thought to be the natural end-point of unrestrained capitalism. The ideologues don't mean by "fascism," the Mussolini brand, but rather an ill-defined psychological inclination to authoritarianism, which (they think) has its home in capitalism and explains stubborn resistance to the postmodern ideological program.

The word "Fordism" is used among writers in the post-Gramsci[1] Marxist tradition, often as an epithet to describe the artificiality of capitalist machine production that makes machines of people, too.[2] You're to imagine assembly-line workers who attach a particular part to cars going by, over and over again, and that's it; that's their job, and they're reduced to production units dissociated from real life and work satisfaction. The critique is that we commodify everything including workers; everything is transactional and therefore adversarial, and workers (all of us) are dehumanized into what counts as contentment with meaningless Fordist jobs because we distract ourselves with sports, entertainment, titillation by sex or violence, porn, emotional nationalism, drugs, outlaw Bohemian fashion and chic, and other nonsense forms of self-effacement. This leaves us, as long as we have prosperity, soulless machines living in a simulacrum of reality. Our biggest concern is safety and security; we run scared of any perturbation in our surfeit of sugar-coated fatty God-hating blandness.

So far, this is all reasonable criticism, which is among the reasons to listen and understand what gives rise to cultural Marxism in the first place. "Cultural," it must be emphasized, to distinguish economic or classical Marxism. On the subject of economics, Marxists are like little children playing with matches in a barn full of hay. Culturally, it's true that Western culture includes vast territories of vapidity. But it's not the result of Fordism keeping the workers down in poverty. It's because we all fall into that kind of vacuousness if we don't actively resist it. We tend not to actively resist it because (a) we've forgotten God; and (b) in prosperity without self-discipline, many will relax into self-justifying indolence, often accompanied by a swagger of imagined countercultural coolness.

Critique of neo-Marxist critique should address first its anti-God

---

1   Antonio Gramsci, discussed infra Chapter 27, urged Marxist principles applied to cultural development rather than economic conditions as in classical Marxism.

2   Gramsci used the word this way in his "Americanism and Fordism" essay published in *Prison Notebooks*, 1934.

materialism, but even in the materialist realm, neo-Marxist postmodernists get it wrong, for example, by ascribing Fordism to "capitalism." "Capitalism" is in quotation marks here because there's no such thing. Capitalism just means prosperity resulting in wealth that is then applied to further wealth production, exactly what you do when you buy stock or put money in an interest-bearing account. There's no system as such called "capitalism" in a free economy, because it's just the result of innumerable uncoordinated decentralized economic decisions, freely made rather than extractive like the takings of government. Marx popularized the word "capitalist" by using it to describe a theoretical stage of materialist economic history. It's not a top-down economic system like socialism or communism. It's just what happens when there is no management. Freedom, in other words.

In the prosperous West, we don't live under capitalism now, unfortunately, precisely because we do live in an economic system significantly managed, what we could describe as liberal or democratic socialism, and have done so for a couple of generations now, basically commencing after WWII. This has been a horrible development, a betrayal in America of its founding principles which is now destroying the country. In 1961, Dwight Eisenhower warned Americans about the danger of the developing "military-industrial complex." He was right. He was describing government/private relations that would burgeon into the Machine, the ideologically aligned government and big business culture-shaping engine of anti-religious tyranny that is now engulfing us.[3]

"Capitalism" is now a catch-all word, when not amplified in volume by using "fascism" instead. But then it's not clear that those who sneer at capitalism actually know what it is; still less fascism, other than stuff-we-don't-like. But to be fair, there's plenty to not like. Not just soul-deadening automated jobs but also the vapid cultural landscape and isolation and loss of community. The neo- and cultural Marxists are certainly right to cringe at that, but none of it is the result of capitalism properly defined to mean people making their own decisions in life without being hectored and harassed and plundered by coordinated power centers of big tech, big media, government, and Wall Street, the Machine that coerces a one-think ideological collective.

---

3   We devote Chapter 23 to the social conformity function of the Machine. The ideology of postmodernism carries within itself the means of its propagation, but in addition, the Machine advances anti-religious ideological hegemony on a very practical level. The Machine consists, as we've noted, in corporate power centers including but not limited to governments of democratic socialist regimes.

The Bible teaches us we have independent and individual moral agency. In this way, Christianity holds to selective salvation; meaning that you personally "choose this day" whom you will serve. We individually own our salvation or perdition, because that's how important we are and so that's the reach of our freedom.

The order of the day, by contrast, is group agency, which really means no agency at all. We're reduced to robotic implementers of automation dictated to us from on high. You know you're seeing this concentrated collectivism when people are divided into groups. This is what makes it neo-Marxism specifically: tribalism rather than fealty to universal principle. Individuals don't have agency, in the regnant ideology; instead, groups purportedly do: not capitalists vs. proletariat, these days, but race vs. race; alphabet people vs. cisgender normies; women vs. men; nationalist populists vs. multicultis; us against them.

But this isn't the real agency that God put into us personally. It's only analogous, in that coerced consensus makes it seem like the group "thinks," but groups cannot exercise agency. Individuals can, but that also means they can cede it to their tribal group identity and agitate for dominance of the group. In the power struggle, abstract partisan ideas are in play, not universal principles. And only the anti-God materialist metaphysical point of view is allowed, unless it's the innocuous and vague variety of religion which expresses we-are-the-world therapeutic "spirituality," resolutely agnostic concerning the spiritual/material duality of human nature. Fear of the Lord is for hicks, in the new dispensation.

There is an interesting quasi-religious component to the hard-left manifestations of postmodern philosophy. "Fascism" is the original sin for postmodernists. One member of the Frankfurt School of thought, Theodor Adorno, even invented an "F-scale" to attempt to measure the degree to which someone has a tendency to fascism psychologically and subjectively. The word "fascism" is no longer used to mean old-school Mussolini-style totalitarianism, the self subsumed into the state to build a super-state vis-à-vis other states. It's a stand-in for everything postmodernists don't like about bourgeois culture. It more or less equates to "capitalism." And both "fascism" and "capitalism" more or less equate to evil.

The profound irony is that postmodern philosophy takes us right to the heart of fascism—the real kind. The essence of fascism is absorption of self into the powerful Machine of the state inextricably allied with big tech, big media, and big business. The new fascism is just like the old, but without the hyper-nationalism and pagan symbolism. The eerie resemblance of hard-left tactics to those of right-wing totalitarians—political correctness, cancel culture, the bracketing of public discourse,[4] the Overton window,[5] suppression of speech—all seem lost on those who declare themselves anti-fascist. These thought-control devices result in a sort of gnosis accessible only if one is plugged into the collective, a system of signs and symbols untethered to objective truth, arcana that can be learned as a code. Part of its attraction is its secret knowledge aspect. One belongs by being able to decode. Everything is a dog-whistle. Understanding the language code even as it shifts is what makes one enlightened and accepted. Postmodern process thinkers are the Druids of our time.

To those who subscribe to objectivity of truth, left-wing communism and right-wing fascism are more alike than different. The original sin of fascism is thought to be "other-ing" people groups and that sin ironically justifies other-ing those who commit it. Interestingly, the original sin of fascism is perceived as cutting through each individual heart,[6] much like sin does in Genesis religions. It's there to be eradicated, in the self as much as in the surrounding society, by any means at hand. Fascism is now vaguely understood to mean also the building or sustaining of barriers between people, because any such barrier interferes with the communitarian project, and perpetuates capitalist alienation. Hence, the antipathy to border walls, immigration enforcement, and even property rights.

Binary oppositions are the way of the world, they cannot be eradicated, so even while eschewing oppositions of every kind, postmodernists inconsistently create new ones, including an opposition necessary to give heft and moral gravitas to their social movements. Foot-soldiers of Antifa and BLM imagine an opposition much larger than it actually is, though it must be said their actions create actual enemies in greater numbers, too. People feel threatened by Antifa violence, naturally enough, and may come to believe its premises. A combination of

4 Rawls, John. *The Law of Peoples/The Idea of Public Reason Revisited*, Cambridge, MA: Harvard University Press, 1999.

5 The setting of boundaries around what counts as acceptable public discourse. For origins of the phrase, see Giridharadas, Anand. "How Elites Lost Their Grip in 2019," *Time Magazine*, Nov. 21, 2019.

6 An assumption behind Adorno's F-scale, but see also the introduction by Michel Foucault to *Anti-Oedipus/Capitalism and Schizophrenia* by Giles Deleuze and Felix Guattari (1977).

imaginary white supremacists, real white supremacists, and theoretical systemic racism rises to exacerbate an oppositional divide. A real enemy then exists, and opposition to that enemy provides meaning and purpose; a metanarrative to replace universality of values. Thus, racialist group identity politics emerges, contrary not only to American founding ideals and the Genesis worldview, but to the Frankfurt School neo-Marxists who said they were trying to avoid this very thing, yet created it.

This happens because of the oppositional structure in the human mind and in reality, and especially in the fundamental opposition of us to God. Every attempt to avoid oppositions ends up reinforcing them. The Antifa/BLM phenomenon is an example. Oppositions are the basis for their ideology; they're not overcome in the course of postmodern deconstruction. And so it is with postmodern deconstruction more generally, whether that of Foucault, Derrida, Deleuze, Rorty, the Frankfurt School, and on and on and on. They are all species of attempted deconstructions of the ideological metanarrative sponsored and supported by religion, of course, but also capitalism and more generally Enlightenment rationalism that informs Western civilization. The point of their deconstruction is to bring down hierarchies of value that support, in their view, power interests. But in the course of deconstruction to end war, they engage in a build-up to bring war. They form a new construction that has all the features of the old but without consensus on universal and transcendent values. Both reflect the Genesis reality of hierarchical value formation through the informational tensions inherent in oppositions in values, ideas, concepts, and things. It's the reality of the world. Postmodern theorists attempt to provide intellectual heft to movements that destroy putative structures of oppression only to replace them with new, and real, structures of oppression. It's all war against God.

Over time, Herbert Marcuse has emerged as perhaps foremost among the Frankfurt School thinkers. In the fashion of Rousseau, he thought advanced technological societies tended to be totalitarian. The United States only masquerades as a non-totalitarian state; our freedom from fascism is illusory. He made some valid criticisms, especially in characterizing the effect on its citizens of being born and bred to be consumers, taxpayers, and workers, rather than perceiving life as an end unto itself. There is value in this understanding, because Americans (and also to some degree citizens of other prosperous liberal Western nations) who escape the trap of government dependence are, in fact, sated with technology and plenty, and tend to spend half their waking time working, and half consuming, with precious little time left for contemplative, relational, aesthetic, and spiritual pursuits. We are, in fact, a taxpayer farm, in the eyes of bureaucrats, and a pool of consumers, in the eyes of corporate strategists. The myth of hard-working go-get-em opportunity-seekers feeds a cycle of work to enable ever-greater consumption.

That's how capitalism plays out for Americans, in this post-Christian era, but the Marcusean cure would be worse than the disease. Marxist disruption of this hyper-efficient state of materialist economic affairs is not the answer. Genesis is. What is a person? Why are we here? What values are eternal, and what is the significance of God's creation and sustenance of us, in this life of plenty, in light of our sin—not "fascism," but actual sin—how should we live, in the light of reality about God-imaged human nature that Genesis discloses? These should be the subjects of our pursuits, not endless ever-expanding consumption and a treadmill of running after the next glittering but disappointing prize, and the next, and the next. We can only eat so many hamburgers in a lifetime. If we shift our attention from crass consumption to the more scarce commodities of privilege, prestige and social rank, we're in even worse shape, emptying ourselves of substance by repudiating the only Author of it.

Frankfurt School thinkers Theodor Adorno and Max Horkheimer[7] argued that alienation under capitalism corresponded to increased wealth. Community is diminished as wealth increases. Isolation follows. The imagery is a box, like the house box and the car box and the TV box and other kinds of boxes by which we separate ourselves from others. The excessive stuff we get with prosperous capitalism reduces community. Society is hyper-efficient as with Fordist assembly lines. But at what human cost? Alienation results from work and from the products of work. The reward for soul-sucking work is getting paid just enough to go home and consume, and breed new consumers, and continue the work/consume treadmill. Mass media is a product that helps people recover from their awful jobs. It's of poor quality but takes us out of this world because that's what people want. It provides a mythology to substitute for that of religion. Celebrity and soaps and superheroes, and so on, are part of its pantheon. People are distracted, in this system, from the fact that close human interaction is what they're really missing. Always the ad is about that, really, not the product. We buy a brand of beer because

---

7   Adorno: 1903-1969; Horkheimer: 1895-1973.

we see an ad with a happy group of friends sitting around drinking. It's not the drink, it's the community people want.

But again, is that the fault of "capitalism," by whatever definition? Sure, this is an accurate description of the worst influences on us in a mostly religion-free prosperous culture. And yes, we should (individually) undertake to resist its potentially dehumanizing effects. But not through utopian socialism. There is no cure without God, and any attempt at a Godless sociological cure in otherwise liberal society will inevitably end in tyranny. This is playing out in real time right in front of us.

For Marcuse, new products in the twentieth century changed everything. It commenced the birth of the culture industry. We produce cultural artifacts, pop culture, popular but empty. But for Marcuse and other Frankfurt School postmodernists, it's the other way around. Products are designed to produce the want. We choose from a limited selection of what's made for us. Accordingly, art should avoid this trap, not being what is most likely to be popular, but what is provocative and deep. This means art should exist for leftist critique of culture, however, not to reflect transcendent ideals including beauty. The reason, for Marcuse, is that we grope after false novelty, as with cars that have very slight changes each year so we have the feel of novelty even though the form of the car is essentially the same. Phony pop culture contributes to sameness. We hear the same songs written over and over again, with only minor variation. They are formulaic. And unfortunately, life imitates that art. The sameness of it all becomes a part of us. Romance in pop art is a good example. It sets people up to think the arc of their life story is complete once a romantic connection is made. It seems briefly like satisfaction of the need for community, but it perpetuates the cycle. The culture industry works to make everyone the same person; assembly units like the assembly-line products we consume. People follow the same pattern of sameness that the culture industry presents to us: a symbiotic self-reinforcing sameness.

Here's the thing. So much of what the Frankfurt School teaches is absolutely true. There is social and work alienation, and it is self-perpetuating. There is a drive to hyper-efficiency that automates not just production, but people. It drives further work alienation, in the psychological sense, though not the economic one of traditional Marxism. There is, to be sure, a culture industry. But is that attributable to an evil system that we label "capitalism?" Or, is it just the form the evil system of the world takes in this prosperous and Godless age?

It takes some effort for us to recognize this particular brand of alienation and exploitation for what it is, that's true enough. But the question as always is freedom. We become vulnerable to the dumbing-down sameness of the vapid cultural landscape because we relax into it, and we do so precisely because we don't look to a higher calling, such as what we would find in religion. But of course, religion doesn't move us away from alienation and anomic pointlessness and toward greater community and greater sense of meaning and purpose, unless God is real. We're only brought into rapt attention to His presence and His love for us if we reject the moral therapeutic deism of this age, and accept God as He is. We accept God on His terms or we reject Him. Those are the only options.

The capitalist response to Marxist critique, from a materialist stance, might be: so what? Maybe there is exploitation and alienation, but it's a far cry from the kind of exploitation and alienation experienced by feudal serfs or chattel slaves. And what's the alternative? Intentional poverty? Nobody is totally free. Everyone is constrained in some way, whether or not the constraint rises to the level of "oppression" or not. Nature used to viciously oppress us. We overcame the limits of nature and improved life. Harnessing control over nature is a part of capitalism, and volatility in the experiences of life are part of nature, so systems have evolved to satisfy consumer demands which have the effect of controlling human behavior, too. We enjoy the benefits of an advanced civilization if there are motivations for participating in the system. That's not capitalist exploitation, that's minimizing coercion but otherwise putting people into the position of willingly pulling at the traces, so to speak.

If we were deeper inside a Soviet-style totalitarian regime, we'd certainly be victimized by insidious dehumanizing ideological demands. That's Orwell's *1984*. But are we dehumanized in the same way in a nominally capitalist regime on which is superimposed ideologies of feminism, racialism, and sexualization of everything? Our society is Huxley's *Brave New World*, but it's possible, at least, to break out of, just like the savage broke out of the soma-saturated society of that dystopia of meaninglessness. That's what Christians should do—break out of the (quite true) invidious dehumanizing impact of sameness culture that the Frankfurt School highlights, but without accepting its philosophical prescriptions.

CHAPTER SEVENTEEN

Sexual Revolution

A VISIBLE CONSEQUENCE of postmodern critique is the sexual revolution of the twentieth century, by which the expectation of self-restraint with regard to sex outside of marriage was cast aside and replaced with an ethic only of consent and against exploitation. It is crucial to understand the function of the sexual revolution: it is to diminish and ultimately extinguish the family and, thus, to advance neo-Marxist ideology.

To understand this function and its purpose, we should perceive that separating individuals from their associations with others serves to atomize them into socially more malleable units. The most significant association which would prevent their complete social absorption is the family. So the family must be eliminated, but this must be a gradual operation. A general loosening of expectations in society occurs, enabled first by rejection of God, or by re-imagining Him. Traditions of moral value passed down through the family are weakened along with the family itself, and as the family weakens further, traditional values weaken further, in a mutually reinforcing downward spiral.

"Tradition" should be understood as objectively formed values, not just deference to the way things were formerly thought about and done. Augusto Del Noce[1] referred to the latter as "traditionalism" in order to distinguish it. His mid-twentieth-century views on the evolving sexual revolution were particularly insightful and prescient, citing as he does

---

1 *The Crisis of Modernity*, Montreal: McGill-Queen's University Press, 2015, pp. 144-45; 160-61.

Wilhelm Reich[2] as the most explicit expositor of the philosophical principles giving rise to sexual revolution, even more so than postmodernists like Marcuse and Freud and the innumerable cultural influencers who adopted their ways of thinking, wittingly or no. Reich was quite explicit in making destruction of the family the goal of sexual revolution. Del Noce observed that from Reich's perspective, "*the abolition of every meta-empirical order of truth requires that the family must be dissolved.*"[3]

Postmodernism is Marxism, if we understand "Marxism" to include not just its classical form of economic socialism, but its cultural applications following Antonio Gramsci,[4] the Frankfurt School thinkers, and philosophical pragmatists absorbing the remnants of atheist existentialism. It is important to understand postmodernism in this way because, as with all Marxist evolution of thought, it consists of critiques of logocentrism and objectivity, seeking to replace them with process philosophies that throw off transcendence.

Marxism has a reproduction problem, however. Part of the reason classical Marxism has never been applied successfully is that its progress was slowed by the ongoing recurrence of taught tradition, to include absolute and universal principles of right and wrong, and of the dignity of individuals in contrast to various forms of collectivist corporatism. The shift to "we" perspective is set back in each generation; religion continues to rear its ugly head; people continue to engage in rational thought oriented to objective and universal principles; the conscience continues to motivate recognition of property rights, tolerance, independence, and sexual self-restraint. These are impediments to neo-Marxist re-calibration of mankind into an entirely social animal.

Postmodern forms of cultural or neo-Marxism arose because of the reproduction problem. Marxist thinking evolved so that its reproduction was to take place in re-evaluation of social norms in increasingly religion-indifferent Western societies. These were understood as necessary because societies evolved well past the classical Marxist set-piece of bourgeois/proletariat duality that was to lead to revolution and utopian socialism. But even with innovations of process philosophies of becoming, and cultural critique, and rebel chic, there remained the competing bourgeois method of self-reproduction: the family. To supplant traditional society's values, its means of reproduction must be eliminated.

---

2 In various works, including most pertinently *The Sexual Revolution*, 1936.

3 *The Crisis of Modernity*, transl. by Carlo Lancellotti, Montreal: McGill-Queen's University Press, 2015, p. 161 (emphasis in original).

4 Mentioned in the previous chapter, and discussed more thoroughly in Chapter 27.

By removing the competition, socially formed norms could prevail over objectively formed norms. The family had to go.

Feminism has been an important part of that evolution. Feminists act to advance what they conceive to be the interests of women; they don't necessarily self-identify, individually, as neo-Marxists. But the feminist tie to Marxism is contained in the oppressor/oppressed paradigm reinforced culturally; in this case, the oppressor being the male-dominated social system of patriarchy. Marx himself seemed to understand that inequality between the sexes, even "inequality" in the limited sense of not being the same, was a fundamental obstacle to a fully formed vision of socialist utopia. He regarded the family unit as one in which wife and children were "slaves" of the husband. The sexual division of labor in the family was a root cause of labor division more generally, by which power structures arise and the powerful alienate workers from the fruits of their labor.[5]

There is a sense in which women came to be thought of as the "means of production" in Marxist terms. She is the "factory" for creating new workers to be oppressed in their turn, and the "factory" is owned by the dominating male in the traditional family unit. In family relations, the male stands in for the bourgeois capitalist oppressor; the female stands in for the oppressed proletariat. In *The Dialectic of Sex* (1970), Shulamith Firestone made just this comparison, expanding from the philosophical perspective of Simone de Beauvoir (*The Second Sex*, 1949). She argued that women must seize the "means of production," exclusive control of sexual reproduction, for a just and liberated society to emerge. Technology, in the form of birth control and relatively more safe (for the mother) abortion, would finally enable a break from the historically oppressive biological family unit. The false consciousness of family closeness and social stability must be disrupted, so that women can finally see the alienation to which they are subjected in traditional families.

This idea of "false consciousness" is central to Marxist and neo-Marxist thought. It is the justification for forcing the shift from individualism to socialism because the oppressed, like women in the case of feminism, don't sufficiently feel their chains to develop the desire to break free on their own. Their alienation is so thoroughgoing that they don't grasp their own oppression. They must be "forced to be free," to use Rousseau's phrasing, and the thinking of Émile Durkheim and postmodernists like Zygmunt Bauman, Richard Rorty, and others.

---

5 *The German Ideology* (published 1932, written c. 1846).

False consciousness isn't limited to groups that will be taught to consider themselves oppressed. Children in general are inculcated with traditional values inside the family unit. Those traditional values give them a "false consciousness" because they deviate from deconstructionist Marxism. Children are thus thought to be absorbed into the oppressive capitalist structure with a false consciousness reinforced by religion, most of all, but also by consumerism, tribal loyalty, a limited and even bigoted form of "love," and other fascist values that inhere in capitalism, and in this way come to accept bourgeois values and fail to see the glories that would attend liberation of the libido and liberation of mankind more generally from the oppressions and alienation imposed by family structure.

Feminism serves the breakdown of the family through substitution of a sameness paradigm in place of a complementarity paradigm. Step one is to create dissatisfaction with the primacy of the home (that is, family) economy. This was a purpose, for example, of Betty Friedan's 1963 book, *The Feminine Mystique*. The work of keeping a home was eased by labor-saving technology and partial outsourcing of child-rearing, so that practical barriers to women's participation in the work force were reduced. Maintaining a home life came to be seen as unfulfilling, and in any event, unnecessary.

At the same time, the economic interdependence resulting from occupational specialization increased. The value of the home economy was diminished in favor of the work-for-paycheck economy. The one-earner family economic model gave way to the two-earner family. This meant less time and energy to devote to caring for the family, but this loss became normalized and was offset by the rewards of ambitious striving for career success that was formerly men's domain. Families over time have come to be regarded as consumer economic units. The materialist imperatives of the age justify outsourcing physical, intellectual, and spiritual development of children. The project of making a whole human being has given way to the parents' projects of self-actualization, but children still watch and learn, so they follow in their parents' footsteps, with the result that the Marxist critique of automated "Fordism," even in families, is made valid. We lose sight of the importance of families to child-rearing.

While the family has been denatured in this way, there has been relentless lobbying for equality of men and women in the workplace. On the surface, this certainly seems unobjectionable. If the contributions are the same, the pay and advancement should be the same. But as a result of typical postmodern definition slippage, equality in the work-place has come to mean equality of "representation," meaning that we are to affirmatively support equal participation of men and women in the workplace. This is why there is relentless narrative bullying about the under-representation of women in various jobs—never the dirtiest and most dangerous jobs, just the ones that appeal to high-status women. But when we encounter this, we'd do well to ask: why? What social ben-efit accrues to having equal numbers of women and men as university presidents or senators? The benefit, such as it is, is left unspoken: it is to encourage elimination of the traditional family economic structure with Dad going to work and paying the bills and Mom making a home. There's nothing inherently wrong with any of the combinations people freely choose for themselves: the traditional one-earner structure, or the traditional structure in reverse (with the one earner being the wom-an), or the two-earner model. But to say there's nothing wrong with any of these ways of living is also to say that people should be left alone to choose for themselves rather than being hectored into a new social norm so as to eliminate all gender role differences.

The same end is in sight with the relentlessly repeated pay gap sta-tistic, wherein we're to repeat a mantra that women make only a per-centage of what men do. Perhaps 82 cents on the dollar. Time and again, the pay gap statistic has been shown to support a lie. It's presented as evidence that women don't make the same pay for the same job. But that's not true. It represents only the ratio of median annual earnings of women to men. Mathematically, it must be less than 100 percent if even a miniscule percentage of the population adopts a traditional home economy model. When one corrects for the type of job chosen and time of entry into and exit from the workplace, and the prevalence of single mothers scraping by with relatively menial jobs, and other factors hav-ing nothing to do with external sex discrimination, it becomes clear that the pay gap statistic doesn't prove unequal pay at all. It only means there are more women who enter the workforce later, or choose lesser-paying career paths, or regard their role in the family as their primary career, so that the outside job is secondary, perhaps only a temporary supplement to family income. The pay gap only proves that many women prefer a traditional role in their families. A presumptive sameness of roles within the family is the real goal behind advocacy to close the purported pay gap, not equality for those in the work force. The goal is a new social norm of women in the work force—further diminishing gender differ-ence in the family—not equality once they're there.

The sameness paradigm has the effect of removing the separate roles of father and mother within the family. They become just two equal parents. Thus, the distinctive voices of masculine and feminine are eliminated in favor of a model of interchangeable co-parenting. In this way, the model of gender sameness is passed on to the next generation rather than the model of gender complementarity, and as a result, the unique contribution of the family unit—including, but not limited to, reinforcement of ontological male/female difference—is diluted.

At the same time, child-rearing is progressively more often outsourced because that is considered just as good as child-rearing within the family unit. Perhaps better, in fact, because "experts" step in, and human beings become diminished so that they are less in need of the cocoon of loving intimacy the family can provide but which experts can't. The outsourcing occurs with public schools and ever-expanding public childcare, transportation, school meals, extracurriculars, and so on.

It's important that we think through the consequences of outsourcing child-rearing. Inside the family, through the medium of love, parents pass on traditional values and at the same time foster resilience and critical thinking, exposing the child gradually to stressors which will challenge those values. In this way, they grow and learn to thrive in a heterodox (that is, non-totalitarian) environment. But what if the child-rearing is so thoroughly outsourced that "society" instead inculcates values? A one-size-fits-all therapeutic mentality is imposed, and there is insufficient challenge to the orthodoxy. Children grow up more vulnerable to ideology, hyper-sensitive to challenges to received orthodoxy and less capable of understanding another's point of view. The passing on of transcendent, objective, universal principle, within families, is replaced by the passing on of social norms, inculcated institutionally. This is true for busy two-earner families, and is true in a more pinched and penurious way among single-parent (usually mother-led) families.

The new norm is that the village raises the child, but of course, there is no village, there is only the Machine, and the traditions passed down are not objectively true values, but rather ideology. Especially the self-perpetuating ideologies of feminism and further breakdown of the family, in service to the liberation neo-Marxism aims for: a re-make of society in which our perspective is shifted from "I" to "we," in which social norms rule rather than objectively true universals by which we have freedom to self-govern and yet live in an ordered society under the rule of law.

The sameness principle serves a set of gender ideologies that follow on to feminism, especially in the LBGTQ etc. context. Though the outward categories of male and female necessarily remain, they are softened and considered changeable. It would seem the feminist/gender ideological alliance rests on conflicting ideas, but they are united intersectionally against the common enemy of heteronormative "patriarchy." The Ts and Qs and non-binaries remain in the alliance even though they would go further in elimination of gender categories. The Ts recognize the categories, by repudiating one to travel to the other. The Qs and non-binaries seem to be engaged in denying the categories, but implicitly recognize them by virtue of repudiating them. Their position is one of critique, remember, as always within Marxist postmodernism engaged in deconstruction of stable categories, to replace them with ill-defined and malleable new social norms, a devolution from scary mountain to welcoming river.

Inequality in all forms is the target, but "inequality" is susceptible to two different meanings, as is often the case with postmodern definition slippage. On the one hand, it can mean unequal treatment before the law, or before the judgment of the surrounding culture. On the other hand, it can mean simply difference; the opposite of sameness. On the latter definition, the cure for "inequality" is sameness. This kind of "inequality" collides head-on with gender difference. There is no more fundamental difference among humans than that between male and female. It is natural, ontological, ineradicable. But if we manage to obscure it nonetheless, this serves utopian ideological ends. This accounts for the stridency of the transsexual movement. It's not about rights for a sexual minority. It's about attempting to eradicate all difference in favor of an all-encompassing vision of socialism.

Any of these forms of attempted compromise of gender categories serves to confuse, in an even more fundamental way, the traditional purposes of a family. Feminism reduces male and female distinctiveness, as do LGBTQ etc. gender ideologies. They do so by division of putatively oppressed groups. These divisions shift individual perspectives from self to group; a first step toward the advent of true socialism. The individual self formed in families would impede this move.

Feminism and gender ideology are not the sole explanation for destruction of the family, or by which the sexual revolution has advanced. Sexual permissiveness in general coincides with those trends. Generally speaking, it is gradual relaxation followed by entire elimination of the norm that sex is proper only inside marriage between two people of the opposite sex. That traditional standard is rooted in the Genesis model of marriage, whereby a man and woman come together in marriage, a bond more significant and more binding than partnership, and in that marriage, the full scope of humanity is manifested rather than just the separate gifts of men, or of women. Marriage meant sexual license, with children often resulting, and a stable environment already in place for their growth and flourishing.

Marriage and sex became untethered, both as cause and effect of the weakening of the family. This resulted not entirely from traditional Marxism, but also from Sigmund Freud's psychology of sexual tension and the neo-Marxist critiques of Herbert Marcuse, Wilhelm Reich, and many others, who, from various angles, were concerned with sexual repression in one form or another. All were resolute atheists, so they disregarded or rejected out of hand the premises of Genesis; in fact, the Genesis model was considered the problem to be fixed. The goal of disrupting the family *per se* was explicit or implicit, but in any event, a natural and necessary outcome in the march to liberation.

The value of sexual restraint, including the restraint of saving sex for marriage, shores up the family as an enduring institution for rearing children. Loosening of that restraint results in loosening the bonds of marriage. Sex is often thought to be of central importance, to marriage traditionalists, not necessarily because it is more pleasurable in that context, or because of generalized conservatism, but because human nature is such that exclusivity of sex to that relationship reinforces the particular importance of the marriage union to its members and indeed to civilization. A man and a woman are more tightly knit together emotionally if their sexual relations are exclusive, each to the other, both during and before the marriage. Marriage serves civilization by providing a stable locus for the passing on of objective and eternal values to children. It is beneficial to the married individuals themselves, freeing them from jealousy that would distance them and erode marriage to the equivalent of a business partnership "with benefits," that regards children, if any, as add-on consumer items.

Sex can be regarded as merely a physical act, but the physical act has attendant emotional consequences, especially for the woman. Much of current feminism involves a reckoning between "sex-positive" and sex-difference in ways of thinking about male/female relations. But all of this relates to the physical act, primarily. Another way of thinking about sex is on a more idealized plane, in which sex means something more than the physical act. Effectively, sex is thought of as recreational only, or as meaningful. But meaning may amount only to a self-generated imputation of significance to the act, as when we assign to it notions of love or even commitment. But even this self-generated imputation of meaning is thin; a wan reflection of the lost and longed-for indissoluble bond between a particular man and particular woman, bone of my bone and flesh of my flesh, which we know intuitively is a higher and more noble context for the physical sex act.

In her recent book, *The Case Against the Sexual Revolution*,[6] Louise Perry uses the phrase "sexual disenchantment"[7] to describe the ideological stance that sex holds no special meaning and no inherent value; that its value is only such as is assigned to it by the participants; and that the only basis for restraint is absence of consent. The phrase is an echo of Max Weber's general disenchantment which follows upon the purported death of God, referring to a dimming of the glow of meaning and significance, so that people now live with more despair and less hope than they once did, even as we are materially better off. Applied to the sexual revolution in particular, "disenchantment" refers to the pretense, in Perry's words, "that sex has no special value that makes it different from other acts," and this pretense has proven devastating. "If sex isn't worthy of its own moral category, then nor is sexual harassment or rape."[8] The sexual revolution makes for transactional, instrumentalizing sex which diminishes both women and men, but is especially harmful to women. Perry doesn't explicitly connect sexual disenchantment with Weber's more general disenchantment in a post-Christian society. But there is a connection. Once the link to transcendent truth is severed, our conception of our own significance begins to unravel, and continues to do so. We reject ontological dualism of nature and spirit, and materialist monism follows. Mankind, then, is just a really smart animal, capable of reformatting reality. Sexual disenchantment is then inevitable, and is followed by sexual monism, the project of transsexual activism. Perry's contribution is valuable, however, because, as George Orwell wrote, "we have now sunk to a depth at which restatement of the obvious is the first duty of intelligent men."

While feminist and gender ideology movements have attacked the traditional family structure from the top down, so to speak, "sex-positive" movements for children in recent years have undermined the values-formation of children from the bottom up, by normalizing

---

6 Medford, MA: Polity, 2022.

7 Perry attributes the phrase to Aaron Sibarium from his essay, "Three Theses About Cuties," *American Compass*, September 23, 2020.

8 Perry, Louise. *The Case Against the Sexual Revolution*, p. 160.

non-marital sex in all its variation, and exposing children to it. The invasion of innocence means the walls of the inviolate family are already breached. The family purpose of rearing children in age-appropriate ways is compromised. The horse is already out of the barn, and over the fence, and across the pasture. The family becomes more dispensable because its central function is diminished: that of readying the child for adulthood, strengthening him or her as he or she grows, inculcating eternal values and an ability to face extremes of ideology with toleration but critical thinking in adulthood. The out-sourcing of child-rearing diminishes this function by making children progressively more available to ideologues who actively seek to liberate them from what they regard as hidebound traditionalism in sexual matters.

The project of liberation backfires. Women and men both suffer in the crisis of meaninglessness and loneliness that predominates as a result of the sexual revolution. Children grow with a stunted vision of the significance of sex and an inability to perceive a transcendent Source for all values, including, most fundamentally, those that inhere in ontological male/female difference.

The essentially Marxist goal of tearing down civilizational structures in order to re-make mankind anew is advanced by the dissolution of the family. The Marxist problem of reproduction of ideology is mostly solved by it, not only because reproduction of objectivity and universality of values is impaired and nearly vanquished, but because a re-imagination of the self naturally takes its place. Anomic lives in silos of isolation are ready grist for the totalitarian mill.

Postmodern deconstruction rests on a foundation of critique, which is distinct from "critical thinking" in its ordinary sense of thinking carefully and rationally about the implications of a proposition. "Critique," as meant by Marxists, or "critical theory," as meant more specifically by neo-Marxists, means deconstruction. It goes beyond careful evaluation, as discussed in Chapter 14. Its purpose is to deconstruct so as to set aside the existing structures of society, variously labelled traditional, bourgeois, capitalist, or fascist.

Frankfurt School theory is a technique for confronting assumptions underlying the capitalist "system," by which is meant really the objectivity of truth and goodness and beauty that inhere in the Genesis worldview. So, for example, what about the marriage centrality of that ancient text? All the bit about Eve being "bone of my bone and flesh of my flesh?" Man made from dirt; woman made as the flowering of the dirt-digging man? And the cultural norms of chastity and monogamy that support those basic ideas?

To Herbert Marcuse, at mid-twentieth century following Freud, being human means repressing impulses and acting on what's best in the long run. We are rational but with primal desires we could act on constantly, but we have a choice to not act on instinct. Subordinating passions to rationality is valid. Civilization, to Freud and the Frankfurt school, means recognizing the benefits of living in community, and agreeing on norms to repress impulses destructive to that community. It means rational self-control.

Superficially, this sounds unobjectionable, but note: this means social norms are not rooted in any objective ultimate truth. They're just the agreed-upon rules of engagement, so to speak, to participate in a society. They're thought to evolve naturally in social processes. That means they're not handed down from on high by a putative God. And so, the norms can be adjusted to social circumstances. Slavery, for example, is and has been acceptable according to cultural norms in various places throughout history, including the United States, well into the nineteenth century. Then it was rejected. Now, approval of slavery would be out of the question, at least in prosperous liberal Western democracies, though we tend not to see it when it takes forms like sex trafficking or exploitation in less-developed venues.

Critical theory developed from Frankfurt School thinking which was resigned to the continuing resiliency of capitalism, but sought to limit what were perceived as its excesses by limiting the creation of cultural norms that protect power interests and tend to oppress. The idea was that some repression of freedom is necessary, but there should be limits, so critical theory is supposed to work in oppositional tandem with capitalism. The question is: what cultural norms should be maintained, and which ones are unduly repressive so that we should re-visit whether they ought to be cultural norms?

There's a serious flaw in this approach that seems to go unnoticed. The assumption critical theorists make is that there is no objective right and wrong, there are only cultural norms: actions and attitudes we socially come to regard as right or wrong. This is what happens upon rejection of God, and of transcendence, and of objectivity. Critical theory exists to curb our cultural norms when they veer too far in unsavory directions, like with the normalization of slavery. But what makes it unsavory? By what criteria is a particular cultural norm undesirable? If they're only cultural norms, rather than objectively right or wrong, why second-guess them? If everything is a matter of cultural norms, why is there a need for some sort of check on formation of cultural norms?

The answer, of course, is that there is objective right and wrong. Slavery, in our example, is wrong. A proper check on excess in cultural norms is appeal to universal principle, not formation of an antagonistic layer of social norms, as with critical theory.

The flawed critical theory assumption leads to disastrous results. We have to wonder what horrible idea might become normative next. Polyamory? Sex change mutilation of children? Too late to put the brakes on those. How about pederasty? Increasingly, there are suggestions that certain forms of it are not always and everywhere bad. Where is the critical theory to put a check on that? What's happening is that critical theory technique is employed to combat objectively wrong morals after all, but only selectively, to serve postmodernist ideals.

One mid-century result of the influence of thinkers like Marcuse was re-examination of traditional sexual morality as to whether it is unduly repressive. There was, for most of history, a ubiquitous cultural norm against promiscuity. Family was supported by the taboo against sex outside marriage. The need for social goods of stability in relationships and rearing of children justified what Marcuse (and others, of course) regarded as repression: taboos that arise solely as a matter of social norms. For sexual liberationists, you're not wrong to have feelings of sexual desire, or to decline to sublimate them so as to pursue them promiscuously in a society liberated from internalized sexual constraints. The historical sacrifice of eros to "monogamic reproduction" (in Marcuse's phrasing) and full-time work perpetuates the binding up of people in an ongoing system of intensifying unfreedom.

Inherent libidinal forces, for Marcuse and for Freud, are the driving motivational force for mankind's striving. These forces take the place of religious seeking after meaning and purpose, and secular philosophical ideas for fundamental human motivation, such as Hegelian historical telos through dialectical synthesis,[9] Schopenhauer's concept of will,[10] Schiller's aesthetics,[11] Bergson's *élan vital*,[12] or Nietzsche's will to power.[13] "Being is essentially the striving for pleasure," Marcuse wrote.[14]

---

9 Georg Wilhelm Friedrich Hegel (1770-1831).

10 Arthur Schopenhauer (1788-1860).

11 Friedrich Schiller (1759-1805).

12 Henri Bergson (1859-1941).

13 Friedrich Nietzsche (1844-1900).

14 Herbert Marcuse, *Eros and Civilization/A Philosophical Inquiry into Freud*, Boston: Beacon Press, 1955, p. 125.

Marcuse correctly believed the libidinal forces had been harnessed by a process of sublimation into full-time work and cultural norms of monogamy and chastity, but he also believed this was a form of repression and that release of the libidinal forces would bring about a full flowering of human potential. Not all sex all the time, necessarily, because eros would become sublimated into agape, and mankind could evolve to be more free and more in harmony with society.

It's important to remember that the Frankfurt School explicitly engaged in a critique of Western logocentrism, as does postmodernism more generally. It is not a ground-up philosophical system to explain reality, in other words, but rather a criticism of reality as understood in Western societies. The purpose is to highlight dehumanizing tendencies in culture and identify them to religious logocentrism, to the end of replacing them with utopian ideology. First decouple feelings of right and wrong from a transcendent Source. Then couple them to socially formed cultural norms. Then they are modifiable, and can be re-directed toward the postmodern vision.

The effort involves re-making mankind; individual men and women and not just society or politics. The target of the critique is quite explicitly religion and its resulting logocentrism. More human promise can be realized, on this premise, by subordinating logic and reason to the instincts; to aesthetics; to a frame of mind that departs from ordered, rational, propositional objectivity, to find rest in abstraction, receptivity, creativity, and instinctual impulses. In short, a descent from the mountain to the river; from the act of division of heaven and earth to the formless void; from the spirit of God to the "waters" over which His spirit hovered.

The logos, for Marcuse, was a "logos of domination," and so he was committed to a replacement reality principle. The logos—rational, propositional objectivity—was to be no longer conceived as the essence of being, and in this way, could be challenged. With Nietzsche, Marcuse held that in Christianity the life instincts were perverted and constrained. The decline of man coincided with the artificiality and alienation of capitalist production resting on repression. Freedom would come from the throwing-over of the logos of domination.

This is essential Marxism: invoking the principle of power, to the exclusion of all else, to critique Christian-originated democratic liberalism and the sort of person it is thought to create. Critique is the point, not ground-up construction, in all variants of Marxism which feature so prominently in postmodernism. Hence, "the Great Refusal" advocated by Marcuse against the repression created by logocentrism. It is an attitude of negation; of tearing down rather than building up.

Marcuse directed hostility particularly to the "monogamic and patriarchal family," institutions he thought existed to perpetuate sexual repression.[15] Marcuse's hostility to traditional family structure and sexual mores amounts to rejection of reality as disclosed in Genesis and in Biblical revelation as a whole. We're expected to find sexual restraint to be merely a cultural norm, developed as a means of repression, which can now be modified with the advent of birth control.

Extramarital sexual license is not objectively wrong, on this reading. But what is? Slavery? Child sacrifice? These have been within cultural norms, in certain times and places. Abortion is culturally acceptable in many quarters, now, but we might come to see it as unethical in the same way slavery once was. The truth is that all these practices are objectively wrong, not made wrong just by social convention. We correct those practices by more refined thinking among objective principles; we don't make them right by trying to reconstitute mankind.

Every civilization has had its share of particular evils to contend with, like the sexual licentiousness and unfounded resentment and soul-destroying addictions in the present age. We cannot find any civilization in history, nor in the present, that is free from some sort of evil that is, nonetheless, within a cultural norm. So what does that mean? Well, for a postmodernist, it might mean it's necessary to burn everything to the ground and start over. But even if that were possible, it wouldn't work. We are what we are because we're made that way, not solely because we're the product of cultural influences of time and place. We regard cultural norms as such because we live in time, and so our past is relevant. But we regard some things as objectively right or wrong, notwithstanding their occurrence or non-occurrence in history.

Critical theory exists because of recognition that things become entrenched in social norms that are not right. Of course, that means absolutes, but absolutes were rejected on turning to the relativism of postmodern cultural evolution. So which is it? If all morality is a matter of social conditioning, why criticize any of it? Critical theory interrogates the culture for norms that are outdated and should be changed, but why should they be changed, if there are no absolutes?

So with the sexual revolution: the norm of chastity and monogamy was rejected because, it was felt, we've moved past the conditions for its

---

15   Ibid., p. 201.

imposition; now it's unduly repressive, so we should normalize instead a replacement set of sexual ethics. But again, why? If there are no absolutes, then what difference does it make which set of "cultural norms" are operative at any given time?

Really, if we follow Marcuse concerning sexual repression, shouldn't we also consider what else is merely normalized now? And what makes it a norm: objectivity or cultural evolution? If the latter, there's no authority for "repressing" anything: slavery, female genital mutilation, sex trafficking, child porn, or anything else. If the expectation of sexual rectitude is only a form of repression imposed as a social norm, then perhaps it seems logical that we could reexamine it so as to loosen the repression and normalize more laxity in sexual matters. In this way, the postmodern narrative of ethical relativism replaces the moral objectivity that inhered in most thinking in all of history before the twentieth century.

Understanding the objectivity of morals as opposed to the social construct of them is necessary before even getting to sexual questions specifically. The question is whether the Genesis paradigm of marriage is objective and real and binding and moral, or whether the postmodern paradigm of relativism, "cultural norms" and ethics in place of morals, obtains. If we renounce objectivity, there is no reason not to go further, and normalize sex with children or choosing to be another sex, or rejecting the binary polarity of sex altogether. There is necessarily no God involved in the postmodern view, only society responding censoriously or indulgently to ethics as fashion.

Critical theories presuppose that the objectivity of truth and morality has already been rejected. In that milieu, we're concerned with "ethics," because "morals" are reserved for the absolute. And yet, there are absolutes, and they emerge incongruously within the postmodernist system of thought. Immorality is reserved for instances of judgment or intolerance or bigotry or chauvinism or other kinds of "othering," because these are the postmodern absolutes.[16] In time, it will also be thought immoral to insist on objectivity of truth and good and evil and the existence of God. It will be absolutely wrong to insist on absolute wrong.

---

16 As well articulated by René Girard, *I Saw Satan Fall Like Lightning*, Maryknoll, NY: Orbis Books, 2001, p. xix.

CHAPTER EIGHTEEN

Process and Flow

THE POSTMODERN impulse to process philosophies is general, but is expressed variously. For another illustration, we can look at the work of Gilles Deleuze and Félix Guattari.[1] As with all postmodernists, Deleuze and Guattari critiqued the modernist assumptions of objectivity. They argued that most philosophers built "identity" as forms of stable reality. They rejected this premise, asserting there were no external stable forms to point to, to adequately yield identity. We should instead focus on difference. Their attempt to move from identity to difference was an attempt to move from substance to process, from mountain to river, rather than the hierarchal meaning-making of differentiation characterizing the present work, which would take us from the river in the direction of the mountain in apprehending reality.

Deleuze and Guattari advocated a new way of thinking, but not just by tacking on new ideas to old forms. They meant to reject old forms altogether, to look to movements and flows of ideas intersecting like "rhizomes," analogous to intersecting and interacting root systems in the complex but unseen underground biology of plants. Difference generates meaning, in this way of thinking; not similarity, whereby an object or concept is mentally fastened to others on the basis of identity, commonly held criteria, so that a hierarchy emerges.

The main trouble with this approach is that the proffered metaphysics of difference is the same as (rather than being in opposition to) the metaphysics of identity. Both involve not just differentiation, but the

---

1 Most notably, *Anti-Oedipus/Capitalism and Schizophrenia*, NY: Penguin, 2009 (first published in US 1977).

same form of differentiation, because to identify as the one thing, one must differentiate it from the many. The ancient problem of the "one and the many" is not evaded in process philosophy, but merely re-framed. Structure is supposed to be the suspect product of a metaphysics of identity, in other words, to be deconstructed through a metaphysics of difference. But calling it difference rather than identity is a rhetorical shift, not a substantive one, and so it does not explain how power interests are protected in the social structure itself. If they did so under an identity paradigm, they continue to do so under a difference paradigm, because they're the same thing. An attempt to reverse the significance of universals, or the problem of the one and the many, fails. Social structures cannot be said to exist to protect the powerful at the expense of the weak under a metaphysics of identity any more than a metaphysics of difference. As always, in quintessential Marxist fashion, the hidden purposes and resulting false consciousness is presumed, not discerned.

And why? It can only be because structures reflect transcendent meaning, purpose, and hierarchy, and spiritual truth behind them. Postmodern process philosophies like that of Deleuze and Guattari bottom out at hatred of God. But as we have noted, religion is not attacked directly, not only because doing so is not yet strategic, but because relativists who have thrown over objectivity don't see any harm in the rubes having an imaginary friend so long as religion continues its freefall into social irrelevance. Why bother to bell the cat if it is too old and infirm to be a threat anyway?

One can, nonetheless, see in the thinking of Deleuze and Guattari intriguing glimpses of the Genesis reality peeking out from behind their reactive perspective. Difference does indeed generate meaning, but not in the way they conceived it. Differences in category generate meaning, it is the natural product of this-not-that delineation that we make in every waking moment, and which is generated in the objective reality around us. This actual meaning-making by opposition generates hierarchy, not the mutual attraction of identity.

Suppose I live in a house almost identical to my next-door neighbor's, two boxes that look the same. Instead of passing over this scene in favor of something more varied and meaningful, we might look at differences, from one house to another, in their occupants and those occupants' ideas, and allow those differences to reform the way of living until the houses no longer look all the same. Meaning would emerge in difference, rather than in sameness-inducing external values causing us to place like with like. The thinking of Deleuze and Guattari might have eventually taken them back to a Genesis worldview, but they argued instead for a shift from the ontology of being that resulted in this awful cookie-cutter environment, toward an ontology of becoming, by means of truncating what they imagined as the valued goal in a hierarchy, and allowing process to take over.

We might ask, "What's wrong with this project?" New York City is vibrant in a way a typical suburb is not, precisely because difference was not constrained (nor identity required) in its development. Its development predated the advent of zoning laws, and the city became what it is as the result of innumerable unmanaged decentralized decisions concerning property rights, before sclerotic urban planning set in. Deleuze and Guattari had some things to say about urban planning, urging it as an example of how an ontology of becoming works out, in contrast to an ontology of being. We might regard it as an emphasis on process rather than on static vision.

In some ways, they end up sounding like political conservatives suspicious of central authority, for whom the very phrase "urban planning" is suspect, presupposing, as it does, top-down management of growth toward a particular static vision. For political conservatives, the higher value is individual freedom over collective control, letting the chips fall where they will in the outcome, in this case, urban geography. For Deleuze and Guattari, likewise, the higher value is rhizomatic growth; a free flow of ideas rather than a static point of reference. In the applied field of urban planning, both Deleuze and political conservatives (generally) would prefer undoing the whole project in favor of urban non-planning—or more accurately, diffuse limited individual planning rather than centralized planning by authority.

Deleuze and Guattari say they get there through an ontology of becoming, as opposed to an ontology of being. That is, localized values emerge through an infinite number of decisions in process rather than movement toward a static hierarchical value structure. Political conservatives get there from the opposite direction: a hierarchical system of values, but those prioritize individual freedom rather than restrictive communal collectivism. In reality, they're the same thing—not opposites. Deleuze and Guattari seem to suggest (and in doing so, echo ideas of other postmodernists) a radical shift in metaphysics from an ontology of being to one of becoming, but their examples (as with urban planning) depend on return to universal values, which inhere in an ontology of being.

This is their way of describing their resolution of the age-old conundrum of how things can be both one and many. Like Heraclitus observed long ago, how can one step in the same river twice? It is but one unified river; an ontology of Being. The river is, just as God said to Moses "I Am." But your feet are wet because they step in a flow: not two rivers, but a continuous becoming of multiplicity, analogized in water. Deleuze and Guattari (as examples of postmodern process philosophers) seem to be saying, "Embrace the becoming; the flow; the difference, the individuation that inheres in the waters." And further, "Reject the being, the stasis, the identity, the wholeness of the one river."

But ultimately, this is only a viewpoint shift; it doesn't change the nature of the river (nor reality as a whole). It just highlights our ability to observe it in two different ways at the same time. The philosophical problem of the one and the many remains; we have not transcended it by taking up process philosophy, as if it were a substitute for seeing things integrated in a hierarchy formed by objective values, concepts, and ideals.

The difference in these two ways of thinking is instructive. What Deleuze and Guattari oppose is structure which oppresses (in the urban planning example, with bad urban geography). They perceive this structure as resulting from the tendency toward hierarchy in value formation; the mountain impulse rather than the river. The hierarchical way of thinking disclosed in Genesis could support an authoritarian metanarrative, but only if it is taken too simplistically. In the Genesis worldview, the solution is to double down on mental and moral division and differentiation, refining one's understanding and value formation upward in the direction of ultimate good, and ultimate beauty, and ultimate truth; that is, to God, in whom all these values reside and originate and pour forth.

A sound understanding of the principles first articulated in Genesis doesn't lead to Nazism. It leads to intellectual discernment and a desire individually to be more; to be better. What is more and better is defined by this-better-than-that refined distinctions, referencing absolute and universal vertical principles. This way of thinking, manifested broadly across society, gives us the best of both worlds: freedom for expressive individuality, and self-controlled respect for value-laden limits and boundaries on conduct. All as necessary to self-constructing oneself as a better person, and only then, secondarily, a resulting better society.

An understanding of the process orientation of postmodernists is necessary to distinguish a thesis of the present work: namely, that if there is a God, there is a dualistic, transcendent reality of spirit and nature, from which flows a repeating dualist, oppositional structure to things and concepts and values, and hierarchies of universal values result, along with refinement of reason. Why impute bad motive to this perspective? It only makes sense to do so if (a) there is, in fact, no God who creates this way; or (b) religion is a knowing falsehood proposed to protect some entirely human interest, such as social structures of power.

Why not instead take the God proposition as true, and consider objectivity on that basis? As always, what happens with postmodern thinkers is first a rejection of God. All else follows. God is of another ontological substance and is transcendent over that which is of the world, and because the world is a pale image of that transcendent reality, it is inferior. This is the first step in a value hierarchy which forms our entire architecture of nuanced moral discernment. Once God is rejected, we can reconsider everything else about the dualist, transcendent paradigm, and that's exactly what Deleuze and Guattari did, and for that matter, so also Marx, Freud, Nietzsche, Marcuse, Adorno, Derrida, and Foucault, among other false luminaries of the postmodern world. Once God is rejected, the whole hierarchical, dualist, transcendent ontological system is suspect. Bad motive—to sustain the hierarchy for the benefit of the powerful—is therefore imputed. There is self-evidently no God, it is believed, so the philosophy which follows from the first words of Genesis is suspect.

To attempt to smash the hierarchy, Deleuze and Guattari would adopt what they understood to be Baruch Spinoza's consideration of traditional theistic ideas of transcendence and immanence. Transcendence involves a dualist reality in which a superior ideal is embedded in a realm beyond time-bound physical material, as in Platonism and orthodox Christianity. From this concept of transcendence comes an entire hierarchy of values, informing our conceptions of the good, the true, and the beautiful, and the relation of abstractions (concepts, principles, virtues, values) to physical things.

Immanence is a distinct ontology of substance by which God is understood to be wholly within the world in a process of ongoing creation. And if not God, somehow the principles, virtues, and values themselves. Spinoza, according to Deleuze and Guattari, attempted to overcome these competing origin stories, and cited a third, "expression," a purely process-oriented conception which attempted to do away with considerations of origin and first principles of reality altogether. Deleuze and Guattari built on this Spinozan concept in their efforts to entirely replace the ontology of transcendence. The idea was to get rid of substance hierarchy, which naturally flows from transcendence, to adopt a "univocal" or one-substance perspective. This is a grand way of insisting on monist materialism as the full explanation of reality. That is the default postmodern metaphysical view, in direct opposition to the dualist metaphysics presented to us by Genesis.

Immanence is a confused term in the Deleuzian world. What it really means is the presence of God whereby He participates in change within the world rather than standing aloof from it once having created it. "Expression" would seem to be a restatement of the process feature of immanence rather than a distinct ontology of substance, but in any event, it provides for a conceptual emphasis on process rather than substance, which is why Deleuze and Guattari adopt the term. Spinoza's point of view is that God is within all, rather than within and also transcendently outside. This is a monist conception of reality, one substance, just as Deleuze and Guattari say. And it's true that the one-substance or univocal conception of God brings into question the hierarchical value formation associated with dualist metaphysics. But this approach does not eradicate value judgments, it just re-locates their origin to social, process-derived values; a subjectively derived social metanarrative to replace objectively derived religious metanarrative. Deleuze and Guattari take a theistic analysis and apply it to an atheist-imagined theory of social change.

Transcendence in the context of talking about God's existence does not negate His immanence. These are presented as irreconcilably in conflict, but the conflict is resolvable in contemplating the nature of God, who is not limited by human paradox as we are. Spinoza was focused on the nature of God, not the nature of how things and ideas move and evolve and change within social systems. He might have gone further than he did, to develop the ideas Deleuze and Guattari later did, but to do so, he would have had to renounce God altogether, and apply a theist term (immanence) where it does not belong: to atheist social theory. Deleuze and Guattari effectively engraft a new meaning onto the word "immanence," meaning a shift of attention to change and dynamism and process, to explain social change rather than God active in the world.

The Bergsonist[2] conception of time in the Deleuze/Guattari analysis is part of this same confusion. It is quite true that all of the past, in a sense, is contained in the present moment, but only in the mind of God, for whom all of the future is also contained in the present moment. This

---

2 Henri Bergson (1859-1941).

perhaps describes God's perspective;[3] in fact, it is in this way we can begin to conceive the paradox of free will and predestination being transcended. If the Bergsonist call to think temporally rather than spatially means thinking of past, present, and future as a continuum in which all is connected, this is a good thing; it means adopting as best we can a God-perspective, whereby we see the entirety of our lives as one large project that we are in the process of creating, but creating with a goal of pleasing God, who takes back our life in His time.

Deleuze and Guattari were so thoroughly collectivist that they urged a perspective of "machines," rather than individuals, which sounds scary, but they meant something like the various sub-systems of the world that operate in conjunction, not "the Machine" of the present work, the neo-fascist collectivist ideological conglomerate of state, big tech, big media, and Wall Street. The machine referred to by Deleuze and Guattari means not just groups of people, but movements of ideas that operate politically. It is another form of shift away from an individual perspective; it is individual agency cast onto something larger and no longer human, just as identity politics is a shift from individual agency to tribe.

This process philosophy is in service to leftward movements in politics, as with all postmodern thought, and that means essential collectivism. Deleuze and Guattari called themselves Marxists even though a central theme of their philosophy was to avoid grand sweeping narratives,[4] including those presented by Freud and Marx. Their book, *Anti-Oedipus*,[5] was partially a critique of those schools of thought in favor of ideological flows and rhizomatic thinking; ways of thinking which would be subsumed into the postmodern paradigm of "liquid modernity."[6] They were Marxist in the sense that they were anti-capitalist. They were anti-capitalist because in their view, capitalism had done its work in history, "deterritorializing" in some ways, only to reterritorialize, so

---

3 This theological conception is sometimes called "Molinism," after Luis de Molina, a sixteenth-century theologian.

4 As suggested in Chapter 11 supra, concerning postmodernism generally, the term "postmodernism" is sometimes arrogated specifically to philosophies for deconstructing metanarratives, rather than to neo-Marxism, because Marxism is a metanarrative. Like so many words in the postmodern era, the word "postmodern" itself can have distinct shades of meaning. The precise concept in play should drive understanding, not a confusion of concepts traveling under the same label.

5 *Anti-Oedipus: Capitalism and Schizophrenia*. NY: Penguin, 2009 (first published in U..S. , 1977).

6 Bauman, Zygmunt, *Liquid Modernity*, Malden, MA: Polity, 2000.

the systems of capitalism must be swept away also, in favor of the pro-cess-oriented ontology of becoming.

Godlessness is necessary to this conception. The subject, the indi-vidual, is the point of perspective because of the heavens/earth dual na-ture of mankind. "Machines" don't have that God-imaged reality. The subject is properly the individual political unit and perspective. Desire, or life force, whether Schopenhauer's general will or Nietzsche's will to power, is a social force to postmodernists, not an individual one.

Deleuze and Guattari, in some places, describe what would tradi-tionally be individual freedom, but they do so in the context of ma-chines, non-individual systems. These machines are real, certainly, but individuals freely join or oppose the machines. Machines are further reducible to individuals. Machines are composed (or should be com-posed) of voluntary associations, rather than top-down imposition of social structures. The philosophy turns back on itself, here, because transcendence is the vehicle to this kind of freedom, not an obstacle to it. That is to say, social systems are indeed flowing, dynamic, rhizomatic, and have machine characteristics, if static structures are not imposed on them. But even in flows, rhizomes, and machines, there is internal struc-ture. The water all flows one way; the machine is formed to advance a particular goal, the rhizomes exist to facilitate voluntary unguided in-teraction for mutual benefit. There are ends in view, in other words, in these various free movements and interactions.

A transcendent structure with commonly held hierarchical values facilitates this, because without common referents for value, control and unfreedom arises from other directions that are even more static and hierarchical, but also tyrannical and brutal into the bargain. Examples: oppression from crime (rather than laws and law enforcement); political tyranny (rather than individual freedom and equal opportunity); priva-tion (rather than a rule of law underpinning market force provision); loneliness and isolation (rather than community achievable despite in-dividual difference).

Postmodernism can be read as a brief for open-minded thinking about how we should resist patterns of thought that bind us to free-dom-inhibiting tradition. As for that, who would disagree? Many of the concepts are perfectly valid even within a world of transcendence. They may rest on objectivity even when disavowing objectivity. Concept cre-ation is not a repudiation of objectivity, it is just a more refined form of discovery of objective truth. It is valid, for example, for Deleuze and Guattari to say that difference precedes identity, but that is just another way of saying reality (and our grasp of reality) depends on successive differentiations of this-not-that, exactly the basis of binary differentiation that forms the mountain of objective, transcendent, hierarchical recognition of values they write against.

Rethinking the process of history in terms of "machines" rather than individuals is valid, but only in the understanding of social processes, which is ultimately all the philosophy of Deleuze and Guattari is about; which is to say, it is just one note in a postmodern, deconstructionist cacophony. Understanding machines and flows is a way to move off the perspective of the subjective individual, which means it is a way to move toward collectivist change rather than individual change, which means it moves us toward structure, not away; and toward hierarchical control, not away; and to more restriction on freedom, not less. Likewise, with the "flows" and "rhizomes" of Deleuzian thinking. These are just ways of describing the interconnectedness of things. In that way, it is useful, but only for understanding the workings of the world and making us more mindful of the consequences of the various interventions we make, so they are not reflexive according to some misguided static hierarchy of social rules.

Though Deleuze and Guattari try to move away from fixed metanarratives, they just create new ones in their place, like all postmodernists. The Spinoza-derived theory of truth creation in process rather than transcendence means, literally, that truth and purpose and meaning arise from action, just like the pragmatists long held, and so the action is Sisyphus moving the rock up the hill, not pausing to reflect why. Just do it.[7] Enlightenment rational thinking is replaced by action, by Spinozan "expression." Rather than replacing Enlightenment reflection and its attendant search for meaning in the transcendent, this move is intended to create a new form of reflection. But try as they might, Deleuze and Guattari don't move us away from structural interest-protection and away from strife, but rather toward it. Not away from ideology, but toward it.

We've discussed the work of Deleuze and Guattari in particular, in advancing the notion of the mountain and the river, because they write of flows in place of hierarchy, and becoming in place of being, analogies in keeping with the river portion of our analogy. But postmodern

---

7 A slogan of the sporting goods company Nike, appropriate because Nike was the Greek goddess of victory. Victory over what? It doesn't and didn't matter. It is the concept of victory in the abstract that is celebrated. The moment by moment success of Sisyphus, straining against the rock, success without purpose.

thought more generally moves to the river, dangerously approaching an imbalance. If we comprehend Genesis correctly, we see that embrace of the river to the exclusion of the mountain is every bit as dangerous as the reverse.

CHAPTER NINETEEN

Life Force

FOR ONE DEVOTED to materialism as a totalizing worldview, the usual explanation for every motivation of human beings is their programming wrought by naturalistic evolution. "Naturalism" is, in this context, a synonym for materialism. Naturalistic evolution supposes we are more fit for survival and reproduction with a combination of traits to suit that end.

But why do we care about survival and reproduction? What drives us? Inherent libidinal forces, as argued by Marcuse and Freud? Hegelian collectivism of dialectical synthesis? Marx's materialism combined with group alienation to produce a buzz of negative angst? Schopenhauer's concept of will? Schiller's aesthetics? Bergson's *élan vital*? Nietzsche's will to power? This is a non-exclusive list of theories devised over the last couple of hundred years to explain it without God. But none of them are adequate.

These notions have developed post-Enlightenment precisely because the question only comes up once God's love is removed as the explanation. They are all efforts to add back the active ingredient, so to speak, once the life on which it acts is denatured. Trying to make bread with no yeast, and casting about for a substitute. What breathes fire into us as human beings? And what breathes fire into the equations, the mathematical and scientific descriptors of our physical universe? They're the same question, really. In a Godless reality, the motivation for human beings is a complete mystery, and it turns out the same is true for material things other than human beings. For non-living stuff, the issue is not "motivation," exactly, but certainly it's the impetus or driver for movement, causation, and the very existence of things.

In the postmodern era, the problem persists, but instead of reverting to the Greeks (who, after all, presupposed some sort of transcendence[1]), postmodernists bootstrap a squished-down transcendence through process philosophy. Emmanuel Levinas does this, for example, by finding a buzz of mutual consciousness arising from alterity—the otherness of individuals and society itself.[2] Giles Deleuze and Felix Guattari attempt this as neo-Spinozans, imagining an alternative to transcendence and immanence in social "expression."[3] Zygmunt Bauman imagines a "liquid modernity," the mountain pulled down in favor of the river.[4] Jean Baudrillard posits a social hyperreality.[5] And all base the locus of their theory on society rather than the individual.

Social consciousness is real enough, but ultimately, it bottoms out in the same way physical reality does. Philosophical pragmatists like Richard Rorty and John Dewey, and deconstructionists like Jacques Derrida and Michel Foucault, elevate leftist social activism to life purpose. But what's below that? Only the Marxist buzz of negation, not really an explanation of anything. They all start with a conclusion and work their way backward until they're standing at the edge of a cliff with only cold depthless eternity behind them. It's all conceptually ungrounded, ultimately, just like our understanding of physical reality is ungrounded because our mathematical and scientific efforts describe but do not explain it.

Postmodernism has been and remains an effort at self-creation, once God is removed from the imagination as Author of meaning and Sustainer of mankind. One could say that all postmodern thought is an effort to find meaning and a reason to strive, once God as Source of meaning is extracted, in the imagination. "Meaning" is used here in its most general sense, as when we question the meaning of life, and what it means to be human, and why we are here. Is there a purpose to our existence, or are we flotsam generated in a sidestream of blind, purposeless matter in motion?

---

1 "Transcendence" as used here means a sense of presence or purpose or mindfulness outside the physical order of things. It could be God, perhaps the aloof but necessary God of Aristotle, but it could be the pagan pantheon or a vague sense that there is some sentience Beyond, necessary to an adequate explanation of our reality.

2 *Alterity and Transcendence*, New York: Columbia University Press, 1999.

3 Supra, Chapter 18.

4 *Liquid Modernity*, Malden, MA: Polity, 2000.

5 *Simulacra and Simulation*, Ann Arbor, MI: University of Michigan Press, 1994 (first published in French 1981).

This general sense of "meaning" includes the question of what drives us. Why do we do anything we do? In an everyday sense, this is easy enough. We get out of bed every day and go to work so we can get paid so we can buy food. But there's more to human motivation than that. Animal hunger drives us, but so do instinctual impulses like sex, prestige, acceptance, compassion, and love. And yet, these too are merely descriptions of different strands of human motivation. The larger question is motivation itself. Why do we strive to do anything?

It's possible to glimpse the driving force disconnected from quotidian impulses. Why would an older person plant a fruit tree if he will likely not live to see it bear fruit? Why do we want a better world for our children? Why is it that the moment we achieve some goal in life, we immediately formulate the next one, before the glow of our last success has even worn off? Why are we never entirely satisfied with what we have and what we do and how we impact others? Why am I writing this, and why are you reading it? Something more than animal impulse impels us.

In the Genesis worldview, God is identified as the Source of this striving. There's little left to be said. We are the way we are because God made us this way. Mankind was made to work in the garden and commune with his Maker. Misuse of God-given moral agency did not eliminate that central motivation, but re-oriented its expression, sometimes in ways necessitating recalibration altogether, as with the Flood. We are warned about ongoing distortions of proper motivation, for example, in the stories of Cain and Abel and the Tower of Babel. But generally, we are not in a quandary about the ultimate source of human life force. Being made in the image of God, we carry an agentic impulse toward full human flourishing. All of our striving is a desire to return to the garden; to resolve that first alienation and return to ongoing communion with God.

This is how we can understand Jesus to fit into the grand plan. In Him, we find spiritual rest, though life in the body may be difficult. Marx and the neo-Marxist postmodernists are right to focus on alienation. They just misapprehend its source. Its source is disruption in our communion with God.

As early as the nineteenth century, thinkers were aware of, and remarked upon, the increasingly prevalent waning of religious belief. Many of those able to see above the news of the day to longer civilizational trends developed a vague and tentative awareness that removal of a personal God, or even "God" as objective embodiment of a hierarchy of value, would be deleterious in ways not yet clear. Once God was conceptually removed, a conundrum emerged. If God is not the source of mankind's life force, what is? In a materialist paradigm, in which people evolve in all their complexity through the purposeless process of material, life force remains unexplained. It is not enough to say that people desire to live and to reproduce. The question is, why?

One or the other of these is true about human conduct: agency or determinism. Either we make choices, such as the choice to live and strive and love and have children, or there is no choice, and even our sense of choosing is predetermined falsity, in a universe that unfolds as it does because it was always going to unfold that way. If all is predetermined, we can fold our hand, leave the chips on the table, and go home, because what is the point of striving?[6]

If we have actual instead of merely apparent agency, however, is there some reason for it, and are we in some way accountable for how we exercise it? We certainly act as though we have agency, in our good choices and bad. The exercises of agency occur on a time-line, in a complex pattern according to goals we construct. We are in a process of life-construction whether we spend our days smoking dope with our buddies, or our years studying medicine to render help to our neighbors. The question here, though, is not how we construct our lives. The question is why we engage in any construction process at all.

This is the question of life force, and some thinkers began to wrestle with it in a world they imagined to be Godless. Henri Bergson (1859-1941) straightforwardly attributed it to a mysterious *élan vital*. This is merely descriptive, however, not explanatory. It served as a placeholder, a necessary puzzle piece in larger attempts to explain a Godless reality. The concept of *élan vital* was eventually mostly dismissed or ignored. Gilles Deleuze and Felix Guattari resuscitated it for their purposes but without adequately explaining its source. Bergsonism explicitly rejects a natural law of moral universals, substituting in its place a proposed reality of creative evolution residing in the intuition. It springs from an effort to explain life force without God, but also leftist negation of ratio-

---

6   But, but, but: predestination! There is undoubtedly a paradox between our conceptions of free will (or agency), on the one hand, and the theological principle that "those whom He foreknew He also predestined to be conformed to the image of His son" (Romans 8:29). Paradox is not the same as contradiction, however. This, among other paradoxes in theology, is not resolvable with facile one-liners. There is evidently some interactivity inside the mind of God and that of people who seek after Him. We can say physical determinism is distinct from spiritual predestination. Beyond that, and resisting temptations to deviate from the purpose of this book, we leave this question to another day.

nal, hierarchical value formation supporting social structures thought to protect power interests: the essence of postmodernism more generally.

Sigmund Freud (1856-1939) found life force in the libido. The sex drive is of foundational significance to human beings even in the Genesis worldview, but it is there constrained through sublimation into a higher ideal of love, hence the first man's literal and figurative embrace of the first woman endowed with human agency as "bone of my bones and flesh of my flesh." Freud believed sexual tensions to be foundational to human personality and to human striving.

Herbert Marcuse followed Freud in constructing his theories of social repression and liberation. Marcuse acknowledged the process of sublimation, but expanded it to the entirety of mankind's structure of adherence to cultural norms like work and chastity and monogamy. He advocated release of the libidinal forces in the formation of a new kind of person more fully actualized than his repressed forbears, and society, likewise, emancipated. What he got, of course, was the '60's sexual revolution, moral lawlessness, sterile relationships, and more, not less, personal alienation.

Aesthetics are sometimes expressive of the dynamism of a life force, if not the force itself, in the philosophies of thinkers like Friedrich Schiller (1759-1805), Marcuse, Theodor Adorno (1903-1969), Deleuze, and somewhat surprisingly given the pragmatism he is most known for, John Dewey (1859-1952). The tension between sensual and rational, or between rational and intuitive, is said to create the life force. Not that we live for beauty, necessarily, but that beauty has some effect on us equivalent to the transcendent sense in religion, suggesting something higher, better, and aspirational, but just out of reach, and so the life force consists in that ever-reaching.

For Arthur Schopenhauer, aesthetic appreciation could constitute a kind of still moment as a respite to the imperative of the general will tugging us along a bumpy road of survival. Friedrich Nietzsche built on Schopenhauer's general will to develop his will to power, a more targeted vision of what the life force in people really means. Nietzsche is often cited as a pivotal thinker on the shift away from God. He famously wrote "God is dead," not so much to express his personal conviction, but to remark upon the implications. This is what he actually wrote:

> God is dead. God remains dead. And we have killed him. How shall we comfort ourselves, the murderers of all murderers? What was holiest and mightiest of all that the world has yet owned has bled to death un-

der our knives: who will wipe this blood off us? What water is there for us to clean ourselves? What festivals of atonement, what sacred games shall we have to invent? Is not the greatness of this deed too great for us? Must we ourselves not become gods simply to appear worthy of it?[7]

Nietzsche was intensely aware, therefore, of the implications for our understanding of reality, once we unimagine God. Much is left unexplained, including, but not limited to, the life force. Following but expanding upon Schopenhauer's idea of a noumenal generalized will, Nietzsche posited the will-to-power to describe the urge impelling people forward, but again the idea is descriptive rather than explanatory. Atheist existentialists, through the mid-twentieth century, generally followed Nietzsche on this point, tacitly or explicitly, and a necessary life-force of some kind is presupposed but not explained in the subjectivist existentialism subsumed into postmodern thought.

Some thinkers return to the problem rather than ignore it, however. Peter Sloterdijk (b. 1947), a contemporary German philosopher, addressed it from a Nietzschean perspective, in *You Must Change Your Life*.[8] To engage a positive life of "Practising," Sloterdijk repeatedly refers to "vertical tension" originating in ontological dualism.[9] Without this vertical tension, values collapse. The vertical tension is symbolized in the torso of Apollo, and derives from this mode of hierarchical value formation. Not through the work of a putative God, however: "Being itself is understood as having more power to speak and transmit, and more potent authority, than God, the ruling idol of religions."[10] The noteworthy point for our purposes is Sloterdijk's recognition of the need for a replacement source of vertical tension, the impelling life force toward positive "Practising" if we have killed God. The torso speaks to us precisely because the ground of all being is beyond ourselves.

We are considering how one explains life force or generalized human motivation in the absence of God. Libido, will-to-power, aesthetics, vertical tension from Being itself. Another is suggested here, and it is further suggested that this explanation surpasses all of the foregoing in the generality of its application, in its tacit ubiquity. A word for it is "collectivism," but another is "socialism." Though left undefined, "socialism" carries baggage; it is employed here because it better juxtaposes

7 Nietzsche, Friedrich, *The Gay Science*, sec. 125 (1882).
8 Cambridge, UK: Polity, 2013 (published originally in German, 2009).
9 Ibid., pp. 11-13.
10 Ibid., p. 22.

individualism.

Individualism, as opposed to socialism, is a matter of perspective. Suppose you set out to paint a landscape. Anyone later looking at it will assume the perspective you create for them. If they're mountains, are you in the valley looking up at them looming over you? Or are you a thousand feet above them, seeing them as a repeating pattern of peak and vale marching off into the hazy distance? Similarly, when assessing a conceptual mystery like life force, do we see it as a personal and individual phenomenon, looming large in subjective consciousness, or as a social one, in which we are but one lesser node in a larger expression? We are social creatures, after all, not merely in the sense that we form associations with others, but in the more fundamental element of intersubjective consciousness. One could look at the phenomenon of life force individually: "my" life force; or socially: our species' life force.

Socialism, the word, is often associated with Marx and his dialectical materialism. History has not unfolded as Marx predicted, and the underlying principles have been reapplied in numerous settings around the globe, all with disastrous results. Economic socialism is tried again and again in part because it ought to work, on the presuppositions those on the left hold concerning human nature. But it's also revisited because it appeals to negative instincts of resentment, for those who deem themselves downtrodden, and to the power hunger of elites, for whom it is a useful framework for domination and control.

Apart from these political realities, however, there is an instinctual element to the leftward lean into socialism. "Instinctual" in its most literal sense, because Enlightenment rationalism is rejected in postmodern thought, in favor of an inner groping for satisfaction of emotionally felt needs. We might say the mountain gives way to the river. The spirit of God gives way to the waters over which He hovers. Entropic return to matterless form and formless matter. Retreat from the heavens to the firm footing of earth. Ethereal idealism to tangible earthy urgings. Immanence replacing transcendence. This is not just a movement toward the resting, unconstrained, creative, unconscious primal id. It is a movement also away from hard-edged objective principle that constrains and represses. Marcuse expresses this desired movement in his way; Deleuze and Guattari in theirs. Importantly, it is not merely a shift in emphasis among propositions weighed by rationally thinking people. It involves unearthing buried psychic material to form a new kind of person, much as the Bolsheviks sought to usher in Soviet Man as a new creation.

In this way, people don't just wake up one day and decide, propositionally, that socialism in economics and culture and politics is the way to peace and plenty and happiness. The idea is to provide conditions for change in people; to promote change from the outside in. Those conditions include identification with the collective, and the collective is to be ever-expanded as the "other-ing" of people groups is overcome and discarded as a relic of caveman tribalism.

In a world that dismisses God as yesterday's fictional avatar for hierarchical power interests, how is one to find personal meaning in life? In the individualistic world without God, the lightness of being becomes unbearable, and a socialistic world becomes more attractive. The thought is that my life might be meaningless, but the collective life of humanity is not, and it rolls forward on a meaningful Hegelian movement of becoming, toward humanity's perfection, at least insofar as the project is not interfered with by retrograde fear-driven traditionalists, with their insistence on selective salvation and a God who divides and differentiates and judges. The movement of history seems to be meaningful, and so participation in that movement is meaningful. To some, a Rousseauan "general will" seems to both explain and provide meaning to life, better than a merely descriptive individual "will to power" or *élan vital*, and certainly better than a God glowering at me from just beyond the veil.

CHAPTER TWENTY

Individualism and Socialism

A CRUCIAL DIFFERENCE in perspective divides postmodernism from the Genesis worldview. The socialist perspective on the one hand and the individualist on the other. We can make sense of this difference if we begin with careful definitions, and then grasp how the free/unfree distinction is related.

First "socialism." The word conjures the traditional Marxist vision of a way station on the road from capitalism to communism, in which the means of production are collectively owned and centrally managed by the state. Understood this way, one might recognize as socialist the move in Western liberal democracies increasingly toward centralized planning in which the government takes responsibility for the economy, centrally controlled banks manipulate the media of exchange, and public/private partnerships blur the line between public coercive extractive transactions, on the one hand, and private voluntary mutually beneficial commercial transactions, on the other.

This traditional understanding of "socialism" has to do with the movement of material goods and services. Marx was concerned primarily with material conditions of the proletariat vis-à-vis the bourgeois. He thought the evolution to communism would occur through dialectical materialism. In Hegelian thought, on which Marx relied, the thesis/antithesis/synthesis was formed in social resolution, interpreted and expressed through society's elites, Druidic determiners of synthesis through gnostic discernment. This was an early form of philosophical pragmatism in which the direction was established by the culturally powerful; the synthesis formed accordingly, and then the next synthesis and the next so that society moves forward like a river with its roil and direction formed from social process but necessarily guided by a higher plane of understanding among intellectual elites.

"Socialism" must have broader meaning than it does in traditional Marxist dogma, however, if we are to understand the postmodern outlook in contrast to that of Genesis reality. Though postmodern thought incorporates Marxist ideas, its socialist outlook runs deeper than old-school dialectical materialism. It relates to a perspective; a disposition; one might almost say an instinct that is counter to the individualist conception of self and freedom. This deeper meaning of socialism is employed here, because it dovetails with an opposing "individualism" that is similarly unbound by formulaic political dogma, relating also to a perspective or disposition or instinct. Thus, we can meaningfully contrast these two inner dispositions. To be clear, these are the meanings of "socialism" and "individualism" in the discussion which follows.

Genesis is not a textbook on individualism. Nor is the Bible in its entirety, for that matter. There are instances in which the perspective is "we," as with God's choosing the Hebrews as His. But the irreducible self as locus of moral agency is implicit in the whole unfolding story. We have individual responsibility before God for our acts and omissions. We are told to look up to God for values and understanding, not to the side at our fellow men and women. We are individually responsible for what we do.

The story of Cain and Abel is sometimes cited for a kind of socialist outlook, in that Cain queried God: "Am I my brother's keeper?" The answer is "yes," we're to look out for one another. But this story isn't about implementing a socialist perspective. Cain was individually guilty in the first place, and individually suffered being cast out, mirroring the casting out of his parents from the garden. The story is about unfounded resentment on the part of Cain (among other things), not socialism.

Even the Flood story contrasts Noah's obedience and salvation to the destruction of the rest of mankind. It reinforces the proclivity of mankind to sin, resulting from the broken relationship with God. If there is a socialism in the Bible, it is in the "we" who are not God and so depart from His guidance and so miss the mark in rightly orienting our lives. That's the universality of mankind's sinful nature, however, not the socialism of a shared "we" perspective in all things.

If we think of Christianity as merely a philosophical movement (rather than the salvific delivery available to mankind), we would have to see it as a delivery system for certain Jewish ideals into the wider world. Among them, equality. Individualism is necessary to the very concept of equality. If the locus of our moral imagination is all of mankind in the abstract, there is nothing to equalize. Acquiring a conviction of equal moral worth is necessary precisely because our moral outlook is individualistic, and so also our sense of agency apart from moral considerations.

Too often, "equality" is thrown out in social discourse, as if everyone were already on board with what that word means. The problem with "equality," the word, is that it is not incisive enough by itself to get at what is really meant when people march in the streets or make law or scream it at each other. The conceptual problem is this. When you hear "equality," ask: equality of what? Citing Amartya Sen's analysis, James Otteson puts it this way:

> Do we mean equality of opportunity? Equality before the law? Equality of individual liberty? Equality of material resources? Equality of condition? Equality of welfare? Equality of capability? As Sen shows, championing any one of them will entail, in at least some ways, sacrificing others. We cannot have equality of material resources, for example, without sacrificing at least some equality before the law—some will have to have their resources taken from them so that it can be given to others, which means the law will have to treat different people differently, granting legal rights to some that it denies to others. Similarly, equality of resources will conflict with equality of welfare, because some people require more resources—perhaps they are disabled, for example—to enable them to enjoy the same welfare as others who require less resources. Equality of capability will run afoul of equality of resources because some will require greater education, training, or other assistance in order to fulfill their capabilities than will other people.[1]

People differ innately in intelligence, agreeableness, talents, and innumerable other variables; and extrinsically in status, wealth, and intangible resources like strong families, education, and industriousness. Equality cannot mean attempting to level individual differences so that we are the same, or are compensated for the ways in which we are different, as if I could trade some of my industriousness for your intelligence so we come out the same on some imagined common medium of ex-

---

1   James R. Otteson, *Seven Deadly Economic Sins: Obstacles to Prosperity and Happiness Every Citizen Should Know*, Cambridge: Cambridge University Press, 2021, pp. 94-95; Sen, Amartya, *Inequality Reexamined*, Cambridge, MA: Harvard University Press, 1995.

change. Equality must mean equal moral standing, responsibility, and dignity. Not sameness.

Illustration. You're walking down a city street and you take a short-cut through an alley. Along the way, you're assailed by a person wielding a baseball bat. In recovery, you think about this episode. Are you angry at the assailant? Is he morally and legally responsible? The assailant was arguably merely an instrumentality, just like the bat. The bat was wield-ed by the assailant, but the assailant was "wielded" by the combination of influences on him that brought him to this pass. Maybe he's in mate-rial poverty. Maybe his material need is heightened by a need for drugs, which is, in turn, generated by a sense of alienation, in turn the result of an uncaring society corrupted by bad old capitalism or something. A so-cialist outlook might take you to this kind of passivity in the face of evil. We're all in it together, you might think, and perhaps the fault lies with corrupting evil in society at large rather than the person with the bat. A socialist outlook might likewise take the assailant to passivity in the face of his own moral responsibility, a condition enabling him to strike out in contrived Cain-like resentment, returning real evil for imagined evil.

There are two irreconcilable ways of thinking. The individualist way ascribes moral responsibility to the attacker, because he is a human be-ing choosing evil. The socialist way lets the assailant off the hook, but also imagines him with diminished moral agency. He's just one element in a chain of causation, not a moral agent with equal dignity and worth and responsibility to other moral agents like you. On this thinking, all of our time-bound experience is merely a series of innumerable interlock-ing chains of material causation, unfolding in an automated way among people, things, and ideas. It's you who mentally let him off the hook, in this scenario, but that's not an act of moral agency on your part, either; you just recognize the inevitability of physical and conceptual cause and effect. You were in the wrong place at the wrong time, by happenstance, the same as if you happened to be standing on the wrong beach when the tsunami came in. It just happens, it's no one's fault. And this is the way of the world, in this paradigm—the way of materialist determin-ism. If you have a "good" heart, you might advocate for social reform to ameliorate the material conditions of people including those who might take up bats against their neighbors, but why? What makes your heart "good?" Why feel an uplift in what you call the "soul," or desire moral approbation from society? Good and evil are not transcended, in this worldview. They're both eliminated, such that the "why is there evil" question is rendered meaningless.

This might seem like an extreme example, but is it really? Either we have moral agency, like Genesis teaches, or we don't. An on/off switch, not a dimmer switch. We don't have moral agency on a spectrum. If it presented on a spectrum, that would mean some have more than others—the very essence of inequality, of differentials in moral worth among individuals, re-paganizing us in stratified conceptions of human worth.

Individualism and socialism are often debated in terms of freedom. To those who hold a Genesis worldview, it seems self-evident that the exercise of agency, including, but not limited to, that form of agency we call "moral agency," is an exercise of freedom. In modern times, debates between left and right have often devolved to whether certain activity is the product of individual agentic choice, or is irreducibly social. This is most readily apparent with economic activity, as to whether an instance of it should be public or private. There is no reason the purchase of clothing, say, should be public. But reasons are readily apparent for the raising of an army.

It's puzzling how "freedom" could ever be associated with socialism. But it often is, in postmodern thinking, so we should set about understanding it. We'll find that freedom in the individualist conception means independence; in the socialist conception, interdependence. In the individualist conception, the minimizing of social constraint is in deference to universally held moral values; in the socialist conception, social constraint serves the end of re-making the individual. To understand these differences in our conception of freedom, it's best to take a step back in history and then return to the postmodern era. We also need to remind ourselves that what makes the postmodern era the postmodern era is rejection of God.

The history of ideas flows continuously. It is not demarked by one-off events like the conversion of Constantine or the voyage of Columbus or the trial of Galileo or the storming of the Bastille. Ideas move and reshape and spread and constrict over time. Some are submerged, never to reappear; some take hold and dominate for centuries. Some, like the realities revealed in the Advent and Resurrection, have permanent effect. Because ideas are fluid, we naturally express them with handles, like events that exemplify them, or thinkers associated with them, but we should keep in mind that these are just markers. People expressing a line of thought, or events manifesting their hold on people in a given time, help us comprehend larger movements of ideas. The Reformation did not begin with Martin Luther's act in 1517 by itself, for example, but was in ferment long beforehand, among others besides Luther, and afterward, it unfolded in ways unexpected by Luther. And yet, we look to that date or to the name Luther to give definition to the Reformation and its historical impact.

In the West, genuine Christianity was pervasively influential through the medieval and Renaissance and Reformation periods. The beginning of modernity is often pegged to about 1600, not because of a particular event, but because of Reformation-induced loosening of religious authority combined with bold advances in scientific inquiry of natural processes, as with Francis Bacon and Isaac Newton. René Descartes (1596-1650) significantly contributed to the individualist perspective in knowing and to questioning metaphysical assumptions through reason.

Thomas Hobbes (1588-1679) wrote early in the modern period. His contributions to political philosophy were important for how they affected our conception of freedom. He leaned to a materialist and mechanistic understanding of human beings. In *Leviathan* (1651), he argued for a strong central authority to answer the uncertainties and discord of war and civil conflict. It was necessary, he thought, because the alternative "state of nature" involved "continual fear, and danger of violent death; and the life of man, solitary, poor, nasty, brutish, and short."

Hobbes is sometimes considered a proto-fascist. Though he espoused a social contract theory, his conception of the parties to that contract were, on the one hand, individuals competing for self-preservation and, as a result, brutish to their neighbors, and on the other hand, a despotic sovereign strong enough to preserve peace among them. The individualism Hobbes was concerned with meant an insistence on the consent of the governed, hence contract theory, but the danger of predation by fellow citizens would drive the consent. Hobbes' vision adumbrates postmodern totalitarianism because he imagined people asking for their own domination so as to be protected from all-against-all conflict, to survive in a hostile world. It involved a power orientation in our thinking about terms of social interaction rather than an orientation of love or even mutual respect.

A look back almost 500 years ago to Hobbes is also a look forward to the near future in postmodern Western liberal societies. The absence of a cohering faith in objective principle means subjectivism in all things. We fail to see ourselves in others and so render ourselves unable to love one another. We splinter into as many truths and moralities as there are people, and so power is the only organizing principle. Into this environment, security seems to require despotic control. Habitual deference to lingering outdated principles like equality causes us to observe the forms of democracy, but social narratives develop to support metanarratives of ideology in place of unchanging objective principles. The narrative reinforces power concentration, not only in government but in certain commercial power centers like media and tech commerce and big business, and these become mutually reinforcing as the Machine exercises control over our lives. We come to expect, and get, social control by narrative.

We should hold in mind that Hobbes' early advocacy of strong power reposed in the state was meant to protect weak individuals. It will resurface in the thinking of fascists, called by that name, in the early twentieth century, and this will be directly relevant to postmodern conceptions of freedom.

Social contract theory for power negotiation between individuals and state remained an important idea after Hobbes. With John Locke (1632-1704), it had a more generous cast. Locke advocated religious toleration, but his vision of liberality vis-à-vis the state required a commonality of ethical principle, which religion in that age could still provide. Locke's political theory was profoundly influential, including with respect to the formation of the United States.

By the late 1700s, religious skepticism could be openly expressed, and was so by many, though Catholic or Protestant orthodoxy was still dominant. Political ideas to be included in American founding documents were in popular circulation and were heavily influenced by Jean-Jacques Rousseau (1712-1778). Those ideas quite explicitly prize individualism. Rousseau himself pivoted away from individualism, however. He explicitly made a jump not undertaken even by more overt religious skeptics of his time, in considering mankind to be essentially good except as corrupted by society, contrary to the Genesis principle that mankind is inclined to sin. If we carry an innate inclination to sin, as Christianity holds, then individual attention to higher God-ordained principle is the right prescription for dealing with it. If mankind is basically good except as corrupted by society, however, then the source of evil is social, and to deal with it one must assume a socialist perspective.

Indeed the Rousseauan vision extrapolated to today may lead one to conclude the only cure for individual evil is dissolution of self into the sea of humanity, taking on an "oceanic feeling" of thorough-going "we" perspective; the striving for social rather than individual consciousness, to coincide with political socialism of wealth redistribution by a self-appointed elite. With no longer even a pretense of God-imbued individual dignity, perhaps "we" are better off if there are simply fewer of us, an attitude manifested in abortion activism, euthanasia, and anti-natalism in its various forms.

Rousseau developed a notion of the "general will" for society and wrote that if individuals resist this general will, they should be "forced to be free."[2] Because the state, in his vision, would secure the general will, the individual would be freed from private claims upon him. This idea seems paradoxical if we equate individualism with freedom. But as we will see, Rousseau's incipient pairing of socialism with freedom will recur in postmodern thinking.

Rousseau's social perspective was a natural result of social contract theory for government, which he emphasized, as had Hobbes and Locke before him. Social contract theory is equated to freedom, of sorts, because voters have a say in who governs them. But they don't really have a say in the scope of that government, other than to choose one lordly overseer instead of another. That's not the same kind of freedom as personal autonomy, freedom to succeed or fail without government or social interference. The vote does not free the individual from the dictates over him that his fellow citizens vote in.

The movement toward democracy that social contract theory supports is freedom only in the social sense that Rousseau had in mind. Democracy, unqualified by protection of individual pre-political rights, only shifts power from the sovereign to the collective, as opposed to the individual. For there to be individual freedom, the power of the collective would also have to be limited, and that's what the American founding documents undertook. Without that limitation, individuals do not have freedom because they are subject to the collective will, enforceable through the power of the state.

Rousseau is often cited for his view that mankind is basically good. Of course, people in all ages have tried to come to grips with the fact of both evil and good in human nature; it's not as though Rousseau, in the eighteenth century, suddenly switched the presumption for all of us, from evil to good. But the question whether people are "basically" evil or good was back in play, we might say, in Rousseau's time. That thinking strongly influenced the Romanticism of the ensuing nineteenth century, and, of course, the Marxist and more generally postmodern reversal in which people are believed good except as social power structures corrupt them.

2   Rousseau, Jean-Jacques, *On the Social Contract*, translated by G.D.H. Cole. Mineola, NY: 2003 (first published 1762).

If we believe everyone is basically good, where does that leave us when confronted with the Genesis reality that we defy God and do evil? It means what we observe falls short of what we expect, exactly the definition of frustration. So much of life then presents as disappointment and literal disillusionment. In the postmodern era, our tendency is to expect good and be beaten down by evil rather than expecting evil and being delighted by good. It's no wonder that the prevailing attitude in the current age is one of suspicion, cynicism, and despair.

A socialist perspective was the result of the thinking of Hegel, as discussed in Chapter 12. His *geist* was a spirit of the age which evolves teleologically through time as the result of repeating dialectics of thesis, antithesis, and synthesis. This central idea in his philosophy does not proceed from the psychological, subjective inner being, as did that of Descartes and Emmanuel Kant (1724-1804), and as would that of Søren Kierkegaard (1813-1855) and (inconsistently) the later existentialists. Hegel's ideas proceeded from a top-down way of thinking about society. It was necessarily socialist in perspective.

Following Hegel, Marx was concerned, from a socialist perspective, with the movement of ideas in history. His "socialism" would be a historical stage following the individualist power negotiation with the state. It would take some time for Marxist ideas to set the world aflame, but they did so at the outset of the postmodern period, around the turn of the twentieth century. They include the paradoxical notion that socialism means freedom. Marxism would be the theoretical basis for hard-left ideology well into the twentieth century, gaining momentum in the Soviet Union, China, and many other places.

Marxism gained adherents among Western democracies deemed "liberal" in the sense that people were liberated from despotic sovereigns by social contract participation in government, respecting a specified range of individual rights exempt from government control. The totalitarian impulse in Marxism was not well recognized for the first half of the twentieth century but became so with revelations of Stalinist brutality and then post-war evils in China and many other places. The totalitarianism of fascism was impossible to overlook, given the bellicose eruptions in Spain, Italy, Germany, and Japan. The resulting worldwide conflagration of 1939-45 combined with communist and "national socialist" genocides made the twentieth century the bloodiest century in history, by any measure. It was a war of liberal vs. illiberal; individualist vs. socialist. Liberal democracies, on the one hand, and illiberal fascism and socialism, on the other.

In retrospect, the ideologies of communism and fascism seem more alike than different. Both involve subjugation of the individual to the collective. Both regard human beings from a social rather than individual perspective; both associate that socialism with freedom; and both theorize individual freedom in state strength. How could that be, if more power in the state necessarily means less power in the individual? The answer on both the hard left and the hard right is to remake the individual, and redefine freedom.

To track this redefinition, let's first understand the traditional meaning of "individual" and "freedom," the definitions employed in the liberalism that so animated political developments in the late 1700s in the West. An individual is the inviolable self, the irreducible locus of conscious awareness and subjective experience. In various ways, we interact with other individuals and with society, but the me/you and me/they barrier is never breached. An individualist would take freedom to mean that self is independent and unconstrained.

No one wants external constraint on their own freedom. But the intersubjective element of human consciousness means we live in societies, so that means interdependence in personal relations and commerce, which in turn means law and social norms to limit trespasses of various kinds among neighbors. We desire self-governance on the part of others in society because in its absence, chaos and brutality reign—another kind of external constraint. Absence of self-restraint across society makes individuals less free, just as Hobbes imagined: an ungoverned brutish mankind in a state of nature. Maximum individual freedom would, therefore, come from minimal external constraint combined with a high degree of individual self-control across society. That maximum state of individual freedom degrades with greater external constraints, in the forms of excessive government control, unnecessarily conformity-demanding social norms, and lawlessness among our neighbors.

Dependence is a kind of constraint. We have a high degree of dependence on society around us, to get what we think we need to live. This is so partially because the range of goods and services we consider essential to life is quite broad in the prosperous West. But it's also because the degree of specialization and automation attenuates us significantly from the ability to produce what we need on our own. Our hunter-gatherer days are long behind us. Even growing food in variety is beyond the knowledge of most of us. Consequently, in this commercially specialized age, we tend to measure independence in dollars rather than real wealth, but even if we're rich in dollars, we're dependent on a society supporting dollars as a reliable medium of exchange. Dependence and external constraints are encroachments on individual autonomy and, therefore, on freedom. Actual personal freedom is never absolute. Freedom is limited in every society; it is always a matter of degree. And yet, it remains a fundamental aspiration of human beings, even as we unconsciously fritter it away, one marginally insignificant socialist advance at a time.

In the postmodern era, commencing around the turn of the twentieth century, the drift from objectivity to subjectivism in truth-formation was related to the socialist tendency to think of humanity from a top-down perspective, because truth was thought to be formed in pragmatism toward social goals.[3] The individual rights-securing function of government in the American founding documents became ever more ignored or re-interpreted. Instead of thinking about what makes me individually more free, I am more likely to think what makes "us" more free. Society was increasingly seen as the source of such individual expression as a person might have rather than an impediment to it. This is group identity. The socialist perspective means we're more likely to see individuals, including oneself, as instantiations of the body social which forms the context for the individual rather than seeing society as a collection of individuals.

The latter perspective was meant by Margaret Thatcher when she remarked in 1987:

> There is no such thing as society. There is a living tapestry of men and women and people and the beauty of that tapestry and the quality of our lives will depend upon how much each of us is prepared to take responsibility for ourselves and each of us prepared to turn round and help by our own efforts those who are unfortunate.[4]

This was a rare cry for return to reality, an island of sanity in a sea of Durkheimian sociology. Emile Durkheim (1858-1917) was an influential sociologist who argued for the reality of "social facts," recognition that an individual reacts to matters of public movements or opinions in the same way he reacts to other features of physical reality. An em-

---

3 *Dangerous God*, Chapters 11-14; see also the necessarily socialist approach as reflected in the philosophies of John Dewey (1859-1952) followed by Richard Rorty (1931-2007).

4 Interview with *Woman's Own* magazine, September 1987.

brace of Durkheimian "social facts" means embrace of a metanarrative socially generated, not just a shift to a socialist outlook in contrast to the individualist. It is more significant than a general mood in favor of socialism and rejecting individualism.

The shift to the postmodern age has a religious character. Durkheim, and later others, articulated what amounts to a project of deification of society itself. The sustained project of removing the divine from the imagination has resulted in a secularism that doesn't just exclude God but replaces Him with society itself, now conceived as something mindful and distinct from the teeming individuals who comprise it. It is not the same as the paganism of ages past, or the casual atheism of a post-Christian society still under Christian influence. The social deity replacement has become doctrinal itself. In Roberto Calasso's words, it is:

[A] way of thought that adheres to its own principles no less than the religions that have gone before it. And places its faith no longer in transcendent beings but in a body described as humanity.[5]

---

5 Calasso, Roberto. *The Unnamable Present*, NY: Farrar, Strauss and Giroux, 2017.

CHAPTER TWENTY-ONE

Pragmatism

SOCIALISM BOTH ENGENDERS and is the result of philosophical pragmatism. Each depends on the other and on repudiation of transcendence.

Philosophical pragmatism means ends justify means. Marx was an early promoter of pragmatist thinking, though in his time, it was not labeled "pragmatism" nor regarded as an independent school of philosophical thought. In 1845, he wrote a set of theses, concise thoughts on how he would build upon the work of Ludwig Feuerbach, especially Feuerbach's criticism of religion in *The Essence of Christianity* (1841). Consistent with Marx's other writings, his "theses" outline a pragmatist approach to philosophy:

> The question whether objective truth can be attributed to human thinking is not a question of theory but is a practical question. Man must prove the truth, i.e., the reality and power, the this-sidedness of his thinking, in practice . . . [Thesis 2].

> Philosophers have hitherto only interpreted the world in various ways; the point is to change it. [Thesis 11]

"The point is to change it?" What point? Whose point? Change the world to what? What Marx does here (as in all of his writings) is subordinate his utopian goal to the process by which he would achieve it. Truth is formed in action. Our thought processes are to conform to our political goals, rather than allowing our political goals to be formed according to rational thought processes based on objectivity of truth.

For this reason, Marx and later permutations of Marxism emphasized "praxis," the combination of truth and practice, because static theory alone is the domain of philosophies of being, which Marx's (and pragmatists') philosophies of becoming were supposed to replace.

Although Marxism is quintessentially pragmatist, the label "pragmatism" and the concept that truth might be formed in action was developed more fully later, around the turn of the twentieth century, by Americans John Dewey, Charles Peirce, and William James. Although these three are thought of as the founders of pragmatism, and pragmatism itself as an American innovation, it has these deep antecedents in Marxist thought though early pragmatists did not necessarily consider themselves Marxists. Pragmatism (along with existentialism and atheism) is a pillar of postmodernism.

Richard Rorty,[1] a more recent philosophical heir of John Dewey, was an articulate advocate of the idea that democracy is a collective; that the collective has a utopian communitarian goal; and that leftist revulsion against alterity in every form is the only proper reason for democratic participation. Like Dewey, Rorty believed human beings should regulate their actions and beliefs by the need to cooperate with others rather than to stand in right relation to a non-human authority, like religion or the putative God it celebrates.

Beliefs, pragmatists like Rorty hold, are habits of action rather than attempts to correspond to reality, and therefore are to be "justified," and justified to the rest of society, not God, because it is the rest of society with whom we must move in unison to achieve "happiness" rather than ethereal wispy truth that transcends but may not make us happy. Happiness in this vision means not being tortured by thoughts of meaning and purpose more significant than prosperity and getting along with our neighbors. The postmodern pragmatist vision rejects the primacy of beliefs derived from evidence and reason concerning objective truth and replaces it with beliefs directed to other ends like collective "happiness."

Rorty would have us give up on trying to represent reality accurately. The difference between nature and social constructs is unhelpful, he thought. We should instead distinguish which among social constructs has more utility. Of course, as always, the question is utility for what, and the answer for Rorty is a vague "inclusiveness." There is no real essence to us. We are all fluidly "becoming" rather than static "beings,"

---

1 1931-2007.

and the movement is to social harmony rather than ultimate universal principle.Social justice movements from every angle are the approved vehicles to move us to the goal of "inclusivity," and it makes no difference whether these movements rest on mere social constructs rather than reality. At least one irony here is that even as the pragmatist rejects universal principles inhering in objective reality, he invokes certain of those principles—like "inclusivity" and against "bigotry"—to make the argument.

Pragmatism, according to Rorty relying heavily on Dewey, is the idea that the conditioned is all there is. Thus, like Marx, philosophical pragmatists are materialists,[2] believing matter in motion is the whole of reality, and even ideals like truth and honesty and the concept of reason itself are mere social constructs which we perceive, but otherwise have no footing in reality. "The conditioned," therefore, means daily life in the body, excluding the sublime, the transcendent, the eternal, and certainly the God who is said to embody or emanate those things. Human beings, according to Rorty's pragmatism, "have nothing to know save their relations to each other and to other finite beings."[3] He urges that we be satisfied with the conditioned, giving up the quest for the infinite, but at the same time urges that we be content with beauty, as though that were not the most obvious and prevalent sign and symbol of the infinite he urges us to give up. Happiness is our only goal, not truth.

Pragmatism is a philosophy built around advancing the leftist vision by any means. It is a posture of negation, a process philosophy to advance the underlying but unstated goal of socialism. The negative stance to hierarchy and transcendence is its purpose. A Left Bank bohemian chic attends this purpose and so it is often styled anti-authoritarian. Rorty, for example, was quite explicitly "anti-authoritarian" in that he advocated emancipation from non-human authority. Non-human authority means most particularly God, but also social structures like religion formed as a result of belief in God, structures falsely (according to pragmatists) assumed to originate in ontological hierarchy. Rorty believed bad old religion reifies what are, in fact, only products of human practices, projecting them onto a non-human source of authority called "God." Religion serves, in other words, only to cement power interests, just as Marx asserted. This Marxist perspective is central to pragmatism, as it is in postmodern thought more generally.

---

2   Brandom, Robert B., in Foreword (p. xvii) to Richard Rorty's *Pragmatism as Anti-Authoritarianism*, Cambridge, MA: Belknap, Harvard University Press, 2021.

3   Rorty's preface, *Pragmatism as Anti-Authoritarianism*, p. xxx.

This is why rejection of God is the crossing over from modern to postmodern thought. Religious assumptions about the nature of reality support a correspondence theory of truth; that is, objectivity in truth/falsity; right/wrong. This foundation in turn supports hierarchical social structures. For postmodernists, religion must be rejected so that objectivity can be rejected, and objectivity must be rejected in order to install in its place a process-oriented engine of change toward socialist goals.

Rorty: "We need to make a distinction between the claim that the world is out there and the claim that the truth is out there."[4] On the contrary, truth is objective regardless of theories stating otherwise. Postmodernism posits non-objectivity of truth, but that is a false statement about truth. It is equivalent to this statement: It is objectively true that truth is not objective. The assertion about truth—that it is not objective and is in any event irrelevant—is made on the criterion of objective truth. The contradiction disproves the central pragmatist axiom, and, in fact, proves its opposite: that truth is, in fact, objective.

But presenting it as non-objective serves the postmodern advocacy stance. Jean-François Lyotard wrote: "Our hypotheses, therefore, should not be accorded predictive value in relation to reality, but strategic value in relation to the question raised."[5] To say that a hypothesis should not be accorded predictive value in relation to reality is to say that the hypothesis is not objectively true, which is what postmodernism says about itself as well as everything else—even though it is necessarily saying this particular hypothesis (that there is no objective truth) is objectively true. The purpose of roundabout ways of speaking of truth, as with Lyotard, is to hide the inconsistency. It is to explicitly place postmodern hypotheses in service to advocacy instead of truth.

The justification for this throwing-over of truth in the postmodern age seems to be something like this: If knowledge is a construct of power, then knowledge itself can be attacked just like other structures of power. "Knowledge" is not objectively available to us all, but is formed in a power struggle. Hence, the primacy of social narrative and the metanarrative ideology, which the struggle produces. With this mindset, so what if we "re-describe" and twist things to mean something slightly different and more congenial to a postmodern outlook and continue to ratchet disingenuous discourse in a leftward direction? It's not dishon-

---

4 Rorty, Richard. *Contingency, Irony, and Solidarity*, Cambridge: Cambridge University Press, 2009, p. 3.

5 Lyotard, Jean François. *The Postmodern Condition: A Report on Knowledge*, Manchester: Manchester University Press, 1991, p. 7.

est; it's fighting fire with fire. Ends justify means, always, in the pragmatist view. The power system generates "knowledge" that is not objectively true, and so a critique of that power system can just as validly create its alternative "knowledge" that is no less "true" than what it critiques.

Because of this sense of justification in dishonestly re-characterizing debate, and detachment of language from meaning, language is intensely scrutinized so that it can be used both offensively and defensively rather than as a neutral conveyer of information. In this way, language itself becomes the battleground rather than just the instrument for the exchange of ideas. Rules develop for how we can speak about certain things: political correctness. Those rules incorporate substantive leftist meaning into discourse. It's politically incorrect to say racial disparities are caused by anything other than racism, for example. Not because it's true in an objective sense, but because the language is monitored to advance ideology rather than to present objective truth; there's no such thing as truth outside that which is socially formed. Violating the rules imposed by postmodern ideology immediately places one outside the discussion, as not being fit for polite society.

Cynicism at the heart of postmodern theory is evident from the fact that it fundamentally rests on the supposition that things are as they are to protect dominant systems of power: a conspiracy theory with no particular conspirators. This stance of negation is shared among those inclined toward Marxist theory. It is like-minded disposition to deconstruction of a society that doesn't make one happy. Postmodernism is about ways of seeing the world, not truth claims, so it "refuses to substantiate itself and cannot, therefore, be argued with,"[6] as we saw in our consideration of the hermeneutics of suspicion (Chapter 14). The continued existence of constraints on personal autonomy imposed by hierarchical value systems constitutes a standing affront, feeding frustration, rage, and tantrums rather than principled debate.

Pragmatists see religion as a problem because, of course, it presupposes objectivity of truth, but also because it infects people, in Dewey's words, with a "sense of sin." Rorty sets forth this idea as foundational to his development of pragmatism, but what does "sense of sin" mean? The religious doctrine of sin? Guilt? That human depravity is merely a social construct? That there is no right and wrong? Hard to say, but whatever it means, it is understood to be an impediment to giving oneself over to the collective, because the sense of sin causes one to look outside oneself

---

6   Pluckrose, Helen and James Lindsay. *Cynical Theories*, Durham, NC: Pitchstone Publishing, 2020, p. 38.

for the cure. It points us to transcendent truth, so it must be disrupted and re-directed. We're all morally wonderful all the time, but if we do slip up, we don't transgress eternal moral values, we transgress values formed in the social flow. We don't really excise the "sense of sin" because God placed it in our conscience, but we shield ourselves from that guilt-induced unhappiness if we are dissolved into the oceanic feeling of socialist approval as a means of coping with the sense of alienation we feel. Just so long as we don't have to face God over it.

The "non-human" sources of authority decried by pragmatists include God, religion, idealism, Platonism, transcendence, and other such conceptions of truth outside ourselves. The postmodern push is to rid ourselves of this impediment, so that we abandon the specter of transcendence and give ourselves over to radical immanence, deriving all our sense of well-being horizontally from the well of human relations founded on goodwill, whereby we negotiate a social consensus that does not appeal to anything outside those relations. Rorty, among other postmodernists, saw the Enlightenment as being about throwing off the yoke of religious authority, with the following result:

> In the last two centuries, it has become possible to describe the human situation not by describing our relations to something ineffably different from ourselves, but by drawing a contrast between our ugly past and present and the more beautiful future in which our descendants may live.[7]

Without religion underpinning our assumptions about reality, what do we have? For pragmatists like Rorty, it is human freedom, what he thought results from dispensing with religious moral instruction, replacing it with individual autonomy. But then it turns out that the individual autonomy is not that at all, but a collectively-formed commitment to socialism. Morals are replaced with ethics, and ethics are not objectively discernible: instead, they're collectively formulated, and defined as practices which will serve this universal commitment.

Rorty was devoted to "democratic politics," which for him meant bringing into existence a "utopian, inclusivist, human community."[8] Democracy is not, therefore, a procedural means of weighing out competing principles in representational government but rather a vehicle for bringing about a communitarian paradise. What does "inclusivity"

---

7 Rorty's preface, *Pragmatism as Anti-Authoritarianism*, p. xxix.
8 *Pragmatism as Anti-Authoritarianism*, p. 47.

mean? It means the opposite of bigotry, but is that it? Are we to love our family members no more than the other eight billion people on the planet? Such watered-down "love" is not love at all. And what does it mean to "include" people, if not sharing in guaranteed rights vis-à-vis the state, or common deference to universal moral standards, or to the objectivity of truth? Rorty does not disclose what he thinks inclusivity means, but he's quite clear that whatever it is, it is movement to social-ism, using democracy not to mediate competing opinions concerning principles, but to advance an inexorable leftward movement to collec-tivist utopian ideal.

The purpose of democratic policies is therefore socialism, in the postmodern vision. Democracy is a vehicle to selfless communism. Pragmatism ushers in totalitarianism, but interestingly, serpent-like, it is presented as the prevention of totalitarianism. Totalitarianism is the abnegation of self in favor of the state, and that's what postmod-ern thought is directed to, except that the state now overruns its banks so that power is shared in various ways with non-public institutions to form the ideologically simpatico Machine. Postmodernism is a totaliz-ing ideology presented as the cure to totalizing ideologies.

Rejection of God and commitment to socialism is to be made uni-versal through coercion, ultimately. Here's how:

> There is no way in which the religious person can claim a right to be-lieve as part of an overall right to privacy. For believing is inherently a public project: all us language-users are in it together. We all have a responsibility to each other not to believe anything which cannot be justified to the rest of us. To be rational is to submit one's beliefs—all one's beliefs—to the judgment of one's peers.[9]

Let's understand this appalling assertion. Individual freedom of thought is to be eliminated by having all our beliefs submitted "to the judgment of one's peers." Why? And to what end? Rorty doesn't say, but asserts this is required "to be rational." Rationality doesn't fit the prag-matist view at all, however, because the word refers to routines of logic in the mind oriented to objective truth. So the word is employed instead to mean that which points to socialism, because socialism is taken to be the goal of right-thinking people. Collective consensus is substituted for objective truth as the orienting criterion for thought. In the pragmatist mind, the collective consensus is formed by social process, so it's not

---

9 *Pragmatism as Anti-Authoritarianism*, p. 21.

eternal and pre-existing, nor there to be discovered rather than invented.

That process, for pragmatists, involves social negotiation of beliefs. It is significant that "beliefs" are the subject of that negotiation, rather than truth. Truth—in its traditional definition of correspondence to reality—is no longer relevant. "All of us language-users are in it together," ("it" being the formation of socially-held belief) because language is the medium for the social negotiation of belief. We're told we have an obligation to each other concerning our beliefs, though this is nowhere in any pragmatist thought adequately explained, other than with the vague assertion that we are social creatures. We are, in one sense, but how does that mean we have to "justify our beliefs to each other?" This idea couldn't apply to one's belief in objectivity, obviously. Objectivity, and perforce religious belief, is voided *ab initio* in pragmatism, as it is in postmodern thought more generally.

What more chilling assertion could there be than, "We all have a responsibility to each other not to believe anything which cannot be justified to the rest of us?" Your very beliefs are to be constrained to that which is socially approved. The process itself eliminates belief outside the process, which means you're prohibited from any belief in authority of any "non-human" (God-created) construct of ideals or principles or metaphysics. The anticipated socialist utopia is the authority, in other words, and we are all subject to it.

To say truth results from social negotiation is to presuppose a universal submission to the general will of Rousseau's imagining. That would only be possible, however, through universal rejection of objectivity in truth and morality, and that means no religion. It means universal compliance, and that means universal acceptance, and that means abnegation of self in favor of the collective, and that means totalitarianism. Evidently Rorty, like other postmodernists, was particularly concerned with the rise of so-called "strong-man" leaders as the sign and symbol of that form of social organization we must avoid at all costs. So long as that element is absent, the totalitarian aspect of socialism can be overlooked. This cure means a kind of relaxation into an "oceanic feeling" form of socialism in which no one can rise above another as an authoritarian because we've all together ceded our individualism to the collective.

Understanding the distinction between authoritarianism and totalitarianism is crucial for making sense of this perspective. Rorty and the post-modern left are concerned with the rise of oppressive authoritarian centers, rightly enough. Their models for that form of authori-tarianism feature powerful individual leaders like Hitler or Mussolini or even Franco. Former President Trump is reviled and feared because he's seen as fitting that mold. The fear on the left is a fear of powerful individuals atop hierarchies of ideological hate for "outsiders" of some description—in this day, splintered identity groups who see themselves oppressed at the hands of white heterosexual males. Hitler's regime is the archetype authoritarian oppressor, not only for its strong-man hier-archical character, but also for its racialist foundation. Postmodern ide-ology re-employs that same kind of racialism, however, pitting women and minority racial and sexual identity groups against white heterosex-ual men, instead of pitting one set of universal values against another to work out a way of living together in peace.

While authoritarianism is top-down oppression like that just de-scribed, totalitarianism is bottom-up subsumption of self into the col-lective. In the Marxist or Rortian vision, that collective is not seen as a vehicle of oppression but rather as a vehicle for inclusive communitar-ian socialism. This is their "democracy." So for Rorty and other post-modernists, the prevention of authoritarianism entails socialism. Not classical Marxism, which dealt with material conditions of the proletar-iat, but an expanded version which re-makes the person. On this vision, oppression by the collective is literally inconceivable because the self is to be adjusted not to see it as such. We instead seek ecstatic oceanic feel-ing, so long as we are vigilant against the rise of Hitlers. In this way, we run straight into the clutches of Stalins, however, because the pragma-tist "anti-authoritarianism" is totalitarian. It takes us full circle to losing ourselves in the collective, this time the Machine rather than Mussolini's state, but it's all fascism.

The utopian vision is unobtainable, as the etymology of "utopian" suggests. The socialist vision takes us to an all-against-all battle for su-premacy because truth is truth, and some will resist being subsumed into the Machine. The Machine is the vehicle for this collectivism and would be so even if we could move past the limitations of nations into a one-world government. A one-world state is still a state, just one that is more all-encompassing and more soul-extinguishing than any of the lesser fascisms thus far foisted upon mankind and embodied, as always and ever, in a Stalin or Hitler or Mao who rules by coercion, genocide, and fear. Pragmatism is fascism, presented in pastels of polite bourgeois self-righteousness.

Nor is a withering away of the state possible, as conceived by Marx and retained as a footnote in some postmodern utopias. Contra Dewey, it is not the "sense of sin" that introduces an urge to power in human beings. The urge to power resides within already. It is self-controlled through adherence to objective principle, or it is not. Religion induces motivation by moral principle, constraining the savage within. When religion is extinguished, the savage yet remains. Postmodern neo-Marxist thought, as with pragmatism, seeks to eliminate the savage by eliminating the person in whom it resides.

The protean applications of Marxism in postmodern thought are supposed to kill the cancer of spiritual vapidity, living parasitically in the capitalist host, but always they do so by killing the host. And then, it turns out the disease itself isn't dead after all, but proliferates pandemically when the host dies. The dead "bodies" lie all around us: Venezuela, Cuba, the Soviet client states, Cambodia, and many others. Those "bodies" infected with Marxism but not yet dead are weak, anemic, and vulnerable. This includes most of Western Europe and the United States, at this hour.

CHAPTER TWENTY-TWO

Democracy

SOCIALISM IS ADVANCED in our political life under the benign banner of "democracy." We should understand how this works, because we now live with two competing visions of democracy. One is a textbook definition of procedural protections in governance, including especially elements like viewpoint diversity by free speech debate; integrity of process in the vote; deference to the resulting majority; and constitutional protections against majority tyranny.

The competing vision of democracy doesn't necessarily clash point by point. It involves, instead, a distinct paradigm, and it is substantive rather than procedural. It is essential socialism, the "we" disposition in contrast to individualism. "We" must unselfishly find and share common ground, not selfishly fight for individual interest. In this vision of democracy, free speech is not a priority, nor is the right to dissent. The priority is consensus, and it's not considered oxymoronic to coerce that consensus, because the thought is that we are moving to unity in the form of erasure of boundaries among people, so it is humane to force people into it because they will then discover a better world.

How could people come to such radically distinct notions of what democracy means, on a personal, subjective level? One's personal self-awareness, the locus of consciousness in the individual self, would seem to be self-evidently irreducible and the necessary unit of all decision-making. On the other hand, our social nature means that society, too, is in some ways considered a unit of decision-making. The political question is what type and degree of decision-making should occur in each.

The Bible teaches that we have independent and individual moral agency. We are individually morally responsible, and so the scope of our individual freedom should coincide with that degree of responsibility. One might reject the premise, however. If there is no God at all, then are we individually morally responsible? Because if not, one might conceive a society in which agency, moral and otherwise, shifts from the individual to the collective. Even among those who have not rejected God, there may be an instinct for melding into the collective as a matter of religious belief. The ecstatic vision of losing oneself in God's love can be confused with a sense of belonging in society.

A vivid illustration is provided by the Indian mystic Ramakrishna (1836-1886), describing an oceanic feeling as the essence of religious transcendence. A salt doll goes to measure the depth of the ocean but melts away entirely in the water and is then unable to measure the ocean's depth.[1] This feeling of oneness equates to ultimate socialist collectivism; religious ecstasy coinciding with dissolution of self into the collective. One might describe this as a desire for ultimate immanence; in fact, the word "immanence" is used in this peculiar sense in much writing from the left. Instead of referring to the presence of the divine in the world with us, the word is used to refer instead to the feeling of social unity overwhelming us in flooding love and communitarianism. A loving social envelopment is confused with God's love, for those disposed to a river disposition and inclined to feel more than reason, a sense of God's presence. For people of this religious but socialist disposition, God's transcendence is imagined minimized and His immanence maximized.

Of course, people don't have a spectrum switch in their minds for these descriptions of God's presence, like for treble and bass on an audio player. They're more a felt sense. Immanence is the warm bath of human fellow-feeling which coincides, in religious socialists' minds, with the presence of God. For them and for post-religious socialists, transcendence is the harsh scowling disciplinarian brandishing the belt for a good spanking if you don't behave.

This goes a long way toward explaining the huge divide between those on the left and those on the right, be they religious or irreligious. And it goes a long way to explaining why there are religious people on both left and right. Each may be guided more by their mountain or

---

1   Related in a letter from Romain Rolland to Sigmund Freud in 1929, cited by Roberto Calasso in *The Book of Books*, New York: Farrar, Strauss and Giroux, 2019, p. 275. Note that individual initiative and purpose, measurement of the depth of the ocean, is also lost in the self's dissolution, and so is not available to the collective. Dissipation follows dissolution.

river psychological dispositions than by creeds to which they say they subscribe. A religious person might internally emphasize justice, and the resulting bloody Crucifixion, and gritty reality existing apart from personal feeling. Or a religious person might internally emphasize mercy, and Pentecost, and the sustaining love flowing through our reality. Each may miss the totality of the Christian story by looking solely to the mountain or the river; to the horizontal or vertical beam of the cross. And each side looks with puzzlement and exasperation on the other.

Ours is a post-Christian society in which many would say they want nothing to do with religion, and therefore, they might contend, the immanent/transcendent distinction is irrelevant. It's not, though. For one thing, the sense of immanence and transcendence remains in the culture and in personal experience, even when faith is extinguished. For another thing, the very words are re-purposed for effect, as occurs routinely in the postmodern world. Definition slippage is the first sign of God-evasion, just like we would expect if we pay attention to the stories of the serpent in the garden, and Cain and Abel, and the Tower of Babel, and other foundational paradigm-setting stories of Genesis.

Immanence and transcendence are words in today's public discussion that are misused by being unmoored from their religious origin. They have no application outside religious worldviews, but are used, nonetheless, by those who consider God non-existent or irrelevant. On the left, immanence is that warm social glow; it means values and truth are formed horizontally in flows and processes, the essence of postmodern philosophy trying to replace transcendence. Transcendence, for those on the left, is the discredited vertically formed hierarchy of value and objectivity of truth, the enemy of feel-good communitarianism which represents our utopian goal—and it is all about love, they feel, so surely God would approve anyway, if there were a God.

The oceanic feeling of ultimate socialism coincides with spiritual monism, the idea that all of reality is of one substance, there is no duality between material and spiritual. The great metaphysical divide in the West is thought to be between religion and secularism, but it is really between dualism and monism. Monism includes Eastern pantheism, but it also includes materialism, the default metaphysics of postmodernists. By confusing materialist metaphysics with the absence of a metaphysical stance altogether, we come to think of materialism as merely "not religious," a negation rather than a something unto itself. We may continue to engage the negation rather than the substance of what we have defaulted to: a metaphysical belief as substantive as that of the monotheisms, but denying the transcendent; the supernatural; the immaterial.

In this way, we are duped into considering monist materialism religiously neutral and give it exclusive access, politically, to the public square. A political insistence on secularism is not insistence on neutrality. It is insistence on monism, and the default monist view in our society is materialism. Secularism is misunderstood to require materialism. Secularism, on this understanding, is therefore as much a metaphysical view as religion, yet it is treated politically as if it weren't a metaphysical view at all. It is thus confused with neutrality rather than a metaphysics in competition with religion.

Contributing to the sense of social oneness rather than individuality has been the conviction of some that the legacy dualism of Christianity is essentially a selfish creed.[2] Christians often do good deeds, but only because it redounds to their credit with God, or so goes the thinking. This overlooks the heart-change that yields the good deeds and thereby shows a misunderstanding of Christianity. Presumably, the idea of socialists is that throwing our lot in all together, each contributing as he can to the common good, better reflects unselfishness.

This seems to be the break point between democracy as individualists see it and as socialists see it. Democracy for socialists isn't merely representative government. It is a vehicle to ever more complete socialism. The founders of the United States understood the danger of Plato's beast[3] but engaged with it in the form of republicanism plus government limits as the best hope for expansive liberalism. Restraints of limited republican government are not incidental to the American form of "democracy." By rejecting the limits of constitution and religion, we move to democratic socialism. This continued movement to collectivism is what is meant by democracy, to the socialist left. This is why the United States has drifted away from government limited to preserving individual rights and toward government expanded to express social cohesion.

Factoring in the general postmodern belief that the socialist/collectivist vision is self-evidently ethically preferable (on the grounds that it is not selfish like with individualism), it seems justifiable to exercise

---

2 This idea is one among many strands of thought unraveling Christianity in the nineteenth century. See *Dangerous God*, Chapter 9.

3 Plato alluded to the population in a democracy as a "beast" potentially motivated by interest rather than principle, an early recognition of the danger of plebiscite democracy as reflecting the will of the majority moment to moment, without underlying constraining principles to protect the minority, like republicanism and constitutionalism. *The Republic of Plato*, transl. by Allan Bloom, Basic Books, 2nd edition, 1968, Book VI, 493b, p. 173.

power rather than appeal to objective truth in the effort to prevail in the narrative, and to coerce, or deceive as necessary, to attain that power. After all, it is the best thing for the backwoods dissenters; they just haven't figured it out yet and will thank their socialist betters later. This level of hubris might seem unbelievable, but it's exactly where the thought contributions of Hobbes, Rousseau, Durkheim, Rorty, Bauman and others take us.

The question, as always, is: who decides? Collectivists (socialists) need all-in participation, but individualists want collectivists to mind their own business. The Rousseaus and Rortys and Baumans of the world aren't overtly strutting around trying to make themselves Il Duce. They're trying to force a shift in human nature to recognize a collective "who" to do the deciding for all of us. Our liberty is to be collectivized and offloaded to the cloud, and henceforth, the cloud decides what "we" do and what "we" think. Don't worry, the cloud is managed by good guys. This is either toxic hubris or unfathomably naïve faith in the milk and honey of human kindness, impervious to the experience of all of human history, not to mention the instruction of Genesis. Every move in this direction—every one—has ended in tyranny. But next time will be different.

Pragmatists like John Dewey and Richard Rorty elevate "democracy" to the place of God. Theirs is a substantive theory of collectivism, not a mere procedural rule of governance in which the voice of the governed is represented. To grasp the significance of this, we must back up to the origins of what we called "democracy" before postmodernists commandeered the term.

It has always been true that those with political power must show some deference, even if merely symbolic, to the will of the people governed. People in the lower strata of society traditionally wanted to be left alone and especially wanted not to be lorded over by those who consider themselves superior by accident of birth. A noble without a spirit of *noblesse oblige* would be destined for a fall.

In the pre-democratic hierarchical West, a system of vassalage developed under kings, wherein one's rights and privileges in society were governed by position in that hierarchical vassalage. The Magna Carta of 1215 was a marker for increasing accountability on the part of rulers, in which the then-king of England compromised his kingly authority in order to secure his position, conferring certain rights on lesser nobles.

The idea of a people's voice in government continued to develop, to the point that "social contract" theories of government came into vogue during the Enlightenment era. The central point of social contract theory is that people are self-sovereign but voluntarily confer a portion of that sovereignty onto a ruler or ruling class for practical reasons. As thus conceived, representative government meant individualism, because it means basic human rights reside in the individual, not the collective.

In Chapter 20, we noted the progression of social contract theory through Thomas Hobbes to John Locke to Jean-Jacques Rousseau, to examine its effects on individual freedom. Social contract theory suggests there is an implied agreement between the people, on the one hand, and their government, on the other. Its positive aspect is that it supposes people own themselves; they are self-sovereign and not mere subjects of a king, who would otherwise have all earthly authority over them. Government, therefore, has only such authority as it acquires from the people. This is contractual in nature because it imagines people voluntarily ceding a portion of the authority that originates in them, in exchange for the rule of law and the benefits of social living in peace. In other words, this theory supposes the government is an agent for the people, rather than a lordly ruler.

But social contract theory is limited in an important way. Implicit in the notion of social contract theory is a presumed unity of the populace. That is, we imagine the handful of rulers on one side of a negotiating table and the entire populace apart from them on the other. Individuals in the population get to vote on a representative or a policy or a proposition, but the majority rules. That's the nature of a democracy. If you are perennially in the minority, with no constitutionally guaranteed individual rights, you are subject to the tyranny of the majority. This is the effect of a democracy not constitutionally limited so that the majority can only vote away so much of your freedom.

Moreover, no one in the society has the option to say "no thanks" to the arrangement. It is not truly a contract, therefore, because the essence of a contract is a voluntary agreement to a set of mutual rights and obligations. Individual participation is limited to the vote, and the vote is limited to choosing representatives who then often act on behalf of the government as against the people, instead of the reverse. Politicians in a democracy coddle their constituency as necessary to retain position, but otherwise see themselves acting on behalf of the government of the society as an entity distinct from the individuals within it. Democracy is a collective enterprise; therefore, it does not by itself secure individual rights vis-à-vis the government. If there is no embedded principle to limit the scope of government, as there was in theory at the founding of the United States, it is whatever the voters through their representatives say it is. People increasingly vote their interests rather than principle. Individual interests carry little political weight, however, so the trend is inexorably to assertion of group interests rather than principle applicable to all.

Because democracy stood initially for the proposition that certain rights are "unalienable"—individual and pre-political—democracy is often conflated with freedom. These are not the same thing, however. Genuine freedom means independence; freedom from constraint; the right to be left alone. The right to vote, standing alone, does not confer that. Here is the problem as expressed by Anthony Esolen:

> People are free not because they get to cast a marked piece of confetti for their distant rulers but because their distant rulers have only very distant things to do with them, if anything at all. Liberty is to be defined not by how many things you or your representatives get to vote about, with your own vote so diluted that it would be like a grain of sand in the Sahara desert, but rather by how many things no one needs to vote about, or no one dares to vote about, because they get done by ordinary people pursuing their own good and the common good in ordinary ways.[4]

Democracy is not coincident with freedom unless the social contract contains a commitment to limit the power of government to certain essential functions rather than whatever power lobbies dream up to foist on other citizens. Democracy without constitutional limitation to essential government function not only does not assure freedom, but becomes the vehicle for extinguishing freedom. This is perhaps true of any kind of government structure people might invent, but in the hands of postmodernists, democracy becomes an affirmative engine of ideological tyranny. It advances the same illiberalism that was extinguished at the cost of millions of lives within living memory.

Not being limited by principle in the scope of its activity, the government expands. Its coercive power over individuals expands. That power spills over government's structural boundaries to non-government power centers, because the boundary between public and private is increasingly blurred. Public/private "partnerships," pervasive regulation and regulation-influence (effectively, negotiated regulation), public

---

4 Esolen, Anthony. *Sex and the Unreal City/The Demolition of the Western Mind*, San Francisco: Ignatius, 2020, p. 110.

funding of private ventures, and unprincipled exercises of taxing and spending authority are among the ways the boundary is blurred. This matters because government is defined by its ability to coerce. Government alone mandates, through the law. Private association is defined by voluntarism. Associate through commerce or by joint effort; or don't. There is no compulsion. To blur the distinction between voluntarism and coercion is a dangerous thing. Doing so becomes the means by which government power and private power centers converge into a Machine monolith crushing individual freedom.

This explains how the government can do things unheard of in the traditional understanding of "democracy," like actively suppressing free speech on matters of public policy. Recent examples include vaccine effectiveness, election integrity, and "diversity" initiatives. Government is no longer confined to procedural democratic principles. It uses its coercive power to advance substantive ideology, with ideologically allied and interest-interwoven non-public power centers like big media, big tech, and government-regulated Wall Street. Hence the Machine of ideological social control.

The seeds of fascism exist in Hobbes' conception of social contract theory, but more insidiously in that of Jean-Jacques Rousseau, who famously conceived the "general will" of democratic society, in contrast to the individual wills of its disparate members. The state, for Rousseau, would be the guarantor against impingements on freedom from structures of prestige and class, but to accomplish this, the state's requirements would be imposed so that citizens would "be forced to be free." The upshot of his vision is a citizenry in which each person conceives himself primarily as part of a whole.[5]

The idea that democracy meant a kind of unity among its citizens rather than merely preservation of pre-political rights was evident in many of the Romantics of the nineteenth century, for example, Walt Whitman, in his *Leaves of Grass*. We're to imagine ourselves each as one leaf of grass in a field, and in this way, the perspective shifts from individual freedom to the beauty of the collective. One must see society as a whole rather than a collection of individual people. Far from advocating wariness over any form of authority, in the way that animated Enlightenment individualism expressed in America's founding principles, democracy became for many, like Whitman, exactly the opposite:

---

5 Rousseau's conception is helpfully discussed in Storey, Benjamin, and Jenna Silber Storey. *Why We Are Restless/On the Modern Quest for Contentment*, Princeton, NJ: Princeton University Press, 2021, pp. 99-140.

a vehicle to enlightened communitarianism.

CHAPTER TWENTY-THREE

Metanarrative

THE VARIOUS elements of postmodern thought (such as those identified at the beginning of Chapter 11) are a metanarrative. That metanarrative prominently includes propositions in opposition to those of monotheistic religion and these include:

—Absence of objective truth;

—Absence of objective morality and, therefore, moral relativism;

—Materialism, so there is no spiritual reality—no God;

—Melting of self into the collective as re-defined freedom.

The natural and organic way for metanarratives to form is to look at the facts on the ground, so to speak, and draw inferences from those facts on an orientation toward objective truth. Then one compiles those facts and inferences into a narrative, and draws inferences of principles that the narrative supports, and those principles collectively constitute the metanarrative.

Example: We might reason from the facts of human nature and consciousness and moral agency, and the natural categories by which the world makes sense to us, including the transcendentals of truth, goodness, and beauty, to infer a supernatural Author of those things, and that Author's ongoing sustaining of them. Then we might look to the facts of the Hebrews as against surrounding pagan peoples, and then the Advent and Resurrection of the Christ, to understand the nature of mankind's reconciliation to God. From these facts we have a narrative, of which the Bible is a part, and that narrative supports principles of faith, hope, reason, and love in a God-infused world, all bound up in the metanarrative of Christian principles. The proper sequence, then, is facts to support inferences to support narrative to support metanarrative.

Metanarrative

Narrative

Facts

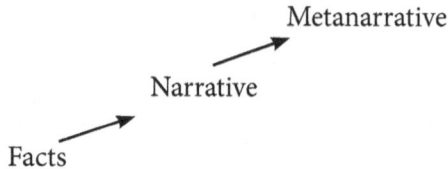

Postmodernism gets this backwards. The metanarrative of an ideology is presented first: overlapping types of neo-Marxism. Then a narrative is developed to support that metanarrative. Then fraudulent inferences are developed from a tendentious reading of selective facts, to support that narrative. Facts support narratives, but as a necessarily incomplete assemblage of facts, narratives are quite manipulable in support of some other end. Facts can be assembled selectively, or otherwise dishonestly, or with unfounded imputations of bad motive, or for ulterior purposes. Facts are often assembled to fit narratives, in other words, rather than narratives being formed to fit facts.

Polemical misuse of narrative can gain traction and apply across an entire society. For example, in recent years in the United States, we've seen rioting, burning, looting, millions of dollars in property damage, and deaths and other instances of violence over what was presented as racial injustice in policing. Are we seeing facts drive narrative which in turn drives metanarrative? Or, is it the reverse: metanarrative driving narrative based on facts selected or deselected for polemical purposes? To say it differently, is the operative narrative driven from below by facts, or is it formed from above by ideology?

In this example, the metanarrative is systemic racism. The narrative formed concerning policing is that innocent black people are routinely harassed, intimidated, beaten, and even killed by police officers who disproportionately target black citizens for brutality. But it turns out the only facts presented to support that narrative are the proportionately higher rates of black arrests and violent police encounters. We're expected from this to accept the narrative as self-evidently true, but the simpler explanation is higher rates of black crime. We might be tempted to relax standards of strict facticity because, after all, racism is bad and has had inter-generational impacts, and so the principles in play are the important thing, not the circumstances of individual police interactions. Testing the accuracy of the facts in this situation strikes those infected with the virus of postmodern pragmatism as quibbling about inconsequential details, at best, and at worst, insistence on logocentric objectivity as another manifestation of systemic racism.

But if we ignore or distort objective facts on which the narrative and in turn the metanarrative are based, we mistake the cure for the disease. Narrative divorced from fact on issues like this is a means of deceitfully diverting attention from the rot in society caused by ideological socialist policies and deconstruction of cultural norms that result in indolence, self-indulgence, and anomic pointlessness. The real problem is not racial at all, but more vulnerable segments of the population suffer the consequences disproportionately. The effects show up in crime and police encounters, but also in other measures of well-being like literacy, employment, drug use, and destruction of families.

Another example is in the ongoing debates in the United States about elections. Fairness in voting means both equal access and election integrity. Competing narratives develop. On the one hand, there are too many restrictions relating to voter identification, mail-in voting, waiting periods, and the like. On the other hand, the integrity of the vote is compromised because there are too few checks against abuse. The resulting competing metanarratives are voter suppression vs. voter fraud, an unsubtle binary deliberately left unrefined because oversimplification serves polemical and hence political purposes.

When the postmodern left speaks of overthrowing white supremacy, what is the object? We're first to accept that there's a racial hegemony that imposes its cultural values on others. Superficially, that seems like something we ought to address, until we dig more deeply into what "cultural values" are in play. It really means replacing Western liberalism with power centers we will call the "Machine" redistributing wealth, removing the individual from the center and replacing him with the collective, redefining virtue, and recognizing only government-granted positive rights, rather than natural pre-political rights; all in service to a goal of greater social control. Again, it's not really about race at all. "White supremacy" is a strategic ambiguity in word use, to fraudulently build a metanarrative congenial to the goal of remaking mankind.

The New York Times' 1619 Project is likewise an attempt at re-shaping narrative. It is a retelling of U.S. history as one of slavery and oppression rather than emancipation and freedom. Aside from recasting selective facts in a new direction, it is Marxist in its essential pessimism, negation, suspicion, and division.

Another example is the "vaccine moment" of 2020-22. The whole episode has been one long push and pull to control the narrative. Many Americans were surprised to hear the President of the United States actively suppressing speech, in violation of the cherished First Amendment, on a subject about which he and the rest of the government had much to say.[1] It should be obvious to anyone that the underlying facts don't control the narrative; instead, authorities wielding power attempt to do so. Here is Paul Kingsnorth, writing from Ireland:

> Internment. Mandatory medication. Segregation of whole sections of society. Mass sackings. A drumbeat of media consensus. The systematic censoring of dissent. The deliberate creation by the state and the press of a climate of fear and suspicion. What could possibly justify this? Perhaps the combination of a terrible pandemic which killed or maimed large percentages of those it infected, and the existence of a safe and reliable medicine which has proven to prevent its spread. This, of course, is what we are said be living through. This is the Narrative.

> But it is clear enough by now that the Narrative is not true. Covid-19 can be a nasty illness, and should be taken seriously, especially by those who are especially vulnerable to it. But it is nowhere near dangerous enough—if anything could be—to justify the creation of a global police state. As for the vaccines: well, let's just acknowledge that vaccination has become a subject which it is virtually impossible to discuss with any calmness or clarity, at least in public. As with almost every other big issue in the West today, opinion is divided along tribal lines and filtered through the foetid swamp of anti-social media, to emerge monstrous and dripping into the light.[2]

Increasingly, the underlying facts don't seem to matter. The "narrative" is what we rely on, and we're increasingly tolerant of it being untethered from supporting facts. This isn't just the result of limited attention span or the hurly-burly of the news cycle. It results also from the philosophical pragmatism[3] that is at the heart of postmodern thinking. The ends justify the means, in pragmatism, even as the ends are camouflaged through misdirection and deceit. It's easy to see how this naturally devolves into all-against-all social battle for ideological dominance.

Postmodern ideologies exist to spur rebellion against what the ide-

---

1 And attempted to install a "Disinformation Governance Board," instantly and rightly dubbed by critics as the "Ministry of Truth," after the fictional propagandist entity in Orwell's *1984*.

2 "The Vaccine Moment/Covid, control, and the Machine," January 2022. (www.paulkingsnorth.net/vaccine).

3 Pragmatism is the subject, especially of Chapters 21 and 22, but it is an element of all postmodern philosophy, in that it is a process philosophy that first abandons universal principle.

ology presents as injustice in social structures. Justice, in the postmodern view, involves social re-negotiation among groups of people, and that negotiation turns on power. The religious metanarrative, by contrast, discloses that the line between justice and injustice runs through the heart of every individual, not between groups labelled oppressor and oppressed. Justice must be an appeal to universal principle, therefore, not to social group power negotiation.

The feminist narrative is that sex differences are entirely social constructs and, as such, should be dismantled to correct injustice. Is the narrative factually true? It may be counted as true by women frustrated with sex-role expectations of traditional society. But it may be counted as untrue by women who prefer a social environment that reinforces traditional roles. The narrative results in pressure to conform to expectations of sex-sameness in home and working environments, but many see this as debasing the utility of partnerships of differing sex roles, especially in regard to child-rearing. The feminist narrative is that all of history is one long story of unjust oppression of women, and correction of this injustice requires elimination of sex differences. This is possible, it is thought, because sex differences are all social constructs and, therefore, amenable to deconstruction. Similarly, distorted narratives are behind other movements that rely on a paradigm of oppressor and oppressed, like anti-colonialism, multiculturalism, anti-racism, and LGBTQ "equality."

In the postmodern imagination, metanarratives are suspect and to be deconstructed. As we have seen, however, that deconstruction only results in a replacement metanarrative. For hundreds of years after the Resurrection, the dominant metanarrative of Western civilization was Christian religion. That was in the process of change as the twentieth century dawned, and Christianity continued to decline, despite the evident horrors of competing ideologies that resulted in the mid-century wars. In the postmodern age, the metanarrative of religion has been increasingly suspect, and is deemed ripe for deconstruction. This has not left us without a metanarrative, however, as some postmodern writers seem to have intended. It has left us instead with a socially formed metanarrative that bends toward the very fascist and communist totalitarianisms that were the subject of the mid-century devastations.

It would seem obvious that to understand anything, we must start at ground level with objectively verifiable facts. We might say that a certain event certainly happened at a certain point in history. Or that race is a biologically insignificant variation in the human species. Or that men and women differ innately in some respects. Facts can be misrepresented or misunderstood, and often are, but they are less manipulable than the inferences we draw from them at the levels of narrative and metanarrative.

Narratives are not always and everywhere suspect. They are quite useful, in fact, because no one is in command of all the facts of history and of the present, so we have to depend on explanatory narrative as the next level of abstraction. But narratives become a social battleground once we de-privilege the objectivity of facts and truth and morality. This explains the calumny postmodern ideology introduces into public discourse. We might, for example, express nationhood in the United States as a people-group escaping religious tyranny founding a religious but religion-tolerant "city on a hill," later incorporated on Enlightenment principles of liberation from political constraint of natural rights. Or alternatively, the property-grabbing aspirations of a powerful racial people group, colonizing new land by means of subjugating less powerful racial groups.

In orthodox Christianity, facts are presented: the nationhood of Israel with its conflicts, conquests, and religious ritual developed over time; God's interventions into space-time on behalf of His people; the life, death, and resurrection of Jesus. The narrative that emerges is God's creation of people, special within His creation; His faithfulness to His people; the need of the people for redemption from a world of self-inflicted sin and pain; and redemption in the resurrection of the Christ. The metanarrative is theology, which forms the principles which explain the narrative. Those principles include an explanation for the Source of truth and morality and aspirational ideals; and a supernatural reality supervening upon the natural reality we most immediately know.

In the same way, metanarratives are constructed in contexts other than the religious. National Socialists in 1930s Germany conceived of the world in neo-pagan terms of struggle and conquest; of blood and soil. The narrative believed to support that metanarrative was the existence of a pure and untainted Aryan race being defiled over time by incursions of inferior races, most notably the Jews, who, in their view, invented God and thereby eradicated paganism through the bloodless cerebral abstraction of transcendence. Accepted as facts supporting that narrative were economic travails, unjust humiliation at Versailles, the conviction of self-evident racial superiority, and the rise of a Führer to embody the nation of purified irrepressible Übermenschen. In a similar vein were the nationalistic metanarratives of Fascist Italy and Imperial

Japan.

Socialism and communism and neo-Marxist cultural movements rely on metanarratives, but they typically aren't understood as such by postmodernists because they are thought of instead as means to de-construct metanarratives of the right like Nazism, a dark instinct of the weak-minded which recrudesces from time to time so that we must be ever wary of it. But metanarratives of the left, though every bit as dangerous, seem to be invisible to postmodernists, and this makes them vulnerable to what is really the same totalitarian impulse.

In traditional Marxism, facts on the ground in the early nineteenth century included a seemingly intractable class structure following upon the serfdom that had formerly tied peasants to the land, and then rapid industrialization disrupting those social structures, motivating peasant movement toward centers of capital concentration like factories. The narrative was one of exploitation, wherein the workers were oppressively treated like elements of capital themselves, in the eyes of the property owners who used that capital for wealth generation (hence "capitalists"). Revolution was asserted to be the only way to disrupt the cycle of oppression because alienation of profit from workers' toils was thought to keep them down. The metanarrative included these principles: resolute atheistic materialism, wherein a person's awareness and agency is circumscribed by his conditions in life; a Hegelian historical telos in which serfdom gives way to capitalism, which gives way to socialism, which gives way to communism; and ongoing conditions of oppressor and oppressed classes sustained by the purported lies of religion and the propertied social hierarchy.

The spirit of Marx is still with us and so also the basic outlines of this metanarrative. Sin does not infect people, according to this mindset, nor does religion extirpate it. Those who would preserve their power and money and prestige sustain systemic structures like religion to mislead people into acceptance of their oppression. Self-awareness and agency are in actuality limited to economic concerns, as they must be within a resolutely atheist, materialist worldview. The paradigm of oppressor and oppressed is re-applied in this age to various neo-Marxist movements of feminism, sexual liberation, racial re-segregation, and, of course, corporatist economic socialism centering power in the Machine, just like in fascist ideology.

This neo-Marxism employs postmodernist deconstruction techniques to free us from what are regarded as diseased ideas about human nature and a theoretical God. The goodness of humanity is crowded out by the social ills of striving for power, money, and prestige, as Jean-Jacques Rousseau thought, rather than the badness of humanity being refined out of us by our individual striving for universal ideals, like the Bible teaches. Deconstruction of this diseased society is called for, to cull the bad presumptions of religion and the false freedom of capitalism, thereby freeing mankind to live in a more natural state of harmony and plenty.

So goes the metanarrative, resting on a narrative of oppression, resting on the "facts" of perfectible mankind in a godless reality. In this way, new metanarratives based on the oppression narrative are generated: male oppression of women through the patriarchy; heterosexual oppression of sexual minorities through binary heteronormativity; white oppression of racial minorities through systemic racism, colonialism, and nationalistic chauvinism.

The shift to postmodernism around the turn of the twentieth century results from lines of thought in existentialism and pragmatism. Pragmatism places formation of truth and morality in action; that which "works" to bring about social progress. But there is endless disputation about what constitutes progress. "Truth" is then contingent on bogus consensus, in turn formed by the push and pull in society, which like a ship with no rudder scuds along with tides and weather, while all who are shipboard run around with passionate intensity, as if what they do matters.

What emerges is this: a battleground for dominance, not about what conceptions of truth and morality will prevail, but about what constitutes truth and morality in the first place. One must understand the role of metanarrative to make sense of it. In a discussion between any two, the metanarrative constitutes the third point, to which both appeal. It occupies the place religion once did.

Religion, or at least   Social (not religious)
Objective truth   metanarrative

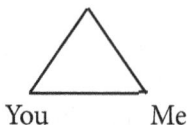   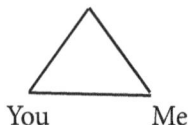

You   Me   You   Me

Operative metanarratives include patriarchy, systemic racism, heteronormativity, nationalism, and ever-opportunistic incipient fascism which society must vigilantly hold at bay. The metanarrative of systemic racism deflects attention from conditions that directly contribute to racially disparate social outcomes, like single parenthood, poverty, indifference to education, and so on. The metanarratives of patriarchy and heteronormativity conflict with ontological sex duality and marriage as Genesis presents it. The metanarrative of anti-fascism recasts evil as resistance to socialism.

If you listen to debates about truth and falsity, and about right and wrong, you will discern the same form that prevailed when truth was objective rather than relative. That form is reference to a third-party arbiter, so to speak. But, being relative, the nature of the arbiter is in question. That's what it means to be relative. We don't just live among people with differing opinions on various subjects. We live among people with wholly distinct worldviews, informed by distinct metanarratives. To understand others, we must first identify their operative metanarrative. Only then can a discussion take place with mutual intelligibility.

Christianity / God-within-me / Communism / Materialism / Will-to-power

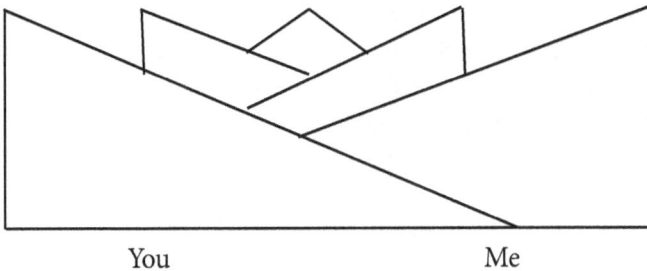

You   Me

We no longer have common ground by which to measure truth or morality. We're only using the form of objective truth to have the discussion. A particular proposition of truth or morality can be considered objectively true and morally right only insofar as one adopts the entire worldview of which it is a part. We always use the form of objectivity in the discussion, but objectivity (as opposed to subjectivity or coerced consensus) may not actually be part of one's worldview.

A project of postmodernism is to critique metanarratives of hierarchical meaning, like religion and political fascism. The point is to dissolve them and instead find meaning generated from non-hierarchical flows and processes. But in practice, new metanarratives are created with new hierarchies, because that's the way of the world. This easily observable phenomenon seems to be invisible to postmodern thinkers, however, perhaps because the operative theory is that all hierarchy can be eliminated. One after another socialist experiment fails, but hope springs eternal that next time will be different. The dissolution project has been corrupted in all past attempts, the thinking goes, but next time, we'll successfully collapse the hierarchy in favor of utopian equality.

As Genesis teaches, however, truth and goodness can't be redefined, ultimately, because they are real and objective in reality. They can't be theorized out of existence into less scary flows and processes. Efforts to relativize truth and goodness cut against the grain, producing disharmony, cacophony, chaos, disorder, irrationality, illiberalism, oppression, and violence. The days are ever darker, and this is so because of encroaching collective evil; principalities and powers arrayed against us oppressively.

The way to trigger the wrath of evil in this age is to transgress the post-truth narrative. It needn't be about a particular issue that has long been in debate, like abortion. It could be about something seemingly a matter of objective science, like the appropriateness of pandemic protocols. When some subjects just can't be discussed without wrathful attacks to un-person the speaker, we're witnessing a broad-spectrum descent from individualism to socialism; objectivity to subjectivism; mountain to river. It's not just an out-of-proportion disagreement. It's not just a one-off episode of evil manifesting in the world. It is a sign of spiritual principalities and powers at work against speakers of truth in the world. Narratives are a weapon of something more sinister than the left/right divide inside generally liberal Enlightenment values. It's not just ideological, it's diabolical. Speaking specifically of the pandemic narrative, Naomi Wolf wrote:

> [T]his edifice of evil is too massive, too quickly erected, too complex and really, too elegant, to assign to just human awfulness and human inventiveness.[4]

We should apply this assessment to postmodernism more generally.

---

4 Wolf, Naomi, "Is It Time for Intellectuals to Talk about God?," *Independent Institute*, independent.org, Feb 3, 2022.

CHAPTER TWENTY-FOUR

The Machine

W HAT DO WE call a narrative that omits important facts and emphasizes less important ones? We call it a false narrative. The language of the serpent in the garden. A cause of the crumbling of the Tower of Babel. Narratives are stories we tell ourselves about who we are. But they can be developed and advanced in politics and culture to shape rather than merely describe who we are. They can be contrived to advocate a particular metanarrative.

We tend to think of mainstream media as the carrier of our shared narrative, and that was perhaps true before the increased political and cultural fracturing after the 1960s, and then the advent of the Internet and then social media. Media bias has been an increasingly common lament in recent decades, but in the last half-decade or so, the spurious neutrality of mainstream media has become odious. Blinkered, but straight-faced, presentation of news operates to build and impose social narrative rather than present facts to let the narrative form itself. Here is how one commentator, Freddie deBoer, describes the process, in the context of media's collective yawn over government-influenced shaping of narrative by Twitter:

> I'm interested in how these orthodoxies develop within media. I'm interested, in other words, in the Maw. The Maw is, broadly speaking, the expression of the culture war as operationalized by the consensus opinions of media. The Maw is the aggregate of opinions of paid-up journalists and writers and pundits and, specifically, the opinions they will allow. When a big story breaks, there's an initial feeling-out period where the media talks to itself and decides what the consensus opinion

will be. As time has gone on, this process has gotten faster and faster, so that now the media consensus and the expectation that all decent people will glom onto it develop in a matter of minutes. . . .This is the Maw at work—it's the expression of culture war in what the media sees as a respectable position to hold. In the Maw, nothing independent survives.[1]

To understand what's going on socially in our world, it's now necessary to mentally filter legacy media according to our understanding of the kind and degree of the presenter's bias. If we listen at all, we must not listen for content directly, but instead listen to how the story's told and for the interstitial silences of what's left out. Our purpose in listening must be to perceive movements of ideology—metanarratives—rather than to acquire relevant and reliable facts.

More independent purveyors of opinion now carry more weight among those paying attention—not because they're thought less biased, but because they're thought more honest. These presentations make no pretense of neutrality. We still have to infer the operative facts, but the spin is more visible. By listening to opposing opinions, one can discern the competing narratives and reason our way to the metanarratives they represent. This is not to say the truth is somewhere between opposite poles of opinion, necessarily. It is rather to say opposing presentations of overt opinion inform us as to competing narratives in play, and from there, we can grasp the competing metanarratives they support. Meta-narratives are the principles distilled from one's worldview; from one's *weltanschauung*.

Presenters that make their worldview more visible include think-tank essayists, bloggers, writers, YouTube speakers (perhaps now more likely found on Substack or Rumble); radio talk shows; late-night TV talk; and magazines or e-zines unapologetically presenting not just a story, but a way of thinking of things. Some of these media formats are accessible to stand-alone individuals—amateurs, we might say—engaging with whatever public might find them, often starting out on social media platforms at relatively little cost.

This might seem an ideal *laissez-faire* market for debate, in which small-d democracy can flourish, but in this age, there is a stronger instinct to quash perceived bad speech than to respect the principle of free speech, including "bad" speech, attempting to overcome it in the public

---

1 "The Twitter Files and Writing for the Maw," substack.com/freddiedeboer, December 12, 2022.

discussion with good speech. Democracy, as we saw in Chapters 21 and 22, is susceptible to two distinct and irreconcilable definitions. More speech supports democracy understood as a set of procedural principles of governance. Less speech may serve democracy understood as the socialist principle of utopian communitarianism. The socialist vision has gained ground against the classically liberal vision, stirring the instinct for thought control on both right and left. Thus, from every corner, left and right and interest-driven, there is hand-wringing about the need to control against misinformation, disinformation, and malinformation.

Who do we imagine is to do the controlling? One could say the government, because it alone has coercive power. But that's simplistic, in this age. A more descriptive term is the Machine: a corporatist partnership that includes the elected elements of government, but also its administrative state, along with big business, big tech, big media, and other ideological cultural influencers. These allied power centers advance postmodern ideology by disabling personal autonomy and fostering ever greater automation and interdependence. A collectivist perspective in all things is heightened by fast assemblages of big data, instant and vastly detailed information via Internet, hyper-specialization in individual economic efforts, and a relentless drive to efficiency through automation. Central banks tinker with the economy as one large engine. Financial credit scores become stand-ins for Chinese-style social credit scores, as does the ubiquity of instantly available information on everyone through relentless data-mining. Money is more represented in electronic exchanges than in cash. And so, developments to eliminate cash altogether (as recently bruited in the UK) are technologically closer to possible and would make us ever more dependent on computer algorithms for needs of daily living. These developments enhance the tendency to approve collective, centralized manipulation of individuals.

The Machine's goal is the advance of ideology, and that ideology includes the element of social control: of consumption of goods, medical care, the economy, travel, civil legal compliance, criminal law enforcement, and so on. Individuals cease to think in terms of personal autonomy, and begin to think instead in terms of privileges granted by the Machine.

The mechanism of Machine control (and another reason the word is descriptive) is automation: literal automation, in the case of interconnected technology, but also human automation, in the case of algorithmic living in an atmosphere of increasing social and commercial interdependence.

Ideologically aligned big business is heavily regulated by government, but the regulation is not merely an assertion of power by the entity that legally coerces, on the one hand, against entities subject to that coercion, on the other. Rather, regulation is, for the most part, mutually beneficial among such entities. For big business, costs of compliance are more than offset by reduction of risk and of incursions of competitors. Government regulation of business is for the most part an expression of power negotiation among partnered components of the Machine.

In addition, even ostensibly private commerce becomes joined to government within the Machine in the forms of public contracts, public/private partnerships, and ideological like-mindedness. The ideology is advanced in various forms of preferential treatment by identity group rather than universal value and in other expressions of ideology like "stakeholder capitalism" and "ESG" corporate governance and investing.

"ESG" is instructive on this point. It's not just a term to describe motivations for corporate activity other than profit. Together the three letters mark a company's compliance with doctrines of postmodern ideology. "E" refers to environment-friendly corporate practices, but that's taken to mean climate ideology, which is in turn taken to mean Machine control over means of production and consumption to avert or mitigate what is constantly presented as a catastrophic environmental crisis. The totalitarianism, which the global control would require, is ignored or else deemed a worthwhile concession to make given the severity of the putative crisis. Or else totalitarianism is the real point of it all.

The "S" (in ESG) refers to social. Socially conscious corporate policy doesn't mean general good citizenship. It means the whole array of progressive principles intended to remove inequality and move us toward sameness, including systemic racism, aversion to "populist" or "nationalistic" ideals, ongoing feminist antagonism against the patriarchy, and hostility to traditional family structures which might tend to delegitimize same-sex union and the identity-before-essence metaphysics of transgender ideology.

The "G" refers to corporate governance, scrutinized for the degree to which it promotes progressivist ideology from within. As with all postmodern ideology, it therefore contains a self-replicating gene, so to speak. The mechanism for further ideological advance is in this way encoded in the ideology itself. ESG is among the means by which political progressivism is leveraged through unelected power centers of Wall Street and the administrative state. In this way, the Machine imposes destructive postmodern ideology with no meaningful political recourse. We can't vote out of office the business groupthink that advances progressive ideology through ESG corporate policies.

Similarly, an insidious partnership between government and ostensibly independent private media outlets is obvious to anyone with eyes to see. Many media organizations lend their willingness to spin news to the ideological ends shared with government's entrenched regulating administrative arms. Social media organizations have become the most obvious co-ideologues, engaging as they are in "content moderation" that inevitably serves to control narrative.[2] Increasingly, the government controls narrative through willing accommodation by social media.[3] Social media fetters speech in the name of "content moderation," under direct influence of the government, or the indirect influence of simpatico cultural elitism, or, failing those, the government's glowering omnipresence. In this way, we further cede freedom to the collective in supine surrender of our freedom of speech, which is inextricably bound up with freedom of religion, as America's First Amendment suggests.

It's hard to argue this isn't an attempt at thought control through narrative:

> One could argue we're in the business of critical infrastructure, and the most critical infrastructure is our cognitive infrastructure, so building that resilience to misinformation and disinformation, I think, is incredibly important . . . .

These were the words of an appointee to the American Cybersecurity and Infrastructure Security Agency in November 2021.[4] "Cognitive infrastructure?" That means narrative, and "resilience" means controlling it. Misinformation/disinformation efforts by government, especially in league with ostensibly private media, recall us to the prescience of George Orwell. Not just in the way we're to think words don't mean

---

2   The inference is inescapable from government forum "debates" of recent years, as with the Senate interrogation of Mark Zuckerburg about Facebook's "content moderation." The purpose of both sides was to limn the scope of content moderation, not to debate whether content should be "moderated" in the first place.

3   See, e.g., Klippenstein, Ken, and Lee Fang, "Truth Cops," *The Intercept*, theintercept.com, October 31, 2022. The subject matter is exactly that on which co-ideologues most want to control narrative, such as the origins of covid, the effectiveness of vaccines against it, racial justice, U.S. withdrawal from Afghanistan, voting integrity measures, and the nature of U.S. support of Ukraine.

4   Ibid.

what they mean, but in the way concepts are conflated and thereby hidden so that the poison has taken effect before we realize we've swallowed it. At this writing, numerous lawsuits wend their way through American courts, criticizing government interference with free speech through pressure on ostensibly private social media. But litigation is a slow and grinding process, and the metanarrative is halfway around the world and rapidly evolving while litigation is just getting its shoes on.

Across liberal Western societies, there is an increasing sense of unease at this state of affairs; in particular, the interdependence of commerce combined with ideological hegemony of the Machine. Here is Alana Newhouse:

> Ask yourself why, in fact, so many corporations now all support the same roster of causes. Ask yourself how all channels of discourse in America suddenly flow in the same direction, making local and institutional and communal distinctions that were once defining seem vanishingly trivial. Why do all universities have the same politics and curricula and trigger warnings and quotas? Why must all hospitals and schools have them too? At what point does one accept that all of these causes and crises are related, that the closeness of their relationship to each other is quite strange?

> A new and decadent power center has been built, made up of the federal government and a constellation of corporations and non-profits that operate as connected wings of the same sprawling complex. The people who control the key platforms and networks are aggregating power to themselves at the expense of everyone else. . . . [5]

The "new and decadent power" is the Machine.

The ideology propagated by the Machine amounts to a state religion. Writing on the sex identification component of the ideology, Mary Harrington remarks:

> [I]f something looks like a duck and quacks like a duck, it's probably a duck. And when a movement with an instantly recognizable symbol [e.g., the "pride" flag], a distinctive metaphysics (identity precedes biology, all desire must be celebrated) and a calendar of feast days celebrated by governments, corporations, universities and public bodies acquires the ability to punish those who deface its symbols, the only possible thing you can call it is an emerging faith—one with a tighten-

---

5   "The Jews Who Didn't Leave Egypt/A lesson from the past about choosing freedom over servitude," *Tablet*, tabletmag.com, April 14, 2022.

ing grip on institutional power across the West.[6]

A first principle of America's founding was separation of church and state, summarized in the First Amendment to the American Constitution. The point was to prevent religious tyranny like that experienced by early colonists before emigrating from England. Religious liberty was founded on Enlightenment values of religious tolerance, separating governance from private views we regard as religious. To modern eyes, the scope of that tolerance might seem fairly narrow. It applied to the range of religious practice extant at the nation's founding: essentially, the various stripes of Protestantism, plus Catholicism, with a sprinkling of deists and freethinkers among the cultural elite of the time. The point of the non-establishment and free-exercise clauses of the First Amendment was to prevent government adoption of one of the religious viewpoints at the expense of others. Western religions of the time advanced a metanarrative, a set of principles that combine as a *weltanschauung*, a worldview concerning the metaphysics of transcendence, the moral make-up of human nature, and the ethical principles on which individuals interact with others and with government. A religious worldview can be termed a totalizing philosophy by which one makes sense of the world and navigates his way in it. Christian religion consisted in totalizing metanarratives about the superintendence of the world by a God both transcendent and immanent in this world; a moral imprint on the conscience of people from that God; an inclination to sin in the heart despite that conscience; and redemption from sin in Christ. There were varieties of theological belief within this basic framework.

The postmodern worldview rejects these religious premises but is similarly totalizing in its apprehension of reality. It denies a transcendent God, and metaphysical duality, and attempts to shift truth and morality formation to social process. It is monist in its metaphysics; that is, holding there is only matter in motion comprising reality. It perceives human nature as being mutable and essentially good except as corrupted by influences of individualistic selfishness among others in society. It prioritizes society over individuals, in perspective. We are to be concerned with social consciousness, socially formed values, and social justice.

Postmodernism addresses the same questions as religion, concerning what it means to be a person, and the sources of morality, and the

---

6 "Blasphemy is Dead, Long Live Blasphemy/The 'marketplace of ideas' was nice while it lasted," reactionaryfeminist.substack.com, October 26, 2022.

principles on which we interact communally. It is a worldview every bit as dogmatic as religion, with every bit of the potential for tyranny. We wouldn't call these fundamental tenets concerning reality a "religion" only because we use the word "religion" for belief systems that feature God or gods, with attendant doctrinal metanarrative reinforced in group rites and practices. But postmodernism is certainly a worldview, one that is every bit as totalizing in its perspective on reality, and certainly comprising doctrine reinforced in metanarrative and group political activism.

We avoid government sponsorship of a religion because it creates fertile ground for tyranny against other religions. The exact same principle ought to apply to worldviews we don't describe as "religious," and for the very same reason: they consist in dogmas and doctrines that, when engrafted onto government, result in tyranny against those who don't subscribe to them. Postmodern ideology should not be sponsored by government for the same reason religion shouldn't be.

But it is. Government not only sponsors postmodern ideology, it propagates it through its politically unaccountable administrative shadow, and the ideology is then echoed in the power centers of big media, social media, big tech, and Wall Street. The worldview of this Machine is supported by institutions of education intent on extirpating competing worldviews from among the next generation. In this environment, religious worldviews are actively suppressed, and the postmodern worldview is actively and exclusively sponsored. Why shouldn't the concerns that animated the principle of separation of church and state apply to the worldview presented by postmodern ideology? Why are only religious worldviews excluded from Machine activism?

A hedge against identification of the Machine, and the means of its growth, is to classify criticisms of it as conspiracy theory. In this way, critics of the obvious consolidations of power and ideological conformity are likened to flat-Earthers and Holocaust deniers. No one wants to be thought of as a tinfoil hat-wearing conspiracy theorist. But it's not conspiracy theory to point out ideological alignment among social power centers. It's not conspiracy theory to point out the blurring of boundaries between public and private, which creates the environment for it. Conspiracy theories posit a secret plot of some kind. There is nothing secret about the shared illiberal ideology of cultural elites, or the dilution of checks on their partnerships in power. They don't overtly call for overthrow of metanarratives based in transcendence. But those competing metanarratives are crushed by the Machine, implementing its metanarrative of immanence, materialism, metaphysical monism, and cultural and economic socialism. Those not in sync ideologically are pushed to the margins. Anyone can look and see what ideas are in play; there's no need for secrecy, nor for a cloistered cabal to hatch the plan of world domination.[7] The ideology does not result through the exchange of ideas in reasoned debate. Rather, the ideology itself dismantles the ability to engage the debate in the first place.

We form an understanding of social narrative from a variety of sources, including entertainment, broadcast, print, and social media. But information technology contributes to making us a mile wide and an inch deep. We're all instantly in the know about the same thing, even though what we know is shallow and mostly meaningless in a larger sense. One individual's capacity to know what is going on is limited, of course, in that we all have the same 24 hours in a day that George Washington, Abraham, and Jesus had. We rely on a process of distillation in media. That means we necessarily rely on the summations and opinions of others, and what we think we know is attenuated from ground-level facts. In earlier days, we had better command of facts, but we commanded facts about a relatively narrow sliver of the world. Now we have broader perspective but command fewer facts, so we more heavily rely on the inferences and "narratives" developed by others.

It's common now in politics to strive to "control the narrative." The "narrative" is not a straightforward presentation of facts and principles. It's a story developed from selected facts to support a disguised metanarrative. We're expected to rely on the accuracy of the narrative, though we know it is contrived. We tend to worry that others will not see the contrivance, or recognize that false narratives amount to creative partisan lying. And so we ratchet up the decibel level with our own contributions to try to overcome the distortion.

---

7   Consider, for example, the open and explicit plans of the World Economic Forum, available for anyone to read, such as Klaus Schwab's and Thierry Malleret's *COVID-19: The Great Reset*, Forum (World Economic Forum) 2020. An excellent treatment of its implications is contained in Michael Rectenwald's *The Great Reset and the Struggle for Liberty*, Nashville: New English Review Press, 2023.

CHAPTER TWENTY-FIVE

Liberal to Illiberal

W E PAUSED OUR discussion of individualism and socialism to explicate the concepts of metanarrative and the Machine, so as to better understand how the socialist perspective is advanced in what we have long thought of as liberal Western societies. Now we turn to the question whether they can truly be considered liberal any longer.

In 1919, Benito Mussolini identified fascism as the shift from individual agency according to liberal social contract theorists, to social agency in the totalitarian state:

> Liberalism denied the State in the name of the individual. Fascism reasserts the rights of the State as expressing the real essence of the individual. (...) The Fascist conception of the State is all embracing; outside of it no human or spiritual values can exist, much less have value. Thus understood, Fascism is totalitarian, and the Fascist State—a synthesis and a unit inclusive of all values—interprets, develops, and potentiates the whole life of a people.[1]

This is the Fascism of the Italian political party by that name, but also small-f right-wing fascism more generally. "Fascism is totalitarian." It explicitly calls for the individual to be subsumed into the state. But so did Maoist and Stalinist communisms, which we regard as being on the extreme left. Those states were unquestionably totalitarian and unfree. So how could one associate the socialist perspective—of the fascist right or communist left—with freedom? The answer has to be that we don't,

---

1 "The Doctrine of Fascism," *World Future Fund*, http://www.worldfuturefund.org/wffmaster/reading/germany/mussolini.htm.

we merely redefine the words we use.

It is inescapable that the most important tenets of postmodern thought coincide with fascism. In both, individual identity is a myth because identity is socially formed. Culture makes the person, not God. Both conceive law and cultural norms and social institutions as merely masks for the naked exercise of power. Logocentrism, the centrality of the word, is suspect, because language is the medium over which all our interactions take place, rather than emotion and intuition, and so (to postmodernists) language has an alienating impact that must be overcome. We're to believe Western civilization has been corrupted by linear, objective, hyper-rational abstract thinking, and so must be replaced by a return to pagan immanence, natural close-to-the-earth living, and an easy-going, guiltless sexuality.

In Western democracies in the twenty-first century, we tend to think we're far removed from fascism, forgetting that what makes fascism fascism are just these thought trends, which can and do appear in ostensibly liberal democracies. Identity politics have become ubiquitous, and the identity is not with those who share universal principles, but rather with those of the same race or sex or sexual proclivity. It is a return to tribalism, even as we inconsistently mouth values of multiculturalism, tolerance, and openness. The political stance of parties we consider to be on the left present arguments entirely inside a paradigm of deconstruction, just as with both Marxists and fascists. Because reality is thought to be socially constructed, men can imagine themselves women, and vice versa, and huge swaths of this generation now in childhood are sexually confused. A crisis of meaning has so overtaken illiberal postmodern societies that they don't reproduce at replacement rate.

In his *Liberal Fascism*, Jonah Goldberg defined fascism like this:

> Fascism is a religion of the state. It assumes the organic unity of the body politic and longs for a national leader attuned to the will of the people. It is totalitarian in that it views everything as political and holds that any action by the state is justified to achieve the common good. It takes responsibility for all aspects of life, including our health and well-being, and seeks to impose uniformity of thought and action, whether by force or through regulation and social pressure. Everything, including the economy and religion, must be aligned with its objectives. Any rival identity is part of the "problem" and therefore defined as the enemy.[2]

---

2 Goldberg, Jonah, *Liberal Fascism: The Secret History of the American Left, from Mus-*

Susan Sontag, no particular friend of the right, declared "communism is fascism."[3] She wrote:

> [I]t is generally thought that National Socialism stands only for brutishness and terror. But this is not true. National Socialism—more broadly, fascism—also stands for an ideal or rather ideals that are persistent today under other banners: the ideal of life as art, the cult of beauty, the fetishism of courage, the dissolution of alienation in ecstatic feelings of community, the repudiation of the intellect, the family of man (under the parenthood of leaders).[4]

"[T]he dissolution of alienation in ecstatic feelings of community." This is the utopian vision for fascism, and for communism, and for democracy as postmodern thinkers envision it.

Fascism is associated with the right, and our danger is clearly from the left, but we should not continue to think of fascism and communism as the extremes on a single linear spectrum. If we look at Mussolini's definition and compare it to the political ideology postmodernism takes us to, it's clear they're the same thing. The words—fascism and communism—are often used more like emotional markers than actual totalitarian theories. Something to hurl at one's enemy for emphasis. Fascism and communism converge, in every important way, and together they stand opposite (classical) liberalism. Liberalism means hands off the individual. Both fascism and communism mean totalitarianism: the individual subsumed into the collective. The important extremes are not fascism and communism, but totalitarianism and individualism.

Individualism allows for heterodoxy because there is yet a common belief in transcendence, or objectivity, or God, or logocentrism. That is, there are abstract principles to which we all subscribe, and we self-govern by them. By common deference to these external principles, we maintain our individuality yet live peacefully together. But if we don't self-govern by objective principle, then we attempt to govern each other by a grunting all-against-all push for what we will then describe as social consensus. The social consensus is binding on all, so it's not really consensus. It's coercive. It is achieved by giving up individuality to the collective. This is a feature common to both fascism and communism,

---

solini to the Politics of Meaning, New York: Doubleday, 2007, p. 23.

3   Herzog, Wagner, "Susan Sontag—A Leftist to Be Admired," *Merchants of Air*, August 23, 2017, merchantsofair.com.

4   Sontag, Susan, "Fascinating Fascism," *New York Review of Books*, Feb. 6, 1975.

as they were understood in the twentieth century. Like postmodernism, they are avowedly socialist and materialist—no one seems to remember that anymore.

Postmodern thought has moved from the theoretical and into the minds of individuals in formerly liberal Western societies. The hope is thin, therefore, that a government like that of the United States will return to governing on objective principles like equality, justice, and so on, rather than on coerced "consensus." We trend to social democracies that are every bit as tyrannical as the old-school pagan strong-man fascism that comes with a comical moustache.

Leftists fear interruption of the program of collectivism, given life by postmodern philosophy. Socialism has been advancing in the United States for generations, not reversed but only throttled back slightly when Republicans are in office. The more blue a person is, the more convinced he is that the leftward socialist program is the only moral telos appropriate in a democracy. An interruption in that program would mean emergent evil, therefore, not just a temporary dial-back in one lost election cycle.

The new fascism is just like the old, except more pernicious and more tenacious. The old involved subsumption of the self into a totalitarian state embodied in a dictator. The new involves subsumption of the self into a totalitarian Machine disembodied from individuals, and formed and sustained in the coercive collective. The "Machine" of the new fascism is not limited to a government. It includes collective-reinforcing big business and especially big tech, with accomplices in legacy media, education, and other social media. It is a Machine because it is not one power center, but like-minded interdependent systems, government and non-government, binding individuals within it through hyper-efficient algorithmic commercial interdependence, technology, various forms of surveillance, and social pressure for speech conformity.

Old fascism:	New fascism:
Strong man leader	Coercive "consensus"
Party orthodoxy	Social orthodoxy
State as totalizer	Machine as totalizer
Individual subsumed	Individual subsumed

Some postmodern thinking also speaks to a "machine" but as some variant of subgroups within society (Deleuze) or the automatism of consumer identity (Marcuse). On this point, the postmodernists are looking almost, but not quite, in the right direction. Their criticisms are valid, but their fixes are collectivist, to remake the person by remaking society first rather than appeal to universal principle. In this way, they miss the inevitable oppression the collectivist Machine poses for the individual.

Fascism, the word, should be understood as descriptive of the current collectivism, but instead is wrongly understood as the symbol of archetypal evil. Postmodern leftists generally posture themselves as activists in opposition to it.[5] We should look past the labels at the reality, however. What does the deconstructionist left really stand for, and what is the fascism they say they oppose? There is actually little daylight between them. The principles underlying fascism—the real kind—are alarmingly similar to those gaining currency in postmodern thought. The fascists of the last century are the intellectual forebears of today's hard-left activists. Both resolutely turn their faces against the word, logocentrism, rationality, reason, transcendence, and, of course, God. Ironically, the very existence of old-school real fascism provides cover for its recrudescence in postmodern power plays. The radical deconstructionist left hides its fascist principles by posturing itself against a straw-man "fascism" only superficially distinct. Postmodern theorists despise the swastika but adopt key principles that go with it.

How can this happen? It can happen by facile left vs. right thinking. As with all such oppositions, greater differentiation and division is necessary to adequately understand. The left/right dichotomy in politics had its uses but now oversimplifies. Both "right-wing" fascism and "left-wing" communism are considered extremes on a spectrum, but they aren't, really. They're competing forms of illiberal socialism, both of which stand in opposition to traditional liberalism of free markets, limited government, and individualism. Their similarities are more significant than their differences.

This is better understood if we take a short step back historically. After the putative death of God in the West—which we can reasonably peg to about the turn of the twentieth century—the concomitant abandonment of objectivity of truth and morality generated ideologies that came to be associated with left and right: communism and fascism, respectively, at the extremes. The liberal West watched with growing unease as those concentrations of illiberal power grew. Enmity between

---

5 See, for example: Michel Foucault's preface to Gilles Deleuze's and Félix Guattari's *Anti-Oedipus: Capitalism and Schizophrenia*, New York: Penguin, 1977, p. xi.

the ideologies resulted in the Soviet Union's uneasy alliance with the liberal democracies against the fascisms of Germany and Italy, and imperialist Japan. For the liberal democracies (the UK, U.S., and others), the hot war was against fascism, and the ensuing cold war was against communism, but both were antagonistic to the liberal West because of their illiberal socialist similarities.

Postmodern philosophy, after the war, mostly continued the baseline assumption against God and, more vaguely, transcendence, and against objectivity of truth and right and wrong. The wars spurred attempts at rejection of overarching metanarrative ideologies,[6] like those on the right, just defeated at great cost. Ideologies of the left, however, were either invisible or were deemed innocuous to those thinkers, so post-war philosophy resumed on lines of Marxist variants critiquing the crass commercialism of capitalist liberal democracies, and/or the putatively oppressive power dynamics endemic to them.

Individualism was the direct target of fascism, as it is of postmodernism now. Mussolini's definition of fascism was most essentially collectivist and self-abnegating (excepting, of course, application to elites). Likewise postmodernism. In both, all of one's being is a social construct, and upon formation of that self, tribal solidarity is found among those who regard themselves similarly formed. Human consciousness is thought to be constituted by social forces and structures of power, and these are expressed in language, the medium for all such social construction. Because the culture forms the individual (rather than the other way around), cultural needs and demands have priority over individual rights and autonomy. Both fascism and postmodern neo-Marxism involve social engineering to the end of reforming the individual. Fascism was a deconstructionist project, just like postmodernism is now. The idea, then and now, is that Western civilization must be dismantled to make way for a new civilization founded on pagan immanence, close-to-the-earth environmental sensitivity, and collectivist solidarity.

A particularly disturbing but also self-proving feature of both fascism and postmodern developments is antisemitism. It's not just that fascists were rabidly antisemitic and now antisemitism is on the rise again. It's that there is a cause-effect relationship between fascist and postmodern ideologies, on the one hand, and hatred of Jews, on the other. Why are Jews in disfavor, to put it mildly, in both ways of thinking? It's because of their "invention of God," adherence to an idea of the

---

6   Indeed, some thinkers make this the definition of "postmodernism," a definition more narrow than that employed in the present work.

transcendent, expressed in the word, a set of ideals existing in reality, beyond the language used to describe them. God supports those ideals from above, but killing off our conception of God does not solve the problem. He remains as an avatar, at least, for the principle of hierarchy in values and ideals. The remaining sense of transcendence is thought to be a cerebral construct at odds with the earthy pagan "blood and soil" mentality sought after by the Nazis, which overlaps in the pagan and environmentalist sensibilities of postmodernists.

Immanence is the idea of spiritual reality in the world. Transcendence is the idea of spiritual reality outside the world. These are sometimes seen as a paradox, in theology, because how could God (or gods) be both? "Transcendence" means exceeding the bounds of one's normal experience, so in theology, it means that which is spiritual rather than natural. In orthodox Christianity, God is transcendent; however, He is also immanent, meaning that He exists spiritually in the heavenly realm but also in the immediate world of our living experience. The latter, immanence, is more obvious in Christianity, upon the advent of the Christ and the principle that the Holy Spirit continues upon the Ascension as "the Helper" among us. Jesus summarized all the law and prophets on two commandments: to love God with all one's heart and soul and mind, and to love one's neighbor as oneself.[7] Obedience to these commandments means experiencing God transcendently and immanently, respectively. Immanence does not exist independently, however. Transcendence must come first.

In Jewish theology, understood before its being proven out by Christ's Advent, God was more readily conceived as existing transcendently, far off up there dispensing law and judgment to serious academic but prophetic minds, sorting it all out for us earth-bound beings constantly looking up for guidance. The fascists, like postmodernists, disbelieve God and disbelieve *in* God, and so Jews were thought to have "invented" Him. Upon inventing Him, they (the Jews) were understood to introduce a false narrative of sterile vertical Platonic idealism, replacing the merry dance of paganism, gods superintending ritual-enforced tribal solidarity, a social oneness of immanence. For this reason, antisemitism recurs in extremes of ideology. The Jews are held responsible for interrupting the merry dance; for substituting bloodless principle in place of healthful vigor, action, and collectivist expression of the will-to-power. In the Jewish (and ultimately, Christian) conception, truth (and

---

7 Matthew 22:37-40.

falsity) and goodness (and evil) are external to us yet binding upon us. They are not determined by nature, or the community, or the self. This is precisely the point of departure for both fascism and postmodernism.

The appeal of fascism is that the sense of alienation we feel can be overcome by collective group solidarity, and organic, collective generation of truth and morality. This is also the appeal of postmodern philosophy.

The metaphor:	The mountain	The river
Man's creation:	God's in-spiriting	Dust
God's presence:	Transcendence	Immanence
Spiritual outlook:	Jews (/Christians)	Materialists

The idea in the existentialist precursor to postmodernism was that meaning is mankind-created, not objective. Pragmatism picks up where existentialism leaves off, transferring the truth-creation to a collective plane. Impersonal cultural forces shape human behavior, it holds, and do so through language—language understood as all systems of signifier and signified, so not just words audible or written, but other systems of communication like dress, art, social norms, and so on. All such "text" can be decoded to unveil power structures in society, and those power structures inscribe meaning collectively. We are shaped by culture, class, gender, ethnicity, and sexual proclivities by the whole collective language system. Individual autonomy is illusory, a product of Enlightenment and transcendence notions of individualism.

Transcendence means that words (and image and semiotics more generally) point to realities beyond themselves. But that idea is considered an illusion by postmodern deconstructionists. The words (and the images/signs reducible to words) are all there is, there is no reality beyond. That means power is the only basis for word (signs) use. This is an anti-logocentric position. Postmodern deconstructionists try to topple the hierarchy created by logocentrism, word-centeredness. Word usage is just illegitimate perpetuation of Western metaphysics, and so devious manipulation of words to deconstruct it seems justified. It is the language misuse by the serpent in the garden all over again.

Why isn't book burning, like the Nazis did, just like the current cancel culture and political correctness and prohibition of offensive speech and bans from social media providers? And aren't these all just new Towers of Babel crumbling to their destruction? All entail destruction in our ability to speak to one another. We build our Towers of Babel and they fall periodically, as they are doing right now in the West. Genesis warned us of this.

CHAPTER TWENTY-SIX

Coercion

T HE PROCESS philosophies that unimagine God are socialist and necessarily so. Their progression in postmodern thought hollows us out from the inside, so there is no God-breathed self any longer to accept or reject God. This is what C.S. Lewis was getting at in *The Abolition of Man*, which he published in 1943. If we deny objective values, then all values are subjective. But if all values are subjective, then the individual who generates his values comes to think of himself as material, in accord with the presumptive materialism of this age. As a material being, he is manipulable like other material things, and some power (like the ideology of the Machine) is permitted to rise up to do the manipulating.

The Machine is zealous for order at the expense of all else, and individuals are manipulated into service of whatever totalizing ideology is at hand: communism, fascism, or the totalizing democratic socialism of the Great Reset. We are currently being herded into totalitarian ideology by self-appointed elites emboldened and empowered by the successful stretching of its muscles in the fear-induced reaction to Covid. The paternalistic reach of the World Economic Forum, the United Nations, NGOs, and other elements of the Machine are not fever dreams of conspiracy theorists, but active movements which gain traction precisely because we mentally disconnect from our God-imaged dignity and come to regard ourselves as manipulable material beings, snuggling into the warm communitarianism of utopian socialism. The trend line is to totalitarianism, just like in Germany and Russia in the run-up to the mid-century catastrophes. Totalitarianism is not mere government oppression. It is the subsumption of self into the collective, in just the way

Mussolini defined "fascism." Tribal identitarian partisanship in place of fealty to universal principle is how we get there.

In the postmodern outlook, the individual, lost in the collective and dependent on it, is nonetheless better actualized, in some way, and so that actualization becomes the definition of freedom, instead of independence and liberation from conformity-inducing power centers. Thus, postmodernists redefine the individual, and redefine freedom. Let's inquire into how they manage it.

A first step might be to distinguish between subjective and objective freedom. Mere subjective freedom can be unfreedom, the thinking would go, as when a slave is subjectively happy with his lot, conditioned to accept it, so that he doesn't feel his chains. Few would agree that slavery should be tolerated because those trapped within it are afraid of change. They are objectively unfree. The slave in our example would be "forced to be free," in Rousseau's vision, by abolition of slavery and a levelling of all members of society into an equality uncorrupted by ambition, prestige, and selfishness.

Slavery is only an extreme of inequality, however, so perhaps a general socialism should be forced to try to eradicate all other differences? We are all caught up in other less obvious kinds of patterns or circumstances that constrain us, after all, starting with economic or social disadvantages we're born into, and for which we are therefore not responsible. Perhaps objective freedom requires a rigorous redistribution of economic resources, and a levelling of social circumstances, a socialist might argue.

The obvious objection to this is that human nature (as disclosed in Genesis) would not support such a move. With such a total shift to socialist perspective, there would be no "I" left to embody human dignity. And a second obvious objection is that it is impossible. Even if we could snap our fingers and make everyone equal in resources all in a moment, in the next moment, we would experience a Big Bang of differentials by every conceivable human measure, because people are so very different, in intelligence, ambition, diligence, values, and in innumerable other ways. No freedom is possible through centralizing a model of humanity to then impose on individuals. Indeed, the social engineering necessary to bring about equality of outcome would backfire, pushing down those meant to be brought up even as it brings down those already up. Inequality cannot be eradicated.

But let's suppose the distinction between "objective" and "subjective" freedom gains traction. The next step is to force changes in social conditions on the grounds that we tend to resist our liberators. The thought is that we become mired in a state of unfreedom without realizing it, as when bad old capitalism creates an environment in which we're reduced to consumer units, and are then in need of liberation from the capitalist machine. We need emancipation on this view even though we individually choose—or some of us do, anyway—the soul-ensnaring enticements of novelty and prestige, and the lures of sophisticated marketing, and repression of eros-driven motivation that might bring us to aesthetics-driven self-actualization.

Because people in capitalist societies are subjected to this sort of persuasion against their own interest of thriving in individuality, and because they respond machine-like, we should remake society along socialist lines, the thinking goes, though it would mean re-formatting those people as if they were computers rather than God-created vessels of consciousness, independence, reason, and moral agency. The point is to put off those features of humanity in favor of a self-conception as members of the hive, living out an internalized ethic of aesthetic motivation to replace their formerly selfish brutishness.

The problem of capitalism is consumerism, which is taken to be the production of desire in consumers, turning them into desiring machines, enabling producers to profit by always looking for desires to answer, in a churning engine of addiction to consumption. Our desire for individuality seems to be satisfied in consumer choices, especially choices of style, which by definition, become obsolete so that they have to be replaced in an ever-evolving self-identification with consumer choices. Manipulation of people through their shopping identity occurs so that their individual dignity is concomitantly eroded.

This is a legitimate criticism of how the prosperous West behaves, having jettisoned God. People do seem to give up their real individuality in favor of this simulacrum. But they have a choice. It is suggested here that they devolve to *homo shopicus* not because of capitalism, but because rejection of God results in an absence of source for higher meaning, which results in an ongoing struggle to find meaning some other way. Perhaps in shopping malls but perhaps, instead, the euphoria of intoxication. Or the thrill of crime or violence. Or sexual titillation. Or the defiant resentment of victimhood. Or vindication of imagined rights in a society driven by rights instead of duties; power instead of love. Capitalism in this age might be a sorry state of affairs, but it's not unfreedom. An overthrow of capitalism is not necessary to return hollowed-out persons to self-respect, and more importantly, an overthrow of capitalism and its material abundance would not bring freedom. Freedom means the unconstrained exercise of individual agency, not repudiation of the self altogether.

We might well ask how anyone could slip into the noxious socialist understanding of "freedom," given that it advances dependence and constraint in diametric opposition to the original meaning of the word, and in hostile juxtaposition to human dignity. One way is to internalize subjective pop psychology by which an individual becomes more actualized if certain individual needs are met. The value hierarchy of Abraham Maslow[1] is sometimes misused in this way. He suggested a stepped-up hierarchy of human needs starting with material needs and then certain emotional needs, then intellectual needs, and so on. Clearly, getting food is more fundamentally necessary than intellectual stimulation, and perhaps the hierarchy is helpful to our thinking about the relative weight of various human psychological motivations. But that does not define freedom. It only describes a theoretical means to psychological wellness. These are distinct and non-overlapping concepts. But it can confuse one into a socialist conception of freedom, because it suggests that freedom increases as one moves up the hierarchy of needs. If only material needs could be met (the first level of the hierarchy), we could move up the hierarchy and be progressively more free. We want people to be free, don't we? So let us (that is, all of us, collectively) meet the needs that move the individual up the hierarchy toward self-actualization.

The obvious objection to this way of thinking is that socialism is not necessary to moving up the hierarchy at all. (In fact, economically it would be a hindrance.) If this is a correct model of human psychological thriving, it is just as valid for an individual to pursue for himself. It does not by itself require a socialist approach. Freedom is not found in having the conditions to self-actualize. Freedom is as much freedom to fail as to prosper, else it is not freedom at all.

Moreover, actualization of the self is pointless if the means to accomplish it diminish the self that would be actualized. Self-actualization must be a project of the individual self; it cannot be a social project because people are too different, and the differences are ineradicable. There are wide gaps in intelligence, good looks, inventiveness, industriousness, and so on. There always will be. And those gaps produce inequalities in income, wealth, popularity, and power. They always will.

---

1   Maslow, Abraham, "A Theory of Human Motivation," *Psychological Review,* 1943.

Those gaps grow wider, and faster, than we'd like to think. This is how people are, it cannot be changed by any amount of social engineering or wishful thinking.

We're urged to pretend it can, however. And more, to pretend the only obstacle is our intractability in resisting our own liberation into the collective. A postmodern article of faith is that we all need emancipation from the unfreedom of capitalism. Marx felt that the bourgeois class structure bred a sense that the status quo is just the way things are, when in reality, it is intentionally a structure to protect power interests. Both workers and capitalists work under a sense of "false consciousness" about reality and their place in it. They need to have their eyes opened, therefore, and that is thought to require socialism.

Most postmodernists persist with some variant of this pernicious Marxist premise of social structures inducing "false consciousness." This is the point of the language theory of de Saussure and Derrida, for example: language is, if not meaningless altogether, then a purveyor of falsehood endemically so that we willingly accept our oppression. Émile Durkheim (1858-1917) similarly wrote of social forces greater than individuals swept along with it. We must be forced to be free, just as Rousseau wrote in the eighteenth century. Coercive collectivism for pragmatic political survival is necessary, just as Hobbes wrote in the seventeenth.

In more recent times, neo-Marxists continue the premise of structural "false consciousness" as justification for forcing socialism on reluctant capitalist society. György Lukács (1885-1971) theorized that prosperity under capitalism is illusory because we engage in a process of "reification," meaning that we acquire a false consciousness in place of authenticity by reifying false relationships with things rather than real relationships with people. Prosperity under capitalism gives us only an illusory freedom. We are ensnared, he thought, by this process of reification of the inconsequential at the expense of the authentic, and so we must be freed by force. Our chains, so the theory goes, exist in our own minds, and socialists ride to the rescue to rid us of them.

Similarly, Theodor Adorno decried the automation of mass media and mass culture in society, which produced consumers conditioned to identification with their consumer choices, a society which produces commodification and conformity. The capitalist processes of commodification occurred through a structural process of—borrowing from Lukács—reification. That is, the commodification principles he critiqued were so central to capitalism that they were taken as inevitable and inexorable social forces, again a kind of false consciousness from which we are freed only by the overthrow of capitalism and installation of some sort of (always vaguely described) socialism.

Postmodernist Zygmunt Bauman, in *Liquid Modernity*,[2] quite explicitly approves of coercion for this supposedly emancipatory goal, actually citing Hobbes and Durkheim. Bauman articulates the postmodern view, when he advocates Durkheimian coercion to comply with social norms: "Social coercion is in this [Durkheim's] philosophy the emancipatory force, and the sole hope of freedom that a human may reasonably entertain."[3] We've come a long way from the individualism of Henry David Thoreau: "I would rather sit on a pumpkin and have it all to myself than be crowded on a velvet cushion."[4]

Importantly (and insidiously), the coercion is not to force people to a point of view against their will, but rather to create as one of the social norms an expectation of internalizing social norms. This is the Chinese model. It is difficult to conceive a more obviously totalitarian proposition. Dissent dissolves with the individuals who would do the dissenting. The coercion is not just to comply, but to want to comply, and the compliance is to social norms, not objective principle. Instead of arguing propositions by a criterion of objective truth, we push and pull for dominance in the social acceptability of ideas. The social norm is the norm because it survives the social battle.

Moreover, postmodern social norms are self-entrenching because they result from critique, which as we saw in considering the hermeneutics of suspicion,[5] is substantive, not merely a principle of interpretation, and indelibly partisan and intolerant into the bargain. It does not tolerate rivals. Bauman cites with approval an endemic "inhospitality to critique," referring really to critique of postmodern critique:

> [C]ontemporary society . . . has invented a way to accommodate critical thought and action while remaining immune to the consequences of that accommodation.[6]

In more direct words, appear to listen to conservatives but actual-

---

2 Bauman, Zygmunt, *Liquid Modernity*, Malden, MA: Polity, 2000.

3 *Liquid Modernity*, p. 20.

4 Thoreau, Henry David, *Walden Pond* (*The Variorum Walden*, New York: Washington Square Press, 1962, originally published 1854).

5 Supra, Chapter 14.

6 *Liquid Modernity*, p. 23.

ly just ignore them. Postmodernism is nothing if not partisan critique, but its self-aware proponents have learned from their own technique to ignore opposition. Hence, for just one example, the relentlessly ideological offerings of National Public Radio in the United States, supported significantly through extractive government taxation.

If we prefer to make our own decisions about what is best for us, we should be on our guard so that when we hear phrases like "alienation," "false consciousness," and "reification" uttered by postmodernists, we can drop what we're doing and race to the parapets to defend our ability to decide what reality is for ourselves. To preserve freedom, it is necessary to fight the onslaught, not engage in endless disputation in words the attackers attach no real meaning to.

The coercive instinct in neo-Marxism is unfreedom. Marxist postmodernists are saying others' view of reality is faulty, and theirs is not, and so they're going to do everyone else a favor by forcing their vision. This is authoritarian, until it becomes totalitarian. The difference is this: under authoritarianism, you're oppressed, but under totalitarianism, there is no "you" any longer to be oppressed.

The battleground is language, but language doesn't really point to anything beyond itself, in the postmodern mind, so anything goes. It's all theory, unattached to reality. Postmodern thinkers engage in argument only because unenlightened rubes might be gullible enough to attach objective meaning to their words. Words are weapons in the one-dimensional immanence of the postmodern imagination. They are not pointers to transcendent meaning, so all dialogue in words "is a tale told by an idiot, full of sound and fury, signifying nothing."[7] Engaging the postmodern mind from a position of objective reality amounts to trying to reason with the serpent in the garden. The serpent isn't there to reason together in good faith by common appeal to objective principle. The serpent is there to manipulate you through dissembling words into catastrophic failure. It's not that we're speaking different languages, exactly. It's that the parties produce words for wholly different purposes. On one side, it's to point to the mountain of objective meaning; on the other side, it's to dissolve meaning entirely in the levelling flow of the river.

In this way, ideologies, rather than ideals, become entrenched. Currently, the ideology includes the metanarrative that there is no God; matter in motion is all of reality; morality is socially created; any form

---

7 *Macbeth*, 5:5.

of alterity is anathema to socialist progress; and dissent from socially approved norms is morally selfish and rightly subjected to relentless bullying. Citing Deleuze and Guattari, Bauman specifically pins his insistence on socialist perspective on the absence of God: "In our modern times, with God on a protracted leave of absence, the task of designing and servicing order has fallen upon human beings."[8] This is standard postmodern fare concerning religion, but it's an interesting formulation for its negative implication: If God is real, then this idea of freedom through socialism is wrong.

In postmodern thought, society takes the place of God, and we certainly needed God, so now we must need society in the same way. In the Genesis worldview, dependence is on God rather than mankind; in fact, dependence on mankind is potentially fraught, as we see in the warnings of stories about the Fall, Cain and Abel, the Tower of Babel, and the Flood. Genesis tells us over and over, in many different ways, if we'll listen, that our dependence is not to be on our individual selves, or on our society, or on all of mankind in the abstract, but rather on God alone.

---

8 *Liquid Modernity*, pp. 21, 55.

CHAPTER TWENTY-SEVEN

Marx, Still

W E HAVE MADE frequent mention of Marx in this discussion of postmodernism. That's because the direction of most secular philosophy since the mid-century wars has been Marxist, loosely defined. Marx was not merely incidentally an atheist materialist. His atheism was the key to all his work, and Marxism is the key to postmodernism. Marx's atheist materialism requires a break from the Platonic/Christian understanding that mankind is in a necessary relationship with God (or transcendence or objectivity) and is only secondarily in a relationship with society, as important as that is.

The right way to understand the significance of Marx's lingering impact was articulated by Spencer Klavan like this:

> For the Church and the West to survive, there can be no "concessions" to Marxism—only a stark refutation of it, rooted in the eternal truths that Marxism has erased from view. For the Marxist, revolutionary struggle determines what is good in the moment, irrespective of any fabricated absolutes. For the Ontologist, exactly the opposite is true: unchanging verities, which we grasp in our imperfect but very real communion with God, set the standard that should determine all our actions in each new era.[1]

Universal ethical considerations, and indeed universals in general, are primary and precede politics, in a world attuned to objective truth and morality. But politics becomes primary, in the Marxist vision, be-

---

1   Klavan, Spencer, "Never Been Tried," book review of English translation of Augusto Del Noce's *The Problem of Atheism," Law & Liberty*, lawliberty.org, August 12, 2022.

cause it is centered on society rather than the individual. Society is not a collection of individuals, on this way of thinking, organically generating a culture and institutions mostly independent of the coercive state. Instead, society is an entity unto itself, and the individual is formed by the society. Our relationship to society is thus primary because it is formative of its individual members. Religion is relegated to the status of hobby or therapy or "crutch" until it withers away entirely.

For this reason, postmodernism, Marxist at its core, is centered on political activism. Politics, not God, is the source of value and truth. In consequence, politically active neo-Marxists relentlessly storm the public square with dissembling narrative, and do so mostly unopposed, because for those not caught up in the Marxist paradigm, political activism is not the point of existence. Those not disposed to Marxist methodology tend to look on in puzzlement. And then they (most of them) tend to eventual grudging acquiescence, because it seems not worth the fight, because the public square is not the magical place of meaning and purpose that it is for neo-Marxists. The lesson, or one of them, anyway, is that not engaging politics in this day means not opposing postmodern ideology, and not opposing postmodern ideology means fascism creeping upon us gradually so we don't see it until it's too late.

To make the same point in a different way, let's place side-by-side the Platonic/Christian vision (even as held by the irreligious who hold to objectivity) and the postmodern vision. In the Platonic/Christian vision, truth and morality are real and objective, not socially formed. The ultimate arbiter of good and evil and of ideals like justice and mercy is transcendent of human beings and of the society of which they are a part.

Postmodernism rejects transcendence and logocentrism and objectivity, following Marx, so for postmodernists, there is no such third-point arbiter, and mankind's social desire equates to immanence over transcendence, construed to mean values are generated in social movements. And so, all of life is political. Atheism is central to this vision because it explains diversion of attention of the susceptible from non-political ultimate transcendence, redirecting it to the roiling river of social activism.

Because politics, not God, is the means of generating human worth in the Marxist vision, activist politics take on a religious fervor. The direction of zealous activism is invariably leftist because of the tendentious posture of negation essential to Marxism and its postmodern intellectual legacy. The religious zeal portends totalitarian intolerance because collectivist politics yields "truth" binding on all. Political activism is socialist in postmodern ideology, not just because old-school Marxism was about socialism, but because centering politics in the human self-conception has that result. The procedural machinery of democracy reinforces the postmodernist centering of social political engagement. The private sphere of life fades away and the public sphere pervades. Dissent becomes intolerable heresy rather than minority opinion.

Christians often find politics distasteful, or at least distasteful when it surfaces in religious practice, precisely because they aspire to look upward, so to speak, for ultimate values, separating the sacred from the profane and relegating matters of governance to the arena of the profane. But by ignoring political and social activism, they cede the operative social environment to postmodern ideology. Absent an awakening into reality, the postmodernist carries on in darkness, and the world, which he believes to be all there is:

> Hath really neither joy, nor love, nor light,
> Nor certitude, nor peace, nor help for pain;
> And we are here as on a darkling plain
> Swept with confused alarms of struggle and flight,
> Where ignorant armies clash by night.[2]

The posture of negation that is Marxism creates a presumption of opposition to the existing order and a tendentious attitude of rebellion against principles which imply transcendence. Marxism does not stand alone as a form of society. It only exists as critique of another, like a virus existing parasitically in a host, and like a virus, it enervates and may ultimately destroy the host. The point is not to sweep away what exists to immediately install a better plan. The point is only to sweep away what exists. It's not at all clear what would come next after successful Marxist activism. For now, it only matters that whatever it is, it won't be what we have now.

Marxist atheism is central to postmodern thought for the additional reason that it is materialist at its core. Materialism is the default philosophy one holds if all religion is rejected. The default monist metaphysics of materialism means matter in motion comprises all of reality. There is no spiritual component of reality as in metaphysical dualism. One implication of the materialist worldview is that it affects profoundly how

---

2 Final lines of "Dover Beach" by Matthew Arnold (1867).

one thinks of morality, as compared to those with a worldview of logo-centric transcendence. Morals are deemed merely evolved tendencies which enhance social living in the monist materialist view, not a set of ideals divinely imbued in the conscience, as in dualist theism.

This idea of morality enhances the lean to socialism, but more importantly, it reverses the Christian presumption about the origin of evil. People are natural and good, except as corrupted by capitalist society, goes the thinking, rather than carrying in the heart the corruption of original sin resulting from the Biblical fallenness of the world. Our felt alienation is externally caused, not internally. On this view, human striving is not a function of individually overcoming corruption in the heart by seeking out an eternal ideal. Instead, we're to perfect society so as to eliminate external corrupting influences, and as a result, the light of human goodness can shine forth.

The postmodern presumption is that the corrupting influences are from religion or "capitalism," and social activism will overcome them. This must take place in a socialist environment with all-in participation, not as a matter of persuasion but as a matter of consensus, therefore, consensus formation of norms is necessary. The consensus must be coerced until the entrenched traditionalists are defeated or die off. Coercion means totalitarianism, of course, but it is only the interim price to pay, in the postmodern vision, to bring us all down to the river to laugh and play in the sunshine.

The postmodern turn from objectivity to relativism is well illustrated in the thinking of Augusto Del Noce (1910-1989), who perceptively explained twentieth-century ideologies culminating in the bloodbath of the mid-century world war. He was remarkably prescient about where those ideological trends would take us. Del Noce was Italian, and his works long remained obscure to English-only readers until translated by Carlo Lancellotti. Lancellotti continues as translator in a second sense, writing and speaking on the content of Del Noce's thought.[3] Del Noce is sometimes described as a "Catholic philosopher," which is too bad, because his work is significant far beyond sectarian interests. He was a philosopher who was Catholic, not a philosopher of Catholic theol-

---

3 E.g., various articles appearing in *Humanum*, located at humanumreview.com (John Paul II Institute), and in various personal appearances, some of which at this writing can be found on YouTube. Lancellotti's translation in 2015 of *The Crisis of Modernity* and in 2022 of *The Problem of Atheism* occasioned other English articles on Del Noce, as well,. For example, see Francis Maier, "Augusto Del Noce and The Problem of Atheism," *Public Discourse*, thepublicdiscourse.com, December 5, 2021.

ogy. He was particularly helpful in dissecting the pernicious impact of neo-Marxists, like his countryman Antonio Gramsci (1891-1937).

Del Noce distinguishes between "tradition" and "traditionalism." "Tradition" he took to be values handed down over time, but specifically those values that are eternal and objective and sourced in the transcendent. "Traditionalism," on the other hand, means only that which is passed down, not necessarily tethered to eternal or transcendent values. Traditionalism, in his usage, therefore meant doing things a certain way only because that's how grandpa did it, which is to assume that values derive from tradition rather than form it. Tradition (as opposed to traditionalism) is to be encouraged because it embodies a universal rationality, the Greek logos, according to which truth and goodness are objective and eternal. Del Noce referred to "tradition" rather than objectivity or eternality or universality because it only made sense that the important ideas are passed down because of their eternality and objectivity.

Anticipating the process philosophy of later postmodernists, Del Noce distinguished tradition's "metaphysics of being" from postmodernism's "metaphysics of becoming." A metaphysics of becoming unmoors universality and objectivity and eternality of truth (and falsity) and goodness (and evil), hence the relativism of the postmodern era. Postmodernism presupposes a metaphysics of becoming because it regards truth as the result of a social Hegelian process of historical dialectics rather than a universal existing above and apart from human history. We see this play out now in the process philosophies of postmodernists like Rorty, Deleuze, and Bauman. Postmodernism, therefore, rejects tradition defined as Del Noce does.

This rejection takes the form of what has been described here as a posture or attitude of negation. Del Noce called it "revolution," thus placing tradition and revolution in opposition, as did Marx. Revolution meant, for Marx, a radical rejection of authority, and that is certainly a dominant feature of postmodernism. Rejection of human and divine authority is one thing, but this Marxist element of postmodernism goes further to reject what lies behind all authority: the objectivity and eternality and universality of truth, falsity, goodness, and evil.

Another instance of the Marxist principle of radical rejection of authority, for Del Noce, is in the aptly described sexual revolution.[4] The sexual revolution involved changing mores made possible by rejection of transcendence. As such, it enabled rejection of tradition as he defined

---

4 Chapter 17, supra.

it. But more, it meant and still means destruction of the family, because family is the means of handing down transcendent and objective values. Its function of handing down values is explicitly what is meant by "tradition." Destruction of the family is not an incidental consequence of the sexual revolution, in other words. It is a purposeful goal, necessary to completing the project of collective shift from objectivity to relativism; from eternal to temporary; from transcendent to socially formed and dictated values.

Rejecting authority thus means not just rejecting Del Noce's "tradition," but rejecting also that which makes it tradition. It means cutting the anchor chain and drifting with the vicissitudes of weather and current, the socially produced values urged by the powerful. And the ideals of the powerful coalesce in the Machine, the system of mutually reinforcing institutions imposing ideological conformity as a condition to participating in the increasingly automated and interdependent commerce of the world.

In essays contained in *The Crisis of Modernity*, [5] Del Noce anticipates a kind of mutation in Marxism, possibly extrapolating from his study of Antonio Gramsci's work. Gramsci did not reject Marxism—he was a communist—but he recognized the need to shift its emphasis from class division and materialist determinism to other forms of social division and revolution. People are motivated by social conditions, but these include ideas and identity, not just material conditions as in classical Marxism. Gramsci sought to shift Marxist emphases accordingly—an evolution to cultural Marxism.[6] Gramsci recognized the greater likelihood of success for Marxism in a "long march through the institutions," including the arts, education, and media. For the last century, this has been the socialist strategy, particularly after World War II.

Before we return to Del Noce's description of Gramscian leftist movements, we should pause to understand the nature of the socialism that would result from Gramsci's efforts, as distinguished from classical Marxism. The shift to cultural Marxism meant a more all-encompassing vision of socialism even than what Marx envisioned. Gramsci's cultural Marxism, the soul of postmodern philosophy, is not merely economically collectivist but collectivist more generally: a "we" perspective in all things. It is, therefore, totalitarian in the sense of Marx's discredited communist phase of history. It is totalitarian in the sense that the self is

---

5 Montreal: McGill-Queens University Press, 2015.

6 A summary on this point is provided by Mark Dooley, "Antonio Gramsci's Long Struggle," *Public Discourse*, June 2022 (thepublicdiscourse.com/2022/06/82558/).

subsumed into the collective, exactly in accord with Mussolini's definition of fascism, except that now the collective is headed by the Machine, without borders, rather than the nationalistic state under a strong-man leader. In this way, hard left communism and hard right fascism merge in the totalitarianism for which postmodernism is the blueprint.

Del Noce understood an implication of Gramsci's thought: the mid-century wars could not extinguish the tendency to totalitarianism.[7] To the contrary, the tendency is marked by "the negation of the universality of reason,"[8] which equates to abandonment of transcendence, objectivity, and eternality of values. The result, writes Del Noce's translator Lancellotti, is that "totalitarian systems monopolize power by affirming that rationality itself is political. They claim that their ideological narrative coincides with rational discourse and thereby excludes *a priori* all forms of criticism."[9]

This is exactly what we see now. To hold that rationality itself is political means that rationality is the product of social consensus, including, if necessary, "consensus" that is coerced. This is the pragmatist form of "democracy"[10] and explains why the postmodern ideological metanarrative seems so impervious to rational critique. It's not that the Christian perspective isn't heard. It's just rejected out of hand as not being rational, so that it lies outside an acceptable band of discourse, or outside the Overton window, disapproved by cultural elites. In this way, it is simply ignored.

Del Noce went further, characterizing how the totalitarian collective would come about: through the "science" of rational automation, the technique employed by what is referred to here as the Machine. This scientistic, technological approach to human activity presupposes a thoroughgoing materialism, so that the questions religion is intended to answer are never asked, and religion is irrelevant except when reduced to bromides invoked as a kind of therapy. The Machine's own metaphysics, reductionist materialism, is set up to be considered neutral, as when religious freedom issues are addressed with the pretense that they stand in isolation, to be examined without contrast to the metaphysics of the Machine. The Machine's rejection of transcendence in this way goes un-

---

7 See Carlo Lancellotti, "Augusto Del Noce and the 'New Totalitarianism,'" *Communio International Catholic Review*, Summer 2017, vol. 44.2, citing Del Noce's *The Crisis of Modernity*, Montreal: McGill-Queen's University Press 2015, p. 230.

8 Ibid.

9 *Communio*, 44, p. 324.

10 As discussed in Chapter 22.

examined. Religion is further emptied of relevance, increasingly supplanted by niceness exuding from vaguely immanent materialism.

Realistic evaluation of competing metaphysics is further avoided by the way postmodern ideology presents all issues as lying somewhere on a continuum of conservatism vs. progressivism. This linear spectrum is inadequate because both imagine a teleological movement from past to future through solely material and political process. This is Hegelian/Marxist historicism, conceived as the force supplanting transcendence to drive immanent materialism. "Conservative" and "progressive" are both contained in this Marxist historicism. They pertain only to the pace at which one proceeds deterministically through inevitable evolution toward socialism. Conservatives seem to be asking only for a slower pace, not a distinct worldview that rejects the inevitability of that progression. "Conservative" and "progressive" are both internal to the postmodern ideology of the Machine.

The real question is whether mankind has an irreducible link to transcendence or is entirely shaped by social influences. Whether we are made in the image of God, or are entirely socially, that is to say, politically formed. Postmodern society doesn't bother to deny religious claims. It denies the relevance of questions to which religion supplies answers.

Grasping the transcendent might make us insist on self-sovereignty, as befits one who is made in the image of God. But the studied indifference of postmodernism to religion helps to induce even religious believers to place their trust in the Machine, instead, and the Machine, in turn, renders us ever more passive. We tend to release such self-sovereignty as we think we have because the automated Machine incrementally removes our autonomous initiative, replacing it with a habit of reliance on the Machine's algorithmic automation. The habit of exercising agency is drowned in the habit of seemingly necessary involuntary dependence. The consequence is that we reflexively turn to human authority for direction, invoking Machine social adjudication as our authority. It becomes increasingly more difficult to preserve integrity in dissent by isolating so as to stay as politically invisible as possible.

We see the dependence most clearly in society at the bottom. That is, the most passive are those who are least resourced and most needful, habituated to the dictates of the Machine and trained to embrace the socialist "we" perspective instead of the dignity of one possessing the *imago Dei*; one made of dust but also God-breathed; one standing in the privileged position ordained by God between the heavens and the earth. The most vulnerable among us are like canaries in the coal mine, but we tend not to see them as such. We watch them suffer and scratch our heads as to why.[11]

Revolution versus tradition is Del Noce's formula to replace the contrived spectrum of progressive/communist left versus conservative/fascist right. As prescient as Del Noce was, however (more than a half century ago), the gathering conflict is not lining up precisely as he imagined because the advance of the Machine has so successfully diminished the sense of transcendence. The political spectrum is now just a quibble about socialist details. The emotional posture of negation—Del Noce's "revolutionary" stance—is so thoroughgoing in our society as to be the new bourgeois. It is the outlook "handed down" now, in accord with the etymology of "tradition." Revolution is actually the dominant mode of thinking and being and feeling now, and tradition, to include embrace of the transcendent, is and will increasingly become the transgressive position; the minority cultural dissent. A revolutionary aesthetic and ideological stance is cool even now, when it is plainly the dominant and powerful majority.

An inversion has taken place. Formerly bourgeois traditionalists are decidedly in the minority. The word "bourgeois" hardly fits anymore; it is thought to mean the privileged class and its toadies in self-satisfied middle-class conformity, but now the word attaches to a bewildered and angry minority, unwilling to cross over to the new dispensation of ever-centralizing power to distribute by social group new totems of privilege and class, and to redistribute private wealth by the exercise of that new power. The minority, attuned to personal excellence rather than ingroup solidarity, seethes with resentment at the advance of the Machine.

We think of revolution as involving "the people" fed up with lordly overseers, pushed beyond the people's limits of patience. The French Revolution is taken as the model, defining all revolution, including the internal psychological disposition of rebelliousness invoked in Marxist attitudes of negation. The current revolution isn't like that, however. The people won't rise up against the Establishment, or against the State, or against the ruling classes by whatever description. The Machine itself revolts, though it is already master of the order which is the subject of the revolt. The Machine is engaged in a push—a final push, if its calculus is correct—to vanquish with finality the lingering traces of fealty to universality of values; to objectivity of truth and morality; to transcen-

---

11 Two works from the U.K. and U.S., respectively, helpfully demonstrate this point: *Life at the Bottom*, by Theodore Dalrymple (Chicago: Ivan R. Dee, 2003) and *The Dream and the Nightmare*, by Myron Magnet (San Francisco: Encounter Books, 2000).

dence; to God.

The stubborn clinging to transcendence by "conservatives" endangers end goals of the postmodern project. It's not dead till it's dead. The Machine has avoided what might be perceived as a Tiananmen Square, thus far, but resistance cannot be long endured because it reveals the lack of unanimity in the contrivance of consensus. Democracy in the postmodern view must evolve to social consciousness replacing the individual; to the self subsumed into the Machine; to a totalitarianism not confined to national boundaries. Consensus must become genuine and not merely a temporary pretense to obscure the harsh reality of coercion.

It would be preferable, for the elite lever-pullers of the Machine, that we all see the light and shed our prejudices and enter the garden smiling, leaving all traces of God-awareness at the gate. But there will, no doubt, be some who remain faithful, allied with those who stubbornly resist giving over the self; who would go to martyrdom before submitting. That is a remnant, the tattered few who will remain faithful after serial purges. The important thing for the Machine now is to get to a tipping point favorable to its goal of consensus in abandoning logocentric transcendence and embracing socialist utopia.

Revolutions have typically been prosecuted by the bottom strata of society against the top. This time it's inverted: the top against those increasingly pushed to the bottom. This is not a future event but is happening now. The Machine advances to extinguish ideas. Ideas are more troublesome than people, for power elites who steer the Machine. It's your soul they want. Like a drunk insisting he's sober, the powerful insist on their humane goodwill as they rob you of self-sovereignty. Our individual agency is both gift and curse, perhaps, but it is reality. It means personal responsibility, but it also means freedom. Our individual agency separates us from the animals. It is the difference between slave and free. Resistance is something people with agency do. The method of the Machine is not to eliminate resistance directly but instead to eliminate agency. We're being hollowed out from the inside. Hollow people don't resist.

CHAPTER TWENTY-EIGHT

Collapse

POSTMODERN PHILOSOPHY is so completely dedicated to the renunciation of objectivity and transcendence that it walls off the most obvious explanation for the vertical value tension omnipresent in our experience. This includes ideas presupposing the reality of God, of course, but also all ideas which require a constancy of categories. To hold that there is any proposition that is unchanging and eternal and objective is to depart from secular postmodern philosophy.

We can align our thinking to objective truth, and perhaps we'll then find God, or if not God, at least a basis for order and tolerance and prosperity and individual flourishing. Or we can align our thinking to postmodern process philosophy which yields a presumption of relativism, and all these goals will be forever lost to us.

Philosophical ideas become disseminated into culture and are there mutated and applied endlessly and sometimes artlessly. They are also borne out in our political movements, large and small. We live them out in our daily lives, often unaware of how our decisions and routines are influenced by big ideas that have filtered down to daily thinking patterns. Hierarchies of ideas and values are thus disseminated, and we may not see them for what they are. Even relativists who reject the idea of objective hierarchies of value live inside hierarchies, because that is the way the world is. Hierarchy in the abstract cannot be deconstructed.

The advance of postmodern ideology is the construction of hierarchy, enabled by increasingly ingrained algorithmic automation. The systematizing way of thinking augments the systematizing ideology it advances. We tend to think on the margins rather than about our lives as a whole and how they compares to other ways of living. And so we may fail to appreciate the cumulative effect of automation on our lives.

Technology, for example, seems to free us from drudgery, but does it really? Participation in the automated systems of the world takes an incalculable amount of our energy and attention, and exacts autonomy in favor of the almighty Algorithm. The cumulative effect of automation habituates us to a way of life that makes us ever more dependent on machines. And not just machines per se but the thing that makes a machine a machine, automation: algorithmic procedure not just inside the machine but in the expectations on us in so many areas of our lives, like learning and following increasingly abstruse legal requirements untethered to demands of the conscience, and the squeezing out of any discretion in how we go about doing our jobs, and byzantine tax regulations we have to hire specialists to navigate, and ever-changing social expectations including the politically correct flavor of the month. If we step back and take notice of how much of our time and attention is devoted to following what amount to algorithms, we see why throwing it all over seems like an impossible step to take. Living and working as a cog in a machine seems like loss of agency. And it is. Loss of agency is the essence of slavery, and it's slavery even if we're duped into relinquishing that agency voluntarily.

It's not an exaggeration to say we work for machines, not they for us. This is true for social machines, like innovation-stifling regulation and the shifting rules of social tribalism. But it's more visible for physical machines. Think of the significance of this phrase: "the system is down." What does that mean? It means a computer glitch brings us to a standstill. We can't complete a routine commercial interaction. We're helpless because the equipment and systems and job expectations make us so. In a situation like that, we find ourselves just as automated as the machines we rely upon. We all work for "the system" now. The system consists of mandatory protocols and procedures, and political correctness, but also interconnected computers, the Internet, portable cell electronic devices, and every industry that depends on those things, which is to say all of them.

This is possible through information technology, specifically, execution of algorithmic actions electronically, over networked computers, in ever-expanding activities of life. Thinking professions automate through computer language, crowding out skilled manual labor, leaving only routinized service jobs until those, too, are automated. It is usual to think of much of our daily commercial life, or interaction with the various levels of government, to be actual algorithmic routines, especially as increasingly enabled by advances in information technology. Many workers now essentially execute algorithms repeatedly, with very little inventive personal input.

Extreme interdependence and automation is also possible because ordinary commerce involves not just buyer and seller, but a host of entities built into the structure surrounding any commercial exchange. If you buy a shirt from a store, it doesn't just involve you and the store and the monetary system behind the medium of exchange. It involves the store's manufacturer, the transporter of shirts, and innumerable other players all involved in that one little transaction. Too many to count, but they include interlocking on-line advertisers, marketers, distributors, jobbers, sub-manufacturers, and so on, and each in large hierarchical corporations composed of people who have no idea how to make a shirt. The simple act of buying a shirt involves the participation of a huge swath of participants in the economy.

The systemic interdependence produces prosperity, which in turn feeds interdependence, symbiotically. We have more because of economic efficiency, and we have economic efficiency because we have more. It would be impossible to locate one person who grows cotton, weaves shirt material, dyes and finishes, and cuts and sews shirts. If you did find such a person, the shirt would be impossibly expensive. You can well imagine that in earlier times, acquiring something as simple as a shirt would involve a much less efficient process, and the cost of the shirt would be concomitantly larger. Maybe a month's labor, instead of an hour's. As it is, most of us in the prosperous West have many well-made shirts, and each of them costs only a little in proportion to one's income or wealth.

Imagine the efficient assembly-line method of manufacture often illustrated by Ford's auto assembly lines. Each participant in the assembly line adds a tiny little bit to the finished car. Now imagine that same idea writ large across the entire economy. The shirt you acquire has innumerable little inputs all along the way. This kind of economic efficiency is—and must be—continually maintained and improved upon. There is an inexorable movement toward ever more efficient manufacture and delivery of shirts, through automation of process.

Human agency plays an ever-decreasing role. We can criticize this state of affairs as dehumanizing commodifying capitalism, and probably we should. But capitalism is not itself the problem. Capitalism, in the abstract, is not even an economic system; it's more like the absence of a system, unmanaged and instead the result of innumerable independent and free decisions.

The problem is in the human heart, regardless what societal structure that heart is placed into. What's wrong with the world is me. Corruption flows from the inside out; our job ought to be to contain it, to cover our mouths when we cough, so to speak, to let goodness thrive. Contrary to what we're told in the therapeutic society, the place to actively suppress evil and actively encourage good is in our own individual hearts. In doing so, we brighten the corner where we are, but that must be counted as enough, because grander schemes to combat evil often generate evil. We bring light and life to the world one candle at a time. We are wrong to presuppose a purity of individual hearts to be protected from corruption through social control, like a massive umbrella covering all of us at once from the lurking fascism of postmodern imagination.

Automation in the economy is concerning but becomes beastly with Machine oversight of its interdependence. Advocates of individual freedom rail against government excess, because unlike power centers of big tech, big media, and Wall Street, government has the exclusive ability to make decrees and enforce them with violence. It alone has ultimate coercive power. It now manages the working economy by regulation which can be enforced partially through financial disincentive but ultimately by taking life, liberty, or property. It engages in public/private partnerships not self-regulated by market pricing. It manipulates consumption and spending and banking through innumerable inputs into the otherwise free economy.

This is not capitalism. It is a managed economy, Machine-run, and the Machine increasingly sponsors collectivist postmodern ideology. The government is one of the players in delivery of the shirt to you. One of its roles is to tax energy out of the economy, in order to intervene again through regulation, so as to cement the cohesiveness—and therefore efficiency—of large established commercial power centers like big tech and Wall Street. Regulation inhibits innovation but (in gigantically grown economies like that of the United States) injects greater efficiency for the largest established providers of goods and services—like those most likely involved in provision of the shirt. The system of automation disfavors small business in favor of large participants in the economy that can carry the regulatory compliance cost. Wall Street overwhelms Main Street. This has the effect of further concentrating economic power and further dehumanizing personal commercial transactions.

The interdependence of prosperous Western economies does not weave us closer together, as we might imagine. The automated nature of production means that among workers, there is an increasing polarization between algorithm creators and algorithm followers. The skilled group in-between thins out, and because that more or less corresponds to the middle economic class, wealth inequality widens and becomes more obvious. Our prosperity in absolute terms is less important than in relative terms, because everyone measures themselves against their neighbors, not against the world and certainly not against history. Even for a person who is richer than 99% of the world through all its history, what's important is the relative wealth of his immediate neighbors. Wealth inequality feeds unfounded resentment and a sense of entitlement. This has a destabilizing effect, exacerbating the tensions postmodern ideologies generate.

This state of affairs feeds the purpose of the Machine, which is control. Control of its own decrees, of course, but as those become increasingly broad, the control encompasses the entire economy and important aspects of our otherwise private lives. The government is a significant participant in the Machine, its contribution being coercive power. Nominally private entities impose ideological conformity and the government enforces it. The government is so intertwined with nominally private commercial interests that it significantly influences economic well-being in ways other than its traditional role of standing behind the rule of law. This goes far beyond a government existing to protect pre-political individual natural rights, as was envisioned in the founding documents of the United States.

Instead of the country consisting of citizens free to self-actualize in every realm, including, but not limited to, the commercial, the political concern now is almost entirely with individuals' material conditions, consistent with the prevailing ideological materialism. Our government-protected freedoms have largely shifted from the freedom to be to the freedom to have. We are diminished by this, to the point that we confuse freedom from want with freedom from coercive power.

This is an awful development. Our first thought, if we find ourselves in need, is not to look to family or friends, but to the Machine, starting with government. Governments of prosperous Western societies increasingly call the shots on how commerce proceeds, but are also increasingly involved in broad areas of our formerly private lives. While it participates in the system of bringing you cheap shirts, it intervenes in your life in countless other ways as well. In the United States, it is now involved in the content of private media. It is amazingly brazen in suppressing speech which dissents from its own messages about how people should behave. Suppression of free speech was at one time the obvious bellwether of overweening government. No longer. We don't even seem to notice it. Part of the reason is the ideological purposes of the Machine, including ideologically consistent social media and traditional media, engaged in generation of false narratives as necessary to effectuate its ends. Whenever we perceive the development of false narrative, we should understand it can only be to generate ideological metanarrative.

The intricate commercial interdependence we have highlighted is not by itself a bad thing. To the contrary, it represents an uncontrollably complex and intricate web of prices which passively but accurately convey accumulated information concerning market value. Each transaction is an assignment of value in the form of price, informed by that web, such that every node of exchange is more or less directly engaged even in a single transaction. There is no need for a source of valuation from the outside, as by some overarching authority, nor would such a thing work out well in practice, as every experiment in price intervention by every government in history has amply borne out.

The point of highlighting here the intricate web of interdependent commerce is not to criticize it as an engine of prosperity unto itself. The point is to show how it can be unscrupulously used to exclude and, thereby, to enforce ideology. The web of interdependent commerce seamlessly binds together all elements of the economy, as with cotton growers, transporters, assemblers, etc., in our shirt example. That binding together is a differentiator against that which is not bound, such as commerce excluded through interventions of the Machine. Machine intervention can be brought to bear not just to skew commercial valuations in certain segments of the web, but to control access entirely. In this way, a disfavored individual or group can be excluded. A way for the Machine to seal off the interdependent web of commerce, so as to exclude, is to passport entry or exit in some way.

The system of the world is powerful, automated, collectivist, coercive, and acquires the means to exclude by imposing conditions on participation. Power begets power, in the world's system. Genesis (in Chapter 11) gives us some inkling of how this alarming circumstance can arise, in the story of the Tower of Babel. It is a story of technology, collectivism, security, and materialism. These are the same features which figure into the system of the world now, resting not on the higher ideals of God, but the lesser ideals of mankind. As occurred in the Tower of Babel story, the power system of the world is repeatedly dismantled, until, in His time, God dismantles it for the last time.

Signs of enslavement to the system of the world include Machine-imposed conditions on participation in society. The Machine arrogates to itself the authority to passport movement within the system. A ready example is China's social credit system, but there is a looser Western version in which we are acceptable if we acknowledge and denounce ideological enemies of the Machine, like patriarchy, heteronormativity, systemic racism, and nationalism. Thought and action must be politically correct so it fits within the Overton window, or the bracketing of public discourse philosopher John Rawls prescribes, or the narrow band of social consensus supporting the dominant metanarrative.

Another Genesis paradigm-setting story demonstrates how this might work. In Chapter 4 of Genesis, we find the story of Cain and Abel. As a result of his awful sin, Cain's livelihood, working the ground, is taken from him. He is sentenced to being a fugitive and wanderer; an outcast from society; so removed from its protection that he could be killed. God gives him a mark, however. With the mark, he can live without further interference. The mark is a passport, therefore; a way of continuing to participate in the system of the world without incurring this-world judgment. Unrepentant sin marks Cain for death in the next life. But the mark lets Cain live in this one.

The passport is necessitated by the Machine's enslavement of individuals. We tend to think of slavery as a subjugation by force, as with chattel slavery. It can certainly include that, but it needn't be so limited. Slavery means loss of human agency. Human agency is the God-given moral authority over one's own actions, whereby we choose evil and we choose good. Moral agency is what distinguishes us from the animals. So removing it pushes people down, closer to animal-like conditions. Externally, anyway. People are still people, so their humanity is suppressed in conditions of slavery, not extinguished. A person made a slave by force is weighted down by oppression, but not dehumanized altogether as he would be if subsumed into Machine-formed totalitarianism.

A person can voluntarily give up agency and make himself a slave. Loss of agency is the key feature of slavery, not merely being forced to do work you'd rather not do. People do work they'd rather not do all the time, because their life conditions require it. It's a universal condition, and we don't regard it as inconsistent with freedom. We're put here on Earth to work, and sometimes the work is tedious or physically difficult. Necessity doesn't make us unfree. What makes us unfree is the loss of personal decision-making. At first blush, it would seem impossible to voluntarily give up human agency, because agency means voluntary decision-making. But it is possible in a circumstance in which one is deceived or manipulated or coerced or dehumanized into choosing dependence.

If you wanted to make yourself a god and control people, how would you go about it? There's old-fashioned coercion and force, but a better strategy is to get them to choose their enslavement. How? You could try persuasion, but that appeals to their critical thinking, and critical thinking is their best defense. You don't appeal to human agency, that's what you're trying to eliminate. Bolshevist bullying is somewhat better, because it degenerates critical thinking and unleashes the miasma of fear, but the coercion may be insufficiently subtle. You want your would-be subjects slavering to comply, not grumbling and covertly dreaming of revolution. So a way to go about it is to redefine free critical thought. Bring about conditions in which it no longer means questioning everything, according to objective principle, and instead means a disposition of critique. Demonize bourgeois capitalism even after it is hollowed out from the inside and remade into postmodern totalitarianism. You don't attack the ideas, you diminish the idea-havers. We want to see ourselves as enlightened, truth-seeking, good people, so present conformity to the metanarrative as the way. Get your subjects to make themselves slaves to the system of the world you've built. Voluntary slaves are utterly docile.

If we relinquish our freedom in serial tiny increments, we become slaves to the world's system. We may do so for illusory security, or for bread, or as a misguided attempt to overcome our first alienation in the garden.

CHAPTER TWENTY-NINE

Rebirth

THERE'S BAD NEWS here but good news too. We can pull out of the day-to-day minutiae and see the larger trends. We can, thereby, appreciate the separation of God from our thinking and resulting erosion of the conceptions of objectivity and transcendence that are necessary to adequately explain our world.

Remember the Flood. We think of it as God's judgment on mankind; He wiped mankind out for its awful sin and essentially started over. But He didn't wipe out mankind. He saved it through Noah just like He saves it through Jesus. All individuals die sometime, including Noah. As bad as the catastrophe was, mankind—in the person of Noah—survived by preparing for and then riding out the catastrophe.

We can do the same. Our catastrophe is the postmodern flood of meaninglessness, of driving out the last vestiges of our sense of the transcendent, of the ultimate awful exercise of moral agency in rejecting God, listening again to the lying serpent and repeating the rebellion that expels us from the garden. We are tossed about on the stormiest of floodwaters, by the loss of truth itself and the compromise of our dignity as God-breathed people formed to exist here between the heavens and earth. We should prepare, and then ride it out like Noah did.

How do we do so without giving in to postmodernism's protean corrosive effects on the concept of transcendence and truth-objectivity? Here are a few suggestions.

First, remember that words matter. We ascribe to words an objective meaning, of course. How could we communicate otherwise? Words are among the differentiators we have been discussing, which produce meaning. But words and phrases may be injected into discourse with deliberate ambiguity, as with the serpent in the garden. This may be strategic, and so we should be on the lookout for it. Now, it's true that words have always been mangled or abused in order to deliberately confuse or mislead. Here's John Locke circa 1689:

> Another abuse of words is an affected Obscurity, by either applying old Words, to new and unusual significations, or introducing new and ambiguous Terms, without defining either; or else putting them so together, as may confound their ordinary meaning.[1]

We all know the flim-flam element of words in advertising, for example, so thoroughly that we effortlessly screen ad verbiage for veracity. Likewise, with political advertising that promises a chicken in every pot.

These are relatively more mundane instances of word abuse, however. You know you are listening to the serpent in the garden when the words you hear are used with deliberate and strategic ambiguity to cloud the interests at stake. Rather than engaging directly on a proposition, the technique is to re-direct and re-define, vesting words and phrases with subtle shifts in meaning, until the new meaning is accepted uncritically in place of the old, to the effect of advancing transgressive, truth-denying goals. Seemingly straightforward words like "racism," "freedom," "justice," "spirituality," and many others become so elastic as to diminish their helpfulness in public discourse. Who would be against "equality," for example? One could substitute "equity" because it seems synonymous, but then we've shifted from equality of opportunity to equality of outcome, a radically distinct concept.

This sounds underhanded, but remember that in a postmodern way of thinking, we're no longer talking about what is objectively true, but rather about truth formation. Truth is socially formed and malleable, so it's not thought underhanded to mold and shape truth through this kind of dialogue. Language is just a game, and it's necessary to play the game. There's no point getting angry and upset with someone in this mindset, who has given themselves over to relativism. If you hold to objective truth, it may seem the new paradigm inevitably invites unending disputation and ideological clash. Indeed it does. But stand firm. Let's live in truth, and not by lies. That's a second suggestion for living in a postmodern world.

The third: be wary of "the narrative." Doesn't it seem this phrase is ubiquitous now? We have some general idea that this means a story; a

---

1 *An Essay Concerning Human Understanding*, III-X-6.

string of facts and inferences that comprise one's understanding on a subject. There's nothing wrong with that, as far as it goes. The Bible is a narrative, after all, revealing the character of God and His relationship to His people. Likewise, we have narratives of significant events in history which, though perhaps tinged with patriotic bias, more or less accurately inform our understanding of how we've arrived at the present moment. But employing "the narrative" can be for more sinister purposes. It's one thing to assemble facts to form a story. It's quite another to form a story and then selectively assemble and spin facts and inferences to support it.

Fourth: consider the origin of the conviction that truth is an objective, "out-there" phenomenon. Why does it seem so hard-wired into us? We are rational creatures. The objectivity of truth is necessary to rational thought. It is what links thought to thought logically. This is so fundamental that even postmodernist advocacy depends on it. Logocentrism is not an enemy to be deconstructed or otherwise defeated, as postmodernists generally believe. It is the air we breathe; the medium in which we live and move and have our being.

And fifth. Our world is alive with transcendent truth, with hierarchical value, with beauty. It is alive because the Creator infuses it with His presence in every waking moment. The presuppositions of postmodernism, if believed, will coarsen our ability to experience this other-worldly Presence. Our world will diminish but not the ingrained spark of divinity we all carry, and so we may stumble around in the gathering gloam increasingly bewildered, frightened, and alone. It doesn't have to be that way. We can maintain a sharp spiritual acuity by constantly reminding ourselves that there is a God who cares, and who is present, and who has a plan for us. God is the answer.

These are things to keep actively in mind, but what about how we conduct ourselves in the minute-by-minute interactions of the day? Where do we start, to rebel against the truth-indifferent onslaught of daily interactions in the postmodern age? Well, we can resolve right this minute to stop lying and stop tolerating lies in others. We can listen to Aleksandr Solzhenitsyn, in his 1974 essay, "Live Not By Lies," reacting to the version of fascist totalitarianism that wrecked the lives of so many in his country. As in his time, "a universal spiritual death has already touched us all." We should resist the post-capitalist fascism our Machine overlords would impose upon us, and that means "refus[ing] to say that which we do not think."

Let us choose against serving falsehood, against supporting or appearing to support ideological nonsense even if it means jeopardy to our acceptance in society, or our livelihoods, or even our very lives. We have to choose, in Solzhenitsyn's words, "either truth or falsehood: Toward spiritual independence or toward spiritual servitude." Courage, not cowardice. Principle, not animal desire to stay fed and warm another day. Allegiance to principle, not expedience. Honor to God, not this-life worry. Insistence on our God-breathed individual dignity, not craven collapse into the collective.

The postmodern story is one of alienation. In Marx, it is the alienation of the worker from the material fruits of his labor. In neo-Marxism, it is the alienation of people groups in resentment against the culture. For the Frankfurt School postmodernists, it was inauthenticity, the result of capitalist commodification of human beings. For Freud, it was antagonism among elements of the subconscious. For Nietzsche, it was docile religious servility in the face of the will to power. The siren lure of socialism is an attempt at dissolution of alienation in ecstatic feelings of community.

The noteworthy thing is not the differences in felt alienation, but the common reference to alienation. There is, in fact, a sense of alienation and in that limited sense they're all correct. But the alienation does not result from atheist psychology or human governance or cultural systems or human commodification. It results from our separation from God. It has been there from the beginning, and Genesis explains it. Our alienation begins with our expulsion from the garden and weighs on us all through this life, inevitably, even as we intellectually grasp that it is overcome in Jesus.

But the completion of that overcoming does not happen in this life in the body. Our purpose here is to make things better. Not by our own lights but by God's. Not by appeasement of social groups making power plays but by recognizing ultimate truth and authority: God infusing love into the world on His terms. His terms are disclosed in His revelations in word and nature and flesh.

Imagine you step into a dark closet to find something you think is there. You fumble around. Scrape your shin on something. Curse the darkness. You can't seem to put your hand on that thing you were looking for. Time to back away and come at this anew. The internal means by which we apprehend the logos and make sense of reality is God's gift of light, and a demonstration of His love. Just turn on the light.

Glossary

The words and phrases in this glossary are defined here as they are used in this book.

Agency/agentic. Agency is an individual's volition and capacity to act. It is best understood in terms of causation. A person's behavior is caused by their intention and execution. To say that people have agency is to say they are beings with the ability to form intent to act, and then to act. It is something more than material cause and effect. It contemplates a being with ability to form the intent, rather than the intent itself being caused. This is most evident in the exercise of moral agency. Human beings choose evil or good, knowing them to be such. Agency, the word and the concept, is important in philosophy but is perhaps more accessible if we consider its legal usage in ordinary discourse. When one person acts on behalf of another, we call him an "agent" of the principal for whom he acts. The word "agent" is used because the principal in that instance delegates a defined scope of his own agency onto the agent, who then has authority to bind the principal. "Agentic" is not so commonly used. It is an effort to isolate the active component of volition, so the word would suggest more impulsive or assertive volition in contrast to that which is more evaluative and contemplative.

Algorithm. Computer language is an algorithm, or more accurately a series of many algorithms, some nested in others, to instruct the machine in a series of logical progressions. But algorithm is not limited to computer language. It is any sequence governed by a series of gates from one decision point to multiple others. Any automated routine is an algorithm.

Alterity. Otherness. It means in particular the ability to see another's point of view; to place oneself in the other's shoes, so to speak. This is essential to social engagement because it is the basis for empathy, and for moral values formation, and it is the feature of person-to person relationship in which awareness of the other contributes to one's self-identification. It is also the basis for intersubjectivity.

Anomie/anomic. A sense of lack of direction or pointlessness, implying mental isolation from society around us.

Binary opposition. Two things discernible and definable by their opposition each to the other. This can apply to tangible things but also concepts, including metaphysical concepts like nature and supernature. Two things or ideas in binary opposition present a duality.

Capitalism. With increasing prosperity, wealth accumulates and if invested comprises "capital"—a means of income generation other than one's own labor, that may serve to accelerate wealth accumulation. Capitalism is sometimes associated with free markets, as in the phrase "free-market capitalism," because free markets, unhindered by non-market distortions, generate reliable valuation in the form of pricing. Markets become less free as non-voluntary exchanges proliferate, as with government regulation, taxation, and direct commercial participation. Free market capitalism stands in opposition to economic socialism, and to managed economies which are a combination of free and distorted markets, as with most liberal Western societies. Economic socialism favors vesting the collective (typically the state) with power to manage the economy. Capitalism is not an economic "system," strictly speaking, but describes commerce in the absence of systematizing economic planning. It is for this reason often equated with economic freedom. For Marxists, "capitalism" refers to a social system which allows for wrongfully extractive wealth accumulation. For that reason, Marxist use of "capitalism" refers to an entire social structure which facilitates wealth accumulation in the hands of a few at the expense of an exploited underclass. More generally, "capitalism" in use by Marx-influenced postmodernists means a consumption-obsessed dehumanizing culture which should be deconstructed in the direction of a more humane and authentic society that will then de-corrupt individuals within it.

Collectivist/collectivism. A psychological disposition to consider oneself and others first as part of a social collective. The opposite disposition is to see oneself and others as individuals, together only incidentally forming a society. Collectivism is closely related to socialism, but collectivism is the more generic term. Socialism refers to the collectivist disposition, but also to more specific political structures that attempt to manage the economy. Individualism is in opposition to collectivism.

Communism. A form of totalitarian socialism in which the self is subsumed into the collective. In classical Marxist theory, the stage to follow socialism. The Marxist theory of economic socialism involves concentration of the means of production (that is, capital) in the state, after which the state will wither away and wealth will be commonly held. Certain societies have been described as "communist," like China and the former Soviet Union, but far from withering away, the state in every such instance has been brutally oppressive. Communist idealists sometimes attribute this to nationalism, the need to maintain the state because of the existence of imperialist non-communist states.

Consciousness. Irreducible self-awareness and sense of self. The mind is in some way connected to brain functioning, at least in part, but the phenomenal or experiential aspect of consciousness is not clearly a brain function. This is the sense of what it is like to be a cognitive and aware agent. We have no answer to the question of why or how cognitive functioning is accompanied by conscious experience, nor how a physical system could give rise to that conscious experience absent a dualist explanation of reality. A non-material entity like conscious awareness eludes scientific investigation because science is by definition the investigation of matter and energy. Hence the "mind/body problem" in the philosophy of consciousness.

Contingent. Dependent on something else for existence. In the philosophy of causation, for example, any caused thing is contingent in that it is the effect of another cause. Contingent stands in opposition to absolute, as with an uncaused cause or that which is not fully actualized and therefore fully or partly potential.

Critical thinking. Testing the truth of a proposition against universal principles. One critiques a proposition by examining it in light of other accepted propositions, and by its own clarity, rationality, consistency, and plausibility, and by considering any other evidence for the proposition. On this definition, the critique is evaluative and not hostile; not containing a prejudice or *a priori* skepticism or presumed ulterior motive. This is important to note because in the postmodern era this evaluative posture is sometimes confused with a suspicious one, in which the proposition is presumed to mask a false consciousness or to be part of a deceitful system of power. On this confused meaning of critical thinking, the "critical" portion of the phrase means tendentiousness. An example is presuming ill will in a religious proposition because the critiquer believes religion self-evidently false and therefore advanced for nefarious purposes.

Cultural Marxism. (See also Neo-Marxism). Postmodern variations of Marxist critique. Classical Marxism has not proven out as a path to communism or socialist utopia, but essential features of Marxism are re-deployed in prosperous Western societies consistent with the thinking of later Marxist theorists like Antonio Gramsci, György Lukács, Louis Althusser, and Michel Foucault, among many others. These include "critical theory" or "social justice" theories which divide people by group and impute oppressor and oppressed status to the groups; and other Frankfurt School critiques of repressed or frivolous bourgeois consumer society; and movements toward collectivism more generally, including a socialism of thought in addition to the socialism of economic conditions that was more traditionally the goal of Marxism.

Determinism. The idea that everything unfolds the way it does because of myriad but finite instances of contingent causation. One version of this is that everything that happens in the universe was "determined" at the moment of the Big Bang or other commencement of the universe, whatever form that took. Force operated on matter in space and on an arrow of time so that everything that happens was inevitable rather than being affected by some outside influence like God or the supernatural, because those don't exist, in the deterministic way of thinking of physical reality.

Dialectical materialism/diamat. Materialism is the belief that tangible things and natural processes constitute all of reality, so there is no supernature and the dualist metaphysics in religion is false. Even immaterial concepts, on this view, somehow arise out of that which is material. Classical Marxism rejects all religion and supposes that human beings are shaped by material conditions. Dialectical refers to Friedrich Hegel's thesis/antithesis dialectic of ideas, resulting in a synthesis which then forms a new thesis to spin off more dialectical evolution, and a purposeful direction to history results. Purposeful direction is sometimes referred to as telos, or teleology. The idea that history itself is a kind of living, driving force is historicism. Marxism is fundamentally premised on dialectical materialism, sometimes shortened to diamat.

Disenchantment. The sense that the world is disenchanted upon removing a conception of God (or gods) from it. All is explained by science, in the disenchanted world, which means that philosophical materialism prevails. There is no particular point to physical reality being what it is.

Dualism/duality. A set of beliefs premised on a fundamental binary opposition. Mind/body dualism is an important type of dualism, as is nature/spirit dualism. Ontological dualism refers to duality being intrinsic to the very existence of things.

Eliminative materialism. In this version of materialism, what we think of as states of mind are eliminated from materialism. The theory is that our brains produce all the consciousness we experience, and there is no mind mysteriously emergent from the brain at all. Everything we experience in consciousness and cognition is a function of neuronal impulses and cell memory in the physical brain.

Epistemology/epistemic. The philosophical question of how one knows something or anything. It often is used to refer to the nature of evidence upon which one relies, in forming a belief.

Eternality. Sometimes used synonymously with universality or objectivity. It refers to a reality not bounded by time, and so unchanging and absolute.

Existentialism. There are many varieties of existentialism, represented in thinkers like Søren Kierkegaard, Martin Heidegger, Friedrich Nietzsche, Albert Camus, and Jean-Paul Sartre. These can be reasonably summarized as subjectivism: the idea that meaning and purpose are individually and subjectively formed.

Fascism. A form of totalitarian socialism in which the self is subsumed into the collective. In its pre-war Italian and German forms, the collective was a militant xenophobic state, and power was concentrated in a charismatic leader.

Fideism/fideistic. The idea that faith alone, excluding even reason and perhaps excluding an epistemic basis, suffices for belief.

Fractal. Repetition of pattern at different scales.

Freedom. On the most personal and subjective level, this is a feeling of being unbound physically or by scarcity of resources or by convention or by social expectation. This feeling is thus defined negatively; that is by what it is not: a feeling of bondage. This suggests we tend to think of freedom as a natural state of being, but by a moment's reflection we can see this is not so. Unfreedom and freedom co-exist in different ways at different times among different people, and it is typically considered one and not the other on the basis of individual subjectivity. We are born into a world of economic scarcity and personal needs and demands on our time and energies that we embrace rather than resist, as when we desire to help others because of "bonds" of love. One view of freedom therefore is lack of constraint, but confusion results from thinking of freedom abstractly as an absolute quality, and the absence of it as being an abridgement of fundamental right. More confusion results from associating freedom with life success. Freedom is consistent with both success and failure. The constrained/unconstrained view of freedom may blind us to the fact that certain constraints actually lead to better thriving and thus to greater freedom, as when we accede to imposed expectations of becoming educated, obeying the law, and following social norms of consideration for others (including recognition of others' desire for freedom). Particularly relevant in a postmodern conception of freedom is its subjective nature: that freedom resides in the individual, and the individual alone accepts or rejects constraint on its exercise. If freedom is a social concept rather than an individual one, however, society can generate and justify socially-imposed constraints, as with a theory that material conditions prevent individuals from perceiving their own unfreedom.

Historicism. Aristotle's theory of causation included a principle of purpose in natural causation, meaning there is a purposeful direction to unfolding events. This means an inherent purposive element to the direction of history. Other philosophers conceived that purposive element as deriving from extrinsic sources, like God, or universal intelligence, or a logos impelling events to larger purpose. In Jewish and Christian theology, God directs events to His purposes. Friedrich Hegel developed a theory of teleology in which human desire for freedom drives events, thus generating purpose and direction to history, in contrast to events unfolding randomly without reference to an overarching direction. Teleology means history can be regarded as a driving force in human and social development, hence "historicism." Karl Marx imagined historical stages of feudalism to capitalism to socialism to communism. Neo-Marxists in the postmodern era similarly assume historical progress impelled by the praxis of process philosophy.

Ideology. A system of cohering ideas constituting a belief system, but the word is typically used pejoratively, to refer to a belief system that cancels rather than encourages critical examination, impairing the ideologue's ability to think independently. The pejorative use also includes a sense of artificiality, meaning a socially constructed theory rather than a set of ideas grown organically. Both fascism and communism are ideologies, and so are various applications of postmodernism, like critical theory and the pragmatist vision of "democracy." An ideologue is one who formulates his entire outlook around the ideology.

Immanence. The divine as manifested in the material world, in contrast to existence outside the world in supernature. But immanence is also used with regard to the source of truth, or morality or virtues, without intending to imply the existence of a deity at all. In the latter usage, the source can be society or evolving social mores or process philosophies that do not draw on transcendence.

Individualism. The "I" perspective. Individualism contrasts with collectivism and with socialism. The consciousness of each individual is the irreducible locus of human attention and awareness and volition. Human beings therefore start with the "I" perspective and do not exist in a hive-mind like bees or starlings or midges. On the other hand, human beings do not typically live in isolation, like bears or sloths. The intersubjectivity of human self-awareness creates society, and we exist with awareness of relationship to society as well as other individuals within it. Some people are more oriented to the "I" perspective through self-reliance, self-governance, and independence; seeing themselves as part of society only secondarily. Others are more oriented to the "we" collectivist perspective, by which membership in society is primary in one's self-conception. The difference creates tension politically. Individualists tolerate government (or the collective of the Machine) of necessity, and bristle at political movements that aim to reform individuals. Collectivists tend to see collective reform of individuals in a positive light, tolerant of the coercive element of collectivism.

Informational realism. The idea that information is real unto itself, and not merely an abstract descriptor we impose on reality. Information is bound up in existence, not an overlay upon it, and is therefore ontological.

Intersectionality. A postmodern Marxist political term. It refers to the intersections between putatively oppressed groups, to harness their power collectively for political ends. A group not included in the intersecting oppressed statuses personifies the historical oppression.

Intersubjectivity. A person is a subject rather than an object. Subject One's self-perception is formed in part from awareness of Subject Two's perception of Subject One. Subject One is aware of Subject Two's subjective awareness, and of Subject Two's subjective awareness being formed in part from awareness of Subject One's subjective awareness. This is the concept of intersubjectivity, which depends on alterity. It creates a mutual self- and other-awareness on the part of each, a mutual other-awareness playback that generates social awareness in an individual. Social awareness according to some thinkers (like Emile Durkheim) is distinct from the subjective awareness of its members, but accessible by them. By it, individuals are aware of the social narrative. "Intersubjectivity" is sometimes wrongly used to be synonymous with consensus. The existence of a social narrative is not the same as individual acceptance of it.

Logos/Logocentrism. Logos means word and logocentrism refers to a culture's centering of the word. But the word in this usage isn't just language. It refers to the logic and rationality that orders thought in a coherent way. The phenomenon of our ability to convey and understand the logic of another lies outside ourselves, therefore is thought to be an objective, extant feature of reality. The idea comes from ancient Greek philosophy and is taken up in Christian theism in that God is the source of rational logic communicable and understandable in language. Logocentrism is a feature of Enlightenment thinking, the "age of reason" supplanting superstition but also ways of knowing that can be described as mythos, stories told to convey deeper truths, especially those not directly accessible with scientistic thinking.

Machine. Government, commercial, and cultural power centers allied to advance postmodern ideology.

Marxist/Marxism. A theory of class oppression devised by Karl Marx and his collaborator Friedrich Engels, based on dialectical materialism, according to which those with wealth invest the wealth (capital) to produce more wealth, and in the process exploit a working class (or proletariat) which is alienated from the fruits of its labor but is paid enough to self-sustain and reproduce the next generation of workers, perpetuating the oppressive system. Marx theorized an evolution in historical development from primitive communism to slave society to feudalism to capitalism to economic socialism and eventually global stateless communism.

Materialism/materialist. A monist view of reality that excludes any supernatural component. All of reality is matter in motion. Metaphysics, on this view, is limited to an ideal/real distinction in that concepts, virtues, and consciousness do not exist independently of brain function, but are an emergent property of it.

Mathematical realism. The view that mathematics is a real feature of nature and not merely a self-contained logic system.

Metanarrative. Principles drawn from narrative, which is, in turn, presumed to derive from facts. This is a three-step hierarchy of abstraction. Enlightenment logocentrism gives way to a form of mythos understanding referred to in the culture as narrative, a story based more or less loosely on facts, and devised to imply a metanarrative of postmodern ideology not directly disclosed.

Metaphysics. Apprehending reality as a combination of physical nature and something else beyond, "meta" to the physics. What is "meta" to the physics is spirit or supernature, but sometimes the word is used instead to refer merely to abstractions not directly grounded in physical nature, like truth, beauty, morality, virtues, and vices.

Metaphysical dualism. The understanding of reality as being comprised of a duality of distinct realms (or "substance"): nature and supernature. Nature includes all of matter and the forces acting on it, including the body and brain, existing and changing on dimensions of space and time. Supernature includes that which is spiritual, not bound by space and time.

Mind/body dualism. In thinking on the phenomenon of consciousness, it is the idea often related back to René Descartes that the mind consists of dual substance, mind and brain. The idea is that these are not coterminous; that the brain is the physical organ but the mind is something distinct, perhaps sharing in the non-physical spiritual world in some way. Mind/body dualism is a specific of metaphysical dualism because the distinction between mind and brain is thought to correspond to the distinction between spiritual and physical.

Monism/monist. In contrast to dualism, monism supposes reality to be of one substance, so there is no distinction between nature and supernature or between God and nature.

Mountain. Analogously, the felt desire for meaning and purpose in life, served by order and structure, both personally and socially; in opposition to the river, analogously representing an internal desire for relaxed unstructured personal freedom and lack of obligation to others or to God.

Mythos. In contrast to logos, mythos is a way of knowing which leans heavily on story, analogy, metaphor, and symbolism to convey deep truths. Often the facts related are not intended to be true, but they may be. In this way a fairy tale can convey a valid and true "moral" without being verifiably factual.

Narrative. A story to support a metanarrative, more or less faithfully based on underlying facts relevant to politics or culture in society. In contentious political usage, parties propose and defend narratives, while attacking opposing narratives, because the respective narratives are devised to support metanarratives, the distilled principles behind activism in politics or culture.

Neo-Marxism. See Cultural Marxism.

Objectivity. The idea that reality is the external world unchanged by our subjective perceptions. Virtues, ideals and "transcendentals" like truth, beauty, goodness, and love, are extant in reality and not socially formed and not changeable by social theory.

Ontology. The philosophy of existence.

Ontology of becoming. A theory of ontology that presupposes the con-

314

tingent as the basis for existing. Social or other process is involved in the very existence of things, in contrast to an absolute, eternal, unchanging basis for existence. A river theory, in the imagery of this work.

Ontology of being. A theory of ontology that presupposes an absolute; God, or some other source of static being-unto-itself, as opposed to an evolving, changing basis for existence. A mountain theory, in contrast to the river, in the imagery of this work.

Ontological dualism. The proposition that physical things, concepts, and values come into existence in dualities.

Postmodernism. Philosophical ideas and their deployment into the culture, especially since about the turn of the twentieth century, which contain these key elements: atheism, a blurring or dismissal of boundaries, Neo-Marxist top-down social engineering, a socialist "we" perspective, and antipathy to social structures which commodify and alienate individuals, referred to abstractly as "capitalism."

Pragmatism. The philosophy which holds that truth is formed in action toward some goal. It presupposes some pre-existing inclination toward which the truth is formed. The ends justify the means, but this precept is reduced to the truth-formation level.

Praxis. The combination of theory and practice in Marxist philosophy. Sometimes the word is used for combinations of theory and practice outside of Marxist philosophy, but the word expresses the pragmatic idea that ideals are formed in action, as in Marx's 1845 "Thesis Eleven:" "Philosophers have hitherto only interpreted the world in various ways; the point is to change it."

Process philosophy. Late modern and postmodern philosophy which presupposes an ontology of becoming rather than being; of dynamism rather than what is regarded as a stasis of objectivity and logocentrism. It generally treats relationships among things and ideas, and movements among them, as the source of reality, as opposed to objective propositional truth. Process philosophy attempts to explain human motivation without reference to God. In most philosophy before the nineteenth century, truth and right and wrong were thought to be objective, even among religious skeptics who did not believe in transcendence as such.

Secular philosophy increasingly struggled to explain, without resorting to transcendence, mankind's motivation to strive in a positive direction, rather than descending into animal impulse, without resorting to transcendence or the presumption of objectivity in truth and moral values. Theories developed for horizontal processes, instead, such as pragmatism, existentialism, and other modes of social truth-formation collectively called postmodernism in this work.

Real/reality. To say something is "real" is to say it is part of reality. A materialist would ground reality in material things and forces acting on them. Certain obviously immaterial things might nonetheless be considered real if they are connected to that which is physical. Immaterial mind, for example, is presumed connected in some way to physical brain. Likewise virtues and vices might be regarded as real because they are brain-produced, presumably as products of evolution. In certain kinds of neo-Marxist deconstructionist thinking (e.g., that of György Lukács), certain commodifying human relations can be seen as illegitimately reified, cementing them as instrumentalities of alienation in bourgeois capitalist societies. Likewise consciousness, inconveniently difficult to explain as a function purely of material brain processes, can be deemed improperly reified by a dualist conception of reality at odds with the atheist materialism that is a foundation of Marxism.

River. Analogously, the internal desire for relaxed unstructured personal freedom and absence of accountability, in opposition to the mountain, analogously representing the need for order and structure to perceive meaning and purpose to life.

Sentience. Intelligence, volition, consciousness, and agency. The word's origins, however, relate to the ability to sense things.

Spirit/spiritual. Of or pertaining to the supernatural. In opposition to physical or material. A confusing use of the word now is to describe a person's lifted countenance or heightened animation, as when especially excited or drinking "spirits" or having school "spirit." Those are actually analogues to the religious ecstatic, but the religious basis for them is mostly lost in our culture, while the analogous use remains.

Socialism. Collectivism, the "we" perspective first, in all things. In this sense "socialism" opposes individualism. But socialism has more specif-

316

ic political meanings, as well. In classical Marxism, it was a political theory whereby the state owns the means of production instead of private interests. Apart from original Marxist theory, socialism more generically means social as opposed to individual ownership or control of the means of production, or wealth, or capital. Socialism was part of Nazi and Fascist ideology, in addition to the left-wing ideologies imposed in countries of Eastern Europe, Southeast Asia, China, Cuba, Venezuela, and many other places. In liberal Western societies, a form of socialism involves the gradual erosion of the principle of limited government, in favor of expansion of government control of means of production and of the conditions of private wealth and capital accumulation. In the United States, for example, the long trend-line has been in a socialist direction, toward ever-greater control, extraction, and direct management of wealth by the state.

Subject. A person, having self- and other-awareness of consciousness, able to participate in the intersubjectivity of social interaction. On this basis, subject is in opposition to object.

Supernature/supernatural. In the dualist conception of reality, this is the component that is not physical, but spiritual. It is transcendent, meaning that it is a feature of the natural world but transcends beyond it.

Telos/teleology. See historicism. Teleology describes change according to the purpose the change aims at, rather than the causes which drive it. The word is therefore used to describe the purposeful direction to the unfolding of events through history. If there is a telos to history, it is the purposes toward which events are directed.

Transcendent/transcendence. To "transcend" is to go beyond or surpass some prescribed range or limit. "Transcendent" in metaphysics means transcending the space and time boundaries of nature. The supernatural component of reality would be considered transcendent because it is in, but not confined to, the natural world. The word "transcendent" is often used somewhat more vaguely, however, being unspecific as to what is being transcended, or how. So, for example, emotionally affecting and uplifting music might be called "transcendent" without necessarily suggesting that it actually originates in heaven somehow. Similarly, the word might be used in the same way as "objectivity" or "eternality" to mean a concept or value not shifting with social theory, or otherwise rooted in the absolute rather than the contingent. We might say, for example, that truth is objective, but to say it is "transcendent" is to go further and say it is sourced outside the system of society and the natural world of contingent things. Transcendence therefore means something more than objectivity; it means there is a source outside our time- and space-bound reality that accounts for objectivity. Transcendence is often contrasted with immanence, on this basis.

Universal/universality. The phenomenon of common characteristics or principles by which we differentiate things and ideas. On the basis of universality, we can group like things with like (philosophically, the point of identity), but to do so, we separate unlike from unlike (philosophically, the point of differentiation or individuation). These are opposite sides of the same coin, therefore. Identification and differentiation exist in the physical world, and in immaterial thought in the consciousness which perceives it. The identity and differentiation that constitute universality exists in complex and overlapping ways. Philosophers have long puzzled over the problem of the one and the many, for example: how one never steps in the same river twice, and yet it is the same river. That there is universality in things, and in cognitive perception of things, is a phenomenon difficult to explain without some form of metaphysical dualism, just as with consciousness and ultimate causation.

Bibliography

Ayer, Alfred Jules. *Language, Truth, and Logic*, New York: Dover, 1952 (second edition published in 1946).

Bauman, Zygmunt. *Liquid Modernity*, Malden, MA.: Polity, 2000.

Breshears, Jefrey D. *American Crisis/Cultural Marxism and the Culture War: A Christian Response*, Centre Pointe Publishing, 2020.

Calasso, Roberto. *The Book of All Books*, transl. by Tim Parks. New York: Farrar, Straus and Giroux, 2021.
_____. *The Unnamable Present*, New York: Farrar, Strauss and Giroux, 2017.

Camus, Albert. *The Myth of Sisyphus and Other Essays*, London: H. Hamilton, 1965.

Chalmers, David. *The Conscious Mind/In Search of a Fundamental Theory*, Oxford: Oxford University Press, 1996.
_____. *Reality+/Virtual Worlds and the Problems of Philosophy*, New York: W.W. Norton, 2022.

Cheng, Nien. *Life and Death in Shanghai*, New York: Grove Press, 1986.

Dalrymple, Theodore. *Life at the Bottom*, Chicago: Ivan R. Dee, 2003.
_____ and Kenneth Francis. *The Terror of Existence/From Ecclesiastes to the Theater of the Absurd*, Nashville: New English Review Press, 2018.

Davies, Paul. *The Mind of God: The Scientific Basis for a Rational World*, New York: Simon & Shuster, 1992.

DeGeorge, Richard and Ferndande DeGeorge, eds. *The Structuralists from Marx to Levi-Strauss*, NewYork: Anchor Books, 1972.

Deleuze, Gilles and Félix Guattari. *Anti-Oedipus/Capitalism and Schizophrenia*, New York: Penguin, 2009 (first published in the U.S. in 1977).

Dembski, William. *Being as Communion: A Metaphysics of Information*, New York: Ashgate Publishing, 2014.

Derrida, Jacques. *Violence and Metaphysics and Writing and Difference*, as cited by Jack Reynolds of LaTrobe University Australia, in his contribution on Derrida to the *Internet Encyclopedia of Philosophy*, iep.utm.edu/derrida (section 5).

Dewey, John. *A Common Faith*, New Haven, CT: Yale University Press, 1934.

Dooley, Patrick Kiaran. *Pragmatism as Humanism: The Philosophy of William James*, Chicago: Nelson Hall, 1974.

Dreher, Rod. *Live Not By Lies: A Manual for Christian Dissidents*, New York: Sentinel, 2020.

Durkheim, Émile. *The Elementary Forms of the Religious Life*, New York: Macmillan, 1915.

Dworkin, Ronald. *Religion Without God*, Cambridge, MA.: Harvard University Press, 2013.

Esolen, Anthony. *Sex and the Unreal City: The Demolition of the Western Mind*, San Francisco: Ignatius, 2020.
_____. *No Apologies: Why Civilization Depends on the Strength of Men*, Washington, DC.: Regnery Gateway, 2022.
_____. "The Unbearable Burden of Being," *Chronicles*, December 1, 2019.

Favale, Abigail. *The Genesis of Gender: A Christian Theory*, San Francisco: Ignatius, 2022.

Felski, R. "Critique and the Hermeneutics of Suspicion," *M/C Journal*, 15(1) 2011. (https://doi.org/10.5204/mcj.431).

Frazer, James George. *The Golden Bough*, New York: McMillan, 1922.

Freud, Sigmund. *Civilization and Its Discontents*, London: Penguin, 2002 (first published 1930).

Gabriel, Markus. *I Am Not a Brain*, Medford, MA.: Polity Press, 2017.

Geary, David. "The Real Causes of Human Sex Differences," *Quillette*, quillette.com October 2020.

Gelernter, David. *Tides of Mind: Uncovering the Spectrum of Consciousness*, New York: Liveright, 2016.

Girard, René. *I See Satan Fall Like Lightning*, Maryknoll, New York: Orbis, 2001.

Giridharadas, Anand. "How Elites Lost Their Grip in 2019," *Time Magazine*, Nov. 21, 2019.

Goldberg, Jonah. *Liberal Fascism: The Secret History of the American Left from Mussolini to the Politics of Meaning*, New York: Doubleday, 2007.

Grenz, Stanley J. *A Primer on Postmodernism*, Grand Rapids, MI.: Eerdman's, 1996.

Groothius, Douglas. *Truth Decay: Defending Christianity Against the Challenges of Postmodernism*, Downer's Grove, IL.: Intervarsity, 2000.

Guénon, René. *The Reign of Quantity & the Signs of the Times*, transl. Lord Northbourne, Hillsdale, NY.: Sophia Perennis, 2001, first published 1945.

Harrington, Mary. "Blasphemy is Dead, Long Live Blasphemy: The 'marketplace of ideas' was nice while it lasted," reactionaryfeminist.substack.com, October 26, 2022.

Hart, David Bentley. *The Experience of God: Being, Consciousness, Bliss*, New Haven, CT.: Yale University Press, 2013.

Herzog, Wagner. "Susan Sontag—A Leftist to Be Admired," *Merchants of Air* August 23, 2017 (merchantsofair.com).

Hicks, Stephen R.C. *Explaining Postmodernism: Skepticism and Socialism From Rousseau to Foucault*, Ockam's Razor, 2017 (3rd ed.).

Hobbes, Thomas. *Leviathan*, 1651.

Hughes, Peter. "The Temptations of Tyranny," *Quillette*, Nov. 16, 2021 (quillette.com).

James, E.O. *Christian Myth and Ritual*, New York: World Publishing, 1965.

James, William. *Pragmatism*, Cambridge, NH: Hackett, 1981 (essay first published in 1907).
_____. *Will to Believe*, New York: Dover, 1956 (first published in 1897).

Jordan, James B. *Through New Eyes: Developing a Biblical View of the World*, Eugene, OR.: Wipf and Stock, 1999.

Josselson, Ruthellen. "The Hermeneutics of Faith and the Hermeneutics of Suspicion," *Narrative Inquiry* 14 (John Benjamins Publishing), 2004 (https://doi.org/10.1075/ni).

Jung, Carl. *Man and His Symbols*, New York: Random House, 1964.

Kingsnorth, Paul. "The Vaccine Moment: Covid, control, and the Machine," January 2022, (www.paulkingsnorth.net/vaccine).

Klavan, Spencer. "Never Been Tried," book review of the English translation of Del Noce's *The Problem of Atheism*, *Law & Liberty*, lawliberty.org, August 12, 2022.

Klippenstein, Ken, and Lee Fang. "Truth Cops," *The Intercept*, theintercept.com, October 31, 2022.

Lancellotti, Carlo. "Augusto Del Noce and the 'New Totalitarianism,'" *Communio International Catholic Review*, Summer 2017, vol. 44.2.

Leach, Edmund and D. Alan Aycock. *Structuralist Interpretations of Biblical Myth*, Cambridge, UK: Cambridge University Press, 1983.

Levi, Carlo. *Christ Stopped at Eboli*, transl by Frances Frenaye. New York: Farrar, Straus and Giroux, 1945.

Levi, Primo. *If This is a Man/The Truce*, New York: Abacus, 2003.

Levi-Strauss, Claude. *The Raw and the Cooked*, Middlesex, UK: Penguin Books, 1964.

Levinas, Emmanuel. *Totality and Infinity*. Pennsylvania: Duquesne University Press 1969.
_____. *Alterity and Transcendence*, New York: Columbia University Press, 1999.

Lewis, C.S. *The Abolition of Man*, New York: HarperOne, 2000.
_____. *The Great Divorce*, New York: Harper Collins, 2001.

Loconte, Joseph. "Mussolini and the End of Liberal Democracy," *National Review* June 25, 2019.

Lyons, N.S. "A Prophecy of Evil: Tolkien, Lewis, and Technocratic Nihilism," *The Upheaval* (theupheaval@substack.com) November 15, 2022.

Lyotard, Jean-François. *The Postmodern Condition: A Report on Knowledge*, Manchester UK: Manchester University Press, 1979.

MacLeod, Adam. "Essences or Intersectionality: Understanding Why We Can't Understand Each Other," *Witherspoon Institute* March 1, 2020.

Magnet, Myron. *The Dream and the Nightmare*, San Francisco: Encounter Books, 2000.

Maier, Francis. "Augusto Del Noce and The Problem of Atheism," *Public Discourse*, thepublicdiscourse.com, December 5, 2021.

Marceau, Jean-Philippe. "Panpsychism and Neoplatonism: Re-Enchantment for Mathematicians and Physicists," thesymbolicworld.com, May 29, 2022.

Marcuse, Herbert. *Eros and Civilization/A Philosophical Inquiry into Freud*, Boston: Beacon Press, 1955.

McGilchrist, Iain. *The Matter With Things*, London: Perspectiva, 2021.

Merricks, Trenton. *Truth and Ontology*, Oxford: Oxford University Press, 2009.

Mill, John Stuart. *On Liberty*, 1859.

Milosz, Czeslaw. *The Captive Mind*, New York: Vintage International, 1990. First published 1951.

Minogue, Kenneth. *The Servile Mind: How Democracy Erodes the Moral Life*, New York: Encounter Books, 2010.

Moyers, Bill and Joseph Campbell. *Joseph Campbell and the Power of Myth, Interview with Bill Moyers*, Episode 2: "The Message of the Myth," at billmoyers.com.

Murray, Douglas. *The Madness of Crowds: Gender, Race and Identity*, London: Bloomsbury, 2021.

Mussolini, Benito. *The Fundamentals of Fascism*, 1935.

Newhouse, Alana. "Everything is Broken," *Tablet* (tabletmag.com), January 14, 2021.
_____. "The Jews Who Didn't Leave Egypt: A lesson from the past about choosing freedom over servitude, *Tablet* (tabletmag.com), April 14, 2022.

Ngo, Andy. *Unmasked: Antifa's Radical Plan to Destroy Democracy*, New York: Center Street, 2021.

Nietzsche, Friedrich. *On the Genealogy of Morals*, translated by Walter Kaufmann and RJ Hollingdale. New York: Vintage Books, 1989, (first published 1887).
_____. *Twilight of the Idols*. Oxford: Oxford University Press, 1998, (first published 1889).
_____. *Will to Power*, 1901.
_____. *The Gay Science*, sec. 125 (1882).

Noble, Alan. *You Are Not Your Own*, Downer's Grove, IL.: Intervarsity Press, 2021.

Del Noce, Augusto. *The Crisis of Modernity*, transl. by Carlo Lancelotti. Montreal: McGill-Queen's University Press, 2014.

Norton, Albert. *Dangerous God: A Defense of Transcendent Truth*, Nashville: New English Review Press, 2021.
_____. *Another Like Me*, Dallas: eLectio Publishing, 2016.
_____. *Intuition of Significance: Evidence Against Materialism and for God*, Eugene, OR.: Resource Publications, 2020.

Otteson, James R. *Seven Deadly Economic Sins*, Cambridge: Cambridge University Press, 2021.

Pageau, Matthieu. *The Language of Creation: Cosmic Symbolism in Genesis*, CreateSpace, 2018.

Perry, Louise. *The Case Against the Sexual Revolution: A New Guide to Sex in the 21st Century*, Medford, MA.: Polity, 2022.

Plantinga, Alvin. *Knowledge and Christian Belief*, Grand Rapids, MI.: Eerdman's, 2015.

Pluckrose, Helen and James Lindsay. *Cynical Theories*, Durham, NC.: Pitchstone Publishing, 2020.

Rawls, John. *The Law of Peoples: The Idea of Public Reason Revisited*, Cambridge, MA.: Harvard University Press, 1999.

Rectenwald, Michael. *The Great Reset and the Struggle for Liberty*, Nashville: New English Review Press, 2023.
_____. "What is the Great Reset?" *Imprimis* (Hillsdale. edu) January 6, 2022.

Rée, Jonathan. Witcraft: *The Invention of Philosophy in English*, London: Penguin/Random House, 2019.

Reich, Wilhelm. *The Mass Psychology of Fascism*, New York: Farrar, Straus and Giroux, 1970.
_____. *The Sexual Revolution*, New York: Farrar, Straus and Giroux, 1986, (first published in English in 1945).

Ricoeur, Paul. "Freud and Philosophy: An Essay on Interpretation," New Haven: Yale University Press, 1970.

Roberts, Alastair. "The Music and the Meaning of Male and Female," *Primer*, Issue 03, (Fellowship of Independent Evangelical Churches) 2018.
_____ and Andrew Wilson. *Echoes of Exodus: Tracing Themes of Redemption through Scripture*, Wheaton, IL.: Crossway, 2018.

Rorty, Richard. *Pragmatism As Anti-authoritarianism*, Cambridge, MA.: Belknap, Harvard University Press, 2021.
_____. *Contingency, Irony, and Solidarity*, Cambridge: Cambridge University Press, 1989.

Rousseau, Jean-Jacques. *On the Social Contract*, translated by G.D.H. Cole. Mineola, NY., 2003, (first published 1762).

Ruden, Sarah. *Paul Among the People*, New York: Image Books, 2010.

Shlaes, Amity. *Great Society: A New History*, New York: Harper Collins, 2019.

Schwab, Klauss and Thierry Malleret. *COVID-19: The Great Reset*, Geneva: Forum, 2020.

Scruton, Roger. *Fools, Frauds and Firebrands*, London: Bloomsbury Continuum, 2015, Tantor Audio, 2018.
_____. *Modern Philosophy: An Introduction and Survey*, New York: Penguin, 1994.

Sloterkijk, Peter, *You Must Change Your Life*, Cambridge, UK: Polity, 2013, (first published in German, 2009).

Smith, James K.A. *Who's Afraid of Postmodernism: Taking Derrida, Lyotard, and Foucault to Church*. Grand Rapids, MI.: Baker, 2006.

Smith, R. Scott. *Truth & The New Kind of Christian: The Emerging Effects of Postmodernism in the Church*, Wheaton, IL.: Crossway, 2005.

Smith, Steven D. *The Disenchantment of Secular Discourse*, Cambridge,

MA.: Harvard University Press, 2010.

_____. *Pagans and Christians in the City: Culture Wars from the Tiber to the Potomac*, Grand Rapids, MI.: Eerdman's, 2018.

Sontag, Susan. "Fascinating Fascism," *New York Review of Books*, Feb. 6, 1975.

Sowell, Thomas. *A Conflict of Visions: Ideological Origins of Political Struggles*, New York: Basic Books, 2007 (first published 1987 by William Morrow & Co.).

Storey, Benjamin, and Jenna Silber Storey. *Why We Are Restless: On the Modern Quest for Contentment*, Princeton, NJ: Princeton University Press, 2021.

Taylor, Charles. *A Secular Age*, Cambridge, MA.: Belknap, 2007.

Thoreau, Henry Walden. *The Variorium Walden*, New York: Washington Square Press, 1962 (first published in 1854).

Trueman, Carl. *The Rise and Triumph of the Modern Self: Cultural Amnesia, Expressive Individualism, and the Road to Sexual Revolution*, Wheaton, IL.: Crossway, 2020.

Veith, Gene Edward, Jr. *Modern Fascism: The Threat to the Judeo-Christian Worldview*, St. Louis: Concordia,1993.

Von Hilderbrand, Dietrich. *What is Philosophy?*, Steubenville, OH.: Hilderbrand Press, 2021 (first published in 1960).

Weber, Max. *The Sociology of Religion*, Boston, MA., 1922 (2nd ed.).

White, Heath. *Postmodernism 101*, Grand Rapids, MI.: Brazos, 2006.

Wolf, Naomi. "Is It Time for Intellectuals to Talk about God?," *Independent Institute*, independent.org, Feb 3, 2022.

Index

www.ingramcontent.com/pod-product-compliance
Lightning Source LLC
Chambersburg PA
CBHW020525270326
41927CB00006B/445